California's Daughter

California's Daughter

GERTRUDE ATHERTON
and Her Times

Emily Wortis Leider

STANFORD UNIVERSITY PRESS
Stanford, California

Stanford University Press, Stanford, California
© 1991 by the Board of Trustees of the Leland Stanford Junior University
Printed in the United States of America

Published with the assistance of the Edgar M. Kahn Memorial Fund

Original printing 1991

Last figure below indicates year of this printing:

00   99   98   97   96   95   94   93   92   91

CIP data appear at the end of the book

Frontispiece: "The Puzzle," portrait of Gertrude Atherton at Montalvo, by her great-granddaughter Barbara Jacobsen, showing Atherton as a puzzle with a central piece missing, 1982? (Barbara Jacobsen)

Quotations reprinted from *Adventures of a Novelist* by Gertrude Atherton, by permission of Liveright Publishing Corporation, Copyright 1932 by The Atherton Company, Inc. Copyright renewed 1960 by Muriel Atherton Russell.

This book is for:
LINDA ALLEN
FLORENCE ATHERTON DICKEY
WILLIAM LEIDER
without whom, not.

Acknowledgments

I would like to thank Florence Atherton Dickey, granddaughter of Gertrude Atherton, for her generous cooperation, patience, and friendship, and for permission to quote from unpublished letters and manuscripts.

I am grateful to the following institutions for access to their collections, and to their librarians and staff for their professionalism and helpfulness: the Bancroft Library, the Library of the California Historical Society, the New York Public Library and its Berg Collection, the Huntington Library, the Library of Congress, the Harry Ransom Humanities Research Center, the San Francisco History Room of the San Francisco Public Library, the Oakland Public Library, Lilly Library of Indiana University, the Montalvo Center for the Arts, Clifton Barret Library of the University of Virginia, Columbia University Library, Houghton Library of Harvard University, Mills College Library, the Beinecke Rare Book and Manuscript Library of Yale University, Princeton University Library, California State Library, Barnard College Library, Temple University Library, Van Pelt Library of the University of Pennsylvania, PEN American Center, American Academy and Institute of Arts and Letters, New York University Library, Stanford University Library, National Library of Scotland, and the British Museum. Every effort has been made to locate holders of rights in illustrations and unpublished letters.

An earlier version of Chapter 6 appeared in *California History* 60, 4 (Winter 1981–82): 332–49. An earlier version of the account of the Authors' Reading for Ina Coolbrith in Chapter 10 was published in *California Living* (*San Francisco Sunday Examiner*), June 21, 1981. In slightly different form, an account of Gertrude Stein's visit to California in Chapter 18 appeared in *California Living* (*San Francisco Sunday Examiner*), November 30, 1980.

It is a pleasure also to acknowledge some of the individuals (and one organization) who have assisted or supported this daunting venture, sometimes called Endless Gertrude: Thomas Huster, Janet Lewis, Kevin Starr, Henry Mayer, Chris Goodrich, Ernest Scott, Jane Somerville, Liz Darhansoff, M. K. Swingle, Gerald Wright, Glenn Humphreys, Ellen Smith, Anita Walker Scott, Barbara Roos, Yves H. Lacaze, Carlos Lopez, Jane Ciabattari, Barbara Jacobsen, Tom Turinia, Alice Wetherow, Peter Doyle, James Sheehan, Doris Ober, Albert Shumate, Eric Solomon, David Schoonover, Judy Breen, and the Institute for Historical Study.

Special thanks to Linda Allen, for her loyalty and generosity of spirit; to Norris Pope for his belief in and commitment to this endeavor; and to William Leider, for initiating an improbable transformation, by which a quintessential New Yorker woke up one morning to find she was becoming a Californian.

Contents

Photograph sections follow pages 112 and 200.

Chronology

1857   *January 29*: Gertrude Franklin, daughter of Stephen and Eliza Franklin, marries Thomas L. Horn in San Francisco.

        October 30: Gertrude Horn (Atherton) born.

1860   *September*: Parents divorce; Gertrude and her mother move to Stephen Franklin's ranch near San Jose.

1864   Returns to San Francisco with mother and grandparents.

1865   *April 13*: Mother marries John F. Uhlhorn.

        May: Death of Eliza Franklin.

1866   Aleece Uhlhorn born.

1867   Florence (Daisy) Uhlhorn born.

1869   Transcontinental railroad completed.

1870   Enrolls at Clark Institute.

        After a suicide attempt, John F. Uhlhorn leaves California.

1873   Attends St. Mary's Hall, Benicia.

1874   Attends Sayre Institute, Lexington, Kentucky.

1875   *August 27*: Death of William C. Ralston.

        Returns to the Ranch, San Jose.

1876   *February 15*: Marries George Henry Bowen Atherton.

        November 20: George Goñi Atherton (Georgie) born at Valparaiso Park.

1877   *July 18*: Death of Faxon Dean Atherton.

        Moves with George and Georgie to Rancho Milpitas, Jolon.

1878   Returns during the spring to Valparaiso Park when George
         is recalled from Jolon for mismanagement.
         July 14: Muriel Florence Atherton born.
1882   *July*: Moves with George and children to Oroville, where
         George runs a grape farm for several months.
         November 28: Death of Georgie in San Francisco.
1883   *March–May*: *The Randolphs of Redwoods* serialized in *The
         Argonaut*.
1884   Writes a second novel, never published.
1885   Writes draft of *What Dreams May Come*. Moves to San Fran-
         cisco.
1887   *March 21*: Death of George Atherton at sea.
         Fall: Moves to New York; writes "Letters from New York"
         for *The Argonaut*.
1888   *What Dreams May Come* (Belford, Clarke)
1889   *Spring*: Visits Paris, staying with the Rathbones.
         Summer: Writes *Los Cerritos* at Sacred Heart Convent in
         Boulogne-sur-Mer, then goes to London.
         Hermia Suydam (Current Literature Co. [U.S.]; Routledge
         [England])
1890   *January 16*: Death of Stephen Franklin.
         Returns to California.
         September 20: Death of Dominga Atherton.
         Los Cerritos (John W. Lovell, Co.)
1891   Researches and writes Californian short stories.
         January: Publishes "The Literary Development of Califor-
         nia" in *Cosmopolitan*.
         August–November: Writes "Woman in Her Variety" columns
         for *San Francisco Examiner*.
         Fall: Meets Ambrose Bierce.
         Winter: Writes *The Doomswoman* at Fort Ross.
         A Question of Time (John W. Lovell, Co.)
1892   *March*: Travels East to report on summer resorts.
         August: *The Doomswoman* published in *Lippincott's*.
         Fall: Writes *A Christmas Witch* for *Godey's Magazine*; settles
         in New York City.
1893   *Summer*: Visits Chicago World's Fair and sees herself en-
         shrined.

The Doomswoman (J. Selwin Tait)

1894 Writes *Patience Sparhawk* in Yonkers; its rejection prompts decision to move to England.

Before the Gringo Came (J. Selwin Tait)

1895 Visits Haworth and other literary shrines in England.

John Lane accepts *Patience Sparhawk*.

A Whirl Asunder (Frederick A. Stokes)

1896 Visits Pont Aven, Brittany.

1897 Meets friends of Oscar Wilde while staying in Rouen.

Patience Sparhawk and Her Times (John Lane, The Bodley Head)

His Fortunate Grace (D. Appleton and Co.)

1898 *November 23*: Death of Gertrude Uhlhorn.

The Californians (John Lane, The Bodley Head)

American Wives and English Husbands (Dodd, Mead)

The Valiant Runaways (Dodd, Mead)

1899 *January 4*: Muriel marries Albert Russell in San Francisco.

February: Moves to Washington D.C.

Summer: Writes *Senator North* in Bruges, Belgium; visits London during Boer War.

October 6: Grandson George Russell born.

A Daughter of the Vine (revision of *The Randolphs of Redwoods*) (John Lane, The Bodley Head)

1900 *February*: Travels to Cuba.

Summer: Stays in Adirondack Mountains, New York.

Senator North (John Lane, The Bodley Head)

1901 *April*: Travels from New York to British and Danish West Indies to research life of Alexander Hamilton.

Breaks with John Lane.

The Aristocrats (John Lane, The Bodley Head)

1902 Travels to Denmark.

Visits San Francisco and is heralded; meets James D. Phelan.

Signs contract with Macmillan; George Brett becomes her editor.

The Splendid Idle Forties (Expanded edition of *Before the Gringo Came*) (Macmillan)

The Conqueror: Being the True and Romantic Story of Alexander Hamilton (Macmillan)

1903   *February 14*: Granddaughter Florence Russell born.
        Visits Trieste and Hungary.
        June: Moves to Munich.
        A Few of Hamilton's Letters (Macmillan)
        Heart of Hyacinth (Harper)
        Mrs. Pendleton's Four-in-Hand (Macmillan)
1904   *March and April*: Visits England; meets Henry James.
        May: Publishes "Why Is American Literature Bourgeois?" in
        North American Review.
        George Brett declines to publish *Rulers of Kings* unless ref-
            erences to living rulers are expunged; Gertrude refuses to
            revise.
        Rulers of Kings (Harper and Brothers)
1905   Muriel visits Munich.
        Winter: Visits San Francisco; goes to Petaluma to write *An-
            cestors*.
        The Bell in the Fog and Other Stories (Harper and Brothers)
        The Traveling Thirds (Harper and Brothers)
1906   *April 18*: San Francisco earthquake and fire.
        May 12: Publishes "San Francisco's Tragic Dawn" in *Harpers
            Weekly*.
        Rezanov (Authors and Newspapers Association)
1907   Resides in Munich, with visits to San Francisco area and Lon-
            don.
        November 2: Publishes "San Francisco and Her Foes" in
            Harpers Weekly.
        November 28: San Francisco Benefit Authors' Reading for Ina
            Coolbrith.
        Ancestors (Harper and Brothers)
1908   *The Gorgeous Isle* (Doubleday, Page)
1909   Resides in Munich, with visits to Chicago and Mount Tamal-
            pais, California.
        July 3: Granddaughter Dominga Russell born.
        August: Publishes "The Present Unrest Among Women" in
            Delineator.
1910   Leaves Munich. Visits England. Returns to San Francisco
            to begin drama on modern woman for Minnie Maddern
            Fiske.

       Tower of Ivory (Macmillan)

1911 Tours U.S. by train with Fiske's acting company.

       Visits London to study British Feminism. Supports Suffrage Amendment in California.

       October: Woman Suffrage Amendment passes in California.

1912 *January*: Play "Julia France" fails in Toronto.

       August–October: Campaigns in California for Woodrow Wilson, at the request of James D. Phelan. Criticized for smoking in public.

       November: Publishes "The Fault I Find with America" in *Delineator*, and "Woman Will Cease to Love" in *Harpers Bazaar*.

       Phelan's Villa Montalvo under construction.

       Julia France and Her Times (Macmillan)

1913 *April*: Publishes "The Woman of Tomorrow" in *Yale Review*.

       Joins Authors' League Council. Poses as "California" for Albert Herter mural, St. Francis Hotel.

       Travels to Italy, then goes to Butte and Helena, Montana, to research and write mining novel, *Perch of the Devil*.

       Breaks with Macmillan.

1914 Muriel's marriage ends; she and children join Gertrude in New York City after outbreak of World War I.

       James D. Phelan elected to U.S. Senate.

       Perch of the Devil (Frederick A. Stokes)

       California: An Intimate History (Harper)

1915 Uses columns of the *New York Times* to voice pro-suffrage and anti-pacifist beliefs.

       Granddaughter Florence attends Elizabeth Duncan School in New York.

       Spring: Hospitalized with bleeding ulcer.

       Stokes reissues *Before the Gringo Came*, *Rezanov*, and *The Doomswoman* in one volume.

1916 *February*: Publishes "What the Day's Work Means to Me" in *Bookman* (New York).

       May–August: In France as correspondent for *Delineator*.

       July–September: Writes "Life in the War Zone" articles for the *New York Times*.

October–December: Publishes "What Is Feminism?" in *De-lineator*.

Helps found war relief organization, Le Bien-Être du Blessé.

Mrs. Belfame (Stokes)

1917   Serves as president of Authors League Fund for needy writers.

Holds Sunday salons at her flat in Morningside Heights, New York City.

The Living Present (Stokes)

1918   Edits pro-Ally *American Woman's Magazine*.

Begins correspondence with Upton Sinclair.

The White Morning: A Novel of the Power of the German Women in Wartime (Stokes)

1919   *February*: Travels to Paris to cover Peace Congress for the *New York Times*. Illness compels her early return to New York.

April: Leaves New York and returns to California to undergo surgery.

July: In Hollywood as one of Goldwyn's Eminent Authors. Writes filmscript *Don't Neglect Your Wife*.

The Avalanche (Stokes)

Paramount releases film version of *The Avalanche*.

1920   *November*: Phelan defeated in bid for reelection to Senate; he returns to Villa Montalvo, where Gertrude has her own suite.

1921   *March*: Publishes "Is There a Moral Decline?" in *Forum*.

Sisters-in-Law (Stokes)

1922   Visits Dr. Harry Benjamin in New York for the Steinach Treatment.

Chooses Horace Liveright as her new publisher.

Sleeping Fires (Stokes)

1923   Moves into apartment at 2101 California Street, San Francisco.

April: Testifies against Clean Books Bill at Albany, New York, hearings.

Black Oxen (Boni & Liveright), a best-seller.

1924   Founds San Francisco PEN.

First National Pictures releases film of *Black Oxen*, with Corinne Griffith.

1925 Travels to Europe with Muriel and Dominga.

   May: Meets Gertrude Stein in Paris.

   June: In Monte Carlo, decides to write a novel about Aspasia and Periclean Athens.

   September: Begins research in Switzerland, then travels to Athens.

   November: In Paris, receives medal of the Legion of Honor.

   The Crystal Cup (Boni & Liveright)

1926 *January*: Publishes "Love Is Not All" in *Harpers Bazaar*.

   March 27: Death of sister Aleece.

   September: Universal Pictures releases *Vein of Gold* (based on *Perch of the Devil*).

1927 *August*: Vacations in Honolulu.

   October: First National Pictures releases *The Crystal Cup*.

   The Immortal Marriage (Boni & Liveright)

1928 Delegate pledged to Al Smith at Democratic National Convention.

   The Jealous Gods: A Processional Novel of the Fifth Century B.C. (Liveright)

1929 *January*: Speaks in Boston on publicity tour sponsored by Liveright.

   October: Travels to Rome with Muriel and Dominga.

   Dido, Queen of Hearts (Liveright)

1930 *March*: Travels to Egypt.

   April–October: Resides in New York City.

   August 8: Death of Phelan at Villa Montalvo.

1931 Dominga joins Dominican Convent.

   Writes occasional columns for Hearst papers.

   The Sophisticates (Liveright)

1932 *January*: Joins San Francisco Art Commission.

   Adventures of a Novelist (Liveright)

1933 Contributes to filmscript, *The Woman Accused* (Paramount).

   Liveright files for bankruptcy.

1934 *The Foghorn* (Houghton Mifflin)

1935 *April*: Hosts Gertrude Stein on her visit to San Francisco.

          June: Receives Honorary Doctor of Literature Degree from
               Mills College.
1936   *Golden Peacock* (Houghton Mifflin)
1937   *March*: Accepts Honorary Doctor of Law degree from Uni-
               versity of California, Berkeley.
          Dominga hospitalized with brain tumor.
1938   *March*: Elected to the National Institute of Arts and Letters.
          Issues pro-Franco statement and withdraws under pressure
               as chair of Thomas Mann lecture in San Francisco.
          November: Visits Algonquin Hotel, New York City; partici-
               pates in Lowell Thomas radio broadcast.
          December: Speaks at anti-Hitler Rally in Carnegie Hall.
          Can Women Be Gentlemen? (Houghton Mifflin)
1939   *February 21*: "Gertrude Atherton Day" at Golden Gate Inter-
               national Exposition.
1940   *September*: Named first of California's Most Distinguished
               Women, Women's Day, Golden Gate International Expo-
               sition.
          Campaigns for presidential candidate Wendell Wilkie.
          The House of Lee (D. Appleton Century)
1941   Moves to top floor of Muriel's house at 2280 Green Street,
               San Francisco.
1942   *The Horn of Life* (D. Appleton Century)
1943   Exhibit of Gertrude Atherton manuscripts and memorabilia
               at Library of Congress.
1945   *Golden Gate Country* (Duell, Sloane & Pearce)
1946   *November 11*: *Life* magazine publishes article, "Gertrude
               Atherton Writes Her 56th Book."
          My San Francisco, A Wayward Biography (Bobbs-Merrill)
1947   Receives Gold Medal from the City of San Francisco.
1948   Dies on June 14.

California's Daughter

Introduction

 Gertrude Atherton never gave much thought to the evanescence of fame, but her life offers a morality tale on that subject. At the height of her writing career —in the last decade of the nineteenth century and the first decades of the twentieth—she was praised by George Meredith and Oscar Wilde, championed by Ambrose Bierce, sought out by Rebecca West, befriended by Gertrude Stein and Carl Van Vechten, and often mentioned in the same sentence as Edith Wharton. Though she was vilified at least as often as she was acclaimed, everyone knew who she was. Prolific, controversial, outspoken, she succeeded unequivocally in attaining the visibility, marketability, and name recognition that had already become marks of renown during her lifetime.[1]

When she was elected to membership in the National Institute of Arts and Letters in 1938, she joined a select company (only 21 other women writers had by that time been so honored) that included Willa Cather, Ellen Glasgow, Edna St. Vincent Millay, and Edith Wharton. But it is on the roster of women writers now largely forgotten and unread that Gertrude Atherton's name finds itself today.

Atherton passionately wanted to be famous, but she cared more for celebrity than immortality. Impatient and hasty, she wrote and published too much, revised and self-edited too little. Her importance lies in her accuracy as a social historian whose life spanned 90

years and in her embodiment of many of the values and fantasies—
particularly those of women—of her time.

Born Gertrude Franklin Horn in San Francisco in 1857, before
the cross-country railroad or telegraph connected it to the rest of the
United States, she died in a cosmopolitan, industrial San Francisco
in 1948. She remembered the day President Lincoln died and lived
to advise visitors on the clothes they should bring to San Francisco
when they came to attend the United Nations Conference. A resident of New York and London during the 1890s and of Munich
in the early 1900s, she returned to San Francisco in time to witness
and write about the earthquake of 1906. Gathering material for her
Washington novel *Senator North*, she attended McKinley-era Senate debates and White House receptions. Although she attempted to
stand outside as an observer rather than a participant in world events,
she could not resist propagandizing on behalf of woman suffrage,
campaigning for Woodrow Wilson and Al Smith, or raising money
for the wounded of the First World War. Very much a creature of
the Gilded Age in her display of willful individualism, aggressive
ambition, audacity, and sense of boundless possibility, she anticipated
the present in her preoccupation with the role of women and her
pursuit of popular acclaim.

She produced more than 50 books, most of them novels, but also
including several collections of essays, short stories, a history of California, two books on San Francisco, a fictionalized biography of
Alexander Hamilton, several historical novels set in ancient Greece
or Rome, and an autobiography. In addition to her books, she wrote
columns for the Hearst press and articles for such magazines as *North
American Review*, *The Bookman* (London and New York), *The New
Republic*, and *Harpers Bazaar*. Her opinions—she had one on every
subject—were quoted in interviews, often accompanied by a sketch
or photograph.

Coming into prominence in the ballyhoo era of early modern advertising, she was among the first American writers to highly value
and actively seek personal publicity. She adored seeing her name in
print. Like the heroine of her autobiographical novel *Patience Sparhawk*, she found that the first sight of her name in the paper created
a kind of addiction, making her ego "as insatiable as a child for
sweets."[2]

As befits someone who often wrote for newspapers, socialized with journalists, and derived many ideas for books from the news, headlines and sensation marked her career from the start. Her earliest novels were considered scandalous for their frank eroticism and their reliance on well-known characters and recent events. "THE LAST PRURIENT NOVEL / GERTRUDE FRANKLIN ATHERTON'S NAKED EXPOSURE IN 'HERMIA SUYDAM,'" shouted the *New York World* in 1889. "Gertrude Atherton Writes Her 56th Book," more decorously announced *Life* magazine in a 1946 picture essay. Between these two newsworthy events she caused a furor by smoking in public at Chicago's South Shore Country Club; she declared war, in print, on what she considered the bloodlessness of William Dean Howells and American realistic fiction. Her husband's bizarre death at sea and shipment home embalmed in a barrel of rum escaped wide notice at the time it occurred but provided much grist for the journalistic mill decades later, when Atherton was well known.

In the 1920s she gravitated toward the innovative publisher Horace Liveright because he used advanced advertising and promotion techniques to sell books. Liveright published her much-banned bestseller *Black Oxen*, which treated the sensational subject of "reactivization," the restoration of youth and seductiveness to an aging woman by means of X-ray stimulation of her glands, a procedure known as the Steinach Treatment.

Atherton craved respect as well as notoriety. She varied her literary performances so that dignified books, solidly grounded in historical research, would balance the charge of unconventionality so often hurled at her heroines. The staid *Doomswoman* silenced tongues set wagging by *Hermia Suydam*. Alexander Hamilton in *The Conqueror* served as foil for intrepid Patience Sparhawk. Scholarly novels of classical antiquity followed the sensational *Black Oxen*.

Like many American writers, Atherton earned her first critical recognition and found her most receptive publishers in England, where she went to live in 1895. Whereas the New York literary establishment had rejected her partly, she felt, because she was a Westerner, British readers were almost as fascinated by the American West as they were by Atherton's second enduring subject, the American Woman. Only when *Patience Sparhawk*, published by John Lane in London after American editors had shunned it, was hailed in

British reviews and likened to *Jane Eyre*, did New York begin to take serious notice. By the turn of the century her career was established on both sides of the Atlantic, and in Europe in the 1920s Atherton's books, in Tauchnitz editions, were the most popular of all American novels, far outdistancing titles by Sinclair Lewis or Edith Wharton.

Although she complained about New York's obsession with best-sellers and sales figures, she drove a hard bargain, pursued financial success, and involved herself actively with the commercial side of the book business.[3] For her, writing was a form of venture capitalism, a kind of mining by which locales and characters could be scouted, developed, and merchandized like veins of ore. She rejoiced when, in the fourth decade of her career, her novels twice made it to the *Publishers Weekly* best-sellers list. In 1923 *Black Oxen* took first place on the list (*Babbitt* was fourth). In 1921 *Sisters-in-Law* appeared on the same list, but lower down, with *Main Street* and *The Age of Innocence*. *The Conqueror*, Atherton's fictionalized biography of Alexander Hamilton, remained in print for decades after its initial publication in 1902 and sold hundreds of thousands of copies. As inconsistent in her attitude toward the public as she was about most things, she courted the widest possible readership while setting herself apart from and professing her contempt for "the mass."

She combined a strident rebelliousness with an aristocratic hauteur. She began a hellion and became an institution. The same person who, as a child at her grandfather's ranch, would place a dizzied, comatose rooster under the bed of an unsuspecting houseguest, in delighted anticipation of pre-dawn crowing, would, as an imperious 65-year-old presiding over San Francisco's writers' organization PEN, require all women attending the official dinners to wear formal evening gowns. Obsessed with gentility and the notion that heredity is destiny, she was herself the daughter of an alcoholic cigar importer and a southern belle of respectable New England ancestry whose two divorces made her a social outcast. The exclusive Atherton family recoiled when Gertrude, eighteen and without a fortune or a visible father, married one of them. The Athertons also bitterly opposed Gertrude's efforts to write and worse, to publish. Ladies did not do such things. But being the victim of snobbism seems merely to have heightened Gertrude's desire to operate from the inside of an exclusive circle, in a position to exclude or feel superior to others.

Fond of invoking Alexander Hamilton's belief that human beings are merely animals walking on their hind legs, she heaped scorn on anyone or anything she judged "commonplace." A racist, she believed not only in the superiority of whites to all others, but in the primacy of the Nordic over other European strains. She was attracted to royalty, outraged by Bolsheviks. She held herself apart. Most of the surviving photographs of her are stiffly posed portraits. Though she lived well into the age of the snapshot, she carefully snipped herself out of any in which she appeared. Even her grandchildren addressed her as "Mrs. Atherton."

Women, she thought, came in two varieties: there were the domestic and maternal sort, useful but humdrum; and there were those like herself, a new breed, independent, gifted, worldly, ambitious, and physically stunning. Atherton's New Woman heroines command a manipulative sexuality used to attract and control. Like them, their creator never stopped trying to make herself alluring. Coming into prominence in the era of the Professional Beauty, she claimed that good looks and magnetism were "almost as valuable an asset for the woman writer of serious fiction as for the actress," because they opened doors, allowing her to enrich and expand her knowledge of life.[4] Her cameo-like profile and erect carriage were celebrated. So was her crown of fair hair. Like Lily Langtry, she loved to display her alabaster shoulders when she posed for artists and photographers and was always partial to low-cut gowns. One reporter described her, at the age of 90, surrounded by young men, "a cloud of tulle floating about her shoulders, which show alabaster above the low décolletage," but the photographer Edward Weston found her grotesque in the role of ancient siren, "bursting out of her bespangled evening gown, pulling the gown off her shoulders, and commanding, 'Do me from this side, my hair is better, and I am always taken in profile.'"[5]

Although she wrote one frankly suffragist novel, another in which women stage a revolution against men, and many others with spirited, bright, and assertive heroines, Atherton was the kind of feminist who complains about how ugly most other feminists are. Delighted to remain free of the yoke of matrimony after she was widowed at the age of 30, she advocated economic independence for women, favored divorce, protested the double standard, but confessed to a preference for the company of men—they were more interesting. Like her heroines, she was attracted to fatherly, even grandfatherly gentlemen of wealth, achievement, worldly experience, and stature in the community. But she never compromised her freedom for such a man, preferring a footloose existence to one of roots, domesticity, and ties that might bind.

Her custom was to go to one location for "background" for a book and then withdraw in isolation to an entirely unrelated place to do the actual writing. She would write about Munich on Mount Tamalpais or about Washington D.C. in Bruges. What she called "the spirit of unrest" possessed her and kept her constantly hopping all over the globe. She spent extended periods in England, Germany, and New York and resided briefly in France, the West Indies, Havana, and Greece. Between jaunts she would periodically return to the San Francisco area, where her family remained.

To many she seemed the embodiment of California, a characterization she sometimes chose for herself. She modeled for the figure "California"—imperious and golden-haired—in the Herter murals that used to adorn the St. Francis Hotel in San Francisco. As a younger woman, she often justified her displays of temperament, cruelty, and spite as the prerogatives of the "savage" West. "It is the instinct of the Californian," she once wrote, "to scalp." [6] She made a career out of being a Californian, returning to its history repeatedly in an interconnected series of novels and short stories. Yet as a young woman she deeply resented California's provincialism and fled like a jailbird to New York immediately after her husband's death. She would not return to stay until she was past 60.

In the waning twentieth century, feminists want role models, and Atherton does not always make an attractive one. Her courage, capacity for work, and independent spirit appeal; her narcissism, competitiveness, worship of power, and lack of compassion repel. But in her own time she was widely perceived as a symbol of New-Woman pluck and achievement. Her productivity and boundless energy offered an antidote to the chronic invalidism to which Alice James and so many other privileged women of the late nineteenth century succumbed. Here was a woman who could, in the name of getting a story, sit in the electric chair at Sing Sing or journey to the bottom of a Montana copper mine. Alice Toklas, twenty years Atherton's junior, grew up worshipping the glamorous, intrepid fellow San Franciscan. Mabel Dodge Luhan, who perhaps contrasted Atherton's devotion to career and the single life to her own unfocused yearnings and her pattern of dependence on a series of men, wrote to her in 1935: "You still remain my heroine."[7]

If it is true, as George Stade has suggested,[8] that in American literature men have functioned as adventurers, women as protectors of the hearth, then Atherton had it backwards. She titled her autobiography *Adventures of a Novelist* and never overlooked an opportunity to slam domesticity and the genteel tradition that enshrined it. But in her "adventures" she sought not wilderness but civilization, not the frontier but the sophistication and romantic color of Europe. She took from the American West its tradition of fearlessness, buccaneering individualism, and impermanence and grafted onto it a Henry Jamesian quest for the cosmopolitan.

Atherton held in contempt anything that was easy, and she certainly did nothing to ease a biographer's task. For all her access to print and publicity, she remained remote and difficult to know. Hungry for fame, attention, approval, she kept her distance from those she knew best. She left no diary, revealed little that was intimate in her notoriously illegible and almost always undated letters. Her most readily summoned emotion was wrath. She felt herself a spectator of life, perhaps incapable of real love and reluctant to display affection. Being "impersonal," she thought, made her a better writer.

The engaging autobiography she wrote at the age of 75 resounds with famous names and spills over with amusing, colorful incidents; it rarely questions, probes, or exposes a vulnerable flank. And nature has joined in the conspiracy of obfuscation. Many letters and documents of Atherton's first 50 years were destroyed in the San Francisco fire that followed the 1906 earthquake. No one is likely ever to know much about her father, or how she dealt with the death of her six-year-old son or saying goodbye to her nine-year-old daughter Muriel when she left her in the care of a grandmother and departed for New York. We do have one treasure trove: the letters she wrote to Ambrose Bierce in the 1890s—often confessional and uncharacteristically introspective—have miraculously survived. They have proved invaluable.

It is by indirections that we find directions out, and Atherton's significant self-revelations often turn up in her novels, where she frequently placed a masked, idealized version of herself in the starring role. She possessed little of the "negative capability," or ability to submerge the self, common to great artists. Rather, she imagined herself in myriad guises. Atherton could not escape herself, but whether she truly knew herself is another question. To know her, while placing her against an ever-varying social, cultural, and geographic background, will be our task.

Who is she, . . . this California woman with her hair of gold and her unmistakable intellect, her marble face crossed by the animation of the clever American woman? What an anomaly to find on the shores of the Pacific! She is not maternal, at all events; I never saw a baby held so awkwardly. What a poise of head! She looks better fitted for tragedy than for this little comedy of life in the Californias. . . . No, a sovereignty would not suit her at all, a salon might.[9]

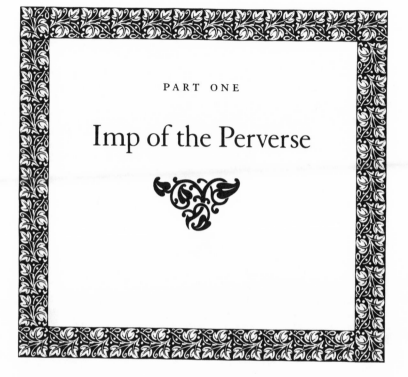

PART ONE

Imp of the Perverse

CHAPTER ONE

A Nomadic Childhood

At daybreak on August 27, 1875, seventeen-year-old Gertrude Horn found herself on a train, traveling back to California after a year of high school in Lexington, Kentucky. She was returning in disgrace, for her great-aunt Mary Bullock, to whom Gertrude's grandfather had turned for help in rearing his unruly charge, had washed her hands of her. The Bullocks, like Grandfather Stephen Franklin himself, were rigid Presbyterians who had been shocked to hear that young Gertrude had been taken to the theater and dancing school in San Francisco and permitted to read novels on Sunday. Brother Stephen had certainly fallen under evil influence. They kept their own children tightly in hand: studies, chores, Bible study, Sunday school, church. They had every hour scheduled, with bedtime strictly enforced at 7 P.M. The cousins found their free-spirited California visitor a revelation and, encouraged by her, played cards in the barn on the sly. They felt bereft when she departed for nearby Sayre Institute, a school whose curriculum included such finishing-school-for-young-ladies accomplishments as wax work, embroidery, painting, music, and French.

At Sayre the girls were expected to keep their own rooms in order, at which Gertrude had balked, just as she had tried to escape her grandmother's sewing lessons years before. (Her grandmother had responded by tying her to a chair.) She cajoled or coerced her classmates into doing it for her, shutting one girl in the closet until she came to terms. She made a bargain with another whereby she provided a weekly composition in exchange for having the buttons of her boots sewn.[1] The domestic arts, she knew from the start, were not for her.

She earned a rebuke from the teacher by writing a story about a boy disguised as a girl who enrolls at a girl's boarding school. Every night she wrote in a diary and left it around, open, to make sure her roommates would read it and ponder her suggestive allusions to her "past."[2] Some 60 years later, a former Sayre classmate was still impressed enough to write Gertrude: "I recall that you were a new species to the girls at school. I think your independence amazed us most."[3]

When she stayed with the Bullocks, she drove her great-aunt to distraction by keeping her hair wild and her clothes strewn all over the floor. More outrageous still, she declared herself an agnostic, flirted in church, and gave every encouragement to the flock of young male admirers she had attracted. At the end of the school year, the Bullocks decided they'd had their fill, a fateful decision that brought Gertrude's formal education to an end before she could complete high school. Gertrude was banished from Kentucky where she could contaminate her cousins no more. Aunt Mary kissed her goodbye at the Chicago train station—entrusting her to the care of a family friend who would serve as escort in those days of the omnipresent chaperon—saying, "You have your points, Gertrude, and I can't help liking you, but I am free to say that I was never so glad to see the last of any one in my life. I think you are headed straight for the devil, but I shall pray for you."[4]

As Gertrude gazed out the window at the snow-covered Sierra peaks, a newsboy burst into her Pullman car to announce a public catastrophe with powerful private reverberations: "Failure of the Bank of California. Suicide of Ralston."

It was not possible. William Chapman Ralston, "the man who built San Francisco," her grandfather's long-time associate and employer at the Bank of California, could not be dead. She had been dreaming about the debut he would give her, a brilliant ball that would mark her formal introduction into San Francisco society, a debut her grandfather could ill afford (as secretary of the Bank of California he was merely a salaried employee) but that would cost a man like Ralston no more than the flick of ash from a cigar. Ralston had stood a colossus of masculine solidity in a universe where all men not named Grandfather Stephen Franklin had revealed their clay feet too many times. This "great man of my childhood" came before her as a vivid presence: "A massive face, clean-shaven above the mouth, and not too much hair below," a piercing but kind and often humorous pair of blue eyes, sandy hair, and "a tightly set mouth which could relax—rarely—into a charming and spontaneous smile."[5] He was an idol embodying ambition, power, wealth, public spirit, enterprise, and boundless generosity: manhood at its summit.

As the railroad car erupted in chaos and night-shirted gentlemen dashed from behind the curtains of their compartments to snatch newspapers in the aisle, Gertrude succumbed to a feeling that "the bottom of the universe had dropped out." To her the Bank of California, that handsome stone building with its roof balustrade, its lofty arched windows, its familiar offices with chairs upholstered in green morocco leather,[6] had stood for the great world itself, and Ralston had presided as king (*Adventures*, p. 43). She conjured an image of Ralston racing his char-a-banc and team of four horses, faster than the train, down the old Mission road each evening to his palatial Belmont residence, where guests awaited him, their bejeweled images reflected in long mirrors imported from Versailles.

Ralston had reigned not only over Belmont but over a financial empire that included a theater, an irrigation canal, tobacco fields, a real estate company, a hydraulic mine, silk and wool mills, vineyards, a sugar refinery, a carriage factory, railroads, a dry dock, and the enormous five-million-dollar Palace Hotel, not yet open at the time of his death. Few could imagine, least of all the romantic, hero-worshipping teenager on the train, that Ralston's genius for landing on his feet had abandoned him and that by the summer of 1875 he was $9.5 million in debt, half of it owed to the Bank of California, from which he had borrowed without authorization. After gambling for control of the Ophir, a Comstock silver mine, he fell victim to a rumor that the mine was barren of rich ore and he himself a ruined

man. There was a run on the Bank of California, until the last coin
in its vaults had been handed out. Bank secretary Stephen Franklin, his usually flawless copperplate handwriting shaky for the first
time, recorded in the minutes: "Mr. Ralston in the chair stated to the
Board that after the most strenuous efforts to obtain coin" the Bank
"had been compelled to close its doors."[7]

When the Board demanded Ralston's resignation the next day, he
complied. It was unusually hot as he walked to San Francisco's North
Beach for his customary afternoon swim in the Bay. He swam into icy
water, farther out than he usually ventured, and by the time rescuers
reached him and pulled his body ashore it was too late. Whether
he died from a stroke or suicide is still debated. But Gertrude could
never entertain the latter possibility. His death had to have been an
accident. His energies were at their supreme pitch of development,
his brain was a perfect machine, equipped for every emergency. No
man knew Ralston better than her grandfather, Stephen Franklin,
and he had placed his unswerving trust—and often his family's wel-
fare—in his masterful employer.

When her train pulled into the San Jose station, Gertrude looked
for her grandfather, whose somber gentleman's attire—black broad-
cloth suit, white shirt with flaring collar, gold-rimmed spectacles,
silk stovepipe hat, and ivory-headed cane—distinguished him in any
crowd and marked him for the Sunday school teacher and Presbyterian church elder he was. He was nowhere to be seen. The chaotic
conditions at the bank, combined with the shock of Ralston's death,
had kept him in San Francisco. Instead, her mother came to greet
her. Her first words to her daughter after a year's absence were, "Do
I look any older?" (*Adventures*, p. 45).

Stephen Franklin's association with Ralston dated back to the
1840s in New Orleans. Restless and—like so many East Coast Protes-
tants—willing to pull up stakes in search of a better life, young
Franklin had left his Oxford, New York, home and set himself up in
the South as a cotton merchant.[8] There he sent for and married his
Oxford sweetheart, Eliza Brown, fathered a son and a daughter, and
prospered to the point where he could afford both a New Orleans

office ("Franklin and Henderson, Commission Merchants," reads an entry in the 1846 New Orleans Directory) and a plantation home in the gulf town of Pass Christian, Mississippi. Ralston, fifteen years younger than Franklin, was a clerk on a steamboat plying the Mississippi River between New Orleans and St. Louis and had called at Franklin's New Orleans office to collect a bill. At this first meeting Franklin judged him "somewhat brisk and offhand," but still "of fine presence, manly and magnetic."[9]

Perhaps Franklin admired Ralston's magnetism and entrepreneurial daring because his own caution made such a marked contrast. He had prospered in New Orleans, but when his business partner speculated and lost $30,000 of the firm's money, he took it as a sign of his, not his partner's, unworthiness. To the Calvinist Franklin, son of a deacon who had donated the room over his cabinet shop for public worship,[10] losing in business could only be viewed as a sign of God's displeasure. "He believed himself to be a sinner of the blackest dye, and predestined to some awful fate, hereafter" (*Adventures*, p. 27).

Still, he had a wife and children to think of, and their material needs could not be ignored. New Orleans, strategically located between the Isthmus of Panama and Eastern ports, was buzzing with talk of Sutter's gold strike in California. Stephen Franklin set out on his thirty-ninth birthday, July 8, 1849, carefully packing the family Bible and the dignified attire that would become his trademark. His wife, son John, and daughter Gertrude would be sent for when they could be assured some measure of safety and stability in the land of gold.

Exhausted by a sea journey that had taken three months, including a mule trip through Panama mud and underbrush, Franklin lasted only a short time at the California miner's rough life. He soon abandoned any lingering hopes for instant riches and began to yearn for his familiar starched collar and the proprieties of civilization. A salaried job in the city, he decided, was what God had intended for him, and he took a series of them in San Francisco, clerking for firms like Shaffner and Kelly while writing columns for the business paper, *San Francisco Mercantile Gazette*. In New Orleans he had been an elder in Dr. William Anderson Scott's First Presbyterian Church. Here in California, where a saloon, brothel, or gambling hall darkened every corner, where Sabbath breaking was tolerated with a wink, and the words "prayer book" signified a man's personal deck of cards, the flocks of sinners fairly begged for salvation. He helped found San Francisco's Calvary Presbyterian Church, calling the eloquent Dr. Scott away from his New Orleans pulpit to lead the fledgling congregation. Concerned about the proper rearing of the young (his father back in Oxford became a school superintendent), he helped establish San Francisco's first orphan asylum.

He waited two years before sending for his family, still worried about whether the place could meet his standards of propriety. The California that had received him was boisterous, masculine territory. In the first years of the Gold Rush the sight of a female in public was so rare that "those whose misfortune it was to be obligated to be abroad felt themselves uncomfortably stared at. Doorways filled instantly, and little islands in the streets were thronged with men who seemed to gather in a moment."[11] By 1851 the *San Francisco Alta* was reporting, "We are pleased to see that each succeeding steamer is bringing to California the wives and families of many of our merchants and mechanics who have preceded them. It looks civilized and Christianlike to see ladies daily passing along our streets."[12]

The city was beginning to make room for the respectable wives, daughters, and sisters who arrived daily. Instead of tents, shacks, and low wooden buildings, substantial family homes began to appear, many built of brick or stone as protection against the frequent fires. Although complaints about sand, wind, and mud persisted, more and more streets were graded and planked, and the steam-paddy cut away sand hills. "Superb carriages now thronged the streets, and handsome omnibuses regularly plied between the plaza and the mission."[13] The sea journey to the Pacific slope, still arduous, became less risky and more predictable, with steamers now operating on regular schedules and the duration of the trip from the East cut down to less than a month.[14]

If physical hardship had diminished, a proper lady arriving in San Francisco in 1851 still faced a rigorous test. "The moral life of California," wrote one woman soon disabused of her high expectations, "is to character what the seven-times heated furnace is to the ore of the metallurgist—only purity itself can come unwasted through it."[15] Perhaps 20 percent of the females around were prostitutes, and a gambling or drinking man (most were both) thought nothing of exchanging an ounce of gold for the pleasure of a woman's company at the bar or card table. "There are some honest women in San Francisco," observed a Frenchman, "but not very many." [16]

In a city with three theaters, a circus, and 150 restaurants, serious pursuits of any kind were easily put aside. "Balls and convivial parties of brilliant character were constantly taking place," masked balls, full dress balls. "The great number of flaunting women of pleasure mightily encouraged this universal holiday." [17] Upstanding citizens cherished a hope that the respectable women now arriving would have a civilizing influence. The Rev. Dr. Scott preached a sermon claiming that what was most urgently needed in the West was neither a railroad nor a steamship line to China, "but the presence of mothers, wives and sisters, and a thorough American home education." [18]

Gertrude Franklin, the future mother of Gertrude Atherton, was just fifteen years old when she arrived in San Francisco with her mother and brother to join her father at Petit's Boarding House. To her father's increasing dismay, she proved too frail to resist the enticements of San Francisco's Vanity Fair. Made of less stern stuff than her Northeastern parents, she had been raised as a Southern belle. From the plantation where slaves had obliged her every wish, she went on to exclusive Eastern schools for the daughters of the elite. Invited to spend school vacations at the homes of wealthy school friends, she indulged her love of pleasure and her delight in being pampered. In San Francisco, her practical mother's admonition that they were no longer rich went unheeded. There was nothing Spartan in her nature, and she possessed, in her daughter's words, "not an atom of common sense."

Gertrude Franklin was "short but perfectly made," with enormous gray eyes, swelling bosom and hips, and tiny waist, hands, and feet. Not endowed with a surplus of energy, she expended whatever she had on the self-beautifying arts, with the goal of attracting male admirers by the score. She would turn heads, she would break hearts, she would measure her success in life by the number and devotion of her suitors. This was the only power she would ever know. With men outnumbering women ten to one in San Francisco, available women, even those less seductive than Gertrude Franklin, had to fight them off. "All danced attendance upon the beautiful Gertrude Franklin," and one young man threatened suicide if she refused him. When telling of this incident, she folded her arms and laughed (*Adventures*, p. 7).

Although an indulgent father, Stephen Franklin had no taste for frivolity, and keeping a belle in frocks and bonnets, hoops and crinolines, boots and gloves, was costing him sums he could ill afford. What's more, he worried that his light-headed daughter might make an impetuous match with a man as unlucky in money matters as he was, and less honorable to boot. San Francisco teemed with adventurous young men, cut off from distant families, who got money any way they could.

In this era of windfalls and downfalls, an unexpected bonanza came the Franklins' way. The New Orleans business partner who had speculated and lost the $30,000 had recouped. Evidently a man of scrupulous honesty, he made full restitution to Franklin, who bought a farming property of some 30 acres near San Jose—60 miles down the San Francisco Peninsula—which everyone called the Ranch. Hoping to deflect his daughter's attention from the godless ways of the city, he installed his family there. But Gertrude Franklin was miserable at the Ranch and begged to return to the city. She showed no interest in anything but clothes and social life, and her parents never seem to have even attempted to make her self-sufficient in any way. Their only solution was to marry her off, as quickly as possible. Since she would always be financially dependent, they reasoned, she had better marry rich.

If we are to believe *Adventures of a Novelist*, Thomas Lodowick Horn was the last man in the world Gertrude Franklin would have chosen as her mate. "My mother protested that she hated Yankees . . . , liked neither Mr. Horn nor his name, that she didn't want to marry yet; she was only nineteen and having a wonderful time. She wept; she would never marry a man unless she loved him" (*Adventures*, p. 8). Horn was urged on her not only by her parents, but by William Chapman Ralston, whose judgment in financial matters seemed impeccable. When Ralston, with his future banking partner D. O. Mills, took it upon himself to plead Thomas Horn's suit to Gertrude Franklin, she was bound to pay heed. She was made to understand that her father entirely lacked the ruthless competitiveness necessary for success in California. Youth passes quickly, they reminded her, and with it woman's best chance to marry well. The prosperous and promising tobacco merchant Mr. Horn alone among her many suitors deserved her consent.

Protesting her way to the altar, Gertrude Franklin, a native of New Orleans, married Thomas Horn, a native of Stonington, Connecticut, aged 25, on January 29, 1857, in a simple ceremony performed by Dr. Scott. What his estimate of Horn's character was we don't know. We do know he shared the materialist ethic. In a pamphlet called "The Wedge of Gold: or Achan in Eldorado," he had written: "True religion is not a declaration of war against wealth, refinement or elegance of taste and manners. . . . Money is a good thing. A man may be rich and yet be a saint." [19]

The rich Thomas Horn, whose Dutch and Alsatian forebears were shippers, whalers, and pirates, made no claim to sainthood. As a San Francisco Vigilante in 1856, he joined the unauthorized military operation that took the law into its own hands, hanging 4 men and deporting 30 others. He displayed none of the sense of public responsibility, or *noblesse oblige*, that Scott, Ralston, and Stephen Franklin all believed should accompany affluence. That part of his income not poured into the elegant Rincon Hill residence he shared with his new wife was invested in drink.

Rincon Hill and South Park at its feet composed the city's choicest enclave, an elite neighborhood of Italianate, Greek, or Gothic Revival houses, each with its own flower-filled garden. The hill has since been cut through, then leveled to make way for the freeway approach to the Bay Bridge, but then it rose about a hundred feet and boasted a magnificent view of the city, the Bay, and the harbor crowded with clipper ships and steamers.[20] In addition to the view, it offered a sunny, relatively fog-free climate and a respite from the bustle and wildness of the waterfront, Portsmouth Square, or Montgomery Street. There were no saloons or gambling halls on Rincon Hill, no brothels to tarnish the staid, upper-class atmosphere. The *Elite Directory* of San Francisco declared there was "little that was stylish or correct in the city" except in this vicinity,[21] and the socially ambitious citizens who gathered there, many sharing a Southern background and a sympathy for the pro-slavery Chivalry side of the Democratic party, agreed.

Thomas Horn's home, not far from the Gothic mansion built by his brother and business partner Benjamin Horn, stood on the east side of Second Street, near Harrison. Its French windows and double parlor, its horsehair furniture adorned with antimacassars, bespoke propriety, stability, respectability. But the menage within soon proved itself jerry-built. The Horn marriage anticipated a miniature Civil War, with a Yankee husband and a Southern wife engaged in daily, hostile confrontation. Although Horn "permitted his young wife every extravagance, she hated him increasingly; he took to drink, and as my mother was in hysterics most of the time while I was on the way, it is a wonder I was not born an idiot" (*Adventures*, p. 8).

To all appearances, 1857 was a placid year on the Pacific Slope. "As compared with the preceding eight years," wrote the chronicler Theodore Hittell, "1857 was quiet and dull. There was no remarkable mining excitement, no great speculation or panic in business. . . . Thieves and murderers stayed away for fear that the vigilance committee might resume power. Business continued to suffer under the depression that began three years before."[22] In that unremarkable year, almost nine months to the day after her parents' marriage, a girl given her mother's name of Gertrude Franklin Horn was born on Rincon Hill. Anyone scanning the San Francisco newspapers for an announcement of the October 30 birth will look in vain. Instead there are headlines about the previous month's disaster, from which San Francisco was still reeling. The steamer *Central America*, carrying a cargo and passengers from California to New York, had sunk off Cape Hatteras on September 12; 420 lives and $1.6 million in newly minted gold were lost.

Prominently displayed in the *Alta* for October 30 among the advertisements and business announcements is one that reads:

> T. L. Horn
> Having Withdrawn from the firm of
> B. C. and T. L. Horn will
> continue the
> Cigar and Tobacco Business
> Under the Name and Style of T. L. Horn & Co.
> at No. 67 Front St.

What Thomas Horn wanted the world to know that day was that he was launching an independent business, separate from his brother's.

But if his daughter's birth went unheralded, she would see to it that for the rest of her days she would be noticed. Her father, during his brief tenure under the same roof, encouraged her hell-raising proclivities by placing her in the center of the table so that she could kick plates into the laps of the assembled dinner guests.

Mingled with memories of her parents' quarrels and her father's drinking, Gertrude would retain some wispy images of her first years in San Francisco: wooden sidewalks, cobblestone streets, mud puddles, steep hills, foghorns; the celebrated lunatic Emperor Norton, who wore a plumed hat and gold-braided frock coat and proclaimed himself Emperor of the United States and Protector of Mexico; monkeys in North Beach; lamplighters, dust clouds, fires, jingling horse cars. "All my early experiences seem to have been of short duration," she would write (*Adventures*, p. 42), and the staccato pattern pursued her into adulthood. She perceived her childhood as a series of brief, disconnected episodes played out in ever-varying locations, with a rotating cast of characters. Schools, neighborhoods, and companions came and went. Most people, she came to feel, should not be trusted, least of all any man who happened to be married to her mother. She must learn to trust entirely in *herself*.

Before she was three, her parents were divorced, an event so cataclysmic in her eyes that even at a distance of 70 years she dramatized and isolated it as perhaps the first divorce in San Francisco. In fact, divorce was comparatively common in California in the 1850s and 1860s. Stable marriage was more rare on the mining frontier than elsewhere in the United States, in part because residency requirements were lax, remarriage easy to accomplish, wages high, migratory habits accepted. An 1851 California divorce law permitted either husband or wife to separate on grounds of incompatibility. San Francisco District Court records for 1856, within a year of the Horn wedding, report 260 marriages and 72 applications for divorce. A New York newspaper claimed "there are no people in the world who so practically ignore and hold in contempt the legal marital relations as do Californians."[23]

How, then, did Gertrude arrive at the impression that her mother was a freak, "ostracized as had she been a leper wandering through the streets in a cowl, a warning bell in her hand"? (*Adventures*, p. 9). The answer is that the Horns moved in a narrow, Southern-dominated, socially pretentious world that had its own set of inflexible standards and prejudices. The fact that the larger world of San Francisco and the West shrugged off the breaking of marriage vows did the young mother and her little girl no good. The elite of Rincon Hill and South Park banished a divorcée from their midst and placed her under social quarantine.

Mrs. Horn's decree was granted in September 1860, on grounds of her husband's "habitual intemperance." Thereafter, she and her daughter became the dependents of Stephen Franklin and soon went to live under his roof at the Ranch. It would be more accurate to say that the little girl went to live in the country with her grandparents, and her mother took time out from her San Francisco social life to visit the Ranch when the spirit moved her. Although society matrons like Mrs. Hall McAllister had crossed Mrs. Horn off their lists and stopped paying calls, male admirers continued to beat a path to her door. Her daughter would never forget, and would spend the rest of her days attempting to rival, the sight of "some ten or fifteen buggies hitched under the large oaks and sycamores surrounding the ranch house. The young men drove sixty miles on the Sundays when she was there and spent the day" (*Adventures*, p. 9).

San Jose in the early 1860s was a sleepy agricultural community in the Santa Clara Valley where palms, olives, almonds, and fig trees flourished in sun-drenched orchards. Gaslight had just been introduced, and the railroad was under construction; those who could not command a private carriage took the stage coach into San Francisco. The Ranch itself, three miles from town, had 33 acres, 30 of them "unimproved."[24] There were wheat fields, farm hands, a mule, and one lonely ox.

Little Gertrude romped around in a gingham frock, copper-toed boots, and sunbonnet with blonde braid protruding. From her absent mother she was learning that domestic chores were a bore and should be performed by others. The person she relied on for her daily care was her work-weary grandmother, Eliza Franklin, a thin, small woman, "very trim and erect, but prematurely old. Softened by those years of luxury in the South, she was unequal to the hardships of pioneer life." Since servants were hard to keep so far out in the country, she cooked for the farmhands and did most of the housework (*Adventures*, p. 9). Watching her sink under the weight of too much responsibility, Gertrude came to think of her as the personification of all she wished never to become.

At the Ranch Gertrude was both spoiled and neglected. Her mother's friends lavished gifts on her when they visited, but only her grandmother, distracted by so many other duties, made any attempt to control her. What she craved was the constant, engaged attention of her parents, and this she rarely had. Occasionally she traveled to San Francisco to visit her father, who was back in business with his brother. At best he was a shadowy presence, fading into an invisible one.[25] Her mother always had more important things on her mind— her social life and her appearance. Gertrude grew up feeling, as that other sometime Californian Gertrude Stein would about her own childhood, that by and large she brought herself up, embodying the wildness, independence, and freedom of the West.

Her one sure way to hold center stage was to act the hellion. When dressed for company "in white with a blue sash," she promptly found a mud puddle to roll in. She ran away daily and "discarding my shoes and stockings, played with my humble companions in the hay in the middle of the creek. When I returned, covered from head to foot with mud or barnyard filth, I regaled my grandmother, after the perfunctory spanking, with tales of imaginary adventures in which Indians and fairies played the major roles" (*Adventures*, p. 10). (When the impeccably groomed Mrs. Horn visited, Gertrude's predilection for dirt must have especially galled her.) She threw temper tantrums in public dining rooms, buried the silver in the garden, and habitually got into fights with boys. During the twice daily family prayers she would station herself behind her pious grandfather and devote herself to the braiding of her hair. "I was the angel child in appearance, with golden curls and eyes of seraphic blue, but I must have been a little fiend" (*Adventures*, p. 9).

In describing herself as a devil or "little fiend," Gertrude made use of one part of her religious education that stuck. Stephen Franklin provided a vocabulary of sin and retribution, but had no success in connecting the words, in Gertrude's mind, with Christian piety or altruistic conduct. She grew up regarding most religious people as hypocrites and considered prayers, Bible lessons, and church sermons

as forms of punishment. She could make no sense of her grandfather's insistence that God rewards the virtuous. How could that be
so, when so many scoundrels prospered and he himself, a model of
kindness and religious devotion, had to struggle along?

His efforts to run the Ranch profitably met with little success. A
pitiless drought overtook Northern California, leaving grain crops
scant and causing farm animals to starve. At the same time, Grandmother Franklin became gravely ill and could no longer carry her
burden of work. When Ralston offered Stephen Franklin a regular
job as secretary of the newly formed Bank of California, he accepted
gratefully. Carrying his ailing wife on a mattress on the floor of the
stage coach, he moved his family into a leased row house on Stockton
Street.

Enriched by Comstock silver and a growing population of refugees from the Civil War, San Francisco had become a booming
financial capital. There were new hotels, new millionaires, and street
railroads that brought the suburban neighborhoods into commuting
distance from downtown and the waterfront. The Pony Express had
already come and gone, replaced by the cross-country telegraph. San
Francisco now supported 4 carriage factories, 12 daily newspapers—
and 231 whiskey dealers.[26]

In 1865, the year following the Franklins' return to the city, two
momentous family events occurred in rapid succession: Gertrude's
mother remarried, and her grandmother died.

The wedding came first, joining the former Mrs. Horn to John
Frederick Uhlhorn, an aristocratic Easterner who worked in San
Francisco in the Quartermaster's Department. Being related to the
millionaire Lorillards of New York, he was considered quite a catch.
The fact that his family had sent him packing, if known, seemed
less important than his Dutch pedigree. With his erect posture and
Dundreary whiskers he was "exceedingly handsome according to the
canons of the day" (*Adventures*, p. 12). Society considered him noble
for marrying a divorcée who had a young daughter and not a penny
to her name. At a quiet ceremony attended only by Ralston, his partner D. O. Mills, little Gertrude, and Stephen Franklin, the old man
held the child's hand firmly and admonished her that she would be
slippered if she did not behave herself.

"My mother looked very beautiful in a lavender silk gown over a small hoop and trimmed with long loops of guimp. Her warm brown hair was arranged in masses of curls caught at the nape of the neck with a jewelled ornament. Her immense gray eyes looked like stars. . . . Mr. Uhlhorn stood very straight and imposing beside her" (*Adventures*, p. 13). Mr. Ralston, showing no more perspicacity than he had the first time around, declared, "I am sure they will be very happy."

Immediately afterwards, as the newlyweds set out for a honeymoon in Calistoga, Gertrude ran away. When a servant found her, hours later, in a sandlot, and brought her home, her grandfather pulled out a carpet slipper and "delivered two gentle taps." Gertrude burst out laughing, announced she had been spanked so many times she no longer felt anything, and what's more, "I never care, so long as I've got what I wanted first" (*Adventures*, p. 14). Since what she wanted was her mother, it's impossible to apply even a child's logic to this statement. What's apparent is that, by age seven, she excelled at denying and masking her deepest feelings. And her grandfather was no match for her. She loved and respected him, she craved his approval—and she rode roughshod over him. He could, and did, lock her in the closet on this occasion. But he could harness her will no better than he could tether the wind.

The turmoil of the wedding would forever mingle in Gertrude's memory with the cataclysmic national event that took place the following day: the assassination of Abraham Lincoln. In San Francisco, newspapers wore black borders. Shops closed. Bells tolled from city hall, fire stations, and churches. Buildings, private and public alike, were draped in mourning, and people in the street wept openly. Fury as well as grief sought expression. The offices of the pro-Confederate *Newsletter* were sacked, its presses destroyed, and type hurled out the window. Police were ordered to arrest on the spot any person who "should publicly express any approval of the assassination" or make "joyful demonstration of any character whatever."[27]

The Franklins had despised Lincoln and may well have joined other ex-Southerners who lamented Confederate defeats at Richmond or Appomattox. Once a slave-owner, Stephen Franklin loyally supported his pastor Dr. Scott, who had used his pulpit to offer prayer for "President" Jefferson Davis, had been hung in effigy for refusing to fly the Union flag outside his church, and had finally been forced to flee San Francisco until after the war. In the wake of the assassination the Franklin home conspicuously lacked the black mourning draperies displayed everywhere as evidence of solidarity. Failing to mourn publicly, at a time when emotion ran so high, was an open invitation to violence. Gertrude remembered "a mob" starting for their house. "As it appeared at the head of Stockton Street, the next-door neighbors tore up a black gown, rushed in, and hung it from the upper windows."[28] The Franklin household was spared.

The Uhlhorns returned from their honeymoon to the chaotic house on Stockton Street, where Grandmother Eliza now lay confined to bed; she died in May. Little Gertrude not only attended the funeral but was forced to kiss her dead grandmother in her coffin. "The faint smell of corruption mingled with tube roses" (*Adventures*, p. 13) lingered in her nostrils, tormenting her; she felt it would never leave, and she never lost her horror of dead bodies. As an adult she managed to be absent from the funerals of most of the important people in her life.

When the lease ran out on the Stockton Street house, Stephen Franklin went into lodgings, and the Uhlhorns moved into a new, tall brown house of their own on Oak Grove Avenue. Mr. Uhlhorn had entered the brokerage business, and Gertrude's mother was enjoying her happiest days. Society deigned to receive her once again, and she threw herself into a whirl of parties and dinners, balls and receptions. One evening she came into Gertrude's room to say goodnight just before going out. She had on a gown of "bright green corded silk, trimmed with crepe leaves, which inspired me with the ambition to grow up at once and inherit it" (*Adventures*, p. 16). If envy tinges this remark, undiluted hatred colors every reference to her stepfather. They had clashed on sight. He considered her a spoiled brat, and she missed no opportunity to annoy him. After almost knocking him over by hurtling down the banister, she was packed off to boarding school, but she soon returned home, having been ejected for bad conduct.

Back on Oak Grove Avenue she made a practice of sticking out her tongue at her stepfather, wooing the neighborhood children into playing with her by giving them her toys, then beating them up. She threw one down a flight of stairs. Furious at the world, she did not hesitate to express her rage in the traditional manner of boys, with physical aggression. In years to come, she would often liken herself to a prizefighter. She would write: "I have always envied Rider Haggard's *She*, who could hurl a bolt of lightning from her finger-tips and shrivel a man to one long cinder."[29]

No nurse would stay with Gertrude for any length of time, but with the birth of her half sister Aleece, in 1866, came a wonderful Irish woman named Rose Stoddard. Employed initially as a wet-nurse, she continued as the mainstay of Mrs. Uhlhorn's household for the next 35 years. Rose had a ne'er-do-well husband and three children of her own. Informed of Gertrude's record of scaring off all previous nurses, she expanded her enormous chest and said, "She'll mind me or find out the reason why." They were soon friends. Rose loved singing and poetry and encouraged Gertrude—who had been taught to read by her grandmother at age four—to read poetry to her while she nursed the baby. Gertrude was taken for daily long walks and, as a special treat, on visits to the homes of Rose's friends for gingerbread, jam, and a chance to hear gossip about somebody's drunken husband.

Of course Gertrude wanted Rose all to herself and resented the new baby, especially when she took sick and had to be watched constantly. When Mrs. Uhlhorn presented Rose with the gift of a new hat, Gertrude took a pair of scissors and, while Rose held the baby in her arms, quietly snipped it to pieces. Once she put the baby down, Rose responded, first with "a torrent of billingsgate," then with tears. At that display of frank anguish, Gertrude's own tears spouted. "I flung myself at her feet and begged her forgiveness, I called myself all the bad names I had heard at school, sobbed that I never would be a naughty horrid wicked girl again, that I loved her better than any one on earth and that she should have a new hat."[30]

Gertrude rarely expressed remorse or cried, and for her to declare her love directly was a freakish occurrence, reserved just for Rose. Often she would laugh when hurt or upset—as she had when her grandfather hit her with the slipper—displaying a hardness she would continue to cultivate. Tears were virtually banished as she grew older and displays of emotion—excepting wrath—held in check. As an adult she offered a simplistic explanation for what was a not at all simple compound of denial, repression, and defense: "When I was twelve an oculist warned me that I must never cry, for my eyes were in dangerous condition and I would go blind if I did not take the greatest care of them. I had already spent three months in a darkened room, and his words so terrified me that they must have created a permanent inhibition, for I have never shed a tear since" (*Adventures*, p. 125).

Being looked after by steady, maternal Rose was bliss, a state Gertrude rarely achieved. She would continue to seek such motherly types to adopt her and free her from domestic tasks, until her last days. (In Munich, she came to rely on her servant Elise Palmert, and in her last years her daughter Muriel performed this function.) The only real homes she would know were governed by efficient, nurturing women like Rose.

Her mother continued to lavish attention on herself, making a fetish of her beauty and attempting to preserve it by any means she could devise. "She went to bed every night with cold cream on her face an inch deep," and groomed herself with meticulous care. She never "had a hair out of place nor her frocks other than perfectly adjusted. . . . As time passed and her complexion lost its brilliancy, she used a good deal of make-up. . . . She bitterly resented the passing of youth and would have traded anything for its return" (*Adventures*, pp. 33, 34). Gertrude was compiling a mental file on her mother's cosmetic rituals designed to perpetuate the appearance of youth. In time she would retrieve them, having adopted as her own her mother's equation of youthful beauty with feminine allure.

Mrs. Uhlhorn had one mysterious habit. Every so often she announced that she was suffering an attack of "the blues" and must not be disturbed. She would retreat to the sofa in her room with curtains drawn, sometimes for days at a time. All food except broth was refused, and she would not speak. Whether these were bouts of depression, menstrual distress, migraine, or the effects of too much alcohol is unclear. A whispered family secret, never repeated in print by Gertrude, was that her mother "drank."

Liquor certainly occupied a place of prominence in the Uhlhorn household. Whisky, brandy, and gin were used as remedies for every possible malady. Gertrude grew up being liberally dosed with all three, plus port wine with cod liver oil in it, "stout" as a tonic, and raw eggs in sherry.[31] For years after she left home she would not touch alcohol in any form, and the drinking woman became a recurrent character in her fiction.

Mrs. Uhlhorn found another escape route in the novels she read, especially those of "Ouida," in which no one was ordinary and extremes of all kinds flourished: wealth and poverty, beauty and degradation. Romances removed her to a fantasy realm in which the heroine enjoyed limitless power, where nothing seemed impossible, nothing humdrum.

Gertrude caught the fiction-reading habit—the more extravagant the plot, the better. She had always loved fairy tales, which pleased her elders. But when she was caught "gazing entranced at the harrowing illustrations" of a novel called *The Daughter of an Empress* by Louise Muhlbach, her mother snatched it away, saying, "go back to your fairy tales." Determined to continue reading it, Gertrude hid both the novel and herself in a straw hamper. There she read until all light had faded, throwing the adults, who feared her lost or kidnapped, into panic. "I read until . . . I had finished gasping over the painful end of the heroine, knouted to death by brutal executioners. Then, discovering that I was hungry, I tipped over the hamper and crawled out" (*Adventures*, pp. 19–20).

By retreating into a hamper to read romantic fiction Gertrude established a life-long pattern. Fantasy and imagination became associated with physical retreat from the world. In "holing up," escaping to a concealed, private realm, she could become doubly removed from the present and its vexing realities. Novels became her chosen narcotic. She read *Jane Eyre* six times (and the Brontës became an enduring passion), devoured *Little Women*, the Gipsy Brenton series, and Oliver Optic. Inspired to see what she could produce herself, she filled blank notebooks with stories, reveling in the praise they elicited from her teachers and her bookish grandfather.

There were more reasons to seek escape as her mother's second marriage turned sour. Mr. Uhlhorn's business failed, and his fondness for gambling houses increased. He lost everything and sold his wife's jewels so that he could gamble more. Once again, the family felt the sting of social ostracism. "There were no more dinners, luncheons and balls. No more carriages before the door on my mother's 'day.' No more drives to the Cliff House on fine afternoons when all the wealth and fashion of the city turned out behind spanking teams to gaze at the illimitable ocean, the chattering seals on their rock, and one another's clothes" (*Adventures*, p. 20). Mr. Uhlhorn, when home, would glower, his wife weep, and the babies squall. And by now there were two babies. A second half sister, Daisy, was born in 1867 in the second-class Brooklyn Hotel: Mr. Uhlhorn now worked as a bank clerk, and the family moved through a series of increasingly smaller lodgings on unfashionable streets.

Instead of arousing compassion, Mrs. Uhlhorn's misery triggered in Gertrude an ill-concealed fury. How could her mother have been fooled by such a rotter as Uhlhorn in the first place, and why did she now endure his affronts in silence? Gertrude seethed at what she called her mother's "supineness," her utter passivity. "To fight for what I wanted was as natural to me as to accept the gifts the gods provided as my right, and I made no allowance for a character that had not an atom of fight in it" (*Adventures*, p. 44).

While Mrs. Uhlhorn could not have enjoyed her daughter's hostility, she seems to have at least fitfully encouraged in Gertrude the renegade qualities she so markedly lacked herself. One of their many short-lived relocations was across the Bay to Oakland, where for day-school graduation exercises Gertrude and her classmates were told to wear a prescribed costume consisting of a white tarlatan skirt, red flannel Garibaldi waist, and blue sash. Mrs. Uhlhorn, whose one domestic talent was sewing and who placed such great importance on appearance, decided her firstborn would wear nothing of the kind. In the years following the Civil War she still must have thought of red, white, and blue as Union colors, which she wanted none of. Instead she set about making a dress of "fine white swiss, tucked to the waist," and sent Gertrude to graduation wearing it. One of the teachers drew her aside, saying, "Be proud of your lovely dress, and don't worry about being different." For Gertrude it was a moment of crystallization: henceforth she would make it her object to always be "as different as possible" (*Adventures*, p. 22).

Returned to San Francisco, she attended a school hand-picked by her grandfather, a private Presbyterian day school called City Female Seminary. (When someone on the board objected to the word "Female" as "indelicate," the school was renamed, after its director, Clarke Institute.) Clarke took itself seriously as an academic institution, offering its young ladies instruction in an impressive array of subjects including Latin, Greek, reading, recitation, orthography, analysis, versification, cosmography, natural philosophy, rhetoric, botany, chemistry, trigonometry, English and American history, English literature, and moral science.[32]

How much of this demanding curriculum rubbed off on Gertrude in her two years there is a matter for speculation. She certainly never learned Latin, Greek, or much science. She studied as little as possible and lived for recess, when she gambled with her schoolmates for glass buttons in the yard. At last a competitive spark ignited in her. She got tired of hearing the same three girls' names—hers not among them—honored each Friday for high achievement, and "turned abruptly from an idler to a hard student." Before long she heard her name called on the honor list (*Adventures*, p. 30). However, the discontinuity of her high school education could not have encouraged her to concentrate on her studies for very long. In four years, she attended three different schools: first Clarke, then an Episcopal boarding school in Benicia called St. Mary's Hall, then the Sayre Institute in Kentucky.

A new domestic catastrophe took place during her last year at Clarke, one that irrevocably shattered her mother's sense of herself and destroyed any semblance of "normal" family life for Gertrude. At that time the family occupied a small house on Jones Street where visitors never called. Rose, now installed as cook and maid of all work, often set no place at the table for Mr. Uhlhorn, who had taken to staying out nights. Mrs. Uhlhorn, her gray eyes red and swollen, complained she had nothing to wear. One night Rose rebuked Gertrude sharply: she was not to go near the front bedroom. Mr. Uhlhorn was ill. At the first opportunity, Gertrude crept down the hall and peered inside the forbidden chamber. She saw her stepfather sprawled, fully dressed, on the bed, breathing loudly, his eyes closed. Her mother stood beside him, motionless. Terrified, Gertrude shut herself in her room. In addition to fear she was conscious of another sensation, one of detached excitement before an unfolding drama. The feeling would visit her repeatedly, whenever she was about to witness death or disaster: "Mingled with apprehension was a keen expectation of something interesting to come" (*Adventures*, p. 25).

She did not learn until much later that her stepfather had attempted suicide by taking chloroform. He had forged his employer's name for a large amount, probably to pay a gambling debt, and had been found out. When Stephen Franklin learned of the forgery, Rose later told her, he and Mr. Uhlhorn had a tremendous row. Mr. Uhlhorn shouted and swore and called his father-in-law a sanctimonious old fool. Franklin, without raising his voice, called his son-in-law a scoundrel, a blackguard, a gambler, and a thief.[33]

Gertrude lay awake at midnight when her grandfather abruptly reentered their house. Mr. Uhlhorn was swaying on his feet. He wore his overcoat and hat and was holding a bag. His mouth hung open, and his expression was blank. Franklin seized him, hurried him down the stairs and into a waiting carriage. He was put on a ship bound for South America and warned never to return. Although he may have promised to stay out of California, he did eventually return, and in the 1880s turned up as part-owner of a large ranch in Tulare County. But the Franklins never knew of this. They buried him.

Mrs. Uhlhorn considered her own life at an end. She did not speak for days, until a new crisis jolted her out of melancholia. Daisy, her youngest daughter, came down with smallpox and had to be quarantined and nursed. Gertrude was sent away to Paso Robles hot springs for two months, far from the pest house and the stricken homes with their warning yellow flags. (For years, in an effort to protect herself against infection, she wore a camphor bag around her neck.) When she came home, Daisy was out of danger, and her mother had assumed the role of semi-invalid and near recluse. She rarely went out. Other than sewing, she did no work in the house. Rose took charge.

Stephen Franklin found himself once again responsible for supporting his daughter's household. He moved in, bringing with him his private library, some of which were eighteenth-century editions inherited from his father. On an evening that Gertrude came to regard as a turning point, he addressed her sternly: "I have decided," he began, "that the time has come to give a more serious turn to your mind. You are now fourteen . . . and you are wasting your time on stories written for boys and girls. You have a naturally bright mind, wayward as it is, and it is time to improve it. I wish you to become a well-read intellectual woman. . . . You will read aloud to me for two hours every night" (*Adventures*, p. 28).

Gertrude had never even tried to meet her grandfather's standards of virtuous conduct. He now handed her a chance to measure herself by a different yardstick, and she leapt at it. It pleased her to be invested with hope and ambition. If she could not be good, she would excel at being clever. She threw herself into the reading sessions, which became a most valued part of her education. They began with "something light," Washington Irving's *The Conquest of Granada*. She read aloud Thiers's two-volume *History of the French Revolution* and the multi-volume *History of England* by Hume. Of course she complained of boredom, but she did not falter, and was rewarded with a chance to indulge her love of poetry. Together they "did" the English poets, from Chaucer through Shakespeare, then leaping ahead to the Romantics, capped by "safe" selections from Byron.

When her grandfather was away she read the sections of *Childe Harold* and *Don Juan* that he had tried to keep her from. In Byron her hungry, romantic imagination found an idol embodying the ascendancy of the individual. His mastery of his own fate, his rebellion against repressive social, familial, and religious institutions, aroused passionate identification. Solitary, courageous, mercurial, Byron asserted in a way that spoke directly to her soul the individual's power to shape his or her own destiny.[34]

Prodigious in quantity and scope, her reading—what she did on her own combined with what she did with her grandfather—opened a window on the wide horizon beyond her narrow sphere. But it was essentially anarchic. It provided much in the way of information and stimulation, but little focus, selection, or discipline. Like everything else in her childhood, it encouraged her distrust of authority and rigor and buttressed her already pronounced tendency to see herself as the measure of all things. At the same time, reading taught her to live in her head and on the page, rather than with other people. The realm of books offered a safe haven, a solitary home she would never have to share or leave.

CHAPTER TWO

Mrs. George Atherton

When Gertrude arrived at the San Jose train station after her year in Kentucky, Mrs. Uhlhorn awaited her. Gertrude registered surprise; as far as she knew her mother still preferred to live in San Francisco, not at the Ranch. Shaken by the news of Ralston's death and by her grandfather's failure to appear, she found little to cheer her in the still lovely woman's presence, especially when it became clear her mother had not come to the station alone. "What is *he* doing here?" seventeen-year-old Gertrude asked as Mrs. Uhlhorn led the way to a small open carriage whose driver—Gertrude's mother begged her to treat him decently—politely lifted his hat. It was George Atherton (*Adventures*, p. 45).

The young driver with the tawny moustache and the broad black eyebrows appeared to be Mrs. Uhlhorn's new suitor; he was staying at the Ranch until he found "something to do." Stephen Franklin, ever hopeful for the rescue promised by a brilliant match for his luckless daughter, was doing what he could to quicken the young man's ardor and had invited him to visit. George had accepted happily. He had quarreled with his own family over his involvement with Mrs. Uhlhorn—twice divorced and fourteen years his senior, with three children—and was busying himself by taking charge of the Ranch horses (he was an expert horseman) and driving people to and from the San Jose train station.

Despite his youth (he was 24) and apparent lack of purpose, George Henry Bowen Atherton offered the kind of impeccable financial and social credentials the Franklins had always held in esteem. His father, Massachusetts-born Faxon Dean Atherton, was a California land baron who had made a fortune selling commodities to Gold Rush miners and investing his profits in real estate. His mother was Dominga de Goñi Atherton, a diminutive Chilean who boasted of her Castilian blood. Married in Valparaiso, where they lived for many years and where six of their seven children were born, the Athertons had moved in 1860 to California, installing themselves on a sprawling Peninsula estate, halfway between the Ranch and San Francisco, called Valparaiso Park.[1]

Dramatically handsome and possessed of fine manners, George had every intention of marrying Mrs. Uhlhorn, but his family's opposition posed a dilemma; he had no wealth or standing independent of theirs. The Athertons, devout Catholics, would have resisted any marriage to a divorcée, even one closer to George's age and with more secure social standing. They took pride in their lofty position among the most exclusive and relentlessly conservative families around San Francisco. They had utterly conventional standards of social propriety and little tolerance for deviation.

However distinguished his family, George lacked the self-definition or command of a strong personality. The indulged son of a doting mother, he cared nothing for his father's realm—work, commerce, public events, and ideas—preferring the diversions of horses, cards, and pretty women. On seeing him, Gertrude, who of course resented him instantly, entertained briefly the hope that he might at least provide interesting and intelligent conversation, but soon concluded that his intellectual-looking forehead gave a deceptive impression. He liked to talk, but as Gertrude put it, "he never said anything" (*Adventures*, p. 48).

Mrs. Uhlhorn did not mind. She found him charming company, and his attentiveness renewed her sense of herself—now far less secure than it once was—as a femme fatale. She failed to observe, however, as the weeks passed, that a subtle but unmistakable shift was taking place: George was beginning to show romantic interest in her daughter, who had youth in her favor and a provocative manner that beguiled him. To hear her tell it in her autobiography, one would think Gertrude did nothing to encourage him; she was a mere cork upon the waters. "His expressive eyes and signs, his muttered endearments, merely irritated me, and I shut myself up in the library and trained my dog to growl at him if he ventured over" (*Adventures*, p. 50).

The fact is, George livened up a singularly dreary scene. Gertrude and her mother considered living at the Ranch a form of burial, and at that moment, after the recent debacle at the Bank of California, there was no money to maintain a San Francisco address or, we can conjecture, to finance a final year of boarding school for Gertrude. The Ranch resembled a sanitorium these days, since Aleece had a lung condition and was being nursed by Rose Stoddard, under the supervision of a doctor who prescribed Pale Ale. Daisy was too young to provide much company, and nobody seemed particularly interested in how Gertrude occupied herself.

She passed the hours reading, dreaming, and romping with her dog. What should by rights have been "her" year—a year for finishing high school and being feted as a debutante—was turning out to be humdrum. She found George's attentions both flattering and diverting. Moreover, they allowed her to feel more attractive than her mother—a new and exhilarating sensation in a young woman envious of her mother's voluptuous appeal: "She had far more than I, who was a skinny young thing with a general appearance of being washed out. Beside her ripe beauty I looked like a rag" (*Adventures*, p. 45). There can be little question that to Gertrude George's greatest attraction, an attraction she did not consciously acknowledge, was that he provided a way for her to injure and surpass her mother.

But that was not his sole appeal. Gertrude found him "magnetic." His conversation bored her, but her pulse quickened when he entered the room. In her autobiographical novel *Patience Sparhawk and Her Times*, written twenty years after these events, George turns up as the handsome, frivolous mama's boy Beverly Peele, transplanted to Westchester County, New York. The identification in Gertrude's mind between Peele and George Atherton is so close that she uses the same vocabulary to describe George in *Adventures of a Novelist* that she had applied to Beverly earlier. He has the same pouting mouth under a drooping moustache, the same tiresome devotion to horses, a duplicate "intellectual brow" that raises false expectations. Although Gertrude's surrogate, Patience Sparhawk, has no respect for the ardently amorous Beverly (whose name may be a tip-off that in Gertrude's eyes he isn't a "real" man), being near him leaves her weak. She stares up at him, her eyes expanding, and something seems to crumble within her. When he embraces and boldly kisses her, the fury and loathing she professes fall away. Blood pounds in her ears and the very air seems to hum. She must concede that although the man's magnetism is "purely animal," it wields tremendous force (*Patience Sparhawk*, 176).

In Patience, as in Gertrude, a double conflict arises. Angry at Beverly for attempting to make love to her, she is even more furious at herself for allowing her own body's flushed response to overtake her like a tidal wave.

During the long, dull, stormy winter of 1876—America's centennial year—George proposed to Gertrude five times. On the day of his sixth proposal, Valentine's Day, Gertrude was "sitting in the library reading the *Phaedo* of Plato. That I understood little of it and appreciated it not at all mattered nothing; I was determined to be well read. I looked up with a scowl as he entered, in the mood, I could see, to propose. . . . I lowered my eyes ostentatiously to the book and turned my back." But he persevered. Finally, according to Gertrude, she yielded with a shrug. "Oh well, I don't care. One has to marry some time, I suppose. But do leave me in peace. I prefer Plato" (*Adventures*, p. 50).

They eloped the next day. George had the license in his pocket when they left for their customary ride to pick up Stephen Franklin at the train station. Without telling Gertrude, he had arranged to have a Jesuit priest marry them in San Jose along the way. Unprepared for such haste, Gertrude threatened to jump out of the carriage, then thought better of it. "Where was I to meet another man, isolated on the Ranch? I might well wilt away into spinsterhood, always a burden on my grandfather." The excitement of the moment began to take hold as she assumed a third-person detachment, becoming a spectator of the drama that was about to unfold. She could see herself as the heroine of a romantic novel, "dressed in the trains and fancy evening caps then fashionable among married women." Feeling "cynical and Ouidaish," she capitulated.

For the present, she blotted out any scruples about her mother's prior claim. "That I was about to commit a scoundrelly act never occurred to me." She behaved, she would later say, like an overgrown child "whose instinct it is to reach out and take what it wants" (*Adventures*, p. 51). She did not know herself well enough to recognize for what it was the piquancy of beating her mother at the only game she knew, social and sexual competition. It was a victory of power substituted for love and moral integrity.[2]

Once married, the newlyweds faced their obligation to break the news to their families. George, they agreed, should return to his parents' home on the pretext that his father had called him back on important business. Gertrude would go alone to the Ranch. She unburdened her secret first to Rose, who "uncorked the vials of her wrath," hurling epithets at her unrepentant former charge. But Rose agreed not to tell the others right away. She went along with Gertrude's plan to wait until the last possible moment and confess only after George sent word that she should come and join him.

After a week, George informed her that the way had been cleared for her to move to Valparaiso Park the following Monday. Gertrude planned to keep her secret, but Stephen Franklin, down at the Ranch for the weekend, mentioned a rumor he had heard on the train— that Gertrude had married George Atherton—and the truth spilled out.

Her grandfather's usually twinkling eyes turned to blue agates and his face whitened. Before retiring, he addressed her in a voice "as cold as Aunt Mary's ice house." "I have little to say to you," he began. "You have been ungrateful to me and have acted disgracefully toward your mother. There was no reason for secrecy. I never knew you to do anything underhand or cowardly before, and no words can express my disappointment in you. As for the young man—whether he will make you happy or not remains to be seen. I do not think, however, that you will have any trouble with his family. They will be so relieved that he has married a raw girl instead of a woman many years older than himself, they will no doubt receive you with open arms. You belong to them now. I am obliged to return to the city tomorrow afternoon. Kindly keep out of my way meanwhile. It will be some time before I wish to see you again" (*Adventures*, p. 54).

They did not meet again for three years.

The Athertons received Gertrude politely but without the open arms Stephen Franklin had envisioned. True, they were relieved to have been spared the taint of Mrs. Uhlhorn, but they had pinned their hopes for George on "a nice domestic girl of their exclusive set, with a tidy little fortune" (*Adventures*, p. 52). Gertrude was a stranger, penniless, of questionable background, and not Catholic (they would insist on her baptism). But she was young, pretty, and they fondly hoped, malleable.

George's father Faxon, gray-bearded, taciturn, and a classic patriarch, did not involve himself directly with the matter of the elopement. Domestic and family matters were handled by Dominga, whose toy-like appearance—she stood only five feet tall and weighed 200 pounds—belied her tyrannical manner. She was the mother of eight children, one of whom had died in Chile. Three of the daughters—Alejandra, Isabel, and Elena—were already married, and the youngest, Florence, was still at school. Of the boys, Frank, the eldest, was "weak minded" as the result of a childhood fall. Faxon Jr., the youngest, was a young buck of wild habits. George was the first son to marry and his mother's darling.

Dominga wielded her maternal scepter like a Spanish queen, enforcing aristocratic Catholic standards of filial duty and social propriety. Rule one was that the children were to consult her in all matters and respect her wishes. She frowned on ostentation, but the wealth of her friends was taken for granted. In men she expected success in business or a profession, along with distinguished birth. Women were required to combine noble ancestry with domestic accomplishment. Once married, they were to manifest unswerving devotion to home, husband, and children. Her three married daughters had not disappointed her. Alejandra was the wife of Lawrence Rathbone, a major in the Navy. Elena had married into the well-known San Francisco shipping and importing Macondray family. Isabel's husband, in Chile, was a Valparaiso banker.

Her favorite son's precipitous marriage, and his choice of bride, threw her into an emotional tailspin. Mrs. Thomas Selby, a neighbor and future in-law of the Athertons, addressed her as if a death had occurred: "When I heard of the marriage of George, I was so drawn to you that I could hardly keep from writing to you of my sympathy and love to you all. My dear friend, none of us ought to depend upon our children for happiness. . . . This is indeed a turning point in George's life. I do trust that he will be happy and useful. He has married a young and pretty girl, thin maybe, and I do hope they will help each other." [3]

Dominga had no choice but to come to terms. The marriage had been performed by an ordained Catholic priest, was binding in the eyes of God, the church, and the law, and that was that. As Stephen Franklin had put it to Gertrude, she belonged to the Athertons now. However isolated and unwelcome she felt on the inside of that inner circle of her mother's thwarted dreams, in the eyes of society Gertrude had arrived.

Valparaiso Park, the Atherton country estate that occupied much of the original Las Pulgas land grant, sprawled over a vast expanse of choice Peninsula countryside that became even more choice after the railroad made it an easy commute from San Francisco. Once owned by Louis Argüello, first Mexican governor of California, the fertile land now made up a lushly planted haven personally overseen by Faxon Dean Atherton, who cultivated the manner of a country squire. [4]

In true baronial fashion, he looked forward to the time when each of his children would acquire a separate house on his 640-acre estate, whose center would remain the main house, which the family had occupied since 1861. Compared to the opulent showiness of Ralston's Belmont palace, the Big House was an understated affair, a solid, square, two-story wooden structure with simple lines, large, light-filled rooms, plain furniture, and floors covered with matting. The bathrooms were the one luxury; there were two of them. And the setting—in a clearing in woods thick with oaks and bay trees, orchards of fruit trees, surrounded by lawns exorbitantly expensive to

water and gardens dense with roses, fushias, lilacs, and heliotrope—
was a glory. A deep veranda, favorite gathering place of the women
on long summer days, traversed three sides of the house.

The house was not designed to impress, for the Athertons took
their superiority for granted. Gertrude had never encountered such
smugness. "They prided themselves upon having the shortest visiting list in San Francisco, and what they did or had or were was of an
indisputable rightness. Everything suffered by comparison. As none
of the children was a pure blonde, Mrs. Atherton lamented my surface accessories, but consoled me with the hope that my hair would
grow darker with the years" (*Adventures*, p. 60).

Wealth alone did not earn their approval. On the contrary, the garish displays of the *nouveaux riches* aroused nothing but scorn. When
James Flood, a Bonanza mining millionaire, Irishman, and former
San Francisco saloon keeper, bought 300 acres in Menlo Park and
set about building a spectacular "wedding cake" of a white house
adorned with turrets and crenellations, the Athertons sneered. For
many weeks the leading topic of conversation on the veranda of the
Big House was whether or not to call on the Floods when they
moved in. Husbands at last impressed upon their wives that for business reasons the Floods must not be shunned (*Adventures*, pp. 63–64).
Dressed simply, as was the custom among the established Peninsula aristocracy, the Atherton women called at the Flood's frescoed
drawing room. They were received by a silk-and-lace-bedecked Mrs.
and Miss Flood, who served tea in Dresden cups from a service of
Comstock silver.[5]

"Business reasons" forced the Athertons to relax their rigid social
code where people like the Floods were concerned, but could not
be invoked to make them revise a hidebound distrust of intellectual display, particularly if the intellect in question happened to be a
woman's. Dominga considered bookishness unladylike and a breach
of genteel Spanish custom. She lectured her new daughter-in-law
in her heavily accented English, reminding her that reading served
no purpose and set a bad example. She must control her impulsiveness and learn to perform with skill and devotion the duties of a
conscientious wife, housekeeper, and mother-to-be.

Dominga felt a certain urgency in her mission to correct the
defects of Gertrude's upbringing, because George's young wife—

without at all wishing it—found herself immediately pregnant. The Atherton heir she carried would be no ordinary grandchild; it would be the first one born to a son, hence the first to carry the august Atherton name.

In anticipation of this significant offspring Gertrude must be taught to sew, for it was the custom in Spain for expectant mothers of all classes to make the baby's layette by hand. "Gertrudes," as Dominga called her, proved hopeless at taking tiny tucks in linen, but she did learn to embroider flannel petticoats. Dominga sat her down beside her for three hours a day of supervised instruction in needlework, protesting all the while her pupil's pronounced lack of experience or aptitude. "So child you are!" she would say. "So child." Gertrude had never been the object of such concentrated maternal discipline and she did her best, initially, to please. Dominga cowed her more than a little, and there was no way to hide from her watchful eye.

While a separate house on the grounds was being built for them, Gertrude and George continued to live at the Big House. Estranged from her family, pregnant, enjoined to stay away from her beloved books, nineteen-year-old Gertrude suffered a loneliness and disorientation entirely new to her. She had no friends her own age. Alejandra Rathbone was the only one of George's sisters living nearby at present, and she was already in her thirties—"but a few years younger than my mother." Florence was at school and was too young for Gertrude anyway. Elena, the second eldest, lived with her husband, Frederick Macondray, in San Francisco, except during the summer, when she and her children moved in at Menlo. George went into the city every day with his father, who had set him up in the brokerage business. But even when he was home, he could not be called a companion.

Walks in the woods refreshed and delighted her, but she found the household routine stultifying. "Mrs. Rathbone came over every afternoon. Neighbors dropped in"—though there was considerably less company during the rainy winters, when unpaved roads were hard to navigate and those with houses in San Francisco preferred to stay there. "They sat on the wide veranda, sewing, embroidering, exchanging recipes, gossiping. I often wondered if life anywhere in the whole world were as dull" (*Adventures*, p. 62).

Meals were elaborate productions, featuring Chilean dishes Dominga had taught her Chinese cook to prepare. During and after one of these eight-course marathons Gertrude was denied even the pleasure of eavesdropping, for with her own family Dominga spoke Spanish. Perhaps because her pregnancy made her queasy, Gertrude refused to eat the highly seasoned food. The cook had to prepare a separate plate for her, which did not enhance her popularity with him or Dominga.

Like her mother before her, Gertrude became pregnant in the first weeks of her marriage, and she was totally unprepared for motherhood. She had submitted to Dominga's demand that she be baptized a Catholic and taken instruction in catechism three times a week. But nobody taught her the first thing about caring for an infant. In fact, since moving in with the Athertons, Gertrude sensed she was becoming increasingly childlike herself, a feeling fueled by Dominga's assumption of maternal authority.

The baby, a boy named George Goñi, was born November 20, 1876. He seemed to Gertrude a living doll, with her own fair complexion and blue eyes. But he proved to be delicate, moody, and irritable. He had to be bottle fed, and the Athertons kept a special cow just for him. The fiercely protective Dominga hovered over him, as did a full-time nurse. After Gertrude demonstrated her unfitness by holding the baby upside down, Dominga forbade her to hold her own son. Gertrude did not fight to hold him. She resisted her new identity as mother, just as she would every subsequent adjustment to growing older. "I had not wanted a baby and . . . was rather resentful that I never had been a 'young lady' and now never could be."[6]

Dominga's solicitude bordered on the histrionic even without provocation, but Gertrude gave her cause. In absolute and malignant ignorance she had decided to take action against poor Georgie's ears, which had an unfortunate tendency to stick out. When the nurse stepped out of the nursery for a moment, Gertrude (who behaved exactly as if the baby *were* a doll and not flesh and blood) took a concealed bottle of glue from its hiding place and made liberal application behind each offending ear. "Some time later the child was screaming in agony. All the family . . . rushed upstairs. The explanation was not far to seek!" The nurse had attempted to remove the glue with her fingers and broke the baby's skin. "He screamed so that he ruptured himself."

Gertrude, who had been basking in Atherton approval since the birth of their male heir, suffered instant disgrace. Dominga squelched a temptation to slap her and after a stinging rebuke refused to speak to her for several days. When she did speak, her words were harsh: "Never you grow up, I suppose. Si that baby die, you have keeling him. Why George he no marry a girl of good sense?" (*Adventures*, p. 70).

Gertrude's response to these traumas of first motherhood was simply to abdicate the caretaker role entirely, yielding to her own suspicion and Dominga's accusation that she was incompetent and could only inflict harm. Forever after, even following the birth of her second child, she would insist that she had been created with the "instinct for maternity" left out of her. Let others perform the functions for which she had no talent and less inclination.

She also forswore the demands of housekeeping. She, George, a cook, a new nurse, and the baby were finally settled in a separate house that Alejandra had designed. It had just one story and stood in the cove of the front woods. Its enormous living room had a redwood ceiling around a glass skylight. George took charge of running things, but she had insisted on two requisites: red maple furniture and ample bookcases, though as yet she had no books. Living in the woods as they did, they shared their space with abundant wildlife, including fleas, spiders—even scorpions—and harmless snakes, which Gertrude herself would kill with an axe, since she found them loathsome to look at. Aggression was one area in which she required no instruction.

The neighbors came to call—Lathams, Selbys, perhaps even Floods. One of them, a lawyer named John T. Doyle, had an extensive library, and Gertrude prevailed upon him to let her borrow from it. After that he brought her books regularly, and other neighbors lent her novels. An acquaintance wrote to Gertrude decades later of her remembered visit to that house in the woods: "The maple easy chairs and the big table were so stunning in the round room. You were wearing a red robe—reading."[7]

A shadow now hung over the Big House, for Faxon Sr. had been felled by a clot on the brain and was not expected to live. When he died, on July 18, 1877, he was laid out in a small room on the left of the main entrance to the Big House, where George compelled Gertrude to go in and view him. The sight of his wax-like visage and shrunken body reminded her of her grandmother's corpse and left a lingering chill. But for once the Spanish protectiveness of women worked to her advantage, and she, along with the other women, was excused from attending the Requiem Mass in San Francisco, for which a special train had been hired to transport mourners from the Peninsula.

Faxon Dean Atherton left an estate valued at close to one million dollars, including bank, mining, and water stock and extensive property in Alameda, Monterey, San Mateo, and Solano counties. His will stipulated that half the estate would go to Dominga, named as co-executor with agent Alexander Grogan. The other half was to be held in trust for the next five years, then divided among the children. The children were allowed monthly allowances borrowed against their inheritance, but the sum of whatever they borrowed would be deducted from their share in the ultimate division of property. Valparaiso Park would remain Dominga's for the rest of her life; eventually it would be subdivided for each of the seven children. George and Faxon Jr. were specifically encouraged to borrow up to $20,000 each in advances "for approved business ventures."[8]

Instead of being freed by his father's largess, George found himself in immediate legal and financial straits. Like many an indulged son of the upper class, he had been raised with no sense of financial responsibility, and he possessed none of his father's business acumen. A habitual gambler, he was already in default when Faxon Sr. died. He had failed in the brokerage business, and as soon as it became known that his father's death had made him an heir, the creditors descended, demanding instant payment. One even tried to get a lien on the Valparaiso Park property so that a foreclosure sale at the courthouse door could supply the necessary cash. Dominga won an injunction preventing the sale, on the grounds that she owned the property for her lifetime.[9]

As protection against the accumulating summonses, complaints, bills, and writs, George tried the legal maneuver of signing his inheritance over to his wife, so that technically he would be incapable of making good on his debts. This was no more than a ploy. Though he filed a document assigning his wife, "in consideration of love and affection," interest in his entitled estate "free, clear and discharged from any and all debts or obligations of mine," Gertrude never con-

trolled his monthly allowance or borrowed a cent against his inheritance.[10]

She had to beg for every penny she received from George, who
combined the sins of improvidence and—where she was concerned
—parsimony. Dominga provided her simple wardrobe and the baby's
needs. When she asked George for an allowance "he merely smiled
in the superior masculine manner. Women had no use for money.
What had I to spend it on? Clothes? I always looked as well as anybody. Books? He scowled. . . . Books! I spent too much time reading
as it was. I should be learning to keep house and sew for my children"
(*Adventures*, p. 83).

In the few surviving letters Gertrude wrote to George while married she often speaks of money, or rather the lack of it. "I did not
go to Hamm's and engage another girl for fear you would telegraph
again and make me lose another $2.50," she says in one, and in
another, "I am afraid I shall not have any money for Christmas after
all." Her mother's experience of male insolvency and unreliability
was being recapitulated. The indignity of her total financial dependence on a tight-fisted ne'er-do-well left scars that never healed.

For the present, though, she felt she had no choice but to make
the best of a bad situation. Written from San Francisco and always
signed, "Lovingly, Gertie," her poignant letters demonstrate that
whatever her misgivings about George, she was trying, in the first
years, to make the marriage work. "I have written you every day and
have only heard from you once." "Hurry up and send for me and
give lots of kisses to Georgie." "As long as I am going down, I should
like to be settled as soon as possible, and besides it is so much nicer
for all of us to be together."[11] It is hard to believe these docile, rather
colorless words come from the pen of Gertrude Atherton.

Not long after his father's death, George and Gertrude faced a
dramatic change: a move to Rancho Milpitas, 43,000 acres in Monterey County along the San Antonio River near Mission San Antonio
de Padua and the largest of the Atherton holdings. Part of the land
had been settled by indigent Indian, Mexican, and Anglo families
who farmed it in the belief that it belonged to the government. The

Athertons, armed with a court decision in their favor, maintained that the settlers were squatters on private property and would have to go elsewhere. The settlers had hired their own attorney, who was appealing the decision. Meanwhile, they refused to leave, and Dominga prevailed upon her co-executor Mr. Grogan to allow George to take possession, assume management of the cattle ranch, and evict the settlers by force, if necessary.

George set out with his party: Gertrude, Georgie, a nurse named Ellen, and a cook named Fong. From the Salinas train station they hired horses and a wagon and continued in drenching rain over mountain roads and through flooding rivers. They arrived at the village of Jolon at the edge of the ranch, where they planned to stay until one of the squatters' houses was readied for them. Jolon had numerous saloons, wooden sidewalks, hitching posts, and watering troughs along its dirt streets and an adobe inn that was a stagecoach stop. There they attempted to sleep in a windowless room guarded by two sheriffs, who had heard reports of squatters threatening to kill any Atherton who dared to show his face at the ranch.

The next morning eviction of the fifty-odd families began. George and the two sheriffs, armed with pistols, set out without Gertrude, who had asked to join them. The homesteaders, mostly Mexicans, depended on crops for their meager existence. Only a few had sheep, goats, or cattle. At the first farm where they stopped, George and the sheriffs were greeted by six men pointing rifles. They brazenly walked by them into the house and began flinging the few sticks of furniture out the window. No shot was fired. The sheriffs disarmed the squatters, who surrendered in hopelessness. At the other farms none resisted except by cursing. One powerfully built man threatened revenge.

Gertrude had arrived with no clear picture of the squatters' situation, and she was appalled by what she saw a few days after the day of confrontation, when she drove by carriage to Mission San Antonio where the evicted families and their meager livestock huddled together. "The church and yard were crowded with women, children, sheep, and goats. Winter was approaching and it was already very cold," but the Mexican women wore but a single calico garment. "The brown children playing with the goats were stark naked" (*Adventures*, p. 76).

Dominga, who had never seen "any one poorer than a well-paid servant," had no inkling of the devastation her husband, son, and the courts had caused. She had given Gertrude a bolt of calico and two red flannel petticoats to bestow upon the dispossessed as a gesture of charity. Though her own experience of poverty was almost as limited, Gertrude found it impossible to act as Dominga's emissary. She could not see herself "in the role of lady of the manor presenting something like fifty half naked women and wholly naked children with a bolt of calico and two flannel petticoats as protection against bitter weather and compensation for all they had lost" (*Adventures*, p. 77). She carried the offerings back to her room, and the woman who kept the hotel made the presentation later.

Gertrude's compassion was genuine, but it should not be misconstrued as anything like the reforming fervor that impelled Helen Hunt Jackson, who two years after this wrote *A Century of Dishonor*. Gertrude never questioned the pre-eminence of the white rich, the way wealth was distributed or land title established. Though moved by the cruel disparity between a millionaire's superabundance and a poor family's struggle for the bare necessities, she continued to think of the pitiable Mexicans and Indians as an inferior and insensible breed, doomed to remain on the lowest rung of the social ladder. When she drew on the Milpitas experience for her novel *Los Cerritos* (1890), she endowed her dark-haired half Mexican heroine Carmelita with the blood of a gentle-born Anglo-Saxon mother. It is her gentle blood that enables Carmelita to crave more than her squalid environment can provide. She sees the ranch, whose people she wants to help and whose redwoods she loves, as an emblem of social stagnation and finds her way out by marrying a compassionate rich man, a landowner who returns the farms to the dispossessed squatters out of the goodness of his heart. The same year that Henry George was writing *Progress and Poverty*, Gertrude Atherton was offering *noblesse oblige* as the solution to the problems of poverty, land monopoly, and social inequity.

When the last settler had been driven from the land, George and Gertrude left Jolon and moved into an adobe ranch house on the Milpitas Rancho. The countryside was beautiful—hills and valleys, redwood and oak woodland, and a curling, surging river—but Gertrude did little outdoor exploring. It was the winter rainy season, and a particularly harsh one. Temperatures were freezing, and the river kept rising.

George loved the ranch life, but he was rarely home. By day, clad in overalls and rubber boots, he worked the ranch. At night he and the hired men went into Jolon to drink and gamble. Gertrude spent her evenings reading through the novels of Walter Scott, which Alejandra had thoughtfully sent as a Christmas gift. The company of Rebecca, Rowena, and Coeur de Lion, welcome as it was, did not dispel her fears. She worried that the settler who had threatened revenge would burn down the house they had taken from him—the very one they occupied—or attack George. A prowler did creep down the chimney one night, dislodging a tile but departing before anyone saw him.

Worst of all, Georgie was languishing. "He was now old enough to run about, but he rarely even walked; he played listlessly with his toys, or sat staring at the flames [of the fireplace] with eyes that looked old and wise and resigned" (*Adventures*, p. 79). The nurse, Ellen, threatened to quit unless she and the boy could return to Dominga. She took Georgie and departed.

After the incident with the prowler, Gertrude too decided she had had enough and announced to George her intention to leave at once, even if she had to walk to Jolon and take the stage from there to San Francisco, where Dominga had rented a house for the winter. To her surprise, George not only consented readily, but added that he was ready to leave himself. He did not mention that in truth he had little choice in the matter. He had made such a mess of his duties managing the ranch that Mr. Grogan had recalled him.[12]

By spring George and Gertrude had returned to their own house at Valparaiso Park, watched over by Dominga, who had also returned for the warm-weather season. Gertrude found George annoyingly underfoot. He had no occupation, since Mr. Grogan refused to advance him money for any more business ventures. Dominga paid off his most pressing accounts, but even she was beginning to set limits and refused to underwrite another of his bungled enterprises.

She did buy him two horses, which he devoted himself to breaking. He donned overalls and worked in the garden. He got himself hired as a stage driver but was fired abruptly after an accident that killed six men.

Pregnant for the second time, Gertrude was spending most of her hours in reposeful reading. She made a vain effort to interest George in doing the same, but the newspaper was as much print as he could undertake. He did plod along in a copy of *Perevel of the Peak*, a few minutes every day, in an attempt to please her, but still had not finished the book after eight years. Perhaps Gertrude proposed they strike a bargain like the one between Patience Sparhawk and Beverly Peele: "If we are to make a success of matrimony we must be companions. I'll try to like horses, if you'll try to like books. On pleasant days I'll ride and drive with you, and when it storms we'll read together in the library" (*Patience Sparhawk*, p. 219). But any such bargain collapsed. George erupted in rage when he saw Gertrude captivated by a printed page. "He was jealous of the very books I read and if I smiled to myself he wanted to know what I was thinking" (*Adventures*, p. 82).

On July 14, 1878, Gertrude was delivered of a docile baby girl who had "dark blue eyes with heavy black lashes, black hair and features as regular as her brother's." Dominga wanted to name her Guadalupe Florencia, but at the baptism (where Arthur Page, son-in-law of William C. Ralston, became godfather) it was Gertrude who prevailed. Archbishop Alemany turned to her to ask the infant's name. "Muriel Florence," she announced.

Muriel's birth provided an occasion for Gertrude to reconcile with her own family, with whom she had had no contact since her marriage. When the little girl was six months old, Gertrude addressed a note to her grandfather, inviting him down for lunch the next Sunday. He politely accepted and spent an idyllic day with her and the two great-grandchildren. As he was leaving he said, "Go and see your mother." She did, the following day, taking both children—and the nurse "as bodyguard." When Mrs. Uhlhorn saw the baby, she melted. There were no sharp words, and a fragile harmony between the estranged mother and daughter was re-established (*Adventures*, p. 99).

Stephen Franklin had sold the Ranch to Senator William Sharon, heir to the Ralston estate, and was living with his daughter and his two Uhlhorn granddaughters, Aleece and Daisy, on Pine Street in San Francisco. Mrs. Uhlhorn, still handsome and impeccably turned out, seldom spoke and rarely left the house. She made sewing for her girls—which she did standing up—her principal daytime occupation, and in the evenings she read aloud to her father. Rose, who was growing old, still did all the housework and cooking.

Gertrude's sphere, these days, glittered more brightly. George's sister Florence had returned from Europe to make her debut. Debutantes must give parties, and Dominga was a willing hostess. Intensely competitive with other attractive women and resentful of the fact that her early marriage had removed her from the social merry-go-round, Gertrude tried to forget her position as a wife and mother, dancing and flirting with abandon. Since she had cheated herself of the frivolous joys permitted a "young lady," she felt entitled to this small recompense. Clearly, her feelings of loyalty to George and her sense of marriage as a partnership were fading. George's failures had earned her contempt, and coquetry was a sure way to get back at him. He did not enjoy watching his wife dance with other men. "He used to beat his head against the walls of the carriage going home and moan that I didn't love him and that he was going mad" (*Adventures*, p. 85).

Gertrude could now spend much of the winter in San Francisco, for Dominga had built for herself a new house in Pacific Heights, a Victorian extravaganza with a Queen Anne tower. It had a central hall where the young people, including Gertrude, could dance while their elders looked down on "acres of white flesh"—décolletage and tight lacing were the fashion—from a surrounding balcony.

Dominga was not pleased by Gertrude's encouragement of the attentions of other young men at dances, nor was she blind to the evident friction between her son and his wife. In a letter to George written while she was in the city and he at Valparaiso Park, Gertrude complained that "all the people here seem to be sorry to have me here" and proclaimed her innocence. "I did not see B—— as you said you did not want it." She implored him not to "let your mother prejudice you against me and be on your guard what you say to her about me. Remember that I am your wife and anything you say against me reflects upon your children. Also that so long as a man lives with his wife he should be man enough to stand up for her no matter even what he may think of her." She signs off plaintively, "I am not very well. I feel tired all the time."[13]

George made scattershot attempts to confine and contain her.

When Oscar Wilde came to town on his 1882 lecture tour, Gertrude wanted very much to hear and see him, for Wilde's shoulder-length hair and velvet knee breeches were the talk of the town. Pseudo-Wildeisms like "too utterly utter" fell from many fashionable lips and the local florists sold out their supplies of white lilies and sun-flowers.[14] George, scandalized, forbade her to go. He said "any man who walked about with a sunflower and called himself an aesthete must be too improper for a decent woman to look at" (*Adventures*, p. 183).

He must have realized that the diversions of San Francisco posed a serious threat, because he jumped at a chance to move his family to the country one more time to attempt a fresh start. His mother, yielding to his blandishments, reversed herself and agreed to lend him the money to buy what he was positive would be a profitable grape farm in Oroville, on the Feather River in Butte County. Once more the young family, this time with two young children in tow, packed up. But George's ability to fail never abandoned him, and he quickly exhausted his capital on the grape farm. Dominga sent more money and attempted to help find markets for his wine, to no avail.

Possibly as a result of Oroville's polluted water supply, George contracted malaria, compounded by kidney problems. Afraid that the delicate Georgie would also get sick, Gertrude and George sent him home to Dominga, who reported "Georgecito is very contented and has very good appetite. I have to take him to San Francisco to buy shoes and pants and stockings."[15] She reveled in grandmother-hood—"Do not fear that Georgie tires me"—but fretted over her son's health. Her letters never so much as mention Gertrude, but they often express concern for little Muriel, whom she feared would catch "the fever."

Muriel remained robust, but every other conceivable disaster be-fell them. "The house was very old, and battalions of bed bugs marched over the wooden walls day and night," Gertrude wrote. "Lightning struck the telephone [telephones were new and rare] while I was at the instrument and flung me across the room. The thermometer generally stood at 104 degrees and dropped but two or three degrees at night. George got in with a wild set in Oro-ville and sometimes did not come home until two in the morning" (*Adventures*, p. 88).

After a few months they were ready to give up, but even that proved difficult. No one wanted to buy a failing grape farm. Dominga begged George to leave the farm anyway, "for your health and for the short time," and to "rent it as soon as you can. Before the month is past. I am so afraid of the fevers. Take as much as you can of the milk. . . . They tell me this is very good for your disease. Even if you don't rent, get a care-taker and come soon. I write you every day so that you will be happy. . . . Goodbye, I hope every day for a note telling me that you are coming to Mama."[16]

They did find a tenant, and before they left, Gertrude persuaded George to sign the vineyard over to her. For several years she received a small monthly check, the only independent income she knew until she sold her first story.

Back in Menlo, the predictable and insular summer routine— picnics, hayrides, informal Saturday night dances, gossip on the veranda of the Big House—seemed almost pleasant after the Oroville fiasco. George was not well, however. He had a painful kidney stone, and Gertrude was required to nurse him. At night she applied compresses—again like Patience Sparhawk—and administered morphine drops.

They sent young George to stay with Dominga in San Francisco in the fall. Without warning they learned he had come down with diphtheria—which Gertrude blamed on the conditions at Oroville —and in a few days he was dead. There was a brief announcement in the *San Francisco Morning Call*:

ATHERTON—In this city, November 28, George Goñi, son of George H. B. and Gertrude F. Atherton, a native of California, aged 6 years and 8 days. Friends are respectfully invited to attend the funeral today (Wednesday) at 2 o'clock from 1950 California St.[17]

In her autobiography Gertrude reports the death of her son in the briefest of paragraphs, as if at the time of writing she still could not bear to linger in that dark room. Reticence and withdrawal served her well as armor. In her 1899 novel *A Daughter of the Vine*, the heroine Nina Randolph has an illegitimate baby who dies. "Nina did not cry, nor did she speak. When the child was dressed for its coffin, the housekeeper brought it to the bedside. Nina raised herself on her elbow and gave it a long devouring glance." Then she turned her back and stared at the wall.[18]

Alejandra wrote to her mother: "I cannot tell you the grief I felt last night when they woke me to give me the news that Georgie had died. The last news I had of him was that he was better, and it never entered my head that he would die. For him, poor dear, I am not sorry. He must be happier in heaven. But George and Gertie must feel it deeply." She closes with "a thousand caresses." [19]

Dominga, who had been extremely close to Georgie, responded to the loss by becoming even more protective of Muriel: "Last night she slept with me. And today we are going out to find some little clothes." [20] Only with great reluctance did she concede occasional visiting rights to Muriel's other grandmother. Dominga also mollified her feelings toward Gertrude. For the first time her letters to George acknowledge his wife's existence, and she sometimes even sends love or regards to "Gertrudes." For her part, Gertrude felt grateful that if Georgie had to die, at least he was not under her care at the time. Dominga would have blamed her for the rest of her life.

The death of Georgie precipitated the birth of Gertrude Atherton, the novelist. The seed of a novel jumped out of a newspaper account she happened to see in the *Morning Call*. Under the headline "What Am I Bid?" it reported an auction sale of the personal effects of the George Gordon family, formerly of San Francisco and the Peninsula's Mayfield Grange. One of the auctioned items, an old trunk containing Nelly Gordon's satin wedding dress and tiny white shoes, went for one dollar. The idea of turning this bit of news into a novel hit Gertrude like a thunderclap. She felt as if "something was battering at a sealed door" in her brain, and the door "went down with a crash." The "rotten spot" on her brain to which she attributed her bent for fiction had "sprung into action." As she would often do again when a novel came to mind, she felt herself become a passive agent propelled by an overwhelming natural force.

She at once sought Alejandra. The Gordons, she already knew, had been her parents' neighbors in South Park and, after that, when they moved to Mayfield Grange (now the site of a portion of Stanford University), the Peninsula neighbors of the Athertons. Nelly Gordon, an accomplished and beautiful young lady before she succumbed to alcoholic excess, had once accepted an invitation to spend six months with the Atherton daughters at Valparaiso Park. Alejandra would be a fund of information on the Gordons, and Gertrude did not scruple to use her sister-in-law as a source or to write about actual people known to everyone in the community.

Gertrude regarded her eldest sister-in-law as her one Atherton ally. Alejandra had little sympathy for George, and although no reader herself, she encouraged Gertrude's love of books. An unspoken bond between them was that they were both artistic women married to aesthetic clods. Alejandra could paint and design homes. Deft with her hands, she was at work on a piece of tapestry when Gertrude burst in, newspaper in hand, announcing her intention to write a novel based on the Gordons and begging Alejandra to confide everything she knew about them. She stayed the afternoon.

When Alejandra left Menlo for winter in the city, Gertrude submerged herself in writing. Although this was a period of bereavement and formal mourning for her son, she felt happier than ever before. She had found her opiate, her solace, something akin to what she had felt as a child hiding out in the clothes hamper to read forbidden pages. From this moment, writing would serve her not as a means of inward-turning psychological probing or a path to artistic mastery, but as escape from the humdrum or the painful into melodrama, novelty, and sensation.

The excluded George raged openly, stalking in and out of her work room, "pounding on the door if I locked it, and reviling the fates for inflicting him with a wife so different from the wives of others" (*Adventures*, p. 93). He goaded her by saying no one would publish or read anything her pen produced and that it was a disgrace for a married woman to even try to write.

Opposition only fixed her determination, and in three months she was done. She titled the finished novel *The Randolphs of Redwoods* and sent it off to the San Francisco weekly, *The Argonaut*. Within a few days she received a letter of acceptance from editor Jerome Hart, suggesting she come down to his San Francisco office in person to discuss some points of editorial concern. Borrowing fare from a servant, she walked to the Fair Oaks station and flagged the train. She was on her way.

"What an infant you are to have written such a story," said editor-in-chief Frank Pixley when Gertrude entered the Dupont Street office. He and Mr. Hart informed her that as editors they did have some misgivings about her manuscript—it was sensational in both matter and manner, and it touched on events and individuals close to home—but they had decided to run it as their first serial. The two editors argued that she must protect herself by publishing under a pseudonym. The name she chose was "Asmodeus," Hebrew demon and, appropriately enough, destroyer of domestic happiness. It is Asmodeus, in the Book of Tobit, who destroys each of Sara's seven husbands in succession. The choice of this nom de plume and her later use of "Frank Lin" placed Atherton in a long tradition of female writers. The Brontës, George Eliot, George Sand, Vernon Lee, and Olive Schreiner had all hidden behind a male persona. She was now one of them.

Although unreliable as documentary history,[21] *The Randolphs* takes its broad outline from the actual decline of a once wealthy and popular family whose secret and fatal flaw was alcoholism. Mr. Randolph, not himself afflicted, is ruined by his rampaging wife and heartbroken by a cherished daughter—Nelly in real life and Nina in the story—whose mother used to bottle-feed her brandy. Unable to control her thirst for strong punch and champagne and having lost the worthy St. John, who loves her, Nina throws herself away on a fortune-hunting doctor who beats her. Her father dies soon after she marries, an illegitimate child dies, and her mother's fortune ends up in the hands of dissipated Irish servants. Prematurely aged but still young in years, Nina dies when a drunken uncle hurls her down a flight of stairs.

Nobody could charge this lurid first effort with timidity or poverty of incident. Naturalistic in its frankness about the seamy side of the lives of apparently respectable women, *The Randolphs* loudly proclaims its author's upbringing on a diet of romantic fiction. The name St. John and the plot device of a dreadful family secret are lifted whole from *Jane Eyre*. When St. John discovers Mrs. Randolph delirious with drink in an upstairs bedroom, foaming at the mouth and biting those attempting to subdue her, we remember Thornfield Hall and its attic occupant, the bestial Mrs. Rochester. Although set in California, there are no sunny days, and the requisite Gothic graveyard scene finds a place. The landscape against which Nina and St. John play out their melodrama is one of turbulent seacoast, rocky cliffs, fog, torrential rain, and moonlight.

Extremely daring for 1883 are the descriptions of Nina as a siren clad in skintight red silk garments who reclines on a chair covered in leopard skin in "an attitude of considerable abandon." Nina's dark hair, serpentine jewelry, and sensuous undulations are frankly sexual. When she first meets St. John, after imbibing champagne at a South Park Ball, she provocatively leans all her weight against him. "Between the scarlet outline of her dress and the dark blue of her coat her ivory neck and shoulders gleamed more alluringly than ever, and her hair, slightly ruffled, lent an additional softness to her piquant, flushed face." St. John, "not being a saint," kisses her and, meeting no rebuke, repeats the operation "not once but many times," finally kissing "every available inch of her anatomy bared to public view." [22]

After performing a Salome-like dance in solitude before St. John, Nina wonders aloud if she has shocked him. No, he assures her; her conduct has been merely "unconventional" and has offended no one. Morality is relative, he says, and serves society, not God. This passage was singled out by Scribner's editors in New York, when Gertrude submitted the novel to them. St. John's free-love sophistries, they maintained, amounted to an apology for adultery and would surely "give offense to religious persons." [23]

The *Argonaut* editors had anticipated a furor, and they got one. A letter from one reader—one of several published—suggested that the serial belonged in the *Police Gazette.* Another maintained that it was criminal to place these "tales of French morals" before the impressionable daughters "who are to be the wives and mothers of the next generation." Still others thought the ethics of fair play had been violated. "There dwelt in Frisco," wrote one, "a family of three who entertained hospitably and were people of position and wealth. The two ladies of the family had a besetting sin; everyone knew and knows of it—but—all three being dead and buried, in the name of common decency—common humanity—why not let their faults and miseries be buried with them?" The series found defenders, too. One reader suggested that magazines should be edited "for mature and healthy-minded men and women, and if it is too strong for any 'youthful minds,' let those same youthful minds be fed on intellectual pap." [24]

The *Argonaut* editors said in print that they hoped the story had offended no living person and tried to argue that beneath the tale's steamy surface lay a moral. This "piece of San Francisco life, brightly and bravely painted," was in fact "a temperance lecture to a class which does not often enough consider the terrible effects of a pernicious habit."[25] Fiction that appealed to a wide audience could do more to further the cause of temperance than the crusader Frances Willard, who was in San Francisco at this very moment, could by preaching to the converted at the YMCA.

The identity of "Asmodeus" remained secret for many weeks, though speculation flourished. Whoever it was could expect the cold shoulder, *Argonaut* correspondents agreed. "If it be a man people will shun him, if it be a woman, poor thing, she will be formally drummed out of Society to the clack of the indignant dowager's tongue and the fife of the shrill-voiced rose-bud."[26]

When the truth did leak out, Gertrude, as predicted, found herself an unwelcome guest in all the posh drawing rooms she used to frequent. Even Mr. Doyle, the neighbor who had lent her so many books, refused to speak to her; he had been a close friend of George Gordon. Alejandra, the source of so many details about the Gordons, felt betrayed by what she considered a wanton disregard on Gertrude's part for the feelings and privacy of others and kept her former pet at arm's length. The other Athertons (excluding the voluble George) never condescended to make direct reference to *The Randolphs*, but they made their displeasure palpable. Gertrude did not receive the customary invitation to spend the following winter in their midst at Dominga's townhouse.

In their eyes she was guilty of several crimes, but the most glaring was her violation of a sacred tenet of aristocratic life: a true lady does not tread the vulgar path of publication, certainly not to broadcast unseemly backyard secrets. Dominga never tired of saying, "Ladies in Spain do not write," a line (without basis in fact) elevated by the tone and frequency of its iteration to the status of a commandment. One neighbor, Mrs. Selby, saw fit to whisk Gertrude into a corner to confide that her own daughter shared the gift for writing, had indeed penned some exquisite things, but of course she would never dream of publishing them.

Aristocracy implied exclusivity, making oneself scarce. An appearance in print defied its very premise. Why, any member of the common herd might purchase and read the contents of a book, magazine, or newspaper! When Gertrude came to write *The Californians*

(1898) she made the tyrant father Don Roberto a mouthpiece of the prejudice she had battled. An author, he says, is no better than an actor doing monkey tricks on the stage, identifying himself as a fool and bringing shame to his name.[27]

Gertrude had seen little of the world, but by now she knew that the Athertons and their narrow social circle could neither change nor fundamentally harm her. She considered *The Randolphs* a triumph, for it flouted convention and set tongues wagging most agreeably, making her the center of attention. Never again would she cower at the thought of Atherton opprobrium. She would find approval in other quarters. No doubt her budding self-confidence derived in large measure from the fact that she had been paid $150 for her work and sensed she could continue to be paid for her writing. When the editors in San Francisco had handed her the check, she had headed straight for her favorite book store to stock up on histories, essays, diaries, and novels.

When the books were delivered to Valparaiso Park the following day, George walked out of the room in a huff. A proper wife, he later told her, would have turned the money over to her husband to help settle his debts. Gertrude's days of trying to play the proper wife had passed. She no longer feared the economic arena or doubted her ability to survive independent of George. "Money," she would write in a newspaper column, "is a controlling force in married life. When a woman finds that she too can make it, her self-respect becomes colossal and quite swamps the little she has left for man."[28] Subtly but unquestionably, the traditional roles of the sexes within a marriage were being reversed. Stronger, more ambitious and more competent than George, Gertrude could now dominate and humiliate him.

Since she had been exiled from the Atherton's townhouse for the winter, she went to her grandfather's, with George's grudging consent and occasional attendance. He became a more regular fixture when he discovered that his wife was encouraging the calls of a quartet of male admirers. To avoid an open breach she returned to the country with him before winter's end. If we are to believe her testimony in *Adventures*, Gertrude did no more than flirt with her callers: "If I had any inclination for devious adventures I never should have dared, for I am certain George would have killed me" (p. 85). She did gloat over the threatened suicide of one of her suitors. Had not her mother been similarly flattered as a belle? It was power that interested her, more than sex. Since she could not be free of George, she would torment him and dangle as many men as possible, like so many yo-yos, from a cord held tightly in her hand.

Menlo Park in winter offered few distractions as she poured her energy into a new book, a historical novel whose cast of characters included such notables of European history and literature as Cavour, Garibaldi, Napoleon III, Thackeray, and Charlotte Brontë. The heroine, "a melange of Madame de Staël and Madame Récamier and Lady Blessington, was a fascinating and accomplished beauty who is widowed at an early age and goes abroad where she plays a great role in European politics." Gertrude knew she had manufactured a heroine who was "all I should like to be myself" (*Adventures*, p. 101). She was also selling stories and articles to San Francisco magazines, still using a pseudonym, but earning fees. The *Argonaut* tried to profit from past success by signing her work, "by the author of *Randolphs of Redwoods*."[29]

She sent her completed European romance to Houghton Mifflin, who promptly returned it. Spoiled by the effortless success of *The Randolphs*, she had been unprepared for her first rejection and felt "both stunned and angry." She decided to put the manuscript aside for a while and return to it when she had more experience as a writer. While it was stored in the attic, rats ate it.

For the first time she concentrated her attention on contemporary American novelists, whose ranks she was determined to join. William Dean Howells would in time become her literary bête noir —she labeled him the champion of the Commonplace—but for now he seemed exemplary enough, and she cut his portrait from a magazine, mounted it on cardboard, and enshrined it on her desk. Even in anti-intellectual Menlo Park, Henry James was in vogue among the young women, and Annie and Jeannie Selby had bought every one of his books. Gertrude borrowed and devoured *Roderick Hudson*, *Daisy Miller*, *Portrait of a Lady*, *The Europeans*, little thinking she would one day meet and dedicate a book to the master whose "great gift for story" and style "that piques with its elusiveness" she held in awe, though she considered his remoteness a fault. In *The Californians* she has a light-headed debutante claim that Henry James is "singularly like Menlo, just jogging along in aristocratic seclusion."[30]

Gertrude's favorite country companion these days was a neighbor in her seventies, Mrs. Watkins, who shared a love of books; they would lunch together, and then read aloud in the afternoon. It was to Mrs. Watkins that Gertrude confided her longings and frustrations. She would never succeed as a novelist, she feared, so long as she remained confined to California, which she called "a hole, thousands of miles from anywhere. I might as well be on Mars. I should travel and see the great world, but George hates even to go to San Francisco. Even if he could afford it he wouldn't take me to Europe" (*Adventures*, p. 103). Her most exotic journey, to date, had been to San Francisco's Chinatown, where as guests of a Chinese merchant she and George had seen opium smokers, girl singers, prostitutes in galleries, and a Chinese play. Landlocked in Menlo Park, Gertrude participated less and less in local society, preferring to inhabit a world of her own making. She had turned the back room of the house into a study where she could work at any hour of the day or night, provoking George's wrath. She would lock the door, and if he pounded on it, she pretended not to hear.

A fantasy novel set in the remote regions she dreamed of visiting now consumed her. The book, eventually published as *What Dreams May Come*, opens with a description of a deserted garden in Constantinople that evokes memories of a "grand, terrible, barbarous, but most romantic past." The hero, a reincarnation of his grandfather, loves a damsel—also a reincarnation—whose ancestral home is a decaying Welsh castle that stands half in ruin. Ripened by centuries of history, she is the antithesis of an American heroine who (according to the narrator) resembles the first fruit of a new tree planted in new soil.

While Gertrude awaited word from publishers—she sent *What Dreams May Come*, in turn, to every Eastern house she could think of—she resolved to leave Menlo Park. "I hated it as I have never hated any place since. I hated everybody in it—George most of all. I even hated the beautiful woods, where I walked for hours at a time, dreaming my dreams of a future where I would be free to live my own life" (*Adventures*, p. 111).

She told George that if he did not move with her to San Francisco, she would leave him and get a job. He tried to persuade her that she could again stay at his mother's townhouse, but Gertrude did not feel welcome there. She wanted a separate flat in the city, and she offered no alternative. In short order she found one, on California Street, like Dominga Atherton's house, but farther west. Here she encamped, with a maid named Hannah. Divorce was out of the question, but the marriage—more and more a matter of preserving appearances—would exist on her terms. The balance of power had shifted irrevocably. If George insisted on playing the roaring lion, she was the whip-snapping trainer. George followed her to the flat, knowing it to be *her* territory. With alarming regularity she found herself wishing him dead.

A story she published a few years later in the *Overland Monthly* presents her slant on the marriage. It concerns a young woman, Beatrix Melon, beautiful, intellectual, cold, and proud, who has married the ne'er-do-well son of a wealthy family. Without goals or mental distinction, he displays "late nocturnal propensities" and is "averse to exertion in any form." Beatrix "had married him in the romance of eighteen because he was very handsome, had a delightful manner, and was wonderfully irreproachable in the matter of family." In her innocence she had believed that in time he would evolve into "an influential and brilliant member of the community." After some years as his wife she concludes that she no longer loves or respects her husband and that her marriage has failed, "but as she had wilfully made her bed, she would lie in it." Her history falls short of tragedy because Beatrix does not see marriage as the whole purpose of her life or wifehood as her sole identity. "With youth, beauty, wealth, position and brains, the future could not look altogether a blank."

Beatrix will not seek divorce, nor take lovers—though an artist admires her. Instead she withdraws into her house with her books and the occasional companionship of a friend. In time she travels alone out to sea, where she writes a book that sinks in a wreck. "Perhaps it would choke a shark. There was comfort in the thought." [31]

San Francisco, a decided improvement over Menlo Park, still left her hungry for change and a taste of the wider world. She found it isolated and provincial, its society small-minded and complacent, its men too concerned with getting and spending to care much for ideas, music, or books. She attempted to create her own enclave of high culture, using her flat as a meeting place for group discussions of new books, held every fortnight. The informal gatherings eventually became the Fortnightly Club, the first in a series of efforts by Gertrude to form her own salon.

A favorite companion of these days was Sibyl Sanderson, a beautiful and abundantly gifted young soprano whose father, a justice of the state supreme court, took a dim view of her operatic aspirations. Sibyl had scandalized San Francisco society by announcing at a dinner party that she wished to know life "from its heights to its depths."[32] She had returned from a chaperoned trip to Paris with the affectation of always dressing in black, with a small bunch of violets pinned to her left shoulder. When someone asked if that were the current mode in Paris, she calmly replied, "Yes, among the demimondaines."[33] In ability to shock the straitlaced, Sibyl surpassed even her friend.

Sibyl and Gertrude saw one another as kindred spirits, amicable rivals who wondered aloud which would happen first, Sibyl's debut as an opera diva or Gertrude's as the author of a published book. They joined in long walks over the hills of San Francisco, sharing their yearnings for New York or the great capitals of Europe and agreeing that neither one would get anywhere in San Francisco, "this jumping-off place to nowhere."

Sibyl's father finally relented, and she went to study voice at the Paris Conservatory. Gertrude felt abandoned. Everything about San Francisco depressed her. "I used to walk past those long rows of houses, drab, with bow-windows, as alike as a row of lead pencils in a box, visualizing the dull eventless lives of those that lived in them, depressing my own spirits to zero. I doubted if anywhere on earth could one feel so isolated, so 'blue,' so stranded as in San Francisco" (*Adventures*, p. 218). Even her extravagant imagination could not conjure the momentous shift of fortune awaiting her.

George had a Chilean cousin, Alberto de Goñi, who in late 1886 stopped in San Francisco as commanding officer of the naval man-of-war *Pilcomayo*. Dominga gave a great ball for the captain and his crew (at which Gertrude provoked rebuke for appearing in a tight-fitting camel hair gown), and George could not do enough for them. Not having a great deal else to do, he put himself at the sailors' disposal, hosting them every day and showing them the town. George had spent the first five years of his life in Chile and was a favorite of the Chilean branch of the family.[34] His grandfather, who was also his godfather, still lived there. When Alberto invited him to join the crew of the *Pilcomayo* on its return to Valparaiso, George decided to accept.

When he told her his plan, Gertrude suppressed her eagerness to be rid of him, fearing she would only prompt him to change his mind and stay home. With calculation, she took the opposite tack, arguing that he had no business leaving; he should try to make something of himself. The allowance that supported them had dwindled, since he had borrowed against his inheritance and incurred nothing but losses. She goaded him by denigrating Chile and comparing him unfavorably with Alberto, who was "somebody." That settled it. George would go.

George had been at sea three months when the doorbell rang one Saturday morning while Gertrude was still in bed. The servant Hannah admitted Rose Stoddard, who was shown into Gertrude's room. Rose unfurled a newspaper she carried, pointing to a paragraph in the shipping news section:

The embalmed remains of George Atherton were brought to this city yesterday on board the barkentine *Tropic Bird*. It will be remembered that the deceased left this port about two months ago on the Chilean corvette *Pilcomayo* on a voyage for his health, and died on the passage to the Sandwich Islands. The deceased was well known in this city and had a very large circle of friends. The exact place of interment is not yet settled upon.[35]

George had developed another kidney stone after two weeks at sea. Administered a shot of morphine by the ship's surgeon, he hemorrhaged and died; he was 35. Instead of burying him at sea, the officers decided to embalm him on board ship as best they could, in a barrel of rum. It took some persuading, but at Tahiti the captain of the *Tropic Bird* agreed to carry the barrel with the body back to the port of San Francisco, along with a cargo of lime juice, vanilla, oranges, coral, and coconuts.[36]

Gertrude received the news calmly, never shedding a tear. At once she dispatched Hannah to purchase a widow's hat and veil for her and sent Dominga a telegram saying she would arrive in Menlo Park on the 3:30 train. Muriel happened to be with Gertrude at the time, and Gertrude took her along, intending to share a bed with her. She was afraid to sleep alone, fearful, as she put it, that "George would haunt me if he could" (*Adventures*, p. 124). Guilt surfaced: she had made him suffer; she had wished him dead.

Dominga could not be consoled. When she heard that George was dead she tore off her clothes and took to her bed, where she screamed until exhausted. No longer screaming but still distraught when Gertrude and Muriel arrived, she embraced her daughter-in-law and welcomed her to the community of widows. As Gertrude sat beside her, Muriel ran in to offer a slice of coconut. Coconut! Gertrude trembled. What if that very coconut had arrived as cargo of the *Tropic Bird*? She ran from the room. For years she could not look at another coconut.

An elaborate mythology and many jokes have vexed the memory of hapless George H. B. Atherton. As a well-known author, Gertrude would blithely describe her eleven-year marriage to him as "one of the most important incidents of my school life." She would also repeat with glee the tale of his containerization. One myth—utterly without foundation, but with a vigorous life of its own—has the barrel of rum with him inside delivered to Gertrude's San Francisco door. But the real details are grisly enough. The body now shelved with those of his parents, son, and sisters in the Atherton vault in a Colma, California, mausoleum that enjoins visitors from bringing real flowers that may "stain or mar the marble," arrived in San Francisco with the heart cut out. George's long-suffering heart, placed in a jar filled with alcohol, resides in a safe of the Edwards Bank, Valparaiso, Chile.[37]

CHAPTER THREE

A Widow in New York

With George dead there was nothing to keep Gertrude in California, which she had long regarded as a prison. She certainly did not consider Muriel, who was nine, an obstacle to her freedom. Sure that she possessed no gift for mothering and that both grandmothers would more than compensate for her insufficiency, she planned to leave her behind. As for where she should go, the obvious answer was New York. She dreamed of conquering the capitals of Europe, but New York seemed a more practical and more attainable goal. It was the publishing and cultural center of the United States—a position Boston had occupied in the previous generation—and if she expected to earn her living as a writer, to New York she must go. Before she could leave California, however, she must negotiate certain mundane arrangements, such as the matter of her income.

Dominga Atherton controlled her monthly stipend from the Atherton estate, and Dominga, as we have seen, took a dim view of feminine literary aspirations, a view her intractable daughter-in-law's previous conduct had done nothing to dispel. Gertrude called on her in the upstairs bedroom of the turreted San Francisco Victorian from which she had been banished after publishing *The Randolphs of Redwoods*. Just back from a course of sulfur baths at Skaggs Springs, where she had gone as a new widow "to regain her health," the restored Gertrude began to plead her case. "I argued that talents, however unladylike, were given for use, and there was no market in San Francisco for mine." Dominga reiterated her (erroneous) belief that ladies in Spain did not write. " 'But they do elsewhere,' I pointed out, 'and you see their books everywhere, even in your own house.' " The name George Eliot was trotted out as an example of the moral compromise a woman of letters must make; had she not lived openly with a man who was not her husband? "I replied patiently that there were no scandals about other women writers, so far as I knew. Look at the New England group." She may have been thinking of Louisa May Alcott, Harriet Beecher Stowe, and Sarah Orne Jewett. "The word proper was inadequate."

Dominga tried another tack, arguing that Gertrude was still like a child in her knowledge of the world and would be too exposed to danger in a city like New York. It made better sense, she thought, for Gertrude and Muriel to move in with her in San Francisco; they would be well provided for. Gertrude assured her that a life of idleness held no allure; that she wanted to earn her own way and knew she could. Dominga, who "had a keen sense of the value of money, for all her sheltered life," at last gave way reluctantly, on one condition: that Muriel be left with her. Gertrude readily agreed, stipulating only that the Franklin side of the family must share in her rearing. "She must be permitted to see my mother constantly and stay with her occasionally" (*Adventures*, pp. 129–30).

The other elder who had to be placated was grandfather Stephen Franklin, who proffered his own list of misgivings and conditions. He did not wish the favorite granddaughter, in whom he placed so much hope, to brave New York alone. She must take housekeeper-companion Hannah with her. If Gertrude consented to that, he would bestow upon her a gift of $1,000, borrowed from the Theological Seminary. Gertrude made no objection and let pass without comment the old gentleman's plea that she direct her pen toward the improvement of the world and "take a high moral tone."

And so, in the fall of 1887, as President Grover Cleveland led the nation in a celebration marking the centennial of the Constitution, she set out, not long before her thirtieth birthday. Among the group of young friends gathered at the train station to see her off, George's youngest sister Florence, soon to marry Edward Eyre, was the only Atherton present. We do not know whether Muriel came or with what emotions Gertrude parted from her; only that she would dedicate her first book to her and not see her again for three years. Stephen Franklin put in a somber farewell appearance, standing apart from the crowd and pacing the platform worriedly, his hands clasped behind him. It was to be Gertrude's last glimpse of him.

New York in the late 1880s, the hub of Gilded Age cosmopolitan culture and commerce, made a study in contrast: between opulence and destitution, Tammany corruption and Anti-Poverty reform; between Lillian Russell's voluptuousness and Anthony Comstock's Society for the Suppression of Vice; between entrenched Knicker-bocker tradition and machine-age innovation.[1] Along Fifth Avenue the chateau-like residences of millionaires made incursions farther and farther north as the city grew. Lengths of pearls and jewel-encrusted bodices clamored for attention in the Diamond Horseshoe of the Metropolitan Opera House, four years old in 1887 and a testament to the pre-eminence of Vanderbilt new money over blue-blood Astor aristocracy. As conspicuous consumption awaited definition by Thorstein Veblen, Irish squatters in Shantytown coexisted with goats and pigs. On the Lower East Side, tenements swelled with new immigrants from Eastern Europe. The Statue of Liberty, a beacon to the "huddled masses yearning to breathe free," had just been unveiled, and Emma Goldman, a teenaged corset-maker from St. Petersburg, was among the first to pass it as her ship pulled into Castle Garden. A magnet for go-getters of every stripe, New York seemed to offer limitless opportunity. As one of Gertrude Atherton's characters would observe, "No success is worth a tinker's dam that ain't made in New York" (*Patience Sparhawk*, p. 145).

The one commodity in short supply was quiet. Newsboys shouted "Ex-tra!" on streetcorners. People rushed and bustled about their business, bypassing obstacles as streets were constantly being torn up, dug up, or paved. The "El" steamed along Sixth, Third, and Ninth Avenues, belching sparks and smoke, jostling passengers and allowing them glimpses into gas- or kerosene-lit dwellings. Apartment buildings were going up everywhere as the city expanded in all directions, including the vertical.

The residential district of Manhattan did not extend much beyond Fifty-Ninth Street. Madison Square, at the intersection of Broadway and Fifth Avenue, had recently displaced Union Square as the city's hub. Broadway remained the main artery for shops, theaters, and hotels. Along the "Ladies Mile" between Eighth and Twenty-Third Streets, the afternoon shopping hours brought caravans of victorias, landaus, broughams, and coupes. Cable cars and horsecars navigated the congested thoroughfares. In her first New York winter, Gertrude would see all transportation abruptly halted, the city paralyzed and threatened with famine in the great Blizzard of '88.

In 1887 Herman Melville, a native New Yorker, was living out his last years in obscurity, sometimes working as a customs inspector on the docks. Walt Whitman grew old across the river in Camden, New Jersey. Edith Wharton, as yet unpublished, had married a man who matched her social pedigree but cared more for dogs and horses than books. In Wharton's Old New York, as in Dominga Atherton's San Francisco drawing room, writing was still regarded as "something between a black art and a form of manual labor."[2]

The acknowledged leader of American letters, William Dean Howells, had recently shifted his own center of activity from Boston to New York, parting with the *Atlantic* after many years as its editor in favor of an editorial position with *Harpers Weekly* and exchanging his Boston publisher for one based in New York. New York, he would tell a friend, has "lots of interesting young painting and writing fellows, and the place is lordly free."[3]

When they arrived in New York, Gertrude and Hannah went immediately to the quietly fashionable Brevoort Hotel on Eighth Street near Fifth Avenue, a district of wide stone-slab sidewalks and venerable family homes, many still occupied by descendants of the original owners. Only a few blocks to the south was the square where Henry James was born and which, before moving to England, he had extolled in *Washington Square* (1881) for its air of "established repose" and its look of "having had something of a social history," riper, richer, and more honorable appearing than any other quarter in the long, shrill city. Its settled air only made Gertrude more aware of her status as a rank outsider. No one here ever heard of the Athertons of Valparaiso Park.

At the Brevoort, where she might have strolled two blocks north to view John La Farge's new mural in a church being redecorated from plans of Stanford White, Gertrude's first act was to order calling cards imprinted "Mrs. Atherton." For eleven years she had been called "Mrs. George" by everyone. From now on she made it a point to be addressed either as "Gertrude Atherton" or simply "Mrs. Atherton." She wanted all the world to know her independence and self-sufficiency.

Hannah sewed a white widow's rouche into her bonnet, even though Dominga had warned her that wearing such attire was tantamount to advertising for a husband. Gertrude wanted another husband less than anything in the world, but the rouche became her and she kept it. Playing the role of widow suited her far better than the role of dutiful wife ever had.

As so often happened in a new place, Gertrude's initial response to the great city was negative.[4] She complained of the monotony of street after street of Manhattan brownstones, just as she had objected to the rows of San Francisco houses with bow windows. Boredom came naturally, and she projected it onto whatever habitat she surveyed. Also significant: she found herself geographically confused and disoriented: "I never knew whether I was walking north, south, east or west, and was continually asking for guidance" (*Adventures*, p. 139). Even in places she came to know well, Gertrude tended to feel lost. Despite her vaunted independence, she needed help finding her way.

She found the faces of people on the street stern and unfriendly, the conversation crass. "The word 'money' echoed and re-echoed in my ears" (*Adventures*, p. 140). This offended her, but hadn't she too come to New York to make money? Was there so great a distance between thinking a thing and speaking it? She was demanding the same sort of social hypocrisy she judged so objectionable in the sphere of sexual morality.

Her first taste of New York frightened her, and her immediate impulse—one she would repeat time and time again—was to take flight. The Brevoort, in any case, cost too much for an extended stay. Since Hannah had relatives in Hackensack, New Jersey, they decided to rent a house there. Having furnished it and coped with the commute, Gertrude changed her mind and decided to give Manhattan a second chance. After the initial shock the big city seemed somewhat less menacing. As Hannah remarked that so much moving would surely mark them as "queer in the head," they settled into a small flat on Fifty-Ninth Street, far west of fashionable Fifth Avenue. Rents were reasonable in this remote quarter, and transportation to the downtown publishing center—which Gertrude intended to storm—would be manageable by "El" or horsecar. Callers would not be flocking to her door, and she could settle in for a siege of serious writing.

A glimpse of her daily life comes to us from an article in the *San Francisco Examiner* on Californians living in New York: "In a room fairly ablaze with vivid scarlet draperies [red, emblem of passion, turns up often in descriptions of the young Gertrude] one is sure every evening to find Mrs. Gertrude Atherton, a student lamp at her elbow, a pen in her hand, and a very serious and very earnest frown . . . between her brows. Mrs. Atherton is a very hard worker—too industrious, if that be possible. Her daily walk is almost her only recreation, and she writes at least six or seven hours a day."[5]

When not writing, she peddled her wares. She had arrived in New York with the completed manuscript of *What Dreams May Come* in her baggage. She also carried several letters of introduction to New York editors, whom she planned to meet face to face. Calling cards and letters in hand, she set about the task of visiting every editor or publisher who would receive her. She certainly hoped to trade on her charm and striking good looks in these encounters, but did not anticipate what every audition-weary actor quickly learns: the pain of being told "no" to one's face.

Newspaper offices congregated downtown on Park Row, "the great irregular mass of buildings surrounding City Hall Square," where "dense throngs packed the crooked side streets, amongst fakirs with their nonsensical wares, and a bewildering array of gilt newspaper names on the rows and stories of polished windows" (*Patience Sparhawk*, p. 310).

Book and newspaper publishing, it need hardly be said, were conducted on a smaller and more personal scale then than now. Publishers' letters were still written by hand in special copying ink and were then wet and pressed into a vise, between sheets of paper, to make duplicates. Manuscripts were handwritten as well; the typewriter was just coming into use. Telephones were becoming familiar, but required vigorous cranking to get results. Publishers tended to know one another, as did editors their writers. So Gertrude's round of visits shows enterprise but not eccentricity.[6]

She had been warned that Charles Dana of the *New York Sun* would be as formidable in person as he was on the editorial page. A man with a white beard and "the fiercest eyes I ever saw" received her with the news that she was the first woman to visit his office in ten years. (His arch rival Joseph Pulitzer had just hired Nellie Bly, who immediately caught the public eye by writing an exposé on the treatment of the mentally ill, feigning insanity and getting herself committed to an asylum in order to get material.) Gertrude, at this juncture, showed no interest in doing more newspaper work. She wanted markets for her fiction, but Dana held off. The most he could promise was to run a review of her novel if she found a publisher for it.

In the *Century* editorial rooms overlooking Union Square sat Richard Watson Gilder, "tall and dark, with a true American face, keen, narrow and bright." Gertrude might have guessed that Gilder would be unlikely to provide support. He had made a career of upholding the conventional morality of the genteel tradition. "America," he had insisted, "has the purest society in the world. Is not this purity worth paying for with a little prudery?" He had bowdlerized *Huck Finn* to make it palatable to magazine readers and refused to receive Robert Louis Stevenson in his office on the grounds that he lacked the requisite respectability. He told Gertrude there is no liar like an author and showed her the door.[7]

When she called on Henry Holt, he complimented her on her colonial profile but condemned her book as too wild, improbable, and "unbridled." He did think she had talent, however, and he encouraged her to continue writing. She fared little better at the house of Harper, "away downtown on a dirty, narrow street" in a building that resembled "a dilapidated relic of Corinth," with its pillars and its statue. Within, editors sat correcting their proofs "to the tune of the shrieking Elevated." When Henry Harper himself received her, he repeated in person what he had already conveyed by letter —that Harper would never publish *What Dreams May Come*, despite its originality. He showed her three negative reader's reports, apologized and looked mournful (*Adventures*, p. 138).

Mr. Harper did suggest that a newer, less established firm might be willing to take a risk with her novel. He recommended Belford, Clarke and Company, a house with offices in New York and San Francisco, but based in Chicago, at that time considered an outpost of the West. They were developing a list of new authors and had already brought out books by the daring Edgar Saltus, whose works (including *The Philosophy of Disenchantment* and *The Anatomy of Negation*) were considered shocking, sinister, and "French." Leaping at the suggestion, Gertrude packaged her manuscript and submitted it to Belford, Clarke.

While waiting for her career as a novelist to take fire, Gertrude amused herself and her San Francisco readers by writing a weekly "Letter from New York" for the magazine that had given her her start, the *Argonaut*. Sharpening her tools as an observer and social historian, she trained her attention most often on fashionable and feminine New York: morning shoppers along Broadway, bored society matrons for whom the Salvation Army provided diversion: "New York being near the close of the season, having squeezed the social ball as dry as a school-boy's orange . . . has turned to religion with a spasm of desperation." Everyone was reading *Robert Elsmere*, a British religious homily by Mrs. Humphrey Ward. Piety, she suggested, had about as much substance among the elite as the fads for whist, Browning, or Lord Fauntleroy ringlets.[8]

Her California readers were treated to good seats at various theatrical performances: Lily Langtry as Lady Macbeth, Mrs. Cora Potter as Cleopatra. She anointed the Jersey Lily a "real actress" and the "most popular woman in America today." Mrs. Potter, who was to resurface in a much later chapter in Gertrude's life, failed to impress her with her acting, but she certainly could slither: "When she writhes around a sofa or undulates out of the barge she is a national advertisement for physical culture."[9] Seductive women keenly inter-

ested Gertrude, and she had plenty of company. The demure young
girl sacred to Howells and Gilder was by no means the only feminine ideal before the public. Broadway shops displayed photographs
of professional beauties: the Duchess of Leinster, Mrs. Langtry in a
low-cut gown, Mrs. Potter simpering behind curtains and fans, Sarah
Bernhardt scowling from behind the jeweled headgear of Theodora.
New Yorkers flocked to the windows.

Gertrude's New York houses no prostitutes or shop girls, no
sweatshop workers or street peddlers, no strikers, defenders of the
Haymarket anarchists, or Tolstoyan communists. Her one acknowl-
edgment of the immigrant culture burgeoning downtown comes in
an account of a visit to the Yiddish theater, where she was enthralled
by Mrs. Silberman as Potiphar's Wife, transported by the music and
charmed by the air of genial sociability.[10]

A great deal of what she knew about New York came to her
through the daily newspapers, which were courting women readers
with expanded fashion, "human interest," and society coverage and
which, as Gertrude informed her *Argonaut* readers, had been bitten
by the sensationalist bug. If a woman has been knocked down by a
streetcar, "she looks in the paper next day, unless she is killed, to see
if the world has heard of her accident, or if the reporter said she was
pretty." The day had passed when a proper lady's name appeared in
print only at her birth, marriage, and death.

Perhaps, Gertrude conjectured, the rage for personalities signified
a rejection of the cult of the commonplace in fiction, "a reaction from
the thrall of the literary skim-milk realists. Not for years has there
been such demand for sensational novels as there is today. . . . There
is a rebellion against Howells that is almost vicious." Although she
had recently counted herself an admirer, from now on she would
never miss an opportunity to revile Howells and the domestic realism
of his novels, which she equated with tame gentility and boring convention. At least sensationalism provided respite from the suffocation
of dullness.

The craze for names might also, she thought, have something to
do with the changing status of women and their increasing restlessness and hunger for distinction. Among women, she wrote:

Eight out of every ten are possessed with an eager, restless desire to be
somebody, rise above the masses. . . . Look at the women who are writ-

ing, painting, journalizing, creeping into public offices, and flocking to the stage. Those who have not the talent to justify ambition . . . [still] want to be independent, to strike out for themselves, to be something more than domestic nonentities. These teach, telegraph, manipulate the type-writer, copy, become trained nurses, doctors . . . or, when they can do no better, they strive for social position. All this . . . is the result of the great women's rights agitation which has fastened its hooks about the axis of the earth.[11]

The restless desire to strike out for herself was something Gertrude knew from the inside, something that set her apart from the aristocrats in whose company she liked to place herself. Striving ambition marks the upwardly mobile. A true aristocrat can never be an *arriviste*, for the simple reason that she has already arrived. And female members of the leisure class, as Thorstein Veblen would point out, are consumers, displayers of wealth, not producers. Gertrude lived modestly and worked compulsively.

Since she craved celebrity, she noted with approval that authors of both sexes, in this dawning of the era of personal publicity, were being written up in "paragraphs" and turned into "personalities." As she delightedly pointed out, "An author today is quite as much of a public character as an actor, and the millions never tire of gossip about him."[12] Having thus described the public appetite for gossipy paragraphs about authors, Gertrude proceeded to feed it with a detailed account of an Authors' Reading held at Chickering Hall, a benefit for the International Copyright League.[13] She painted a group portrait—concentrating on the way the authors looked and spoke—of the literary ruling class of the United States at the end of the nineteenth century, about whom Ellen Glasgow would write, "I thought of them as old gentlemen, and they thought of themselves as old masters."[14] Gertrude dissected James Russell Lowell and Frank Stockton, each in turn, and took them to task for being undramatic readers, as was "The Great American Author," William Dean Howells, of whose performance she wrote that nobody could understand a word, "but fortunately nobody cared; they had seen Howells and that was enough."[15]

On a subject closer to their hearts, Gertrude informed her California readers that her home state spawned talent in abundance but lacked the atmosphere talent needs to develop and thrive. Sibyl Sanderson, for example, had to leave San Francisco and go to Europe to make her mark as an opera singer. Sibyl's success merited an entire column. Without mentioning their friendship, Gertrude announced: "It will take a long time for San Francisco to digest the fact that the girl whom they remember only as flitting through six ballrooms a week, followed by a train of shallow-pated youths, singing occasionally in a light, brilliant voice at musicales, or making the town ring with her eccentricities, is about to become one of the famous women of the world. But so it is. For a civilization barely forty years old and standing almost at the edge of the world, and the new world at that, to send forth a girl who . . . has compelled two continents to recognize her coming greatness, is an achievement unparalleled in the history of any country."[16]

If Sibyl stood on the brink of international fame, she made a disheartening contrast with Gertrude, who felt herself a nobody. Miserable as her married life had been, as Mrs. George Atherton she partook of the Atherton cachet. Society bored and often infuriated her, but she liked to hurl her barbs from within its silk-cushioned interiors; any snubbing should be her prerogative.

In New York she saw mainly other transplanted Californians. Her one contact among established residents was a Mrs. Burgoyne, a former classmate of her mother. Kind, cordial, and well-bred, Mrs. Burgoyne's present condition was distinctly shabby genteel. "She had been a wealthy woman, . . . but she was far from wealthy now. Her husband had lost one fortune after another, and they were living with their daughter Jessie [who worked for a magazine called *Current Literature*] and several sons in a boarding-house not far from their old mansion on Fourteenth Street, now given over to second-class shops" (*Adventures*, p. 141). In truth, Mrs. Burgoyne's situation came disturbingly close to that of Gertrude's mother.

The refrain "Keep Out" pursued her in publishing enclaves as well. Although she had sold a brief article (on the founding of Stanford University) to *Harpers Weekly*, most of the editorial doors on which she had so eagerly knocked when she first arrived remained vehemently closed to her. And her work for the *Argonaut* carried no weight in New York. The Eastern literary establishment, she felt, remained prejudiced and impenetrable. In fact, she managed to see two novels through publication in less than two years in New York —an impressive record—but the negative critical response to them distressed her deeply, almost canceling out any sense of pride in her accomplishment.

What Dreams May Come—written in California about Wales and Constantinople—had been carried East in her baggage. Its subject, one that would continue to fascinate Gertrude Atherton, was reincarnation, but it also provided a forum for comment on more immediate concerns: the colorlessness of American literature, the shallowness of the American girl ("her flavor is as vanishing as the pistachio"), and the hypocrisy of social convention in late-nineteenth-century America. Gertrude was still married and bristling at that yoke when she put into the mind of one of her characters a long discourse on the arbitrariness of the commonly held definition of sin: "The world smiled upon a loveless marriage. What more degrading? It frowned upon a love perfect in all but the sanction of the church. . . . It discreetly looked the other way when the harlot of 'society' tripped by with her husband on one hand and her lover on the other. A man enriched himself at the expense of others by what he was pleased to call his business sharpness, and died revered as a philanthropist; the common thief was sent to jail." [17]

What Dreams was to novel writing what training wheels are to bicycle riding. It had a preposterous and confusing plot, but provided opportunities for satiric asides, evocative descriptions, and romantic flights into the realms of idealized passion, madness, and a remote and exotic past. Belford, Clarke published it as the work of one "Frank Lin." The pseudonym, this time, was simply her mother's maiden name, divided. Gertrude told an interviewer, bolstering her pedigree, that she was a lateral descendant of Benjamin Franklin and that her nom de plume was a copy of his signature, divided. But the name "Frank Lin" soon vanished. The publisher made no secret of the author's real identity, and three months after the first printing editions appeared bearing the name Gertrude Franklin Atherton. [18]

The book sold well. The *Argonaut* (which had previously given the book the only favorable notice it would get, calling it "clever" and "absorbing") reported late in 1888 that a sixth edition had just been issued, "the previous edition of 35,000 volumes being exhausted." It said that a quarter of the sales were made in California but that it remained "the literary sensation of New York, and promises to be the most successful novel of the year." [19] This last was the *Argonaut*'s own bit of fiction. The most talked about and biggest selling novels of that season, according to *Publishers Weekly*, were Mrs. Humphrey Ward's *Robert Elsmere*, Amélie Rives Chanler's *The Quick or the Dead?*, Olive Schreiner's *Story of an African Farm*, and Mrs. Deland's *John Ward, Preacher*.

Eastern reviewers tended to ignore *What Dreams*, and when they did mention it, they found fault. *Publishers Weekly* grouped it with Laura Daintrey's *Eros* and Edgar Saltus's *Rien* as a member of the sensational school, calling it a "morbid psychological study, treating of mesmerism and reincarnation in a by no means improving style."[20] *The Critic* called it "one of the most aggravated expressions of literary hysteria we have come across," but held out some hope for the novelist's future: "We perceive behind all that is abnormal here a stamina that with proper care and treatment may turn disease to rugged health."[21]

Hermia Suydam followed *What Dreams* by a scant four months. Gertrude wrote it during her first months in New York, and it draws on her experience there. The heroine, a drab and penniless orphan with literary ambitions, lives in Brooklyn with a married sister whose eventless life she loathes. Marriage, to Hermia, seems as boring as an American novel, "correlative with all that was commonplace; with a prosaic grind, that ate and corroded away life and soul and imagination; with a dreary and infinite monotony." It offered, year after year, "neither change nor excitement, nor recognition nor power. Nothing of mystery, nothing of adventure."[22] The attack on marriage marks Gertrude Atherton as a social radical far in advance of the more democratic and compassionate Howells and in advance of her own rigid class bias as well.

Hermia heads a long list of Atherton heroines who resemble the author. She is an ash-blonde who reads, dreams, and has trouble reconciling her fantasy life with reality. Gertrude from time to time succumbed to the feeling "I was not there. Neither I nor these others was really alive. Life was a dream and nothing happened. Perhaps . . . if human beings actually existed, it was a state of suspended animation where they dreamed through eternity" (*Adventures*, p. 128). Hermia experiences the same feeling. She too is clever, restless, and easily bored. She publishes in magazines under an assumed name, and her verses, written with a "white-hot pen," consistently meet

editorial rebuffs for their "unconventionality." She has dared to substitute "red hot lava" for the usual "shower-bath of lemonade," and
her reward is rejection.

Hermia's literary aspirations provided Gertrude a chance to hit
back at conservative New York editors wary of offering readers "the
complex, the radically original, or the deep." When Hermia makes
the rounds of downtown editorial offices, one editor tells her: "You
are too highly emotional. This is a family magazine and has always
borne the reputation of incorruptible morality. It would never do for
us to print matter which a father might not wish his daughter to
read. The American young girl"—here the editor parrots Howells—
"should be the conscientious American editor's first consideration."
Hermia's inhospitable editor argues that people "want to be amused
and entertained, they do not want to think."[23]

Hermia dwells in an imagination sustained by Romantic poetry
and history. She dreams of being loved by Mirabeau or Napoleon,
Aaron Burr, or Cavour; or by a nameless lover to whom she, locked
in a tower, throws down a rope ladder at night. When an uncle leaves
her a legacy of a million dollars, she determines to act out her fantasy: "She would claim her place in society here [in New York], then
go abroad. She would have a house, each of whose rooms should be
an embodiment of one of that strange medley of castles she had built
in the land of her dreams."[24] Her boudoir will suggest a scene from
the Arabian Nights, with walls hung with golden cloth and dancing
maidens pictured on the ceiling. And she, the occupant of this erotic
chamber, will transform herself into a beauty before whom men will
kneel in worship.

She sets about the twin tasks of redecorating herself and her
house, making little distinction between the two kinds of renovation.
(A preoccupation with surfaces, with external appearance rather than
"the woman within," continued to mark and mar Gertrude's thinking about women; this was her mother's cruelest and most abiding
legacy.) Aided by a trained nurse who puts her on a strict regimen
of exercise and diet, a hairdresser, and an elaborate new wardrobe,
Hermia emerges a dazzling siren (whose transformation eerily an-
ticipates the rejuvenation of Countess Zattiany in Atherton's 1923
bestseller *Black Oxen*). Successfully transfigured, Hermia dons a lace
nightgown and removes the pins from her hair. "Tossing her hair

back she sprang forward and kissed her reflection in the glass, a long, greeting, grateful kiss, and her eyes blazed with passionate rapture." [25] Is there a more frankly narcissistic scene in all of fiction? Infatuation with her own image is another link between Hermia and her creator.

The new Hermia becomes society's darling, and all goes according to plan—until she tries to realize her love fantasies. The men in her imagination make those of "actual, prosaic life appear tame and colorless." She allows a debonair and cynical writer of dialect stories to make love to her (the sex scene is discreetly indicated by asterisks, but there is no doubt that it takes place), and the affair continues several months. It then falters, and Hermia's encounter with another man, one she truly loves, awakens in her torments of remorse and "a sort of moral nausea." Her adventurous intrigue causes her so much pain and guilt that she attempts suicide, hardly the response of a loose woman. Though the voice of reason points out the illogic of the double standard ("why, then, is your one indiscretion so much greater than his many?") and the positive benefits she has accrued by having an affair ("your chances of happiness are greater than if you took into matrimony neither experience nor the memory of mistakes"), she continues in torment until her new love dies in the operatic finale.

Hermia repays scrutiny because it represents a serious, though aesthetically crude, attempt to grapple with perplexing questions about sexual morality and a woman's legitimate right to express passion outside of marriage. The heroine-mistress, unlike Edna in Kate Chopin's *The Awakening* (1899), survives her indiscretion and looks forward to a full life. Except for the immature Nina Randolph, she is the most red-blooded of Atherton's heroines. There will be countless future accounts, in future novels, of alluring women, but it will be a long while before we see another engaged in an illicit affair. Whether in response to experience she herself had or to the harshness of public reactions—or both—Gertrude spent the rest of her career in retreat from Hermia's frank sexuality.

When she looked back at *Hermia* some 40 years after its publication, Gertrude admitted she had intended it to stir things up. The critics, she reasoned, had flailed her without provocation for *What Dreams May Come*; this time she meant to provide quarry. In her autobiography she confesses, "I wrote the book more in a spirit of mischief than anything else. If they thought my first poor little effort 'immoral,' let them have something unequivocal to rend with their teeth and claw with their talons" (*Adventures*, p. 147). She acknowledges her love for the fray, her contempt for easy games; an "Imp of the Perverse" drove her to provoke.

In 1888, the year *Hermia* was written, three other novels written by women caused defenders of feminine virtue to cry foul: *Eros*, by Laura Daintrey, *Miss Middleton's Lover*, by Laura Jean Libbey, and Amélie Rives Chanler's *The Quick or the Dead?* In all three, a married woman couples with a man who is not her husband. None of the three—often linked as "the erotic" or "the sensational" school —focuses, as *Hermia* does, on the romantic adventures of a woman never married, nor does any other question the double standard or the desirability of the married state. Although they elicited censure, the three books sold well. In writing *Hermia*, Gertrude was consciously responding to popular currents, as well as her own impulses. She was joining other daring women writers and going them one better.[26]

But however deliberate her attempt to scandalize, she was ill prepared for the outcry that greeted *Hermia*. Even before its publication the *Argonaut* reported that it had been turned down by her previous publisher, Belford, Clarke, "on the grounds of immorality after it had been diagnosed, discussed and branded as the most immoral novel ever written in the English language."[27] It announced that the book would instead be published by Fred M. Somers, editor of a new journal called *Current Literature*.

Somers's name would have had a familiar ring to many *Argonaut* readers. Together with Frank Pixley he had been one of its founders and had corresponded with Gertrude when she began publishing anonymously in its pages. He had subsequently moved to New York, made money on Wall Street, and invested in the periodical *Current Literature*, devoted to current books and writers. When Gertrude arrived in the East, he looked her up. (She described him in one of her *Argonaut* letters as "the best looking editor in New York.")

When every other editor she approached with *Hermia* ran quickly in the opposite direction, Somers agreed to publish it, though book publishing was not his line. After bringing it out, he promoted it in his magazine, describing Mrs. Atherton as a woman "with the natural audacity of the Californian, the intellectual breadth of the Southerner, the uncompromising character of Northern blood. She lives quietly with her maid in an unpretentious uptown flat and writes what she knows to be the truth regarding the environment of her characters, regardless of professional criticism and obedient only to her convictions."[28]

Apparently Somers's interest in his novelist friend went beyond the professional, for Gertrude found it necessary some years later to assure Ambrose Bierce that she and Somers had never been engaged. In her autobiography she refers mysteriously to a man in New York to whom she was "half engaged," adding that she doubted she had ever really loved any man. Somers, she confided to Bierce, had called on her steadily for two years, but in that time, she felt, had gotten to know her only "about as well as he would a Martian dame by telephone."[29] We know little about what passed between them, but we do know that after *Hermia* Somers dropped book publishing.

Critics greeted it with vituperation, though even the most venomous acknowledged that its author had talent. The *New York Times* called it "an aggressive story of that ugly kind which necessarily follows when romance has for its leaven human coarseness." Although "not without force and dramatic power," it was "not fitted to be brought into the family."[30] That was mild and mannerly compared to the blasts of a columnist for the *New York World* who wrote under the name "Nym Crinkle." He devoted an entire Sunday column to the book, under a blazing headline: "THE LAST PRURIENT NOVEL / GERTRUDE FRANKLIN ATHERTON'S NAKED EXPOSURE IN 'HERMIA SUYDAM.' NYM CRINKLE DECLARES SHE HAS MADE A BOLD BID FOR ABUSE, AND HAS REACHED ABOUT THE LIMIT OF LITERATURE." Crinkle claimed that the book cried out for a policeman, not a critic; it was an instance of lawless sensationalism, all the more menacing for having come from a member of the sex that had evolved over centuries as "more delicate, more reserved, more reticent, more sensitive to evil, more refined in thought and action" than men.

Crinkle took aim at the woman, Gertrude Atherton, not the author. Her very body comes under assault when he accuses her of "tearing off all the clothing which considerable decency and conservative instinct have blessed her withal" and exposing a repulsive naked form: "Her genius is varicose, her talent vascular and flabby, her tissues dropsical." She brings the slums to the boudoir and trounces decency in the name of realism. *Hermia* should be condemned as the product of a diseased mind, which should be treated with "pitying pathological consideration." [31]

The Sunday this diatribe appeared in the paper, the sons of Mrs. Burgoyne rushed chivalrously to Gertrude's doorstep and offered to horsewhip the perpetrator, but she held them off. "I had no wish to be made any more notorious than I was already. After they had gone I sat down and read those articles . . . over several times, wondering if I were ruined for life, still more how men could write in such terms about a woman. They might have been written by roughnecks whose major diversion was the prize ring" (*Adventures*, p. 148).

A propensity for double bookkeeping betrays itself here. Gertrude continued to expect men of the press to behave like courtly Southern gentlemen as she flouted prevailing standards for ladylike behavior. She naively assumed she could venture into unpaved precincts without getting mud on her skirt. Although the attack in the *World* was both cruel and unjust, it should not have been unforeseen. Gertrude was less than candid to herself and others when she denied she had courted notoriety or ridden the crest of the sensationalist wave. The fact is, she sought scandal, but got a bigger dose than she had bargained for. When Ambrose Bierce (who at the time had neither met Gertrude nor read her novels) wrote from his literary throne in San Francisco, accusing her of following fads and seeking publicity, she angrily replied:

I think it is very nasty of you to condemn me without a hearing & to bracket me with a crowd I despise, upon no better authority than sensational criticism. For the "blaze of controversy" and the "blare of bugles" I am in no way responsible, further than that I happened to write a book which gave the critics something to talk about. I have never incited a line of advertising or heralding; there is no necessity.

My latest book was intended merely as a study of character. I have often wondered why American authors had never written of men & women (particularly of women) *as they were*. So I thought I would try it, and the result has been a storm I did not anticipate. People do not like the truth, they like the people of books, not of life; and if their mental vision is diverted from its familiar vista they get mad. It is for that the book has made a sensation, not on account of my personality or deliberate effort, and moreover it was written before the erotic eruption. But I would not publish it until it was as good from the literary point of view as I could make it, and the consequence is that I am inevitably bracketed with the rotten and ridiculous school of Saltus-Chanler-Daintrey.[32]

She had no business claiming she had held back *Hermia* while she patiently polished and perfected it. The book was composed in New York, and she had been there only a year when Fred Somers accepted it. Gertrude's defensiveness and deficient self-awareness boded ill for her development as a writer of depth. Though she claimed not to care what people said, she cared profoundly. A weekly New York scandal sheet called *Town Topics*, devoted exclusively to society, had published a paragraph beginning, "If Mrs. Atherton were to ask me 'What Dreams May Come' after reading her latest novel, I should say such as follow an over indulgence in absinthe or hashish." "*Hermia Suydam*," continued the paragraph, "is a very unpleasant drama unpleasantly developed, gloomy as a dream of Baudelaire." Since Mrs. Atherton possessed more power of expression than any American writer in the erotic school, since great artistic heights stood within her reach, "why then does she linger in the ooze about Parnassus?"

Because *Town Topics* reached the elite readers whose good opinion Gertrude coveted, this must have caused her particular pain. She marched down to the editorial office and demanded that editor Colonel Mann retract his scurrilous remarks. He refused and continued to bait her in print: "What is this I hear about California's most gifted daughter possessing an arm sixteen inches in circumference, i.e., half an inch more than [prizefighter] John L. Sullivan's biceps? I should advise Mrs. Atherton to try the gloves as the only effective means left her of answering the last letter from the poetess of passion, and of incidentally following some of Hermia's recipes for the proper and beautifying distribution of adipose tissue."[33]

"That last letter from the poetess of passion" refers to another public controversy in which Gertrude was embroiled, with Ella Wheeler Wilcox, an effusive poet and advice giver, whose volume *Poems of Passion* had sold tens of thousands of copies and whose celebrated recitation at the New York salon of Mrs. Frank Leslie

Gertrude may have witnessed. The maudlin Wilcox made an easy target of ridicule or legitimate dispute about the woman question, since her ideal woman was Gertrude's antithesis, shy and innocent, a devoted mother who listens more readily than she speaks, embodies tact and modesty, and sees herself as above all a keeper of the home. Gertrude might have mocked or attacked her on several legitimate grounds. She chose, however, to meanly disparage her appearance, referring to her in one of her *Argonaut* letters as "a little mouse-colored woman who needs a conspicuous dress to be noticed [at Mrs. Leslie's she wore a white satin Empress Josephine gown] and whose only good feature is a sensitive mouth. She is thin and in a dim light looks quite young."

The ensuing heated exchange of letters between them received national press coverage. Mrs. Wilcox, in answer to the initial assault, replied, "Is it possible you wrote the enclosed item? My eyes are full of tears as I write. . . . You must be rich in friends to unnecessarily wound and antagonize one who was inclined to be your friend." The *San Francisco Examiner* ran the headline: "DAGGER AND HAIRPINS / ELLA WHEELER WILCOX AND GERTRUDE ATHERTON AT WAR / THE PRIESTESS OF PASSION SAYS SOMEBODY BLEACHES HER HAIR / AND GERTRUDE DOESN'T CARE." Lending the dispute all the dignity of a cat fight, it printed the full text of Gertrude's rejoinder, which reveals her as a profoundly isolated and unhappy woman with a well developed capacity for cruelty. "Outside of my family," Gertrude wrote, "and a few friends, people are nothing to me. I care neither for their good opinion nor their bad. My one desire in life is to be left alone—to have nothing hinder my work. Therefore, you may be able to understand that I am incapable of personal spite or malice; people do not interest me enough to arouse either. . . . Having the caustic pen of a Californian, I frequently say things which appear ugly in print. It is the instinct of the Californian to scalp."

Mrs. Wilcox delivered the final riposte: "I think culture and talent impose a certain amount of control on us. The courteous treatment of another and the restraining of brutal impulses is all that distinguishes our manners from ignorant boors." After retaliating for the remark about her mouse-colored hair with a suggestion that Mrs. Atherton owed her lovely blondeness to bleach, she approached higher ground by adding, "We certainly do not need to ridicule another's appearance." She closed, "Hoping and believing that in your next incarnation, if not here, you may suffer exactly as much as you have needlessly and brutally caused others to suffer here, I will take farewell of you."[34]

Gertrude relished the limelight, but she was not enjoying the unflattering glare of the publicity she now faced. She had learned to turn on others the techniques of personal abuse that had been used on her, without any benefit to her reputation. She feared her notoriety would continue to scare off publishers and encourage unsavory gossip. The charges of immorality hurled in her direction left her genuinely baffled. She had plans for a new novel, to be set in California with a heroine named Carmelita, and she wrote to a prospective publisher, Joseph Stoddart of *Lippincott's Magazine*: "You will probably want to know something about its morality, although you are more daring than most. I will frankly say that I have come to the conclusion that I do not know what morality is." She repeated that her only motive in writing *Hermia* had been to tell the truth. "The consequence is that I find myself treated to columns of abuse all over the land. . . . In spite of the fact, my opinion of Hermia has not changed. All this to show you that my moral sense may be awry, before I tell you that I do not think there will be anything improper about Carmelita."[35]

She hastened to let Stoddart know that if *Hermia* were any kind of yardstick, her next book could be counted on to bring some commercial success: "To be practical, *Hermia* is now in its fifth edition although not yet a month old, and you will be sure of selling at least 2,588 copies of anything I write in San Francisco alone. . . . I am California's only native born author, consequently each book I write . . . makes a furor over there." In other words, she was saying, I may be thought immoral but my books sell. Ambivalent, she tried to have it both ways, protesting her innocence and at the same time arguing that scandal boosted sales.

Her notoriety had not actually done great things for her pocketbook. She complained that only 12,000 copies of *Hermia* were sold. "It takes so few books to make a sensation. . . . Every copy is read by at least five people." Her *Argonaut* letters fetched only fifteen dollars a piece, and she calculated that her average annual income from her writing so far added up to a grand total of about $276.[36]

As her second spring in New York approached, she became more and more convinced that she had played out her hand there. She had met a few people, but formed no binding ties. She had published, but still had to struggle for acceptance and financial reward. And she felt the local critics treated her "like a common adventuress." She thought she would receive better treatment in England, "where the libel law is no joke, and whatever they think of me they'll take care not to print it." Disillusionment with New York merged with the restlessness of her nature. Realities always fell short of expectations and her sense of being a spectator, not a full participant in life, always propelled her to new surroundings. A spirit of unrest possessed her: "I was not merely disgusted, I wanted something new, and all my life I had longed for Europe" (*Adventures*, p. 150).

Her sister-in-law Alejandra now lived in Paris (Major Lawrence Rathbone had become American Consul General) and had repeatedly invited her to visit their Champs Elysées apartment. Gertrude decided to accept their hospitality and stop in Paris before going on to London. Other Americans would be flocking to Paris for the 1889 Exposition. Some would be attending Sibyl Sanderson's debut at the Opéra Comique, in an opera Jules Massenet had written expressly for her. Sibyl wanted Gertrude present at her performance, the culmination of a dream they had shared in San Francisco. So Hannah was given notice—Gertrude would not be able to afford taking a servant to Europe—the Manhattan flat was vacated, the trunks packed.

Displaying the "supreme loneliness and craving" she shared with Hermia Suydam, Gertrude boarded a steamer.

PART TWO

Fin de Siècle

CHAPTER FOUR

Europe

"I have no home," Gertrude would tell an interviewer in New York in 1903; "I am a wanderer on the face of the globe."[1] What more apt expression could she find for her quarrel with the Victorian feminine domestic angel than to pursue a footloose existence in a geographic tailspin, stopping only long enough to observe new settings and write during brief residencies in temporary dwellings? Where Edith Wharton would lavish thought, care, and dollars in creating "The Mount," and publish a first book on the decoration of houses, and where Mabel Dodge Luhan would make herself chatelaine of a series of elaborate domiciles, beginning with a Florentine Medici palace, Gertrude Atherton chose an unencumbered path that left her free to follow her impulses and inspirations. She traveled light, ridding herself of unwelcome possessions almost as rapidly as she acquired them; as she once explained to Carl Van Vechten, "There are no attics in apartment houses."[2]

Gertrude Stein (born eighteen years after Atherton) believed that what was American about her generation was that it "does not connect itself with anything."[3] Atherton shared Stein's identification with motion and discontinuity, but recreated it in her life style rather than her prose style. In choosing to live out of a trunk, she allied herself with other intrepid women travelers of the day—such as Mary

Kingsley, who explored West Africa, and Isabella Bird, who crossed the Rockies on horseback—with the lively late-nineteenth- and early-twentieth-century subculture created by far-flung adventurers in skirts. The Women's Building at the 1893 World's Columbian Exposition in Chicago celebrated such; it contained a museum of female achievement that offered a photograph of the Grand Canyon taken by a woman suspended from a rope.[4]

Gertrude *was* intrepid, going off alone to Cuba during a yellow fever epidemic right after the Spanish-American War in search of a novel, and venturing, accompanied by a woman friend, to even more remote and undeveloped islands of the West Indies in search of facts about the early life of one of her heroes, Alexander Hamilton. But most often, for her, travel meant cosmopolitan Europe. And here we immediately confront a contradiction. For what she sought in her disconnected life as a sojourner in Europe was connection and a sense of proximity to the past.

While still in New York she had written a letter to *The Critic* lamenting the poverty of romantic color and background in her native state. "There is no sentiment in California," she wrote. "The place is too young, too crude. It would be like expecting poetry in an untutored urchin of three." Objecting that Helen Hunt Jackson's popular novel *Ramona* (1884) endowed the early California missions with a romantic atmosphere that they did not actually possess, she argued that cold, bare adobe walls looked "hopelessly modern," and suggested "a country whose ancestors have barely passed away."[5] Even the "great forests and terrible mountains" of California, created in a cataclysmic past, "brooded upon the mysteries of the future."[6] The very sunniness of the California climate, she felt, discouraged literary creativity. "Fancy Emily Brontë writing *Wuthering Heights* in California! The setting is all wrong for anything deeper than the picturesque crimes of desperadoes."[7]

Before she ever set foot in Europe, it occupied a hallowed place in her imagination as the locus of tradition and history and the antithesis of California callowness. It promised the mystery of time-worn castles and ruins, the glamor of counts and empresses, the heroism of Napoleon, the sanctity of places enriched by literary idols like Byron and the Brontës. Europe also meant the legacy of Madame Récamier and Madame de Staël, who had used their good looks and intelligence to shape history. Both had conducted salons in Paris near the time of the French Revolution, at which luminaries of political and cultural life gathered. If she had been willing to settle in one place long enough, Gertrude—who did attempt a salon in New York during the First World War, when her daughter Muriel was there to do the arranging—would have liked to model herself on these symbols of sexual, intellectual, and political success.[8] As a mecca for the salon, then, Paris made an appropriate starting point for the Europeanization of Gertrude Atherton.

In the spring of 1889 Parisian boulevards were thronged with visitors to the Exposition celebrating the centenary of the French Revolution and of the Republic. Thousands—including Thomas Edison, Buffalo Bill, Sarah Bernhardt, and the Prince of Wales—climbed the steps to the newly built and controversial Eiffel Tower, an engineering tour de force that announced the ascendancy of technology over aesthetics.

Among the invading multitudes, Gertrude luxuriated as the privileged house guest of Consul General and Mrs. Lawrence Rathbone, who were installed in splendor in a large apartment running around three sides of a court on the Champs Elysées. Just opposite was the fashionable short street where Sibyl Sanderson lived with her mother and three sisters. Gertrude attended her Opéra Comique debut in *Esclarmonde*, a Romanesque-Byzantine affair in which Sibyl had to show her three-octave range to good advantage while veiled and wearing a crown a foot high. The press called her high notes "Eiffel Tower" notes.

Briefly exhilarated by Paris, Gertrude soon found it not measuring up to her expectations. For one thing, the Rathbones were keeping her on a short leash. Here she was, 31 years old, the author of two daring novels, a widow who had been married for eleven years and borne two children, being chaperoned and watched over like a vestal virgin. The Rathbones refused to let her go out alone at night and quailed at the thought that any taint of fin de siècle decadence might seep through their well-secured French doors.

As usual, Gertrude's hackles rose in response to any imposed re-

straint on her freedom. But at the same time, she found herself dis-
quieted by what she thought Paris had done to Sibyl Sanderson, who
was functioning quite openly as the mistress of a much older married
man, the composer who wrote *Esclarmonde* for her, Jules Massenet.
Gertrude could write easily enough about temptresses undulating in
skintight red dresses or seductive boudoirs hung with oriental draperies and carpeted in tiger skins, but a friend's openly adulterous
liaison brought forth in her more than a mild inward shudder. In the
United States, "French" was often used as a smear word by "Mrs.
Grundys" who set themselves up as guardians of propriety. Now,
Gertrude discovered, "French" did signify a different standard of
conduct, one with which she did not feel at all comfortable.

The character Rosita Thrailkill in *Patience Sparhawk* may refer
obliquely to Sibyl Sanderson. Rosita is Patience's old school chum
from California who has come to New York to become "La Rosita,"
a music hall prima donna of questionable virtue. After a separation
of several years, Patience sees in the face of the now celebrated stage
personality a "faint touch of hardness, and the eyes held more secrets
than they had two years ago. They were the eyes of a wanton." Rosita
has lost all traces of "refinement" and mocks Patience for keeping "ideals and things" (*Patience Sparhawk*, p. 276). The shocking
Gertrude Atherton could be quite easily shocked herself. Gertrude
never commented directly on Sibyl's illicit relationship with Massenet, though she once called another singer "Sibyl with the badness
left out." In Paris the friendship between the two ambitious young
women who had walked the hills of San Francisco together dreaming
of Europe and fame cooled, never to be rekindled.

Gertrude scarcely conceived of herself as "good," but in the sexual
sphere she did not want to be, or to be thought, "bad" either. As her
encounter with the Anglo-Irish writer George Moore demonstrates
—in a kind of preview of her far more complicated relationship with
Ambrose Bierce—she could not easily have it both ways. They met
at a Parisian musical salon, which Gertrude attended arrayed in "a
décolleté gown of black velvet, and a head-dress that I fondly believed made me look like Pauline Bonaparte" (*Adventures*, p. 160).
She was introduced to a tall, blond man "with a long colorless face
that looked like a codfish crossed by a satyr" whose name she at once
recognized: George Moore was the author of Baudelairean poetry

and Zolaesque fiction that she may not have read but certainly had
heard of. She and Moore had a New York acquaintance in common and a shared victimization at the hands of Victorian prudes
and literary censors. They had both written about a woman's degradation through drink and been called names in print. Moore, who
had arranged for an English edition of Zola to which he furnished
a preface, had been involved in litigation on charges (leveled at his
publisher Vizetelly, who was imprisoned) of obscenity. Feeling they
had much to say to one another, they withdrew to the dining room
where they could talk alone and enjoy a slightly daring flirtation.

When Moore called at the Rathbones' a few days later, Gertrude
told him she could not receive him there, that "my people were frightfully conservative, and didn't approve of writers anyhow." Moore,
renowned as a womanizer, urged her to meet him somewhere else
and was startled to learn that the California-bred Mrs. Atherton was
forbidden to go out alone. He had thought of her native state as
a land of freedom and unconventionality; how could its people be
"more slavish to Mrs. Grundy than middle-class England?" (*Adventures*, pp. 163–64). Gertrude put him off further by revealing her
plan to leave Paris and go to a convent to write. Moore wrote to the
New York friend, Madame Lanza, "Mrs. Atherton is going to spend
the summer in a convent in Boulogne. I think I may run over there.
She is amusing and talks readily of you."[9] Gertrude discouraged his
proposed visit. She would be able to see him soon enough in London,
she said, and there was no way she could write at the convent with
him around. The reason for her going was to *escape* company.

The plan to retreat to a convent and write a novel arose during
one of those sieges of world-weariness that inevitably followed one
of her rounds of excessive sociability. "I went to balls, dinners, and
musicales. The Rathbones entertained constantly, their Thursdays
were crowded, but I met no one who interested me. Even cosmopolitan Society was much like any other, concerned chiefly with gossip,
charities, dress, the new play, Emma Eames and Sibyl Sanderson"
(*Adventures*, p. 159). The two aspects of Gertrude's social personality,
the gadabout and the recluse, rotated like farm crops. Now it was
the recluse's turn.

Somehow news of her retreat found its way into the pages of the
New York gossip sheet *Town Topics*:

That shining example of brilliant eccentricity, Mrs. Gertrude Atherton, is already, I hear, tired of Paris. Society bores her, shops fatigue her, people do not appeal to her interest and she yearns for an experience. That the one she has chosen will be a surprise to anybody who has endured the torrid atmosphere of *Hermia Suydam* I cannot doubt. There are to be no more journeyings through literary tropics where Mrs. Atherton is the guide—for from within the cool, chaste and quiet walls of a convent is her next novel to be sent out into the world.

Readers of *Town Topics* were treated to a glimpse of the Sacred Heart Convent at Boulogne-sur-Mer, picturesquely set in a garden overlooking the sea and rich in works of art: "Its occupants are women of birth and breeding, and it is the chosen home of titled Roman Catholics of England when they make a retreat." Mrs. Atherton's new novel, *Town Topics* reported, would be a pastoral. "A contrast to her former work seems now to be her chief ambition. The question which naturally arises is: Could the same mind that conceived *The Decameron* have written *The Pilgrim's Progress?*"[10]

Gertrude displayed a curious attitude toward Catholicism. She had married into the Catholic Atherton family and had submitted to catechism instruction and baptism at her mother-in-law's insistence, but she underwent no true spiritual conversion; she merely observed the forms. Although skeptical, detached, and often cynical about the faith, she did continue to form friendships with Roman Catholics, and sent Muriel to convent schools. The nun's gesture of withdrawal from the world and renunciation of its follies attracted her as a literary subject. Her own granddaughter Dominga would become a Dominican Sister, and Gertrude would write of nuns in her autobiography, "they are probably the only authentically happy women in the world, for they have got what they want" (*Adventures*, p. 168). They seemed satisfied—a state to which Gertrude remained a stranger.

At the convent, which had been an old palace belonging to Henry VIII and was built around several courts, she completed the first draft of the novel she had begun in New York, her first with a California setting, *Los Cerritos*. Although set in an "uncivilized" central California ranch (like Rancho Milpitas) in the shadow of a mission, the book includes an encomium to the convent in France: "in the heart of Europe, whose gardens are like the groves of paradise . . . the lilies lie on the lake and the gray stone walls thrust their rough old stones through swarming green. The chapel is arched and dim, and the nuns kneel in their oaken stalls and chant like a celestial choir, while incense floats above and wreathes the pictured windows."[11] It is a romanticized, idealized portrait, at the opposite pole from the frank description Gertrude included in her autobiography, where she complains about stuffy rooms, narrow beds, unpalatable food, and bedbugs.

Los Cerritos has three female characters with whom Gertrude identified in some way: Monica Alvarado Murietta, her daughter Carmelita (the book's heroine), and a reclusive and elegant woman named Geraldine. Monica is only briefly mentioned. High-born and beautiful, lonely and studious, she has been hidden from the world by her hermit father until the night she is carried off by the Mexican bandit Joaquin Murietta—in California folklore a Robin-Hood-like figure—whom she marries. Their now orphaned daughter Carmelita, the second of Gertrude's projections, is a creature of "fire and audacity," brown-skinned and passionate, and also intelligent, proud, and honorable. A child of nature very much like the warbling Rima of Hudson's *Green Mansions*, she has been limited by her isolated life among poor Mexican squatters. Carmelita's instincts are for "higher" things. She befriends and idolizes Geraldine, a sad and mysterious blonde (Carmelita mistakes her hair for real gold) who has renounced society and taken up a secluded life at an adjacent ranch. All three, Monica, Carmelita, and Geraldine, share a sense of alienation and a physical remoteness from the mainstream. Geraldine, who has suffered a doomed and forbidden love affair, particularly resembles a nun.

It turns out that Geraldine's forbidden lover is the very padre —a kindly, philosophical, and bookish mission priest come to the countryside to do good works among the pastoral poor—who has taken Carmelita under his wing and educated her. This relationship between an eager, unworldly, but quick-minded girl and a much older man of letters is one that recurs in Atherton novels; the model was surely her relationship with her grandfather.

As she sat and wrote in the old French convent, Gertrude put into the padre's mouth some of her own feelings of melancholy, ennui, and disenchantment. In answer to Carmelita's question, "What is life?" he responds, "Life, my dear, is a gray plain, whereon are mirages—nothing more."[12]

Although critics, either through indifference or obtuseness, hurled no charges of obscenity at *Los Cerritos* and although Gertrude took the precaution of instilling in Carmelita "an instinct for chastity," (she has her run to the fine lady Geraldine for a long skirt to modestly cover her bare brown legs), the book is far from virginal. Before she meets the man she will love, Carmelita has a sublimated love affair —with a redwood tree, a symbol of male potency and power that suggests "absolute dominion." Carmelita strokes one tree, presses her lips to its bark, and apostrophizes its invincible strength. When she does meet and fall in love with a flesh-and-blood man who is tall and strong, she identifies him with a redwood. She gazes at him "with languid eyes and parted lips. Then a great flame burst from her heart and swept through her body. She gave a loud, ecstatic cry, like a lioness who has found her mate." Crying "I love you," she "flung her arms about him and kissed him full on the mouth."[13]

Gertrude was too convention-bound to act out her steamy fantasies. Protected by convent walls, she gave them free rein on the page.

She arrived in London in the summer of 1889 without a clear plan, having no idea how long she might stay—in fact savoring the idea of being answerable, at last, to no one and free to move at her pleasure. She did have a short-term agenda. While still in Paris she had received word that *What Dreams May Come* and *Hermia Suydam* had been accepted by the British publisher Routledge and had already gone to press.

A Londoner named William Sharp had sent words of praise for her fiction and an invitation to stay with him and his wife Elizabeth in South Hampstead. Sharp's commendation of *Hermia Suydam* found its way into print in the British periodical *The Academy*. "It is easy to understand," he wrote, "how it has passed through so many editions and encountered such a clamor of abuse, for though absolutely void of just cause for offence, it is at once unconventional and true to life. In the main it is written with skill and verve. . . . *Hermia* must be read; it is a significant book."[14] Gertrude's conviction that England would welcome her had been confirmed.

When she met him, she saw William Sharp, her host and champion, as "a big loose-limbed Scot, with a florid mobile face, stone-colored hair brushed up from the brow, and eyes sparkling with animation. He was a little given to posing, but so, I soon discovered, were a good many of the English literati" (*Adventures*, p. 169). Sharp was an interesting man, an art critic, editor, biographer of Rossetti and Browning, and a pantheist deeply attached to his Scots roots. He had visited the United States, and took a lively interest in American writers. His sympathy with women was so profound that he eventually assumed a female literary identity—the reverse of the more usual practice with pseudonyms—and published fiction under the name Fiona Macleod.

He and his wife Elizabeth welcomed Gertrude with a literary salon at which she was guest of honor. There she met minor celebrities like Richard Whiteing and major ones like Thomas Hardy, "a small, delicate-looking man with an air of gentle detachment" who had a distracting way of staring into space. "I was not awed. I seem to have been born without awe" (*Adventures*, p. 170). Gertrude apparently made no effort to talk to the great novelist about anything substantial, such as his trials at the hands of censors. For his part, Hardy showed little interest in Gertrude Atherton until he heard she was from San Francisco; then the bard of Wessex besieged her with questions about the mechanics of the cable car.

The Sharps were close friends and neighbors of a controversial New Woman, an essayist and fiction writer named Mona Caird, who attempted to befriend Gertrude and invited her to come and stay as her guest for a few days. An early feminist keenly interested in legal reform for women, Mona Caird had published several articles that argued the desirability of marriage independent of church and state.[15] Ibsen's *A Doll's House* had just been performed in England for the first time, and Gertrude might have shared in the new excitement about freeing women from legal and domestic shackles; she might have perceived Mona Caird as an ally, but she rarely, in these greedy, self-serving days of launching her own career, could spare a kind word for another living woman writer or anything resembling an organized women's alliance.

Exhibiting what can only be viewed as projected guilt for her own abandonment of Muriel in California, she focused on what she took to be Mona Caird's negligence as a mother. (Gertrude would have a similar response to American feminist Charlotte Perkins Gilman and *her* child, a few years later in San Francisco. In this period she readily endorsed the popular conception of feminists as somehow unfeminine and deficient as mothers.) Gertrude, as Mona Caird's guest, felt outrage at the way her hostess was rearing her six-year-old son, who "had never been cuddled, coddled, punished, admonished, nor coerced by rules of any kind." When Gertrude reprimanded the boy for sitting on her open trunk, he responded—apparently over-whelmed with gratitude for any shred of attention from an adult—with gestures of affection, showering her with hand-picked flowers from the garden (*Adventures*, p. 172).

Vincent O'Sullivan, in his essay on Gertrude Atherton, speaks of her preoccupation with celebrities and the superficial way she handles them in her autobiography. Her descriptions of famous people, he says, tend to be "wholly exterior, concerned with person and man-ner, dress and undress." [16] He chides her for name-dropping—listing a famous name in the index and then dismissing that person after a single episode. Certainly the pages of *Adventures* devoted to her first London visit support these charges. She confesses coming home after an evening out and curling up with *Who's Who* to find out just who she had met. She mentions a well-known name and con-veys the impression of strong friendship and mutual affection, then never alludes to the person again. We wonder what happened to the Sharps, for example. Did she and they have a falling out or merely lose touch? Elizabeth Sharp wrote a two-volume memoir and never so much as mentions Gertrude Atherton. Perhaps she felt she and William had been used for their hospitality, contacts, and support, and then blithely discarded. [17]

Or what about the James McNeill Whistlers, with whom she struck up a friendship after meeting them at the home of painter Walter Sickert? Her portrait of Whistler may be, as O'Sullivan says, concerned with exteriors, but it is a portrait drawn by an apt and eloquent observer, who reveals as much about herself as her sub-ject: "With his white cockade springing upright from his curly black mane, his flashing, challenging eyes, his wiry little form never still, his sharp satiric tongue, and his constant buzzing like a mosquito ready to pounce, he could never be taken for anything but a celebrity of the first rank. Of course he was an egotist, but as there was never a more interesting one, what matter?" She has a way of making herself the heroine of her own anecdotes and sketches, and in her pages she has both man and wife eager readers of *Hermia Suydam* and competitors for her exclusive attention. Whistler, a kindred spirit whom she admires for his talent, wit, originality, and rebelliousness, turns up jealous of a tête à tête between his wife and Gertrude that excludes him. He invites her to his Chelsea studio, where in her presence he remains at his easel for half an hour—"no doubt that I might always remember I had watched Whistler at work"—and honors her as his "charming compatriot" with an inscribed copy of his *Ten O' Clock* (*Adventures*, pp. 174–76).

An invitation to tea she did *not* accept arrived from George Moore. Since he was asking her to come and sit alone with him at his chambers, she "thought it wise to decline." He took offense, and they never met again.

The only bond of any permanence made during this London season was with a tart-tongued woman named Henriette Corkran who came from a family that had known the Brownings and still had a connection with Lady Wilde, the mother of Oscar. With Miss Corkran, Gertrude paid a call on the sad lady who as "Speranza" had written poetry and essays of fervent Irish patriotism and kept a distinguished Dublin salon. Lady Wilde now lived at the edge of poverty in a tiny house on an obscure London street. Into her candle-lit drawing room she swept: "She might have been a queen graciously giving us a private audience." No doubt she had once been beautiful and stately; she was still stately, "but her old face was gaunt and gray, and seamed with a million criss-crossed lines; etched by care, sorrow, and no doubt, hunger. Her dress was a relic of the sixties, gray satin trimmed with ragged black fringe over a large hoop skirt" (*Adventures*, p. 182).

This portrait probes more deeply, and betrays more compassion, than any other in the London scrapbook; the isolated, aging beauty, fallen on hard days, was a figure Gertrude had met before, and could pity. She would remember Lady Wilde as "a leaning tower of courage" and would mail her from the United States an American imitation of Oscar Wilde epigrams by her Chicago friend, Percival Pollard.

In 1889 Oscar Wilde was celebrated as aesthete, wit, poet, dandy, and brilliant talker. (His dazzling success in the theater and his stunning disgrace in the courts still lay ahead.) Lady Wilde graciously offered Gertrude a chance to meet him at her home the following Saturday, and Gertrude eagerly accepted, "for who would not have welcomed in those days the opportunity to meet Oscar Wilde?" But as the day approached, she had a change of heart, the result of her revulsion when she saw a photograph of Wilde: "His mouth covered half of his face, the most lascivious coarse repulsive mouth I had ever seen. I might stand it in a large crowded drawing-room, but not in a parlor eight-by-eight lit by three tallow candles. I should feel as if I were under the sea pursued by some bloated monster of the deep, and have nightmares for a week thereafter. I sent a telegram to Lady Wilde regretting that I was in bed with a cold" (*Adventures*, p. 184). Physical disgust at the human body came readily to the intense but fastidious Mrs. Atherton.

Wilde also represented to her a strain of affectation and preciosity that she identified with "the decadence, the loss of virility that must follow upon over-civilization."[18] Evidently it was possible—Europe demonstrated that it was possible—to have too much of this good thing. Too much preoccupation with style for its own sake, in someone like Wilde; and, among European fin de siècle novelists and poets, too much "morbid" emphasis on despair, failure, depression, and madness.

In her contempt for "effete" dandies and "morbid" novelists and poets lies the hint of a shift in Gertrude's loyalties, a tilt away from previous alliances with the exotic and unconventional and toward conservative morality and "virile" postures. Aesthetic languors clashed head-on with American dynamism, particularly the dynamism of California and the American West. Many Britons shared Gertrude's distaste for the moribund and epicene aspects of fin de siècle European culture and glamorized what they took to be an alternative: the hardy American West. In Britain, at any rate, it began to seem an advantage to become Californian.

CHAPTER FIVE

Becoming a Californian

 In his short novel *The Siege of London* (1882) Henry James introduces a character named Mrs. Headaway who sheds some light on the hospitality Gertrude Atherton received from London in the 1880s and 1890s. Mrs. Headaway is "a genuine product of the far West—a flower of the Pacific slope; ignorant, audacious, crude, but full of pluck and spirit."[1]

The social success of the vulgar Mrs. Headaway quite horrifies James ("European society might let her in, but European society would be wrong"), and he credits it entirely to her novelty and foreignness. To one of her male admirers she seems to be "as little as possible of his own race and creed. . . . She was like an Hungarian or a Pole, with the difference that he could almost understand her language."[2] Since people see her as a child of nature, her want of refinement—her propensity to talk too loud, her inclination to make everything "terribly distinct," and to act from impulses that are "absolutely glaring"—become a virtue. Mrs. Headaway once lamented her origins, once thought it a disadvantage "to live in Arizona, in Dakotah, in the newly admitted states; but now she perceived that . . . this was the best thing that ever happened to her. She practiced the intonations of the Pacific slope."[3]

James perceived Gertrude Atherton as a variant on Mrs. Headaway. When he met her at a London garden party some years after her first London visit, he privately recoiled when she coyly told him that ages ago in Menlo Park, California, she and a young friend had debated whether he preferred blondes or brunettes. His reply to her inanity masked his dislike; it "was so involved, there were so many colons and semi-colons, so many commas and dashes, with never a period, that by the time he had finished I was too bewildered to do anything but stare at him" (*Adventures*, p. 111). He again responded with elaborate courtesy when she wrote asking his permission to dedicate a collection of short stories to him in 1904: "May my name . . . contribute to bring your work better fortune than it usually contributes to bring mine" (*Adventures*, pp. 374–75). In the privacy of his study, however, he expressed other sentiments. Answering a letter from her that requested information about hotels in Paris, he told his secretary, "I abominate the woman." At frequent intervals "he groaned about having to write to her."[4]

James did not record the reasons for his groaning, but we can guess that Gertrude's brash self-promotion, her want of subtlety and disregard for feminine conventions of docility, and her sheer steam-engine-like energy rendered her, in his eyes, "crude." She profoundly discomfited the man who once likened his good friend Edith Wharton to a hurricane. (He did record, and we will return to, his objections to two of her novels.)

But where the American James recoiled, Britons often nodded in approval. In representatives of the American West they found invigorating breaths of fresh air and a climate, as Swinburne put it, "racy of new soil and strong sunlight."[5] In 1887, when Annie Oakley went to England as part of Buffalo Bill's Wild West show, she became a cult heroine. She was introduced to Queen Victoria and received proposals of marriage from a French count and a Welshman whose mailed photograph she returned with six bullets between the eyes.[6] A colorful Westerner, considered the quintessential American, was sure to draw a crowd. "Americans," wrote Julian Hawthorne, "were curiosities, and if they didn't eat peas with their knives and spit on the carpet, they were welcome. . . . If one played the picturesque barbarian, booted, spurred, red-flannel shirted and sombreroed, he would become . . . the centre of the glittering ring and the louder he yawped, the more the great ladies stroked him."[7]

Bret Harte's California Gold Rush fiction enjoyed such popularity in England that he managed to make a living there long after his career had begun to decline in the United States. In the 1880s he was living in London, still turning out stories with nostalgic gold-country settings that had lost any claim to authenticity but retained their romantic appeal; he readily could place them in British periodicals. When a London editor asked for a California story "with a bear in it," he wrote one to order.[8]

Literate Britons tended to think all Californians resembled Harte's characters. In her Menlo Park days Gertrude once attended a formal dinner at the home of the Milton Lathams, to which the visiting Duke of Manchester was invited. Guests—the women arrayed in jewels and Parisian gowns—sat awaiting their distinguished visitor. The duke arrived in hip boots and red flannel. Aghast, he feebly explained that "all he knew of California he had gleaned from the stories of Bret Harte, and he provided himself with what he believed to be the regulation Western costume" (*Adventures*, p. 65).

Ambrose Bierce had to come to England to find a publisher for a collection of his San Francisco journalism titled *Nuggets and Dust Panned out of California*. In London he hobnobbed with the British poet Tom Hood and with other ex–San Franciscans, like Prentice Mulford and Joaquin Miller. Miller, the Oregon-born "poet of the Sierras" turned up in London drawing rooms arrayed in boots, sombrero, and a red shirt, attire which "tickled the duchesses" and promoted his poems.

Although Gertrude preferred black velvet and pearls to red flannel, she was learning, like Mrs. Headaway, to make a virtue of her origin and in her own way to "practice the intonation of the Pacific slope." She began to see herself as a literary Calamity Jane—fearless, independent, and unstoppable—who eventually found her way into her California novels as a plucky heroine like Helena Belmont. In *A Whirl Asunder* (1895), which was written in England, Helena rides around the countryside in boys' clothes, runs to fires, shuns chaperons, and sits up all night under the trees talking to a man. Helena partakes of California's wildness. When she wants something, she goes straight for it, "undeterred by any tradition or scruples." Her foil is a drab, maternal English girl who has been bleached into blandness by "generations of discipline and homogeneous traditions." Gertrude was beginning to define herself, in Europe, as a Californian and to

realize she could translate that new self-definition into book sales
and fame on both sides of the Atlantic.

As it turned out, Gertrude interrupted her first London stay to
return briefly to New York; sooner than she had planned, she had
to answer a summons of some urgency to return to California. Two
deaths, one impending and one already a jolting fact, called her back.

Stephen Franklin, the bookish, pious Presbyterian grandfather
who had taught her, chastised her, forgiven her, and put money on
her, died in San Francisco on January 16, 1890. "It was a fearful blow,
and I went out and walked the streets all day." She would always
regret her failure during his lifetime to justify his faith in her. "I was
but at the beginning of my career, and so far had little to be proud
of. I was a notoriety, not a celebrity, regarded as an outlaw for whom
there was no place in American letters" (*Adventures*, p. 184).

Franklin's death alone would not have called her to San Francisco.
More pressing was the news in the spring of that same year that her
mother-in-law Dominga was failing;[9] since she had assumed primary
responsibility for Muriel's care during Gertrude's years in New York
and Europe, new arrangements needed to be made. And Gertrude
was, despite the rifts and clashes of the past, attached to Dominga and
ever hopeful for her approval. In many ways Dominga represented
the maternal—certainly more than her own mother. Gertrude had
dedicated *Los Cerritos* to her, a gesture that went unacknowledged:
"I wrote to her often, although she never answered my letters" (*Adventures*, p. 186).

Financial affairs too would have to be put in order. Muriel, as
George's sole surviving child, had some claim on the Atherton estate.
Gertrude herself, as far as she knew, had none, since George had
signed over his share of Atherton riches when he borrowed money
for the Oroville fiasco. Dominga was providing her a small yearly
allowance, purely at her whim.

Gertrude left no account—nor is there any record in letters or
a survivor's memory—of her reunion, after a separation of nearly
three years, with twelve-year-old Muriel; she merely reports that her
daughter was then staying in Ross, in Marin County, with Gertrude's

mother and half sisters. Daisy had married John Craig and was expecting a baby. Mrs. Uhlhorn, who had been given a handsome financial settlement from the Bank of California on her father's death, lived now as a member of the Craig household, occupying herself by sewing for the impending grandchild. Aleece had also moved into this largely female menage, where the now elderly Rose Stoddard shared household duties with the same Hannah who had accompanied Gertrude to New York.

On Gertrude's second day home she journeyed to Menlo Park to see some of George's siblings—Florence, Faxon, and Elena—and Dominga, whom she found "shockingly altered. Her two hundred pounds were reduced to ninety, and she was shivering in the warm sunshine on the veranda, within the folds of a padded dressing gown" (*Adventures*, p. 188). No one named the disease that was consuming her, nor did anyone bring up that other unmentionable subject, Gertrude's books.

Gertrude wanted not only to settle financial and emotional accounts with Dominga, she hoped to tap her as a source of information about Spanish California and the prominent landed families of the *gente de razon* who had dominated in the pre-American era when California was part of Mexico. Gertrude had taken it into her head to make a study of a period—Spanish-speaking, Catholic, and aristocratic—whose traces were quickly fading away, like Dominga herself.

She had conceived her first California novel, *Los Cerritos*, while still in New York, at a time when Helen Hunt Jackson's *Ramona* —telling the story of a half-Indian girl raised on a Spanish ranch in Southern California—earned an enviable national success, even though (to Gertrude's horror) its author was not even a native Californian. In England she had found Londoners endlessly curious about and willing to be entertained by Western characters and lore; anything she wrote about early California, she knew, would find receptive British publishers and readers. Recently, back in the United States, a column by the journalist Kate Field caught her eye by asking, "Why do California writers neglect the old Spanish life of that State? Never has there been anything so picturesque and romantic in the history of America, and it is a mine of wealth waiting for some bright genius to pan it out." Reading this triggered one of Gertrude's mental cataclysms. "Forked lightning was cracking in my skull. It illumined a dazzling vista. Bret Harte had barely touched upon that period and its nuggets were mine" (*Adventures*, p. 186).

Regional writing had been flourishing in the United States since the decades following the Civil War. Americans were rediscovering their local identities and traditions, aided by writers inclined to render grandiose, heroic, or picturesque a past so recent it had been overlooked. Writers like James Whitcomb Riley, who used dialect, found a ready audience. (Gertrude had poked fun at Hoosier-style dialect writers in *Hermia Suydam*, but in her introduction to *Los Cerritos* she made a point of establishing her credentials for reproducing authentic Spanish-Californian speech.)

Gertrude did not fall suddenly in love with the state she had so recently lambasted and fled, but she had gained a new perspective on the way the rest of the world viewed California and a new respect for the commercial potential of regional fiction. Always adept at picking up the dominant pulse of the moment, she hoped to turn her study of pre-American California to profit. If she could capitalize on the popularity of local color stories while she was home on family business, why not?

Interest in the mission towns and in the Mexican era in California was definitely on the rise in a nation hungry for myths that were home-grown rather than imports from Europe. Creating a "Fantasy Heritage" was a growth industry. "The Ramona country" was promoted for the benefit of tourists as a nostalgic remnant of a colorful bygone era. Picture postcards by the tens of thousands were published, showing "the school attended by Ramona," and "the original Ramona." [10] William Keith painted the missions, and mission-style architecture, along with Spanish street names, came into favor all over California. In Los Angeles, journalist and preservationist Charles Fletcher Lummis formed the Association for the Preservation of the Missions, blending boosterism with a genuine interest in honoring Southwestern culture.

The canny and resourceful Mrs. Atherton set out with her sister Aleece to explore the mission towns and soak up atmosphere in Monterey, San Juan Bautista, San Luis Obispo, Santa Barbara (where she stayed at Casa Grande with members of the venerable De la Guerra family), Santa Inez, and Los Angeles, "a town of some fifty thousand inhabitants, shabby and sleepy" (*Adventures*, p. 201). Dominga had provided some letters of introduction to survivors of the grandees. She would be able to tell prospective editors of the resulting stories, "I have not only read every history and reminiscence book of Early California, but I have lived in the Spanish towns with the people."[11]

Although she visited historic sites and stayed with descendants of some of the original Californio families, her goal was neither accurate description of the present nor realistic depiction of the old life; it was amassing detail and color that would help her create a compelling Arcadian myth of early California, a lost golden age one could yearn for but never recapture. The need for ruins, antiquity, and a resonant history that had propelled her flight to Europe she could now graft onto a legendary California past.

Previously, when she wrote about the positive side of being a Californian, she emphasized the buccaneer spirit and competitive drive of its gifted citizens, especially those living away from California. In one of her *Argonaut* letters she wrote: "The restless fever of the pioneers lingers in the veins of their descendants, and those who are not striving for gold are working for fame. The moment [a Californian] enters the race, he makes straight for the head of the line. There is a touch of barbarism in this, a near kinship to elemental nature which older civilization may scoff at, but which is the source of California's power."[12] Now, having returned from England, where the mere mention of California caused a stir, she pursued a fantasy Spanish-California that had lived by values at the opposite pole from those of hard-driving descendants of the Forty-Niners. She sought atmosphere, a picturesque languor punctuated by the nonthreatening aggression of bull fights, the festivity of fancy dress balls, the romance of love-struck vaqueros and doñas draped in lace mantillas dancing to the music of guitars.

Many of the scenes she witnessed on her tour of mission towns stubbornly resisted her attempts to fit them into the mold of romance. She found the widow of General Castro, once renowned as a beauty, had grown obese and her *ojos verdes* "looked like bleached gooseberries." In Monterey, their first stop, Gertrude wanted to get the feel of a moonlit *merienda*, or picnic, and asked her hostess to invite several friends of Spanish or Mexican ancestry to join them on a twilight ride in a charabanc; the women should wear mantillas and bring their guitars. "The scene I had in mind was a moonlit picnic of caballeros and donas, young, slender, clad in the colorful and picturesque costumes of Old California."

Instead, her companions materialized as a group of dumpy women "long past their youth, their heads tied up in black worsted fascinators. When I asked them why they had not worn their ancestral mantillas, they said they were afraid of catching cold." Placed by their theatrical director Mrs. Atherton at various points of vantage on rocky pinnacles overlooking the surf, one fell into a pool of bilge water as others complained of the discomforts of sitting on rocks. To Gertrude the women "looked like nothing on earth but so many black turkey buzzards squatting on the rocks, gorged with prey" (*Adventures*, p. 192). Aleece's giggles mingled with the twang of dilapidated guitars. Willing to laugh at her own inflated expectations, Gertrude also had no qualms about revealing her evident contempt for the old, no longer picturesque women she had asked to be her guests. She wanted them to match her preconceptions, and it never occurred to her to draw out from them the tales they might have been willing to tell her—or that she had missed a rare opportunity by failing to do so.[13]

When the time came to use the *merienda* scene in a story, "The Ears of Twenty Americans," she kept the dramatic coastal scenery and the image of the old people resembling buzzards, but suffused the rest in a romantic haze that suited her myth-making purposes:

Russell moved to a lower rock, and lying at Benicia's feet looked upward. The scene was all above him—the great mass of white rocks, whiter in the moonlight; the rigid cypresses aloft; the beautiful faces, dreamy, passionate, stolid, restless, looking from the lace mantillas; the graceful arms holding the guitars; the sweet rich voices threading through the roar of the ocean like the melody in a grand recitativo; the old men and women crouching like buzzards on the stones, their sharp eyes never closing; enfolding all with an almost palpable touch, the warm voluptuous air. Now and again a bird sang a few notes . . . or the soft wind murmured like the ocean's echo through the pines. The song finished. "Benicia, I love you," whispered Russell.[14]

The Spanish-California stories, gathered first under the title *Before the Gringo Came* (1894) and a second time, with additions, as *The Splendid Idle Forties* (1902), are exercises in calculated nostalgia for the pre-Yankee past. As they glamorize a lost Utopia, they hint that the gringo's superior competence, competitiveness, and dynamism made his ascendancy over the idle Californio inevitable.[15]

In these stories of early California life, one area not examined through rose-tinted glasses is the place of women. Story after story expounds Gertrude's view that the Catholic Church and the controlling Spanish-Mexican families conspired to keep young girls fearfully overprotected and shielded from experience. Distanced from their lovers by metal grating at their windows, denied work outside the home, and once married quickly aged by childbearing, they had little to strive for. Life offered so few choices of role: coquette, wife, mother, nun.

Gertrude allowed her heroines to challenge the narrow morality of their sequestered upbringings. The heroine of the story "La Perdida" has been forced to marry, at age fourteen, a crippled old man; she feels no remorse for taking a strong young vaquero as her lover, reasoning that love has provided the only oasis in her sordid life, "a green spot and patch of blue sky in the desert." The Church cannot be right to preach penance for such meager happiness. "Must not the Catholic religion be all wrong in its teachings?"[16]

When she approached the editors of the magazines which eventually published these stories—the British *Blackwood's* and *London Graphic*, the American *Lippincott's*, *Harpers Weekly*, and *Current Literature*—she emphasized their debt to Bret Harte but claimed she went him one better, since Bret Harte had merely glanced at the period she was writing about. She might also have said that she brought to Californian fiction a new point of view, the woman's. Harte used the masculine precedent of the frontier yarn in telling his mining tales; Atherton's lyrical stories have a matriarchal bent. She creates a world in which the women make things happen, while men play the guitar or prance around on horseback displaying their vivid serapes, silver-trimmed saddles, and boots of soft deerskin stamped with Aztec Eagles. Worse, they—like George Atherton—drink, gamble, and go vagabonding, substituting the pursuit of pleasure for ambition. The mothers in these stories rule with an iron will backed by a green *reata*, or lariat. They tyrannize, imposing their strict standards by force. Their daughters become heroines not by meek compliance but by open rebellion, displays of defiant passion, and impiety.

The stories in *The Splendid Idle Forties* draw a harsh distinction between the romance of courtship and the drudgery of the marriages that follow, marriages that bring wives nothing "better" than swarms of children and bondage to "fat, lazy husbands." Ysabel Herrera, in "The Pearls of Loreto," is spared bitter disillusionment only because she dies with her lover as they are hurled from rocks, in retribution for their sin. Benicia Ortega, in "The Ears of Twenty Americans," having defied her mother by marrying the American she loves, dies young after the birth of a child. Elena, in "The Conquest of Dona Jacoba," does marry the man for whose love she has crossed her mother, but another story informs us she was not destined to live happily ever after. Four years and three babies later, she dies of consumption, leaving a husband who had grown indifferent. Romance, the stories keep saying, dies in fulfillment and thrives on yearning.

Taken as a group, the colorful Spanish California stories—although sometimes rudimentary in characterization, crude in their plotting, and melodramatic in effect—helped legitimize Gertrude Atherton's claims as a serious talent in her own eyes and the world's. To Joseph Stoddart, editor of *Lippincott's Magazine*, she speculated, "If I ever get any literary reputation, it will be over these stories, and I should like everything else I have ever done forgotten." [17]

Stoddart not only published her, he provided space in his magazine for a serious evaluation of her novels by a critic named William Walsh, who praised her daring unconventionality and credited her spirit of literary adventure. By taking residence "in old towns and hamlets and diligently cultivating the sad lingering remnant of the original Spanish Settlers," Walsh wrote, she had succeeded in plowing turf "never before utilized in American literature." [18]

She was acquiring new dignity, new status as a California writer of note, which was all to the good. But as a frontier-bred firebrand, she refused to just sit back on a comfortable pillow of respectability. She needed danger, controversy, excitement; and she was about to find Ambrose Bierce more than willing to provide a portion of each.

Earliest known photograph of Gertrude, about 1860 (Florence A. Dickey)

San Francisco, view from Rincon Point, 1856 (Huntington Library, San Marino, Calif.)

Gertrude, about 1867 (Florence A. Dickey)

Stephen Franklin (Bancroft Library)

Gertrude, about 1872 (San Francisco Public Library)

Dominga de Goñi Atherton
(Florence A. Dickey)

George Henry Bowen Atherton
(Bancroft Library)

Valparaiso Park, San Mateo County (Bancroft Library)

Dutton House and Store, Jolon Stage Station (Huntington Library, San Marino, Calif.)

Sibyl Sanderson as Esclarmonde, Paris, 1889 (Bancroft Library)

Ambrose Bierce (Bancroft Library)

Gertrude Atherton letter to Ambrose Bierce, 1890 (Bancroft Library)

Gertrude Atherton, 1891; frontispiece for *The Doomswoman* (California Historical Society)

Lady Colin Campbell, by Giovanni
Boldini, about 1897 (National Portrait
Gallery, London)

"WHY DO YOU NOT GO?"

harles Dana Gibson illustration
r "Mrs. Pendleton's Four-in-
and," *Cosmopolitan*, December
90 (Leider)

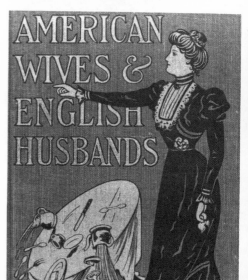

AMERICAN
WIVES &
ENGLISH
HUSBANDS

GERTRUDE ATHERTON

Cover of *American Wives and
English Husbands*, 1898 (California
Historical Society)

Gertrude Atherton at the opera, 1899; pastel by N. Carpomogian (Florence A. Dickey)

Gertrude Atherton portrait by Arnold Genthe, about 1906 (California Historical Society)

CHAPTER SIX

Ambrose Bierce and the Chaste Siren

When she returned to California in 1890, Gertrude had in the back of her mind a plan to meet in person the Bay Area's reigning monarch of wit, Ambrose Bierce. Bierce, fifteen years her senior, was a literary lion of legendary ferocity. His column "Prattle," in Hearst's *San Francisco Examiner*, amused, provoked, and often enraged its many readers, but kept them coming back for more. Simultaneously feared and courted, Bierce named the objects of his stinging judgments and crucified his victims in perfectly turned epigrams. He sometimes signed himself "A. G. Bierce," and it was said that the initials stood for "Almighty God."

Gertrude had not forgotten their collision a while back, when he wrote to her during the flap over *Hermia Suydam*, accusing her of being a sensationalist, a fad-follower, and a publicity seeker, and she answered with a spirited, defensive reply, proclaiming her innocence of the charges and maintaining—with doubtful veracity—that she had done nothing worse than to quietly write a truthful, serious book.[1] Bierce's conduct during the exchange was not exactly exemplary either. He had not bothered to read her novels; he had merely read, and taken at face value, the finger-pointing reviews that had appeared in Bay Area publications.

Now, after a year without contact, they again exchanged letters.

On her return to California, she wasted little time and bowed to no convention in seizing the initiative and boldly addressing him:

My Dear Mr. Bierce:
   I want very much to meet you, but how shall I manage it? My mother-in-law is in Menlo and my own family is over here [in Ross]. Could you come over here some afternoon on the one o'clock train? . . . It is a bore to have to go to the country to call on a woman, but I have nothing else to suggest. There is a comfortable hammock under the trees and when you are tired of talking to me you can go to sleep. . . . I hate you generally, but think you would be interesting. (May 25, [1890])

Bierce, an asthmatic whose health deteriorated when subjected to the fogs and winds of San Francisco, was living in Sunol in the East Bay. He responded with a counterinvitation—she should come to visit him—and a request about her appearance: what did she look like? She replied, "I am a tearing beauty, of course. I wonder you had not heard it before."
   Good looks, their own and other people's, mattered greatly to these two peacocks. Gertrude loved to pose for painters and photographers and to present flattering images of herself to the press and to professed admirers; in her novels she dwelt upon the dazzling skin, eyes, carriage, and costumes of her heroines. As for Bierce, even when living on the various mountaintops to which he gravitated, he lavished hours on his grooming and dress, and was rumored to shave every day "from head to foot."[2] A confessed slave to feminine beauty, he had written to another female correspondent, "If I don't know a woman, I want her beautiful—that is my right."[3] Bierce and Atherton were keenly aware of each other, from the start, as attractive members of opposite sexes, and they engaged in the kind of verbal sparring and playful confrontation that accompanies a courtship dance.
   Mrs. Atherton—to Bierce she was never other than "Mrs. Atherton"—did not immediately act on the invitation to visit Sunol, for the death of Dominga in September had intervened. "Being in mourning I am not paying calls at present, but I shall console myself by going up to Martinez and roaming among the tules at four in the morning. I like that sort of thing better than most men anyway." Perhaps it was a good thing, after all, that they had not yet met. "I feel a pang

of relief at the fate I may have escaped. Think—think! but it is too dreadful for words."

She confessed that his short story "The Watcher by the Dead" had profoundly disturbed her. "That is the one thing I hate you for. It kept me awake for a week, and I have been afraid to sleep alone ever since. This is not intended as a subtle and skillful compliment, but as an honest and feminine appeal." Summoning the image of herself in bed was decidedly provocative, and she did it more than once.

She had moved to San Francisco, leaving behind her relatives in Ross, and taken an apartment on Washington Street, with "a Spanish cook and an occasional Muriel." She told Bierce, "You are well out of San Francisco. I am pretty robust, but the wind smites my nerve centers. Today I am laid up with neuralgia, but cannot tell whether it is the wind or Joaquin Miller. He was here yesterday and told me to do my writing in bed, not to get up until noon. It would keep my backbone warm, which it appears is essential to composition."

They exchanged several letters before the much-anticipated encounter took place. She made it clear that Bierce should feel honored by her desire to meet him. "I seldom ask anyone, man or woman, to come and see me. I care for so little outside my work that I am afraid of boring people or being bored by them." Each year, she informed him, she found herself with fewer friends. But she had decided that he was "more interesting than most people."

They finally agreed on a date, and as the visit approached her anxiety mounted. Perhaps he would dislike her. He had made woman-baiting a kind of second career, after all, missing no opportunity to cavil in print at their lack of virtue or intelligence, the deficiency in the "gray batter of their brainettes." "In order that the list of able women may be memorized for us at meetings," he had written, "heaven has considerately made it brief." Intellectual women, literary women, and the women of the press (the Pacific Coast Women's Press Association had recently formed) were particular targets of his wrath, particular threats to his over-defended manhood.

Bierce's misogyny conflicted with his romanticism. Not only did he find himself powerfully attracted to women, he pursued and at times effusively admired them. He loved playing paternal protector to certain favorites, usually much younger than he and with artistic aspirations. What he looked for in a woman, according to his friend George Sterling, was "a meek and modest mien, and his concession that a woman could wear bloomers and use a bicycle and still remain charming was amazing to his friends."[4] Gertrude had reason to be anxious. What response could she expect from a man who said, "I hate woman and I love women, having an acute animosity to your sex and adoring each member of it"?[5]

She knew she was not his type. He had met her friend Sallie Thibault, who was "intelligent, receptive, sympathetic"—exactly the kind of woman, she suggested, generally favored by men of genius. In contrast, "I have an aggressive sort of personality and am only receptive when I happen to be in the humor." She knew of Bierce's precarious health and had experienced firsthand his irascibility. It seemed likely they would clash: "Tell me if there are numerous trains, so that if we fight beyond endurance, I can go home and not sit and sulk on the platform."

The account of their first meeting that follows relies heavily on her own description in *Adventures of a Novelist* (pp. 202–5). Though her narrative has to be trusted, she has clearly shaped the material to her own ends. She minimizes her own strong attraction to Bierce and her active role in seeking him out. When she made Bierce the model for a character in fiction, he became the most arresting man she had ever seen, with a mouth that is "humorous, bitter, sensual, determined" and an appearance that suggests "virility in every angle"; she is "fascinated, piqued."[6] In the autobiography, he is the one who finds *her* irresistible. She never acknowledges her own ambivalence and seems unaware that she gave mixed cues and played two contradictory roles. She wanted him to fall in love with, but not to make love to, her. She was willing to risk literary scandal and social unconventionality, but not, finally, her "respectability."

On a Monday, probably in January of 1891, clad in "a very becoming blue frock," she arrived at 8:30 in the morning at the Sunol train station, where Bierce greeted her. She had sent him a photograph so that he would easily recognize her, and she had no trouble spotting him. He was "about forty-nine at the time, a tall man, very

thin and closely knit, with curly iron gray hair, a bristling moustache, beetling brows over frowning eyes, good features and beautiful
hands." Despite his attractions, a point against him, in Gertrude's
eyes, was that "he looked too much like my father—what my mother
would have called a typical Yank."

Although his personal life lay in ruins—he had bitterly separated
from his wife, and his older son had recently died at the age of
sixteen in a sensational love duel—Bierce was at the height of his
professional power. Mrs. Atherton's was decidedly the lesser known,
the more untried, talent. She was also a woman, and for a woman to
travel alone to pay a call on "the wickedest man in San Francisco"
was in 1891 a calculated risk. Willing to take that risk, she wanted
Bierce to understand from the start that she had no intention of pros-
trating herself in worship at his feet. When she said as much, he was
less than delighted.

They were not alone at lunch. S. S. Chamberlain, managing editor of the *San Francisco Examiner*, for which Bierce wrote his weekly
"Prattle" column, joined them, lending an air of propriety and elegance. With a monacle in his eye and a gardenia in his lapel, the
former editor of the *New York Herald* and founder of *Le Matin* in
Paris lived up to his reputation for possessing the manner and dress
of an English duke.[7] Chamberlain eased the flow by being "an easy
and brilliant talker." But after lunch, he disappeared. Bierce, pleading ill health, led Gertrude into his bedroom, looking "cynical and
somewhat amused." She "did not turn a hair," but settled herself into
the one comfortable chair, while Bierce stretched out on the bed.

Unwilling to be seduced, she defended herself with a barrage
of well-aimed verbal barbs, which Bierce returned in kind. What
followed was a skirmish of wits worthy of Beatrice and Benedick.
He told her that although her writing showed promise, so far she
had done nothing worth serious consideration. She returned with
an attack on his stories, which "might be models of craftsmanship
and style" and of the technique of horror, but were "so devoid of
humanity that they fell short of true art, and would never make any
but a limited appeal."

Bierce began dismembering the reputations of various highly regarded writers. Meredith was proclaimed indecipherable; he "could
neither think straight nor write straight. His style was atrocious, and

his characters as inchoate as his sentences." Stevenson was "nothing but a phrase-maker; his imagination was so thin that it was all he could do to beat it into a novel of conventional length." Novels were a waste of time, anyway. "The only form in which the perfection of art could be achieved, as well as the effect of totality, was that of the short story."

Bierce's antipathy to the novel, which his *Devil's Dictionary* defines as "a short story padded," was well known. Years after this confrontation, Gertrude returned to the subject to defend the novel thoughtfully, arguing in a letter to Bierce that character is of great importance in fiction, and "character requires the novel"; and that "whatever gives a true picture of the best of one's own times, a living piece of current history done from first hand impression, is of permanent as well as artistic value." But at Sunol, in Bierce's bedroom, in the heat of argument, she blurted that Bierce only opposed the novel because he was incapable of writing one. "You cannot write novels yourself. All short-story writers are jealous of novelists. They all try to write novels and few of them succeed. Any clever, cultivated mind, with a modicum of talent can manage a short story. . . . But it takes a very special endowment and abundant imagination to sustain the creative faculty throughout a story of novel length."

Perhaps she felt she had gone too far with this assault, or perhaps the strenuous repartee had tired her. She decided to change her tactics, soften her tone, and find a way to depart congenially, as a friend, on the six o'clock train. She apologized for being so quarrelsome and confessed to Bierce her great admiration for him; indeed, she considered him a great man. This failed to produce the desired effect. Gertrude never failed to be buoyed by any word of praise, but Ambrose Bierce had the opposite response. He fulminated. His failure to receive national recognition or produce a large body of work gnawed at him. He could not mistake mere journalism for high art. "He was not great. He would not be called great. He was . . . a mere hack. He got so red I feared he would have an attack of asthma."

She could do no more than gingerly announce the late hour. It was time for her to go. His manner relaxed as he walked her to the station. "He became almost charming. He thanked me for coming to see him and apologized for being so cantankerous, said that he had found an irresistible pleasure in arguing with me, and that I was a blue and gold edition of all the poets. The train was late. We walked about the station, conversing most amiably. It grew darker. We were in the shadows between the station and the malodorous grunting pigsty when he suddenly seized me in his arms and tried to kiss me. In a flash I knew how to hurt him. . . . I threw back my head—well out of his reach—and laughed gaily. 'The great Bierce! Master of style! The god on Olympus at whose feet pilgrims come to worship —trying to kiss a woman by a pigsty!' "

The train arrived, and he almost pushed her on board, shouting, "I never want to see you again! You are the most detestable vixen I ever met in my life, and I've had a horrible day."

Both hesitated before renewing contact, yet they found they wanted to remain in touch and corresponded avidly. When his health faltered she expressed sympathy. "I discover that I have an eighth of an inch of heart . . . and it all goes out to you at the moment," she wrote him. "Really I am concerned about you. A little selfishly, because you are quite the most interesting man in California and should be carefully pickled for the benefit of those who want to meet you more than once, but with a decent pinch of abstract sympathy also."

She reproached him for not coming to see her in San Francisco. "I have a charming apartment," she reported. "And a new tea-gown! Primrose yellow—most stunning—but tea-gowns are beneath your notice." She wanted to know when she was going to be asked to visit Sunol again. When he did invite her, she said she would come "when you want me very badly, not before." And she announced she would not come alone a second time; she wanted another woman along. "I haven't much regard for the conventions, but I have some," she said in one letter; and in another: "If I ever summon up my courage to go to Sunol again, I think I will take a bodyguard." When he suggested she bring their mutual friend Elodie Hogan, she balked. Elodie, a transplanted Irish Catholic who was in love with and eventually married the Anglo-French writer Hilaire Belloc, was young and pretty enough to pose a threat. "I am jealous of Elodie and will not take her to Sunol."

Evidently his letters gave her reason to fret about her standing in

his eyes. She urged him to judge her for himself and not be swayed
by what he heard or read about her. "Every once in a while you let
fall something which makes me very uncomfortable, not to say mad.
If I had met you three years ago, before the public began to concern itself with me, we would have got along much better. I would
rather you knew the worst I could tell you about myself than that you
should believe the extraordinary estimates of my character that have
been made by sensational and spiteful people. You have too deep a
knowledge of human nature not to make up your mind for yourself.
. . . As it is I always feel at a disadvantage with you, and am half
afraid to be natural lest everything I say be misinterpreted."

Bierce became her confidant. She sent him long, introspective letters, revealing a vulnerability and self-doubt that she was usually at
pains to conceal or deny. She acknowledged "terrible wants" in her
nature, an inability to feel that she feared marked her as inhuman.
"My imagination carries me everywhere, but my personality is unfinished. I am little more than an embodied imagination, a highly
strung nervous system without a heart, a tablet with inherited re-
pressions on one side, and a sort of magnet-wax on the other. N.B.
There is nothing in my nature which is in sympathy with pigsties."

Her letters keep returning to her wish to become "impersonal."
"Do we ever outgrow ourselves?" she wonders. "If one could only
be mind and sense, with neither heart nor soul!" But it was neither
heart nor soul that kept short-circuiting her friendship with Bierce.
It was body. Gertrude called herself "fastidious." Anything carnal—
Oscar Wilde's mouth, Sibyl Sanderson's liaisons—anything redolent
of the animal, upset and disgusted her. Despite her repeatedly stated
aversion to the "bloodlessness" and lack of passion in American literature of the New England tradition, despite her devotion to torrid
heroines and her preference for low-cut gowns, she was captive to
a rigid, Puritan sexual morality. Her stand-in Patience Sparhawk
would say, "There are some words I hate, the words free-love and
adultery. We can't violate certain moral laws that heredity has made
part of our brain fibre, without ultimate regret" (*Patience Sparhawk*,
p. 365).

As for Bierce, for all his seductive posturing he was the reverse
of a free spirit, haunted and repressed. "He was proud to boast that
no woman, even his wife, had ever seen him in the buff."[8] An abso-

lutist, he made no room for a middle ground. There were angels or devils, nothing in between.

They fought whenever they met face to face. She threatened to drop him entirely. "I shall never go to see you again. You give me the blues. I cannot say why but you do. Although I never by any chance agree with you, I have that regrettable thing called temperament which is sensitive to the influence of strong personalities. Moreover, although I like you tremendously on paper—in correspondence and in the abstract—I do not like you at all when I am with you."

Apparently Bierce was enough taken with her to carry her photograph with him, for a time, and show it around. His sometime friend and collaborator, Dr. Adolph Danzinger, was shown a profile that prompted the German-speaking dentist to write a poem, "Die Nixe" ("The Mermaid"), in the rhythm of Heine's "Lorelei," dedicated to "Mrs. Atherton, the authoress, after seeing her picture." It was published in San Francisco's German-language paper.[9] Such tributes delighted her.

Insults did not, and Bierce was a master of them. However much she proclaimed her "impersonality," she showed herself to be easily hurt. "I pass over your insulting insinuations regarding my personal appearance. I have two men in love with me, and they smooth down the feathers that you ruffle." She confessed, "I am frightfully susceptible to the opinion of others, especially if it is censorious. I have almost no confidence in myself, and do not know my good work from my bad. I only write at all because it is my strongest impulse, in fact the only . . . companion that I have." Injured by something he said that she considered "mean," she told him, "if you are inhuman, the rest of us are not."

She had spurned Bierce's advances, but she was unwilling to renounce her sexual power over him. When his health failed, she wrote, "I am awfully sorry you are ill, and would hold your hand were you here—which joy you must forgo until some future attack." She teased him with references to the two men in her life, but made a secret of their identities: "No, you don't get their names. I will add, however, that I am the least bit in love with each of them, just about as much as I am with you (on paper.)" A few years later, when she had settled in New York and there was a continent between them, she cooed, "If there were flying machines I'd run over frequently and spend a week with you." She would gloss over their history of quarreling and write him that one of her friends "thinks I should go back & live with you—particularly on your mountain—thinks it would be so romantic." Or promise, "some time I'll go back to California just to spend a week with you—if you'll swear not to make love to me."

Distance was the key; it was her requisite for intimacy. She continued to live most of the time in her own thoughts and imagination, where flesh did not get in the way. A letter written in private and in solitude, when she had total control, freed her to be both affectionate and self-examining. Bierce could be relentlessly truthful, and he elicited from her one extraordinary letter. In it she drops her guard completely and confronts the contradiction at her core, the conflict between the impulse to act the femme fatale and her coldness, detachment, and conventional moral scruples. "What do you mean," this letter begins, "by asking if I do not observe the observances?" She continues:

What observances? I do not pick pockets, nor do I betray [a friend], nor do I lie except when it is absolutely necessary. If I were addicted to lovers, I should take a scientific delight in being false to them all. Nature designed me for an Aspasia [10] and then unkindly planted me in a Puritan Conventional household and alloted me an unnecessary share of refinement and fastidiousness. The consequence is that after hammering away at the question for some years I came to the conclusion that the only thing for me to do was sit outside life and look on; to live with my mind and put my personality in a hermetically sealed cell. When I take my pen in hand, I understand character well enough; when I lay it down and attempt to formulate some sort of life for myself I am as much at sea as when I was seventeen. I have not the faintest idea of what is right or wrong. Morality to me is correlative with mystery.

I have known so many men, more than most women of my age, I think, and of all sorts, ages, and conditions. So you see it is better for other people to let me alone . . . to accept me as a mentality. As it is, my intrigues are all mental. There is such a thing as intellectual passion; and that does not drag my warped and unfinished personality out of its cell. All this is very shocking, is it not? But I write it to you alone, so perhaps you will forgive me. I never said as much to anyone before.

This outburst came in the fall of 1891, during one of Gertrude's periodic bouts of disillusion and world-weariness. In San Francisco she had been throwing herself into the kind of manic sociability that she never seemed able to sustain.

She had become one of Bierce's colleagues on the *San Francisco Examiner* and was writing a weekly column called "Woman in Her Variety." She claimed she disliked being a newspaperwoman, but she seems to have relished both the public visibility it afforded her and the contact with newspapermen it provided. She was seeing a lot of the *Examiner* crowd, particularly of the editor, Sam Chamberlain —eloquent, debonair, and alcoholic. She often invited Chamberlain and cronies Ned Hamilton and "Cosey" Noble to breakfast at her San Francisco apartment. Bierce and Dr. Danzinger attended one breakfast, which she presided over in a gown that was "a long, lacy, diaphanous affair." She "daintily held a cigarette between her smiling lips." The food was Spanish, and the table covered with ferns.

The conversation touched on Bierce's recent assault, in "Prattle," on women writers. "With rare exceptions," he had written, "women who write are destitute, not only of common sense, but of the sense of right and wrong—they are moral idiots. A woman may live out half her life, a bright . . . companionable creature, then take to writing for the newspapers and become a sore trial. . . . Never have I known a female antagonist who did not lie and cheat with as little concern . . . as a pig with a mouthful of young larks." What's more, "women of uncommon mental powers are, as a rule, noticeably masculine in figure, face, voice, manner or habit."[11] Gertrude asked Bierce to name his target. "Do you mean any one in particular—me, for instance?" Bierce parried, "You are not particular, Mrs. Atherton."[12]

When Bierce repeated in a letter the charge that she had something masculine in her nature, she countered that what he called masculinity was only self-reliance and strength, "an amount of independence" that circumstances had forced her to develop. He must have commented on her predilection for describing beautiful women in minute detail and hinted that she found women attractive. To that she defensively answered that her descriptions were merely verbal portraits and that she wouldn't care if she never saw another woman. (With characteristic inconsistency, she speaks often, in letters of this same time, about her dear friend Elodie Hogan: "Elodie is blooming! I see her frequently. She is like a small cyclone at times and amuses me much. . . . She is one of the four women I like.")

During her months as an *Examiner* columnist she threw herself into the social ramble: morning breakfasts, afternoon picnics, evenings at the opera, and the constant attendance of Sam Chamberlain. She complained to Bierce that she wasn't getting any work done and could think of nothing but amusing herself "in the most frivolous manner." She invited him to join her and a group of friends on a camping excursion: "Mr. Chamberlain, Mr. Noble, Mr. Stokes, Miss Beveridge, Elodie Hogan and myself are going into the redwood mountains twenty miles behind Menlo for five days. Frank Atherton has a home there in the wilderness and we fish and tramp all day— also we girls wear boys' clothes. I wish you could come. I think you would suit the redwoods." Bierce declined, but he wanted to hear more about the costumes he was going to miss seeing. She explained, "Of course we are not going to wear real boys' clothes. We wear short trousers, long loose leggins & a tunic to our knees. To this fascinating costume I shall add a pink sunbonnet."

As she always found after a season of gadding about, the social merry-go-round began to tire and bore her. "I have been making a frantic effort to interest myself in people . . . but I regret to say it is a dead failure. What a frightful bore the nine hundred and ninety-nine are." She was depressed. "Just now I am rather disgusted with life in general. If I could have small-pox, I think I might do some good literary work."

Undoubtedly Chamberlain's drinking contributed to her black mood. Drunkenness struck a nerve; it had broken up her parents' marriage, and it was ruining this romance. She begged Chamberlain to stop, and he refused. Then she gave him his walking papers, telling him she never wanted to see him again. When he came to New York while she was living there in 1893, she wrote Bierce: "I do not take the slightest interest in Mr. Chamberlain any more. The more I think of it, the more I believe he is an undeveloped hypnotist." She conceded he made excellent grist for the fiction mill and used him as the model for Trennaham in *The Californians*.

If parting with Chamberlain provided one motive for her eager flight from San Francisco to "bury" herself in the country, the failure of her *Examiner* column furnished another. As a columnist she attempted to wear the mask of a bitter, cruel, and blasphemous female Bierce. But she lacked his pointedness and moral authority. She lashed out in all directions, doing her best to outrage and offend everybody. Where vinegar was appropriate, she poured hydrochloric acid.

A column called "Woman in Her Variety" hoped to attract female readers, but it insulted women at least as often as it championed them, calling them more barbarous than men because they are closer to nature and because centuries of legal and social discrimination have fostered irresponsibility and childishness in them. It singled out for praise a woman like Clara Barton, who had "aspiration above the commonplace" and had "taken her life deliberately into her own hands." But it heaped scorn on ordinary women, on the inanities of the *Ladies Home Journal* and the tedium of domestic life. Marriage was labeled unnatural if it lasted too long: "Human nature . . . was never intended to endure one unvarying partner." Incompatibility was branded the greatest marital evil—not adultery—and she judged divorce more honorable by far than a loveless union: "No woman with any self-respect will continue to live with a man after she has ceased to care for him and yet her so doing is applauded by the conservative sisterhood." The financial dependency of married women was deplorable, but at least in California wives were protected by community property laws; in England a married woman was "practically a bondwoman." (Bierce disputed this claim in a column of his own.) If divorce couldn't remove an unwanted husband, there was always murder. Several methods were recommended: serving the victim wine with plenty of glass in it, pouring boiling lead into his ear while he sleeps, or stabbing his eardrum with a knitting needle. (Plots involving actual or contemplated murder of a husband will turn up more than once in Atherton novels.)

Again in a murderous mood, she used her column to savage the downtrodden and their would-be rescuers. "May the devil fly away with charity," she wrote. "People incapable of taking care of themselves . . . should out of pure Christian charity have their heads stuck in a barrel of chloroform. I hate all people who are interested in charities, particularly society girls."

Although she defended the press's infatuation with European

royalty on the grounds that children are brought up reading fairy tales about princes and princesses and that all people long for what is beautiful and picturesque, she found nothing beautiful or picturesque in San Francisco society, which she viewed at close range. "The smarts of California," she charged, "owe their prestige not to a family redwood . . . nor yet to extreme wealth, but to the few years' precedence of dollars over the newcomers. Any family who has had money and entertained for twenty years in this young state is a howling swell." She quotes a young Englishman who told her he would never marry a San Francisco girl because "their mothers were such frights . . . generally fat and coarse of skin and floppy." And she pounces on the chance to embellish the point: "they collapse into a collection of abdomens protruding from various parts of their body, they slouch instead of walk, and frequently they do bedizen."

Such remarks did not endear her to the public, particularly the female public whose readership Hearst was courting. The columns were returning her to a familiar position as pariah. "I am in hot water," she kept telling Bierce. Readers were protesting. "Hearst seems to be worried about the fuss some women are making."

She published and commented on a letter from one angry reader that asked, "Why write at all of your sex if you must do so in such a disparaging, sneering manner?" Such venom, the reader continued, must issue from the pen of a "sour old maid." With what she intended as withering irony, her column responded: "It is true, my dear madame, that I am a sour old maid. I am lean and grizzled and red-nosed and forty-seven." She closes with a melodramatic flourish: "Do you think I have not been the heroine of a romance—comedy—tragedy—a tale of woe and wrong—which would have venomized twenty women! Just wait! Some day I'll tell my story to the world."[13]

Her column ceased when William Randolph Hearst overstepped her limits. Always ready with a new scheme for arousing the "gee-whiz emotion" in his readers, he had increased *Examiner* circulation tenfold with his stunts and sensations, putting baseball news on the front page and printing popular songs in Sunday editions. Now he came up with a bright idea for the Women's Page: combining Gertrude Atherton's acid with the syrup of the maudlin poet and advice-giver Ella Wheeler Wilcox, with whom Gertrude had already feuded in public. The combination would surely produce some entertaining fireworks.

Gertrude seethed. She told Bierce, "Hearst has purchased some letters of Ella Wheeler Wilcox on the supposition that I would fight her and boom his paper nicely. Imagine it!" Moreover, she said, Hearst had had the effrontery to ask her to use her column to address such nitwit topics as "How Women Take Men's Arms." She wrote back, to Bierce not Hearst, that she would not "waste my time with such rot. If he had asked me to write on 'How Women Take *To* Men's Arms' I might have considered the subject." She suspended her column—she would again work for Hearst decades later—and left San Francisco.

Her refuge was the Russian-built coastal town of Fort Ross, north of San Francisco. Here she would nurse the broken heart she intimated she was suffering, drop the company she had been keeping, and throw herself into serious writing. She had to prove she was more than a journalistic viper. The acting-out part of her nature needed a rest; the "good girl" wanted her turn to perform and be rewarded.

The book she threw herself into, *The Doomswoman*, picked up the early California theme of the short stories she had published with such success, but added a literary flourish, attempting to echo themes from Shakespeare's *Romeo and Juliet*. Its hero, Diego Estenega, a Mexican modeled on General Mariano Vallejo,[14] wants California to retain its Mexican character without sacrificing American economic vigor. He berates his people for being dawdlers and drones in a territory filled with gold and rich soil. Its heroine, Chonita Iturbi y Moncada, is Atherton's attempt at a tragic heroine. She has none of the out-of-doors abandon and tart impudence of future California-bred heroines like Helena Belmont, though like them she spurns the traditional maternal role. A regal, dignified, and bookish woman, Chonita personifies the conflicts inherent in the Far West: "She is California, magnificent, audacious, incomprehensible, a creature of storms and convulsions and impregnable calm; the germ of all good and all bad in her."[15] With her blonde hair and "unmistakable intellect, her marble face crossed now and again by the animation of the clever American woman," she looks like an idealized Gertrude Atherton, the self she aspired to be.[16]

"I am working like steam," she reported to Bierce, "and I have come to the conclusion that it is the only thing that suits me. I do not get along with the world at all, but I am always content when I am off by myself in the country and hard at work." She had chosen Fort Ross, she explained, because the latter part of her book is laid there. "It is a beautiful place and very solitary, only the hotel and usual accessory of 'store' and post-telegraph-express office—also a saloon, of course—and a cottage or two in the distance. The cliffs are very fine, and the hills, covered more or less with redwoods, slope almost to the river. I walk four miles a day & don't ever get tired. Am learning to shoot with a rifle."

The Fort Ross cure seemed to be working beautifully. She nursed her dark mood and drank in the dramatic scenery, "with the sea thundering at the base of the cliffs, and the winter wind howling in the redwood forest." From her isolated perch she mailed off manuscripts, wrote to editors, and devoted hours to serious study. Her instructor was none other than Mr. Bierce. Being in one of her contrite and virtuous cycles, she fell willingly into the role of dutiful student, earnestly seeking her teacher's approval as she once had sought her grandfather's. And she found in Bierce the perfect new taskmaster, the man who had set himself up as literary standard-bearer and grammar policeman to the entire Pacific coast. "It is my intention," he had written, "to purify journalism in this town by instructing such writers as it is worth while to instruct, and assassinating those that it is not."[17] Gertrude now added her name to the list of Bierce's "pupils."

Guided by Bierce, she studied Landor's *Imaginary Conversations*, copying out of it the sentences she admired. Bierce directed her to read Professor John Nichol's *English Composition* and Longinus on "The Sublime." She sent him samples of her work for comment: "I have inflicted you with one of my manuscripts, and my only excuse is that I would rather have your opinion than that of all the critics of America put together."

He proposed to help her perfect her prose style, with an eye to what she called increased "precision of thought and expression, condensation and individuality of expression." She assured Bierce that in the matter of style "you and few others have it" and solicited advice from him on minute points of English usage. With his help she was determined to make up for her youthful lack of discipline. "You are quite right," she wrote him, "about early lack of guidance. I do not suppose any writer ever started so wholly wrong. That was partly from having brought myself up from infancy, riding over everybody, and finishing up with Mr. [George] Atherton. . . . It is only in the last year that I have learned to write, and it is to you and Mr. Chamberlain that I owe whatever the results may be."

In addressing Bierce she could assume an abject and submissive tone reserved for him alone: "You are too good to me anyway. I appreciate more deeply than you know your interest in me; but I am equally aware that men prefer being amused by women to instructing them." Like a daughter to an idolized patriarch she said, "some day I hope you will be proud of me."

Their letters passed between one lonely outpost of civilization and another. They were companions in alienation who shared the feeling of never belonging to a group or location. Distinctiveness, singularity, individuality were the words they used for the quality they most prized in themselves and others. Bierce did not wander as far afield as Gertrude Atherton did, but he was every bit as much of a vagabond outsider as he drifted from Sunol to Howell Mountain in the Napa Valley in search of a "breathing place."[18] When Gertrude put him in a story, she made him a hermit who, like the Duke in *As You Like It*, has withdrawn to a simple, natural life in the wilderness, far from corrupt society. She made the heroine (another stand-in for herself) appear, like Rosalind, disguised as a boy. The hermit is the only one who can penetrate her disguise.

Retreat from the world was partly a matter of temperament, partly philosophy. Here were two critics of the tendency of democracy to equalize people and bring them together, two elitists disdainful of the common herd. Both had spent time in England and sympathized with British formality, class snobbery, and literary tradition. They used "commonplace" as a smear word. Recoiling from everyday life in late-nineteenth-century America, they prized what was remote, strange, or special, and affirmed closer kinship with Byron than with their democratic countryman and contemporary Walt Whitman.

While she was at Fort Ross, her novel *The Doomswoman* found a publisher in Joseph Stoddart, of *Lippincott's Magazine*. Stoddart knew and admired Whitman and urged her to read him with care;

he was a great poet. She did "study" him along with her other texts, found him contemptible, and was heartened to learn that Bierce shared her revulsion. "In my opinion," she wrote to Bierce, "Walt Whitman is a hog—a nineteenth century North American ground hog; and with an egotism that would stop a clock." A letter from her to Stoddart calls *Leaves of Grass* "the very sewerage of poetry. The idea—the glorification of the individual, the paean of the human animal, is good, but it is too bad that it should be roared and bellowed."[19]

Howells was another "commonplace" writer they scorned in unison. Bierce chided him for being "absolutely destitute of that supreme and sufficient literary endowment, imagination." Howells, he said, merely "takes notes—as does any other reporter." Bierce challenged the premise of his realism. "Probability!" he scoffed. "Nothing is so improbable as what is true. It is the unexpected that occurs." Howells was impoverished because "he to whom life is not picturesque, enchanting, terrible, astonishing, is denied the gift and faculty divine."[20] Mrs. Atherton cheered him on. Howells, she maintained, was more a "Littleist" than a "Realist." What a bore to parade humdrum life before humdrum, bourgeois readers. A writer should be interested in the exception, not the rule.

Because they were literary allies as well as (at least at a distance) friends, Bierce and Gertrude made a practice of boosting each other's work in print. When *Cosmopolitan* asked Mrs. Atherton for an article on "The Literary Development of California," she included in her piece the names of many writers, but reserved her highest praise for her sometime antagonist: "Ambrose Bierce sits alone on the top of the mountain and does work which twenty years ago would have given instant fame, and yet he is known and published only locally, in San Francisco." She pronounced him, as a short story writer, greater than Edgar Allan Poe.[21]

Bierce had no objection to the favorable comparison with Poe, but he did not like being labeled a California writer. He had little respect for the species and had declined an invitation from Stoddart to have work of his included in the "Californian" issue of *Lippincott's*, along with *The Doomswoman*. Born in Ohio, raised in Indiana, he had fought and lived in the South during the Civil War; his residency in San Francisco had been interrupted by stays in London and the

Black Hills of the Dakota Territory, and he professed no love or special loyalty to the city that had crowned him king. Quite the reverse. He called San Francisco a Gomorrah, a "moral penal colony."

Gertrude tried to convince him otherwise. She did not think the adjective "Californian," which she and Bierce had defended as a legitimate addition to the English language in a debate conducted in the columns of the *Examiner*, indicated any particular kind of writer or writing. "Californian," to her, signified variety. A truly Californian hotel

would quake all the dishes off the table and have a gold mine for the guests to play in. It should have stained glass windows to portray Spanish fandangos, Bret Harte stories, bonanza excitements, land steals, irrigation committees, . . . law court scandals, overdressed "society leaders" and trade winds. A fog should permeate one corridor; another be as red-hot as San Miguel; another bellow with wind; a fourth delivered over to fleas; a fifth a museum for scorpions, tarantulas, grizzlies, seals, panthers, rattlesnakes and other pets for Eastern guests.[22]

Presumably, an equally diverse style would characterize the California literary scene.

But to Bierce, the newly coined adjective "Californian," when applied to writers, indicated mediocrity. He didn't want to be included in Stoddart's "Californian" issue of *Lippincott's*, and he asked to be left out of a catalog on California literature being put together, in anticipation of the Chicago World's Columbian Exposition, by Ella Sterling Cummins. "If you could see your way to leaving me out I should be pleased." The trouble was, there were too many Californian writers, but too few good ones. It was noble of Mrs. Cummins to want to catalog California literature, "but whether the best service that you can render to California's literature is to direct attention to it is another matter."[23]

Of course Gertrude had taken the opposite view, delighting in the prospect of being written up in the catalog and having her etched portrait hung, along with those of Bierce, Joaquin Miller, and Ina Coolbrith, in the Fair's redwood "San Francisco Room." When she read what Mrs. Cummins wrote about her, however, she was miffed at the emphasis on her "unconventionality" and the patronizing tone: "[Mrs. Atherton's] studies heretofore have taken her into the field of the abnormal . . . but as time goes by she will doubtless see enough in the study of normal peculiarity to attract her, and then she will produce something great." [24]

Because praise rarely came from anyone in her native state, she especially prized Bierce's rhapsodies over *The Doomswoman*. From the extreme of rejecting all California writers Bierce jumped to effusive adulation: "In its class," the book was "superior to any that any Californian had done." It was "luminous and full of color. Full of movement . . . too and with something sounding through it that, if not exactly the 'surge and thunder' of genius, is, nevertheless, a long remove from the drone of the mere 'artist.' " Mrs. Atherton alone knew how to write English as spoken by Spanish Californians and to reproduce early California life "before the gold-greedy and dirty-shirted Americans came to vulgarize the situation." Bierce found it pleasing to be praising the book in the *Examiner*, the very place where "Mrs. Atherton's indubitable indiscretions have incurred the red-handed welcome of a giant in a cave, hospitably hungry." *The Doomswoman* marked her sure progress "through the error of youth, inexperience and a certain besetting perversity." Not only was it "sweet and wholesome in point of morality," it was quite simply "the most notable book in our California literature." [25]

These hymns of praise reached her not in Fort Ross but New York. After a few months of feverish writing in that town she had tired of it and told Bierce she was leaving, to "drift out and land somewhere else." She lingered in San Francisco briefly, made arrangements for Muriel's enrollment in a New York convent school in the coming fall, and arrived in the East in time to witness the tumult stirred by the death of Whitman. It was March 1892, and her return to California had lasted just short of two years.

From New York she wrote to Bierce often, full of gratitude for what he had done for her. She told him, "I think you have 'made me' on the Pacific Coast now, sure enough. I am more deeply obliged than I can ever express. You have not only taught me to write, but you have extracted the sting from mine enemies. Nobody will listen to them now." Once she addressed him as "Captain, Oh my Captain!"

She hoped to repay her debt to him as best she could. She suggested the title "Shapes of Clay" (which comes from *The Rubaiyat*) for his collection of poetry and supplied a fund of gossip and anecdotes about the East Coast literary scene, urging him to make free use of anything he liked for his columns. And she took advantage of her position in New York, where she had access to many editors and publishers, to help Bierce get nationally published and reviewed.

"I suppose I am more ambitious for you than you are for yourself," she wrote him, reminding him that his California reputation held small sway in New York. "*Publish in the East*," she urged; "then you get circulation on both sides of the continent. Publish in the West and don't get east of Pittsburg." She considered a New York-based firm a better bet than the Chicago-based Schulte firm, because "it is next to impossible to push a Western publication in the East, the book-sellers won't take it up and the critics leave everything Western at the bottom of the heap."

She fantasized about circumventing the prejudice against Western writers by starting a Chicago-based magazine with Bierce. The project came to naught, but the prejudice was a reality she wanted Bierce to acknowledge. She could help him overcome it by acting as his New York agent. The manuscript she tried to place for him was the collection of poems she titled "Shapes of Clay." Charles Scribner himself wrote her a letter rejecting it, explaining that though the poems were read with interest and appreciation, "the condition of successful publishing of volumes of verse is so difficult that we hesitate to proffer our services in this case." [26]

She had better luck finding reviewers for Bierce's already published work (she wrote one herself for the *New York World*) and promoting him to booksellers: "I was in Brentano's yesterday. Mr. Brentano spoke very enthusiastically of *Soldiers & Civilians*, said that he had sold copies of both English & American editions and that if some *firm* would only buy it and push it, he made no doubt of its success." Voicing suspicion that his writing might be "too strong brandy" for the "effete" East, she also scolded him for not playing politics, refusing to butter up literary kingmakers like Brander Matthews. Matthews, a playwright, critic, and Columbia professor, had praised Bierce in *Cosmopolitan* and was reported to be "grieved because you have never acknowledged his review of your book." She supplied a brief lecture on the realities of literary politics in New York: "In regard to Brander Matthews, you forget that this is the era of log-rolling and that this is the American headquarters. Brander Matthews has acquired what might be called the little reputation by persistent vaunting of his betters and being slapped on the back in return. *Of course* he expects to be thanked at the very least. For heaven's sake spare him in Prattle and give him an autograph letter."

Bierce appreciated her efforts on his behalf, and she kept protesting that there was no need for him to thank her. "I do so much more for myself than I do for anybody else that my zeal in the case of the latter . . . does not keep me awake o'nights. It need not keep others awake either. Besides, when one knows and admires an author, one's self-love demands that others shall know and admire him too." When he sent her a published rumor that linked them romantically she answered, "I should think the scandal mongers would have let up by this time, considering that a continent has been between us for a year and more—worse luck! As for their saying you 'carry' me, that does not bother me at all, so long as it is evident that you think I am worth carrying. *Au reste*—I should like to think I should 'live' one third as long as you will—but that part of the question is not worth answering."

Bierce proved incapable of heeding her advice about cultivating the favor of the literary establishment. He had nothing but contempt for those who played such games, and a prime reason for his gradual drifting out of friendship with Gertrude was undoubtedly his feeling that she played them all too well. He never withdrew the charge he made in his first letter to her—that she courted the public eye over-zealously. In fact, she unconsciously justified the accusation when she wrote occasional self-vaunting letters about how accomplished she was getting at spreading her fame. Bierce craved recognition as a serious writer; he could not see writing to please a wide audience for whom you harbor secret contempt.

Nor could Bierce, the champion of brevity as the soul of wit, forgive Mrs. Atherton's tendency to run on, in novels and letters. He complained about the length of her letters and disparaged her prodigious output as a novelist.

He did read—with little pleasure—*A Christmas Witch*, the novel she published in *Godey's*, in which he appears thinly disguised as a man named Arbuthnot who, in disgust at humankind, has withdrawn to a mountaintop, where his only delights are books, women, and solitude. He is a foil to the heroine Heloise, a precursor of Helena Belmont. Spoiled, impudent, impatient, willful, and adventurous, Heloise shoots at bears, breaks men's hearts as casually as teacups, and gives free rein to her often insulting opinions. Arbuthnot tells her she is merely a brilliant child, a promising but undeveloped intelligence. He might be willing to fall in love with her after the world has ripened her another ten years.

To anyone interested in Mrs. Atherton and Ambrose Bierce, it makes fascinating reading, for it reveals that she cherished the idea of a love that might have been and shows her awareness of her own extraordinary immaturity.

After her move to England in 1895 and his relocation in Washington D.C., the stream of their letters dwindled to a trickle. They continued to send one another copies of their new books, and he would occasionally give one of hers favorable mention in his column. She reported on mutual friends (such as Elodie Hogan Belloc) when she saw them, sent postcards from Germany of the scenes for "The Monk and the Hangman's Daughter," and supplied two British favorites, Horace Annesley Vachell and Richard Le Gallienne, with letters of introduction when they visited Washington. But for the six years before Bierce's mysterious disappearance in Mexico in 1914 not a word passed between them.

Sooner or later the intransigent Bierce came to a falling out with most of his friends and "pupils," and it was inevitable that he should disapprove of the direction Gertrude Atherton took as a popular and prolific novelist. But, according to his daughter Helen, he did retain respect for her intelligence, counting her among three women—the others were Empress Eugénie and George Eliot—whose intellect he admired.[27]

As for Gertrude, she clung to her memory of Bierce, her pride at their connection, and her esteem for his writing, always including him, along with Bret Harte, Mark Twain, and Henry James, in her private American literary pantheon. She loved to repeat the story of the pigsty kiss, carefully omitting any mention of her own trap-setting. He became one of her icons. One of her letters to him, addressed from Munich, admits, "your picture hangs in my salon."

They frightened one another. He was afraid she would prove smarter than he was, stronger and more successful. She was afraid by turns of his censure and his too ardent pursuit. Both feared yielding power and control. Their views of one another, and of the opposite sex, are so defended, so heavy with contradiction, they pauperize the word "ambivalent." They wove nets of inconsistency, two misanthropes in search of company, attracting and repelling, praising and reviling: a man who loved but hated women, whose confused standard of propriety allowed him to blast the morals of a book and then try to seduce its author; a woman who sheathed her Puritan heart in siren's chiffon and who became most intimate when she was the farthest distance away. The wonder is they liked each other so much.

CHAPTER SEVEN

"Our Lady of Transient Fame"

 In her letters to Bierce Gertrude keeps paying him the tribute an apprentice owes a master. Certain he had written some things that would endure, she doubted whether any work *she* had so far produced had any but ephemeral value; some of it embarrassed her. She wrote Bierce, about a piece of drivel she had managed to publish, a novel called *A Question of Time*, "I have not sent you a copy of my new book because I do not think it worth reading. I am endeavoring to write something decent at present [*The Doomswoman*] and am doing it very slowly—instead of dashing it off at white heat after the usual fashion. I write a chapter and then read Shakespeare and think for two or three days . . . then go at it again. It seems to me that the result is more satisfactory. One writes more with one's brains and less with one's senses—one's nerves."

To some extent the California stories, and even more *The Doomswoman*, made claims as serious literary fiction, claims Bierce's rhapsodic praise seemed to justify. Gertrude hoped to be able to combine the writing of what she considered "quality" fiction with earning a living, telling Joseph Stoddart, "I think I shall do nothing but literary work now . . . and if *The Doomswoman* brings me the recognition I hope, literary work would be more profitable than newspaper." [1]

But what if it turned out *not* to be more profitable? Was profit her primary consideration? Recognition? Fame? What kind of a writer did she aspire to become, exactly, and what kind was she capable of becoming? The years in New York, after the Fort Ross retreat and before the decision to move to London in 1895, served as a testing ground. They allowed her to throw herself into the literary marketplace while she engaged in internal debate—sometimes put into words when she wrote to Bierce—about the direction of her career and the nature of her talent.

The easiest of her tasks, the one that came most naturally, was fighting for decent payment for her published work. *Lippincott's* had paid $500 for the magazine rights for *The Doomswoman* (less than a cent a word, by Gertrude's calculation) and she objected to Stoddart, "I must say your firm is not very liberal, because the magazine rates all over the world are 1.5 cents for unsolicited matter and 2 cents for solicited. . . . *You can't have any more of my little stories for less than ten cents a word.*"[2] When the book edition, brought out by Tait, misfired, she complained to Bierce that despite "beautiful reviews" it had sold barely 600 copies.

Gertrude had prized the money-making potential of her writing from the start. From the days of her marriage, when George had withheld money from her while repeatedly bungling his own efforts in the world of commerce, writing looked like a way for her to buy out of the dependency trap and assert her own mastery and independence. But now, five years after George's death and two years after Dominga's, her private economic landscape had assumed a different configuration. She was inheriting the handsome sum of $10,000 from the Atherton estate, but it would be fixed and final. There would be no additional windfalls by inheritance, no more monthly stipend from Dominga. She started with a comfortable economic cushion, but the rest would be up to her. At the same time, she had new obligations to shoulder. She felt financially responsible now, not only for her own support, but that of other female family members.

When she left California for New York in 1892, she knew the specifics of Dominga's will, which left her the $10,000, provided that she transfer to Muriel "before receiving said sum any interest which she [Gertrude] may have as heir-at-law of my son, George, in the house built at Valparaiso Park by my said son. If at the time of [Dominga's] death she shall have been married, the bequest above named shall be void."[3] For once Dominga's controlling nature presented no conflict with Gertrude's. Dominga's wish that she remain unmarried (and in her eyes true to George) coincided exactly with Gertrude's own. Dominga furthered the goal by making separate financial provision for Muriel who, in addition to a share of Valparaiso Park, received $30,000 in a trust to be administered by her godfather, Arthur Page.

If, as she resettled in the East, Gertrude found herself more financially secure than she had ever been, she soon learned of a family disaster that would increase the weight of her burden. Her half sister Daisy Uhlhorn Craig, who now had a baby girl named Boradil (the name of Stephen Franklin's grandmother) turned to her for support after the calamitous collapse of her marriage following her husband's arrest for forgery.[4] Gertrude wrote to Bierce, "My brother-in-law's escapade has thrown the whole family on my hands." Yet another male in the family had demonstrated his irresponsibility and undependability. In response, she took on the traditional male role of economic mainstay and provider.

She turned to her work with fierce industry and professionalism, striving to earn by her pen as much money as she could. She showed an un-Biercian willingness to compromise, to write not just to please herself or serve a muse but to satisfy an editor, meet a deadline, or simply to make a dollar. As she put it in *Adventures*, "Dependents induce circumspection" (p. 222). She joined the Author's Guild, urging Bierce to follow her lead: "It promises to become in time as powerful as the Author's Club in London, which has become a terror to publishers. They could look out for you over here if complications arose." Pressing a point he would refuse to heed, she argued, "the main thing is to be read; to have the public become familiar with you as quickly as possible."

Ballard Smith, managing editor of Pulitzer's *New York World*, hired her to write a series for the Sunday paper on posh resorts like Saratoga (where "forty trains a day empty people like loaves out of a morning basket"), Newport, and Bar Harbor (which she found "slower than Eden before the Fall"). All summer she hopped from one watering place to another, not always savoring the class implications of her role as newspaperwoman in such elite surroundings: "I could not see myself interviewing society women, who regarded reporters as door-mats, wangling my way into lavish entertainments where I should be expected to hobnob with waiters" (*Adventures*, p. 222). But she liked the sums ($280 plus expenses) she could command when the pieces were syndicated and picked up by the *Providence Journal*, *McClure's*, or the *San Francisco Examiner*. She wrote Stoddart, "I have travelled 3,000 miles this month—been to nine watering places and made some money. What I value most is the experience, as I accumulated some good literary material and saw life from the newspaper woman's point of view. Still, I am glad it is over."[5]

She confided to Bierce that she had doubts about the worth of her journalism and was stung when *Examiner* editor "Cosey" Noble criticized her for getting "frightfully hacky," a charge that must have voiced her own suspicions. The dubious work and the sight of throngs of summer tourists gawking at the Saratoga swells sent her scurrying away after two days instead of two weeks, to return to New York full of anger directed outward at "people who are just people" but also directed inward, at herself. She told Bierce, "I don't know how I can go on a paper if I cannot control my moods, and I do not seem able to at all. I hate the proposition of life anyhow, from A to Z. . . . I imagine that domestic women are the only happy kind. I was going to say I wish I'd been born that way, but I don't. In fact if I were given my will, I do not know what I would choose, what gift from life. . . . The only thing I look forward to is to get out of it all."

She found herself accident-prone, unable to sleep (a life-long affliction), and abstracted. In one instance she mistook ammonia for water and swallowed some—which of course made her quite ill; in another she unthinkingly started a fire that spread to the window curtains in her room in a kind of artist's residence on West Fifty-Seventh Street called the Sherwood Studios.

Newspaper work made her feel "hacky," and she hated seeing her writing cut "to make room for illustrations," but at least it provided assignments, deadlines, paychecks, and a ready-made audience. Fiction had to emanate from her imagination, which was not performing the way she wanted it to. "I am in a chaotic frame of mind at present," she revealed to Bierce. "I want to write but I don't know what to write. I have the feeling that I have not discovered my metier and it is high time I had."

One way she escaped her moodiness, depression, and confusion was by accepting a magazine assignment—in this case for a potboiler commissioned for $750 by *Godey's* magazine—and working at such a frantic pace she became numbed and somewhat dehumanized; she could turn herself into a kind of writing machine. To write what became *A Christmas Witch*, she retired to a farm in Milford, Pennsylvania, and turned on the machine. After producing 40,000 words in six days, she could exult in her productivity: "when I finish this thing I shall have written this year two novels, nine stories, twenty-three letters [for newspapers], . . . a number of . . . editorials and three long articles." When she fell into questioning the *quality* of her work, she comforted herself with an accounting of the *quantities* she produced and the sums she'd earned. Didn't the numbers attest success? Wasn't success, after all, what she was after? She wrote Bierce, "I have relegated ambition to the place where it belongs, but success is a magnet which brings you an interesting life, and I propose to have an interesting life."

Aside from the *Godey's* novel—which so displeased Bierce that she promised him she would never try to publish it in book form—she was finding her "fiction tract" disappointingly barren. She had no new novel, "serious" or otherwise, in mind. She did produce a group of short stories which were eventually collected in the 1905 collection *The Bell in the Fog*. A few of these grew out of her summer travel-writing experiences, her observations of the smart set at resorts like Newport and Saratoga and at home in New York. But they did not fully engage her. "I cannot get up sufficient interest to write them out," she confided to Bierce. "I begin and throw the pen aside. The subjects are so trivial, in spite of the fact that they offer good advantage for study of character of a certain sort. They are mostly society stories. What I really want to write is subjective stories . . . which I am afraid you will say is rot."

The "subjective" stories attempt psychological probing, but end up melodramatically and superficially exploring some familiar Atherton themes: the tyranny of marriage; physical transformation of a woman in old age who wants to appear young; the crazed, addicted wife who haunts the living; lives changed by legacies; people who let life pass them by, missing their chance to really "live." Short on nuance or insight, they justify Gertrude's misgivings about them.

But the highly regarded British monthly *Vanity Fair* accepted two of them and paid for them handsomely. Bierce might consider them rot, and so might Gertrude herself at her most candid; but if the world said "yes," that surely meant something positive. Over and over, during these New York years (and after) Gertrude shows an inability to make a distinction between genuine merit and other kinds of ratification: getting published, getting paid, getting noticed. Her hungry but fragile ego overreacted equally to any word of praise or censure from another. As she had told Bierce, "I have almost no confidence in myself, and I do not know my good work from my bad."

Quite true. She should have fought harder for her right to republish *The Christmas Witch*, been less willing to accept Bierce's displeasure as the final word. Now lost to anyone without access to the January 1893 issue of *Godey's* magazine, it has remarkable energy and wit and makes a good read. And she should have buried such atrocities as "The Love Syndicate, Limited," published to great fanfare in the Sunday *World*, or at least published them under another name. But to her, it was paramount to keep working and keep her name before the public, in capital letters wherever possible. More intolerable than producing rot was to produce nothing and be ignored.

She was not ignored. Angling for all the publicity and advertising she could get, she boasted of the "boom" the *World* gave her when it promoted "The Love Syndicate, Limited" with large disc-shaped posters that were displayed for eight consecutive days on newspaper stands and "El" stations all over New York. But, as every performer learns, publicity cannot substitute for the care and affection of friends. Despite growing success, she suffered bouts of abject loneliness, pleading with Bierce to write more often: "You do not know how much your letters are to me. You see, I like so few people —scarcely anyone." She did, as usual, collect a few male admirers, including the British-Canadian short story writer Gilbert Parker, but none of them interested her much. "For all the men I know I don't care a tinker's dam—except each new one a little, while the novelty is on."

Having Muriel close at hand only underscored her sense of isolation. Muriel boarded at New York's Manhattanville convent high school, but spent an occasional day at her mother's apartment. When Gertrude took her to the school to register her, she reported to Bierce that she could not remember either the year or the day of her daughter's birth. She commented, "I'm fond of her, but I'm not maternal," and mused at the dissimilarity between mother and daughter: "Muriel is so unlike me that she might be a changeling. We have not a single taste in common and she hasn't a particle of enthusiasm." Buffeted by the deaths of her father and grandmother Dominga, and by the long separations from her mother, Muriel had turned to Catholicism for emotional sustenance. Gertrude could not resist teasing her about her devoutness and wrote to Bierce: "My youngster informed me yesterday that she had got the third mark for composition on 'The Snows of the Blessed Virgin.' I went into fits of laughter and she was highly incensed."

Any lingering dreams Gertrude had about penetrating the literary inner sanctum of New York were falling away. She disliked the writers who inhabited it, calling them "swells (shams)" and rejected them when they did include her. She registered disbelief when she received an invitation to join a writers' group called "Uncut Leaves" that gathered regularly to read works in progress and numbered among its members E. C. Stedman, Brander Matthews, and Kate Douglas Wiggin. Gertrude lumped them together, in a letter, as "literary ladies and gents whose patron saint is Our Lady of Transient Fame." Did she exclude herself from this sect?

She ridiculed reporter and *Harpers Weekly* editor Richard Harding Davis, passing on to Bierce a story about him that found its way into "Prattle:" "When Richard Harding Davis . . . was in London this summer, he was presented to Mrs. Matthew Arnold, who had read one of his books but never heard of him. Wishing to make herself agreeable, she begged him to send her some statistics about himself as she was writing a book called Unknown Authors."

Davis belonged to another literary club that had asked her to join, the Theater of Arts and Letters. This group, devoted to restoring "literature and drama to the twinship of their birth," presented— to an audience limited to subscribers who were required to come in full evening dress—experimental dramas by such writer-members as Mary E. Wilkins and Clyde Fitch.[6] Behind their backs, to Bierce, Gertrude called them "the Dilettante Review, otherwise the Home for Incurable Amateurs." She said she attended their evenings merely "for the experience and study (principally of human nature.)" She considered them a bunch of pretentious and self-important bores who "couldn't shake up one true dramatic instinct between them, and their plays would be nothing but demi-semi clever dialogue with 'artistic' climaxes. Of course they would be 'literary,' so were their soda-watery books." The only play (by a member) she liked was Wilkins's *Giles Corey, Yeoman*, which she said she appreciated because of her New England ancestry.

When asked to participate in a New York authors' reading, in January 1893, being sponsored by such established figures as Charles Dudley Warner, Richard Watson Gilder, and Julia Ward Howe, she was aghast. "What this sudden humping toward me of Philistia means is beyond my ken," she wrote to Bierce. In a curious inversion, she transforms the established second-rank writers, the "belle-lettrists" who would be expected to regard *her*—the popular novelist and journalist—as a Philistine, into inhabitants of "Philistia."

For all her protests, she apparently performed well at the reading. A San Francisco newspaper account treats her appearance as pure theater, making no mention of what she read, but commenting on her black dress, "which showed to advantage her beautiful arms and neck and set off her golden hair." It reported, "Her voice was clear and resonant but hard. A little training would put her in the front rank of literary locutionists. She was the only author that received flowers."[7]

She continued to feel that members of the Eastern literary establishment waged constant and unremitting warfare against the West, which of course heightened her Western identification. She wrote Bierce (to whom she'd sworn, not so long ago, that she would never return to California), "Yes, I'll go over, bag and baggage to the West." The reason he had trouble receiving his due as a writer was that the Eastern block of critics and editors couldn't handle his power. "You are too strong brandy for the average spirit. . . . What is the matter with the East? Is it effete?"

The West's increasing prominence on the map of the United States was dramatized to the whole world at the Chicago 1893 World's Fair, which Gertrude attended with Chicago critic and editor Percival Pollard, who was making the championship of such Western

writers as Ambrose Bierce and Gertrude Atherton a personal crusade. When he bought a part ownership in the Chicago-based journal *Figaro*, he told Bierce he did it chiefly because "I hope, through
Figaro, to boom the West and Western men in literature. Another
rock for breaking heads against!"[8]

Gertrude did not say a great deal about the Fair and its magnificent White City, other than that "it would take thirty-two years to
see it all" and that she and Pollard (who had published favorable
notices of *The Doomswoman* and *A Christmas Witch*) had become
"great friends." Surely she visited the California Building, a copy of
an adobe mission, its arched entrance hung with chiming old mission
bells, and saw her own portrait in the San Francisco Room. Surely
she stopped at the neoclassical Woman's Building, filled with exhibi-
tions of women's arts, crafts, words, and work, and decorated with a
Mary Cassatt mural "Modern Woman," one of whose panels showed
young women pursuing the flying figure of Fame, "a nude in female
shape, which had supposedly cast off the garments of convention."[9]

Unfortunately, Gertrude attended the Fair as a private, though
honored woman, rather than a journalist; we would know more
about what she thought and saw if she had "written it up" for a newspaper or magazine. Newspaper work continued to take up much
of her time and energy, as she reported to Bierce: "Mr. Duysters
wants me to go to Buffalo and live with the strikers and grapple
with that problem. Ballard Smith wants me to go to live with the
people who don't strike. Mr. Mieux—one of the Cosmopolitan editors—wants me to study Madison Square. Mr. Luther Lancien, a
staid middle-aged gentleman, . . . wants me to tackle a problem not
usually mentioned in polite society. Someone else—I forget who
—wants me to study Lizzie Borden. I shall probably have nervous
prostration between them."

She definitely felt more comfortable with newspaper and magazine types than the Theater of Arts and Letters crowd. At the
New York World she befriended—and found employment from—
Woman's Page editor Elizabeth ("Kate") Jordan, whom she described to Bierce as "really a very fine character—old fashionedly so
—like the heroine of an old Southern novel" (though Jordan was, in
fact, from Wisconsin).

Also at the *World* was a man toward whom—judging from the

frequency and tone of her references to him—she felt more than a casual interest; a man who, as it happened, was married, socially prominent, very much a man of the world, and managing editor of the *World* until he was sent to England as head of its London Bureau. This was Ballard Smith, and according to one associate he had "the air of a baron of the Middle Ages who would brook no delay."[10] He sounds like a version of S. S. Chamberlain, minus the alcohol.

Exactly what happened between them is a matter for conjecture, a puzzle to be pieced together from shards. In one letter to Bierce, Gertrude confesses, "Ballard Smith I like better than anyone." Bierce must have asked what was going on, for Gertrude explained in another letter, written in Far Rockaway in the summer of 1893, "He is not my latest by the way and won't come down here if I can help it. I've had enough of married men." A reporter named Miss Merrien in the autobiographical *Patience Sparhawk*, written in New York during Gertrude's days at the *World*, has this to say about the men of the press:

A newspaper man who is at the same time a gentleman, is charming. It is true they have no respect for anybody nor anything. . . . Their kindness . . . is half cynical, and they look upon life as a thing to be lived out in twenty years. . . . But no men know so well how to enjoy life, know so thoroughly its resources, or have all their sense so keenly developed, particularly their senses of humor. . . . It seems to be a point of honour among them to be unfaithful to their wives. (*Patience Sparhawk*, pp. 317–18)

Is this a portrait of Ballard Smith?

Even though she was a free-lancer, contributing an occasional column or story, rather than an employee, Gertrude requested and got permission to sit at a desk at the gold-domed World building. She told Ballard Smith she was writing a novel with a newspaper background and that she wanted to spend some time in the *World* offices so that she could meet editors and reporters and absorb atmosphere. She used Morrel Goddard, editor of the Sunday *World*, and "a sort of Robespierre of journalism," as a study for her character Morgan Steele, the hard-headed young editor who tells Patience-the-reporter to "keep your eyes open, and cultivate the faculty of observation for all its worth" (*Patience Sparhawk*, p. 315).

The idea for *Patience Sparhawk and Her Times*, her longest and most ambitious novel so far, had burst upon her after two years— for Gertrude Atherton, a long time—of quiescence on her "fictional tract." She took her impatient heroine's name from a Franklin family Bible (the original Patience Sparhawk was Stephen Franklin's New England–born paternal great-grandmother), and got the germ of the plot from a sensational murder trial of 1892 and the coverage of that trial in the press. A novel of the era of sensationalism, *Patience Sparhawk* would never have been written if Pulitzer and Hearst had not mastered—and Gertrude Atherton had not exalted—the craft of selling newspapers with banner headlines about disasters, celebrities, and ghastly murders. If members of society happened to be implicated in any sensational goings-on, headlines got even taller, and profits soared. Eye-witness accounts of prison electrocutions had been newly legalized, and reporters from the *New York World* were among the first to line up.[11]

In the novel, Patience is accused of murdering her husband with an overdose of morphine drops and sentenced to electrocution at Sing Sing. In preparation for writing the jail scenes, Gertrude trooped up to the prison at Ossining and received permission to sit in the electric chair. (She also visited a cell and befriended the sheriff.) "Yesterday," she told Bierce, "I went to Sing Sing and was hung up by my wrists and strapped in the electrocution chair." She found the experience "interesting," although the straps hurt, and "it was not pleasant . . . to reflect that I was sitting in the chair in which several dead men had been."

A quick study, Gertrude surely knew about of the much-publicized trial of Florence Maybrick, a young, pretty American woman found guilty in 1889 of poisoning her husband in England. But the murder that provided the more immediate stimulus, because it was more recent and had received much attention in the American press, involved a medical student named Carlyle Harris accused of administering a fatal overdose of morphine to Helen Potts, the nineteen-year-old woman he had secretly married.[12] According to Gertrude, the press took the accused man's side, but popular opinion went the other way. Everyone was talking about the case, and a friend suggested, "Why don't you write a novel on a similar subject? Nothing interests the public more than murder and suspense" (*Adventures*, p. 224).

But the Maybrick and Carlyle Harris trials could not have ignited her interest had they not found tinder in Gertrude's psyche. It is Gertrude, not Patience Sparhawk, who published recipes for the elimination of an unwanted husband in the *San Francisco Examiner*, Gertrude who once admitted, "Many a time I have wanted to commit murder";[13] and Gertrude who expressed her envy for Rider Haggard's She, who could hurl a bolt of lightning and shrivel a man to one long cinder.

Like her creator, Patience, a stunning and determined, though deprived, young woman from California, marries a handsome and aristocratic man, Beverly Peele, who makes up in temper and tyrannizing for what he lacks in intellect and ambition. As we have seen, Beverly closely resembles George Atherton, and while she was writing the book Gertrude rekindled much of her old fury at him, at the marital bond, and at social constraints on women.

Patience did not actually kill her husband, she is not technically guilty of the crime for which she is tried, but she is shown to be capable of murder. Early in the narrative she comes close to murdering her drunk, promiscuous mother. She has admitted feeling at times that she could kill her husband, and without remorse: "No one has the right to live . . . that can give the world nothing" (*Patience Sparhawk*, p. 328). Like Gertrude, Patience turns to newspaper work as a means of achieving financial independence after her marriage breaks down. She gets a job on the *Day* as a reporter, moving from the elaborate Westchester mansion of her husband's wealthy family into a tiny Manhattan studio furnished with nothing more than a bed and dresser.

Patience not only writes for the press, she becomes—again, like Gertrude—the subject of headlines herself. She adores shocking people, being talked about, "written up," "boomed." When she breaks up a meeting of the Women's Christian Temperance Union with a diatribe against religious hypocrisy, she is thrilled to see it reported in the next morning edition. She gets even more pleasure out of the publicity for the murder trial; headlines like "YOUNG WIFE SUSPECTED OF FOUL DEED!" make her "the sensation of the day," a position she has to savor; not to do so would be "less than American."

Patience epitomizes willful and anarchic self-assertion, a characteristic Gertrude took to be the stamp of the American and especially the Californian. The book is dedicated to the French writer Paul Bourget, "who alone, of all foreigners, has detected . . . that the motive power . . . of that strange composite known as 'the American' is Individual Will."

While writing the novel, Gertrude moved up to Yonkers for one of her retreats from the social world. Enclosing her Warburton Avenue address in a letter to Bierce, she speaks of her new view from a bluff overlooking the Hudson. "This is a beautiful town on hills and cliffs, very old, the avenues lined with maples, and at the edge woods run along the Hudson. My window is opposite the Palisades. But nothing seems very much after California." She set one part of the novel in Westchester County and transferred to Patience her sentiments about the inferiority of the Eastern landscape to her native terrain: "Westchester County, although exquisitely pretty, lacked grandeur and the suggestion of colossal throes in remote ages with which every stone in California is eloquent" (*Patience Sparhawk*, p. 269). Once again, California looked good—from a distance.

In order to make the novel's courtroom scenes authentic, Gertrude began attending a murder trial in White Plains. She found the trial electric and exhilarating: "I never could attend a paltry theater again. The case itself was not interesting—just a policeman who had killed another man in a political row"; but it was the new atmosphere, "the science of the law—which I had never imagined was so fascinating, the dramatic effect of the lying witnesses and of the defendant himself on the stand, and above all watching the lightning-like working of such a mind as Martin Keogh, counsel for the defendant, and listening to his superb summing up" that impressed her. "Keogh got the man off merely by his brilliant sophistry and his eloquence," she reported to Bierce. "He simply sends every idea out of a jury's mind but what he plants there." In her autobiography, Gertrude writes of Martin Keogh—the model for her lawyer character Garan Bourke—"I hadn't the least difficulty making the heroine fall in love with him" (*Adventures*, p. 226). However, she and Keogh never met.

For all its timeliness, *Patience* was rejected by several major American publishers

> on various pretexts. It was too long. Novels at that time rarely ran to a hundred thousand words, and as I was anything but a popular author whose new opus the public was anxiously awaiting, I fancied it was quite likely that some of those publishers thought it hardly worth while to wade through that formidable mass of manuscript. . . . Those publishers who declined it on the ground of not liking the spirit of revolt in the book, or who found it too "sensational," had certainly read it. (*Adventures*, p. 227)

Patience might have been rejected on other grounds as well; it is diffuse and in need of ruthless tightening and cutting. Its heroine, though vital and compelling, is cruel enough, bigoted enough, and self-satisfied enough to alienate even those readers attracted by her intelligence, competence, independence, and pluck. American readers never took to it, when they finally had a chance to read it under a British publisher's imprint. In England, it did make a small furor and was hailed as a prototype of "New Woman" fiction.

The book's rejection by American editors made Gertrude once again consider leaving the country for England, where she felt her work sold better, was taken more seriously, appreciated more, and given a fairer hearing. Oliver Fry of London's *Vanity Fair* had received her stories with enthusiasm, and a woman named Lady Colin Campbell was offering work on a periodical called *The Lady's Realm*. Ballard Smith had moved to England and was assuring her that in London "there was more interest in my personality than in any other American writer, and that he never went to an entertainment where literary matters came out that he was not asked if he knew me, and that he has been asked at least a hundred times to solve a problem contained in a story I wrote for *Vanity Fair*." She only half believed all this, knowing Smith to be "a blarney and embroiderer" who perhaps also suffered from "the effects of seasickness."[14] But she began to make plans, as she put it, "to dispose agreeably" of Muriel during school vacations, so that she could vacate her New York apartment and return to England.

CHAPTER EIGHT

Decadents and New Women

Gertrude had a way of turning up at decisive moments; her arrival in London coincided with the arrest, trial, and conviction—"for acts of gross indecency between males"—of Oscar Wilde. Days earlier he had reigned as London's prince of comedy. Now his name was covered over on the marquee of the St. James theater, where *The Importance of Being Earnest* had been playing to packed houses and ecstatic reviews. The play closed abruptly, and Wilde's books were pulled from library and bookshop shelves. Even newspaper accounts of the trial were silenced after the first days. As London indulged in one of the most virulent of its periodic attacks of moral righteousness, the mood of decadence that Wilde had symbolized faded. The 1890s had not ended, but "the Wildean nineties" had.[1]

As we shall see, Gertrude wasted no tears of sympathy for the "old sinner"—in fact only a few years her senior—whose mouth she had found too disgusting to contemplate. She was destined to encounter Reggie Turner, Wilde's close friend, in Rouen in 1897 and to advise him against coming to Wilde's rescue when he faced destitution and ruin after he emerged from prison. For now, she merely took note of the theatrical trial, clipping early newspaper accounts to send to a New York friend: they "must have been suppressed in the London Post Office, for they were never received" (*Adventures*, p. 233).

This was 1895, the year of the Jameson Raid in South Africa, the year of a Conservative victory in the British elections and of the establishment of "the last government in the Western world to possess all the attributes of aristocracy in working condition";[2] the year of the clash between England and the United States, Lord Salisbury and President Cleveland, over Venezuela and the Monroe Doctrine; the year the fad for marriages between American heiresses and titled British aristocrats—upon which Gertrude Atherton would trade in two popular 1890s novels—culminated with the wedding of Consuelo Vanderbilt to the Duke of Marlborough.

Also in this year, Thomas Hardy published *Jude the Obscure* (and in the wake of critical hostility swore off writing novels), Grant Allan his notorious best seller *The Woman Who Did* (about a woman who refuses to marry the man she lives with), and Joseph Conrad his first novel, *Almayer's Folly*. Harold Frederic, an American novelist and journalist working in London, awaited the British edition of his *Damnation of Theron Ware*. In the United States, young Stephen Crane found his first success with *The Red Badge of Courage*; he would join the small community of American writers living in Britain—among whom Henry James enjoyed preeminence—before his death at the turn of the century.

Late-Victorian London combined an "air of great repose" with an attitude of smug self-confidence made manifest in the stiffness of a gentleman's white collar, the shine on his tall silk hat, and the strut of his carriage horses. "During the long twilights Piccadilly was crowded with broughams and hansom cabs carrying men and women in evening dress to restaurants for an early dinner before the theater or opera; if the night were warm, evening wraps would be flung aside, revealing superb gowns and sparkling jewels." Gertrude did not see, or at least did not comment on, the legions of impoverished homeless stretched on benches along the embankment, but she did see prostitutes, "pretty ladies in feathers and war paint, ready to be picked up by the casual male" (*Adventures*, pp. 231–32).

In this heyday of lavish aristocratic entertaining, of the professional hostess and the Professional Beauty, the name Gertrude Atherton found no place, as yet, either on the booklists of venerable publishers or on the guest lists of Lady Randolph Churchill, Lady Jeune, Madame de Grey, or the new Duchess of Marlborough. Mrs. Atherton hoped to penetrate both the social and the literary arenas. But for the moment, she intended to lie low and spare herself the humiliation of knocking on doors that would not open to her. She had practice as a social outsider and was prepared to remain one for a while longer. No, she would wait, until, as she put it, "I had made my mark" as a literary celebrity. As an attractive American woman, a Westerner, and as a much-published, respected, and discussed author, she would eventually earn her place among the elect. Without compromising her cherished individuality or Californian audacity, she would, in time, sup with Lord This and Lady That.

Her old friends in London, if friends they could be called, had left town. "The Whistlers had gone to Paris to live. The William Sharps were away. I looked up none of the pleasant acquaintances I had made during my first visit, for I was determined to remain in the background until I had really accomplished something. It was six years since I had been in London. . . . London has a great deal to give, but the outsider must give full measure in return: novelty, wealth, or achievement. My novelty had worn off" (*Adventures*, p. 235). Again we wonder what she meant by "achievement." Did she mean writing well or being recognized and celebrated? The distinctions between merit and the various kinds of recognition remained blurred. What was absolutely clear was that, however she got there, she intended to Arrive.

A friend who awaited an entirely different sort of renown was Hilaire Belloc, who came down from Oxford to renew the connection he had formed with her in California during his ardent and anguished pursuit of Elodie Hogan. Elodie's family opposed the match, considering the writer and scholar a poor bet as a future husband, and Elodie, confused about her own feelings, decided to enter a convent in Maryland. Belloc was miserable and in need of a sympathetic ear, which Gertrude provided. She wrote to Bierce on December 19, 1895, "I wish Elodie would come out of that convent and marry Belloc. He has been devoted to her for five years on sporadic encouragement and he certainly is an unusually clever and good fellow."

As for her own love life, Ballard Smith, who had played such a decisive part in bringing her to London, saw her a few times, in "safe" circumstances where others were present, including his wife. She wrote to her *New York World* friend Elizabeth Jordan, "Mrs. Smith is going to give me some dinners. . . . I like her very much and the child is a beauty."[3] Smith did take her to dinner one night "at the house of a friend. . . . When I was putting on my wraps in her room she informed me casually that she had a lover. It was my first experience of the cool insolence of Englishwomen of the upper class, who regard themselves as above all laws" (*Adventures*, p. 236). If Ballard Smith was Gertrude's lover, or at least a romantic interest, she was not going to broadcast the news to anyone. In fact, Smith's tenure in England as chief of the *World*'s London bureau lasted only a year. His health failed, and he returned to the United States; he died five years later, at age 51. Gertrude must have been saddened by his departure—but as usual, she left no tracks.

Friends, in any case, meant less to her than professional contacts, which she was making at a lively pace. Max Pemberton asked for a book for Cassells Pocket Library, and she escaped to Canterbury to write *A Whirl Asunder*. Confined in a tiny room "hardly more than six feet square," before a window kept open as respite from a smoking chimney, she created Helena Belmont, the quintessentially Californian heroine of the open air, who rides to fires (like San Francisco's legendary Lillie Hitchcok Coit), refuses to be chaperoned, and moves freely through the redwood forests.

Oliver Fry asked for some book reviews for *Vanity Fair*. A literary agent approached her, wanting to handle her short stories, but she turned him down on the grounds that she had had great success placing them on her own. As she had discovered in New York, writing to order, just to pay the bills and remain before the public, suited her just fine. Willing and able to produce the potboilers and journalistic ephemera that supplied the money and constant activity she needed, she at the same time sustained her ambition to become a writer of stature. In no way did she see the two needs as mutually exclusive. To her delight, she found London able to offer her something important to her career as a novelist that New York had denied her: a contract for *Patience Sparhawk and Her Times*.

Patience Sparhawk was accepted by John Lane of the Bodley Head imprint in 1895. Lane flourished in London as the fashionable publisher of the day, with his *Yellow Book* and a distinguished list of authors—many of them associated with the Decadents—that included Richard Le Gallienne, Max Beerbohm, and Oscar Wilde himself. ("Uncleanliness is next to Bodliness," quipped *Punch*.) Lane's aesthetic taste and his willingness to take risks with new authors were tempered by a keen business sense and a reputation for tightfistedness. As his contemporary E. F. Benson put it, "he had no objection . . . against thin ice, provided he felt reasonably sure that it would not let him through."[4] Lane did not countenance scandal, although he liked his writers and artists to be timely and controversial. In 1895 it was he, as Wilde's publisher, who withdrew Wilde's books from circulation. When the outcry over Aubrey Beardsley's shocking drawings for the *Yellow Book* prompted Lane to drop Beardsley at once, Gertrude reported to Joseph Stoddart: "I hear there is a warrant out for Aubrey Beardsley. It is believed John Lane went to America to avoid being mixed up in the business, although of course he does not belong to the gang."[5]

Lane also had a reputation as a publisher of women writers such as "George Egerton" (whose real name was Mary Chavelita Dunne) and "John Oliver Hobbes," the pseudonym of Pearl Craigie. His "penchant for women, both as lover and publisher, had earned him the sobriquet 'Petticoat Lane.'"[6] Well aware of the current appetite for books about the independent New Woman, Lane considered publishing New Woman fiction to make good business sense—just as publishing Decadents had. His judgment in choosing to publish Grant Allan's *The Woman Who Did* had been redeemed by impressive sales; the book went through nineteen editions in a single year. Perhaps *Patience Sparhawk* would do as well.

In the public imagination, and in reality, there was a link between the feminists and the Decadents. The New Woman, like the Decadent, subverted social norms and heightened sexual consciousness. As far as most of the late-Victorian public was concerned, "the decadent was new and the New Woman was decadent."[7]

Gertrude, as we have seen, tried to distance herself from the "depravity" and "effeteness" of the Decadents; and she had trouble accepting the sexual liberation that New Woman independence and unconventionality seemed to many to imply. But *Patience Sparhawk* does celebrate both the sexual attractiveness and the rebellious, independent stance of its heroine; it does attack hypocrisy in marriage and the double standard. Gertrude took pride in May Sinclair's assertion, ten years after the book was published, that it had boosted the Emancipated Woman's cause. Right now she was relishing the prospect that the book, as she told Bierce, once published would "rather make things hum." Lane thought so too; otherwise he would never have accepted it.

For his own reasons—perhaps because he was negotiating to open a New York office—Lane chose not to rush the novel into print once he had signed the contract for it. The manuscript sat for two years in a safe at the Bodley Head's Vigo Street headquarters. Gertrude decided to use the time intervening to travel in England and on the continent. Her first priority was to make pilgrimages to certain literary shrines.

She organized for herself a tour of locales connected with English Romantic writers in whose steps she hoped to walk. She stopped in the Lake District, where Wordsworth had lived, and wrote her Wordsworth-inspired—and Biercian—story "The Striding Place," which Henry Harland rejected as too gruesome for *The Yellow Book* but which was published in *The Speaker*. In the town of Linby, Nottinghamshire, "a small straggling village . . . where Byron lay in the family vault," she communed with her early idol, rereading his poetry and reporting to Bierce, "the more I study Byron the more convinced I am that he is the greatest poet the world has known, with the exception of Shakespeare" (October 24, 1895).

She lingered longest in the Yorkshire village of Haworth, where the Brontë sisters—on whose books her romantic imagination had suckled—had lived and written. Although she came to regard Charlotte Brontë's *Jane Eyre* "as an old-fashioned melodrama, the fact remained that it was a pioneer book, a gesture of defiance at the traditions of its era" (*Adventures*, p. 237). Emily Brontë remained to Gertrude heroic, tragic, exemplary. "It was a small thing to be half starved and lonely, afflicted by a drunken brother, and sisters dying of consumption, when consoled with an imagination . . . that must have whispered to her of undying fame. . . . Had she not been one of the few to make the world recognize the genius of woman?"[8] Though she tended to regard living women novelists as rivals, not allies, Gertrude Atherton always thought of herself as a woman writer rather than simply a writer and boldly claimed Emily Brontë as a literary progenitrix.

There was a thrifty and practical side to present-day Haworth, to which Gertrude readily responded, but what really held her were the dark, evocative literary associations of the landscape. Haworth, with its mists, moors, and heather, its mournful graveyard and crooked streets, constituted in her mind the perfect background for drama and romance. It was the exact opposite of California, she wrote, undermining her own efforts to furnish California with a mythic past. "Writers," she predicted, "will continue to go to the dreary moorlands, the dun-colored skies of England for tragedy settings, and for the atmosphere of tradition and history. It will be hard for any writer who has travelled over the wonderful mountains and valleys of California . . . to imagine tragedy in a land of such exultant beauty."[9]

Twelve years before, in creating *The Randolphs of Redwoods*, she had forged a literary and genealogical link between Yorkshire and California. She believed the George Gordon family, on whom she based the Randolphs, had originally come from Yorkshire and that Mr. Gordon, before coming to San Francisco, had been a drinking crony of the dissipated Branwell Brontë. Albert Shumate has shown this to be pure myth, but for Gertrude it was very much alive. While in Haworth she was rewriting *The Randolphs* (which had only been published in serialized form in the *Argonaut*, never as a novel between hard covers) for John Lane, under the new title *A Daughter of the Vine*. The roots she wanted to touch were her own, and they were literary, emotional, and mythic—not factual.

She wrote to Elizabeth Jordan: "I live out on the edge of the moor which is beautiful . . . covered with heather. The [Brontë] family is buried in the church and a museum has lately been opened containing many of their effects. . . . This is the barest, blankest country you can imagine, scarcely a tree. . . . But it is a fine bracing climate and I have written a lot."[10]

Gertrude lacked religion in any formal sense, but she found her own variants of worship and communion. At the little Brontë museum she saw the Nottingham lace wedding veil that had been Charlotte's and the collar belonging to Emily's dog Keeper. She was allowed to touch and peruse at her leisure the manuscript of *Jane Eyre*, which as a girl she'd read six times.

In no way did she feel "ready" for London, but she took rooms there out of deference to an unexpected visitor, her newly divorced half sister Aleece Van Bergen, who had turned to her for help, as had Daisy when her marriage fell apart. All of Gertrude's close kin— her mother, half sisters, and eventually her daughter—experienced divorce or separation. They were uniformly unlucky in marriage, and in this they had Gertrude's complete, even ardent, sympathy and support. Aleece's alimony was too small to enable her to live independently. She never considered looking for work of her own, and she dreaded the prospect of returning to California, where she would have to live with her mother. Never willing to play the role of nurturer, Gertrude again assumed the role of provider, and in this instance, companion.

Gertrude saw Aleece as "a curious *pasticcio*. Almost uncannily shrewd, naturally intelligent, with a quick and rarely faulty judgment of character, she never read a serious book in her life, and her worldly sense extended no further than dressing herself advantageously, holding herself as if she were one of the earth's elect" (*Adventures*, p. 206). She did have "a keen appetite for life, and a gaiety of spirit," and when she submitted, in Linby in Nottingham, that she "had not come six thousand miles to live in an English village," Gertrude agreed to settle in London.

Here she left her sister to her own devices as she sat down to write an article for British readers on American divorce, doubtless triggered by Aleece's recent experience and their mother's long ago. But since it was written by Gertrude Atherton, it naturally reveals more about her own experience as a once discontented American wife than Aleece's or any one else's. "Most middle and upper class women"—Gertrude barely acknowledged the existence of any other class—"are dissatisfied with their men," she wrote. "Divorce is now accepted . . . so long as no scandal has preceded the suit. Today divorce is the rule. And the motive power of the divorce market is women."

Why are urban, upper- or middle-class American married women miserable in their marriages? Because American men "are essentially a race of nervous incessant workers" who have no time to read, reason, or analyze and even less to devote to the rearing of their children. Whereas women steep themselves in "the literature of older worlds," their husbands "have restricted interests." American women "have outstripped men spiritually and mentally." An increasing number become financially independent. Here she abandons any attempt at objectivity and makes her own situation representative of the American woman's:

The typical woman of the U.S. today is a mental anarchist. The reasons for this are several. She is a composite of all the races of the earth, if not in blood, in point of view. . . . She has been thrown largely on her own resources; unlike the women of the old world, she has done her own thinking. . . . She lives in an electrical atmosphere. She is a spoiled child . . . a child of the hour, of the minute; she does not strike roots. Her independence has begot an abnormal amount of individuality.[11]

Gertrude never went through a divorce, but she had experienced the misery of a bad marriage that *should* have been dissolved. The divorced woman, as well as the independent woman, became part of her private crusade.

In London she befriended an aristocratic victim of the divorce courts, Lady Colin Campbell, with whom she fiercely identified. The descriptions of Lady Colin in *Adventures* make her sound like the heroine of a romance by Ouida. A siren before whom "men went down like grain before the reaper," she becomes a fantasy figure of extraordinary beauty, distinction, and tragedy. Irish born, the former Gertrude Elizabeth ("Vera") Blood was "one of the most beautiful women I have ever seen, quite six feet tall but perfectly made, poised and balanced; she reminded one of a spirited clean-limbed race horse. Her eyes and hair were black, her skin of a luminous ivory hue; she had no color save in her lips and used no make-up. Unexpectedly, she had a great deal of animation, and a keen, satiric, brilliant mind" (*Adventures*, pp. 280–81). Whistler, who called her his "lovely leopard," used her as a model for his "Harmony in White and Ivory," and she modeled for Boldini and Burne-Jones as well.

Her five-year marriage to the "thoroughly dissipated" son of the seventh Duke of Argyll had ended in 1886 with one of the most scandalous and publicized divorce trials in British history. She petitioned for divorce, citing her husband's adultery with a housemaid. He counterpetitioned, naming the Duke of Marlborough and three other lovers. The jury found neither party guilty and dismissed both petitions, though she did win a separation for cruelty. She became a widow in 1895, just about the time Gertrude Atherton met her in the editorial offices of *Vanity Fair*.

According to Gertrude, Lady Colin Campbell's divorce trial had cost her her respectability, though at the time they met she lived luxuriously in a handsome apartment off Victoria Street where Gertrude made frequent calls. Lady Colin *had* taken several lovers during her marriage and "amused herself recklessly." In the eyes of British society, her cardinal sin, like Oscar Wilde's, was that she had been found out. The English aristocracy did not require moral conduct of its members, only discretion. The divorce trial, with its attendant publicity, had turned her private indiscretions into public scandal, and she was punished—as Gertrude's mother had been in San Francisco in the 1860s—with social ostracism. From Gertrude's point of view that made her sympathetic in a way the equally reckless, but flourishing, Sibyl Sanderson never could be. Lady Colin's position became even more sympathetic in subsequent years when illness crippled her and she suffered increasing isolation and relative poverty, without bitterness.

Instead of retiring after the scandal of her several adulteries broke, Lady Colin threw herself into journalistic activity, becoming a newspaper travel columnist, book critic, novelist, and editor. Gertrude enormously admired her show of intelligence and mettle. In becoming her intimate, Gertrude affirmed her position as a rebel and social renegade within elite circles. "Ladies of impeccable virtue remonstrated with me, but I replied that I was an American, a writer, a rank outsider, and I could know whom I chose" (*Adventures*, p. 283).

They remained friends during Gertrude's years in England. One evening in November 1898 Lady Colin had arranged a theater party for Gertrude in a box at the Alhambra Music Hall. The American illustrator James Montgomery Flagg was among the guests, and it is he who recorded that Gertrude attended this evening entertainment despite the fact that she had just received a cable informing her of her mother's death in San Francisco. "Gertrude sat partly behind the box curtain as a gesture of daughterly piety."[12] In San Francisco, the local papers gave Mrs. Uhlhorn's age as 61 and referred to her in the headline as "Gertrude Atherton's mother." The obituary reported, "Mrs. Atherton is now in England, but the granddaughter, Miss Muriel Atherton, was with Mrs. Uhlhorn when she died."[13]

Gertrude made no attempt to return to California following her mother's death, but wrote poignantly in her autobiography: "My last memory of [her] is standing by the bed sewing. Hers was one of the stranded lives. She had never left California since her arrival there at the age of eighteen [fifteen, in fact], and rarely San Francisco save for its hated alternative, The Ranch. She had longed to travel, but it was years since she had spoken of this old ambition; perhaps it was forgotten with all the other hopes she had buried" (*Adventures*, p. 220). If her mother's death unleashed a daughter's remorse—for her long absence, her travels, her elopement with George, or for the fact that Muriel, not she, sat beside her deathbed—it remained safely submerged and only obliquely expressed.

Any pangs of homesickness for California were assuaged by imaginative flights back home: Atherton novels written in these years keep returning to Californian themes and locales. There were also social contacts among Americans living in London and even with former Californians, like her old friend from the Napa Valley, Elodie Hogan.

Elodie had left the convent in Maryland after all, had married Hilaire Belloc, and now lived with him in England. Soon after their marriage in summer of 1896, Gertrude wrote to Bierce, "I have not yet seen Elodie and Belloc; I am very curious to see how the match turns out, not only because they are such great friends of mine, but because there was so much that was interesting and almost unique in the courtship and I was in the confidence of both from the beginning. They have wept alternately on my shoulder for five years." By fall, she could report from London, "Elodie is here, changed in some respects, but looking much the same as ever. She is much less 'temperamental' than she used to be, more settled and philosophical. She left her fads in the convent, I expect, and much of her enthusiasm, to say nothing of her brogue. But she is as interesting and likable as ever, and already manifests a decided ability to manage her erratic spouse."

Gertrude journeyed to Oxford to spend a week with the newlyweds. Hilaire had published *The Bad Child's Book of Beasts* and was enjoying a vogue, but his success had not made him easy to live with. An insomniac, he would roam the house at night, slamming doors, or "would relieve his feelings by picking up the boots outside his own door and flinging them down with all his might. If he had been my husband, I should have thrown him out the window at the end of the first week of matrimony; but Elodie was of a more tranquil nature" (*Adventures*, p. 297).

Gertrude came to feel that Elodie's marriage to Belloc eventually cost her her individuality and picturesqueness, as well as her separate literary aspirations. She thought his theories about women to be "as English as possible," by which she meant retrograde; Elodie as wife and mother evolved, in her eyes, into a domestic drudge "submerged in Hilaire, who had what might be called a violent personality" (*Adventures*, p. 298). The disillusionment was apparently mutual. According to Belloc's biographer A. N. Wilson, he and Elodie became critical and condescending toward Gertrude and her work as she fell out of sympathy with them: "To Elodie and Belloc she was something of a joke, and they nicknamed her 'the widow.' " [14]

During the summer of the Belloc marriage Gertrude and Aleece journeyed to Pont Aven, "a gray straggling village" near the Brittany coast of France, where Gauguin had lived and painted in the late 1880s. Given the choice between a boring, "deadly respectable" hotel frequented by frugal British families and another "swarming with [male] artists who were not expected to be at all respectable" (and often brought their mistresses along), the sisters opted for respectability. But they spent time with some of the writers who stayed at the other hotel. Among them was Horace Annesley Vachell, a novelist Gertrude had already met and taken a liking to in London. Through him they met the English poet of the Decadent school, Ernest Dowson. "Decadent" hardly does justice to the deteriorated condition into which Dowson had allowed himself to decline. He had no front teeth, and Gertrude told Bierce that he "never combs his hair nor shaves except when I invite him to tea."

Dowson had taken up permanent residence in Pont Aven. Celebrated in the early 1890s for his intense, sensual verse, he was now, at the age of only 29, an alcoholic headed for complete physical collapse. He had "picked his Flowers of Evil and inhaled their enervating odour." Dowson, according to Vachell, had "a dead-white face and delicate features. . . . The body was thin and frail. Absinthe was slowly consuming it." Invariably drunk by three in the afternoon, he made a piteous sight, "arrayed in the shabbiest of clothes and wearing boots that had once been white."[15] His nightly escapades often landed him at the police station for an appearance before the Mayor.

Vachell convinced Gertrude that with her help Dowson might be saved. She must treat him like a gentleman, invite him to tea, ask him to read his poetry aloud. This plot became the frame for the entirely forgettable Atherton novel *The Gorgeous Isle* (1908), in which a dissipated genius is restored to health, but not creative productivity, by the love of a charming young Englishwoman; since he can only write while intoxicated, she ends up pushing him off the wagon.

Vachell, Gertrude, and an American artist named Mrs. Trulow asked Dowson to tea and rejoiced when he appeared with newly cut and combed hair, a fresh shave, white collar and cuffs attached to his black sweater, and new white shoes. Asked to recite, he treated them all to a memorable reading, over tea cups, of his poem "Cynara," which ends with the beautiful stanza beginning "I cried for madder music and for stranger wine." Gertrude was both moved and impressed by this recitation, in a low monotone, of "a lost soul intoning in space" (*Adventures*, p. 258).

When she recounts the episode in her autobiography, she follows a familiar pattern of self-aggrandizement, giving herself a pivotal role by making it appear that for a moment she controlled the poet's destiny. She trivializes Dowson by suggesting that her brief attentiveness was restoring his self-esteem to the point where he could stop drinking and alter his life. Dowson apparently did reform for a week or so; he did enjoy her company and interest, and he did urge her to remain in Pont Aven for the winter. But there is little likelihood that his reformation would have lasted.

After she returned to London, Gertrude reproached herself— mildly, we imagine—for having abandoned him. Mrs. Trulow wrote from Pont Aven to say that the poet had started drinking again and no longer sported collar and cuffs. When Gertrude groaned, Aleece consoled her with resonant words she would have occasion to test in the future: "No woman ever yet reformed a drunkard."

She saw Dowson one last time, two years later, at a mass for the repose of the soul of Aubrey Beardsley at the Farm Street Church in London. "It was a curious assemblage. All the women were fashionable, all the men looked epicene. The mass was very impressive, and I sat for a few moments after it was over idly watching the people as they moved slowly down the aisle. And then I saw Ernest Dowson. He looked more like a lost soul than ever as he drifted past with his unseeing eyes. And very shabby, very poor. I half rose to follow him, but sank back with a mental headshake. He was a sensitive creature and could have no wish to meet again one who had known him during a brief period of regeneration. He died—miserably, of course— two years later" (*Adventures*, p. 262).

After Aleece returned to California, Gertrude again left London to settle in Bushey, Hertfordshire, in a corrugated iron shack in the back garden of a Scotch family. A British journalist who interviewed her there reported on the plainness of her dwelling: "She cannot work amid luxury, and certainly there was none in the Bushey studio. In some respects it looked . . . like a miner's camp at Klondike."[16]

Her landlady, Miss Bogle, had settled in Bushey to accommodate her brother while he studied at the Herkomer Art School. Two American students of artist Hubert Herkomer, James Montgomery Flagg and Frank Kimbrough (who each later did covers for Atherton novels) often turned up at Miss Bogle's for tea, and Flagg would remember Gertrude as the possessor of "a cold, ruthless brain behind her light blue eyes that were agleam with sardonic humor. She was vain of her long, golden hair and would let it fall over her shoulders after a wash and wander about the garden puffing a cigarette in a funny metal holder slipped over her forefinger. She was delightfully shocking to her hostess." [17]

Gertrude used the Bogle shack in Bushey—which was called "Merryhill Cottage"—as a retreat from London, an easy commuting distance away. Here she worked on her ambitious new novel, *The Californians*, took twilight walks among the hollyhocks, and read proof for *Patience Sparhawk*, which John Lane was finally about to release both in New York and London.

In *Adventures of a Novelist* Gertrude gives the impression that the response of the British to *Patience* was uniformly positive. "Everybody" was reading it, she says, and as a result she began to meet fashionable London for the first time. She quotes with particular pride Sir Walter Besant's words of encouragement and a review in the *Manchester Guardian*, likening the pages on the childhood of Patience Sparhawk to the early chapters of *Jane Eyre* and extolling Patience herself as "the realization of a type, the incarnation of the spirit of independence in a womanly temperament, a figure that will cling to the memory and modify the reader's world" (*Adventures*, p. 266).

English critics surely took her work more seriously than their American counterparts, and they did not—in her case—go in for personal or vituperative attacks. But they could, and did, express shock and disapproval. A reviewer for the *Edinburgh Review* chides Patience for her scorn for the poor and for reporting her emotions "or rather her physical sensations, with a frankness that is nothing short of indecent." And the *London Times* carped that the book carried the taint of vulgarity.

Critical responses to *Patience* in the United States reaffirmed Gertrude's conviction that her countrymen were organized in a conspiracy against her. The *Saturday Review* called it crude, vulgar, and anarchic; *The Critic* found it confused, obtuse, and over-sexed, "yet there is not one honest, strong passion in the whole book." As a novelist, Mrs. Atherton possessed vitality, but too many of her stories were of the lurid and passionate variety, "seeming to demand a refrigerator rather than a bookcase as their receptacle." *The Bookman* accused the characters of talking in essays and said the book gave a distorted picture of American men, women, and morals.[18]

The *New York Times*, not content with the strictures of its reviewer ("The exhibit is too much under electric light"), took the extreme measure of devoting an editorial to *Patience Sparhawk* that challenged the veracity of its portrayal of American life. "We [Americans] do not object to criticism," said the *Times*, "but sometimes we get a little tired of misrepresentation and exact the privilege of the worm." The editorial quotes Mrs. Atherton's complaint to a British magazine that she "cannot write an article without throwing the entire U.S. press into a ferment," and her charge that only two American papers had not "vociferated" at *Patience*. She had stated, "I hope that I shall never do the United States an injustice, but I shall certainly not be deterred from telling the truth about it in every book I write."[19] The gist of the *Times*'s rejoinder was "Balderdash."

Back in San Francisco, a reviewer for the *Call* based his objections to *Patience* on a sense of betrayal. Mrs. Atherton had abandoned her proper task, the romantic treatment of early California themes: "She has sold her birthright—the field of California romantic fiction—for the mess of pottage offered by the devotees of the erotic novel and of sensational journalism." Somebody in San Francisco sent Gertrude a copy of this review, and her answer appeared in print a few weeks later:

I have read your lament over me with much interest. I will not agree with you that I have gone to the dogs because I elect to study life outside California for a change. I have always maintained that our [American] literature did not represent us—for we are the most sensational, heterogeneous and chaotic race on earth, and our novels would lead the outsider to believe that our veins were packed with weak tea.

The only trouble with *Patience*, she submits, is that "it is the most truthful American novel that has been written, and the proof of it is that it has met with angry—in many cases insulting—disapproval from almost the entire U.S. press." As for her alleged abandonment of Californian themes, "What is the use of writing stories which no one will read? I made exactly $12.00 on the book edition of *The*

Doomswoman, and the Lippincott's were so disappointed in the sale of the magazine in which it first appeared that they did not feel justified in bringing it out between boards." Only 100 copies of *Before the Gringo Came* had been sold, and most of the Spanish Californian stories had been published in English magazines. Nonetheless, despite the facts that the East cared nothing for California and the people in California refused to buy her books, she was at present writing another California novel.[20]

That book, one of her most serious and accomplished, was *The Californians*.[21] Much of its power resides in Magdalena Yorba, a heroine who, for once, does *not* resemble the public persona of her creator. Part Spanish-Californian and part New Englander, the proud, dark-skinned Magdalena has a brooding, inward-looking nature. Neither beautiful nor brilliant, she wrestles with inarticulateness and a lack of social grace that belies her thoughtful intelligence. Capable of deep feeling, she falls for the worldly New Yorker Trennaham, who wins, abandons, and at last returns to her. Equally passionate is her hatred of her tyrannical father, Don Roberto, who tries to prevent her going out alone in San Francisco (she defies him to make a rare Athertonian night journey through the city's most squalid streets) and forbids her to read or write seriously. Avaricious to the point of madness, he awakens murderous impulses in his awkward, taciturn daughter.

With *The Californians*, readers of Atherton's novels about California could begin to see that they interconnect; while set in different decades, they share not only a San Francisco backdrop and some recurrent themes, but characters and family names—most of them resonant with Western history: Montgomerys, Tarletons, Yorbas, Gearys, Belmonts. They make up the social elite of old San Francisco—narrow, isolated from the world's nerve centers, complacent, anti-intellectual, inbred. Like the Atherton family, they spend their winters in San Francisco and their summers on the Peninsula or the redwood country to the north. They demand rigid social conformity of their daughters.

One such carry-over, reintroduced into *The Californians* after appearing in *A Whirl Asunder*, is that concentrated essence of California, Helena Belmont, who does exactly as she pleases, riding roughshod over everybody else in the process. She lacks conscience or scruple, but charms because of her originality, spunk, and sense of fun. The pretty, outspoken Helena is Magdalena's foil, rival for Trennahan's love, and best friend. Her father, Colonel Belmont, a profligate Southern gentleman, spoils her, being as indulgent as Magdalena's father is harsh. Magdalena envies her friend's freedom, outspokenness, and ability to turn men's heads. Helena travels all over Europe while Magdalena stays cooped up in her father's house in San Francisco; a "human cyclone," she drives a coach and four and reads Walter Pater in her spare time. By the end of the novel Helena has broken the last in a long string of betrothals and awaits a future as a single woman who will figure in history: she is looking for a revolution to lead.

But the book belongs to Magdalena and her story of disillusionment—with California, Catholicism, and romance—and coming to terms. She finds that the Virgin fails to answer her prayers and that her ideal of a handsome caballero has been displaced by men like her father who care only about money. Her ambition to write withers as she reads Henry James and accepts the limitations of her talent. Even millionaires can be failures, and Don Roberto, Colonel Belmont, and Magdalena's uncle Hiram Polk have all died, unfulfilled, by the end of the book, Don Roberto most spectacularly by hanging himself with the American flag.

Where before Gertrude Atherton equated California's competitive, straight-ahead individualism with admirable qualities like ambition and enterprise, here, through Magdalena, she stops to take a harder look. The pioneer's grasping nature has turned ugly: "Men came to kiss [California] and stayed to tear away her flesh with their teeth."[22] The portrait of California that emerges is a dark and disturbing one, although Helena's cruelty is never as harshly judged as that of the male characters. The critic for the London *Times* complained that the book, though clever and original, "does not add much to the sum of human pleasure. . . . *Daisy Miller* was not nearly so cruel an indictment against a section of American society."[23]

Having written her best book to date (possibly the best novel she would ever write), Gertrude yielded to the blandishments of Dr. Robertson Nicoll, who approached her on behalf of a young publishing firm, Service and Paton. He promised not only to pay her a generous advance but to give her a "boom." That was bait she could not resist. Although she had no idea in mind for yet another novel, she accepted the advance, agreed to a deadline four months later, and returned to France, to Rouen, to begin work.

In Rouen, on the crest of a hill on the outskirts of town, she found her way to a boarding house run by a Madame d'Oliviera. Madame's other boarders, as it happened, were a group of literary Englishmen who had persuaded her never to rent a room to a woman. Gertrude insisted that she could overcome their objections, and she proved correct. The Englishmen were, in fact, intimates of Oscar Wilde. They remain unnamed in *Adventures of a Novelist*, but Reggie Turner and Robert Ross were among them. Both had been with Wilde at the time of his arrest and had immediately fled to France; they again stood by him after his release from Reading Gaol.

Reggie Turner had "a small income which relieved him of the necessity of work, and he loved art, literature and travel. Many of his friends were blinding lights in the literary world" (*Adventures*, p. 277), among them that genius of parody, Max Beerbohm. Gertrude had written a review of Beerbohm's *The Happy Hypocrite* for *Vanity Fair* which had pleased him. Turner wrote to Beerbohm from Rouen:

There is an American novelist staying here, Mrs. Gertrude Atherton by name, and she is the person who reviewed your *Happy Hypocrite*, . . . a criticism which gave you so much pleasure. Fortunately for me she keeps to her room all day except at meals. She seems nice and 35 [she was almost 40] but I shall find out both later. She is a widow . . . and has a daughter in California. It is rather an Ibsen menage.

Turner had heard from Madame d'Oliviera that Mrs. Atherton had confided that she hoped she would not like him *too* much, "a hope," he said, "I quite reciprocate."

Beerbohm's curiosity was piqued. He asked Turner to tell him all about this Mrs. Atherton, and to tell her all about him:

I heard that she had a daughter over the sea, she herself started life behind a bar in St. Louis—then went to San Francisco, where she used to
dance naked in one of the dime-shows. Also she was kept for some years
by President Garfield. When he was assassinated she became an authoress.
This letter is written with a special view to it being read aloud across the
table at déjeuner.[24]

Gertrude probably never heard these witticisms, but she and Beerbohm did meet, at least once, at a London dinner party where he
recommended Bruges to her as an excellent choice for one of her
writing retreats.

    Turner she eventually came to know quite well. They sought each
other out, passing many a pleasant evening at the boarding house in
conversation. He told her he had sat at Oscar Wilde's feet, "listening
to such talk as never before since the Fifth Century B.C. had flowed
from any man's lips." According to Gertrude, he also told her he
now regretted ever having known him, so evil was his influence. He
said he never wanted to set eyes on him again but confessed he had
agreed to meet Wilde in a restaurant in Rouen in a few days. She
urged him not to go, or at least to meet Wilde only to tell him he was
now leading a different life "and he must let you alone in the future."
Turner should not wreck his life "for the sake of an old sinner like
that" (*Adventures*, p. 278).

    According to Wilde's biographer Richard Ellmann, her account
"cannot be sheer invention," although Turner would discredit her
report, much later, as "full of lies." Ellmann speculates that Wilde
wanted Turner to come and live with him, and that Turner re-
belled at that prospect: "he wished to be a friend and not a *copain*."
Although he would rally round Wilde during his last days in Paris
in 1900, Turner did retreat to London, as Gertrude had urged, in
the summer of 1897.[25]

    Gertrude remained at Rouen until she completed her new novel,
American Wives and English Husbands. The idea for it had come to
her after she followed the advice of Madame d'Oliviera to travel to
a particular church and pray. The book sprouted into being shortly
thereafter, and Gertrude—somewhat mystical about the springs of

creation—considered it a minor miracle. "Who knows anything of the psycho-mental process? Catholics to whom I have told the story insist that it was a direct answer to prayer. Perhaps it was" (*Adventures*, p. 276).

American Wives, like her earlier *His Fortunate Grace*, exploits popular interest in the international marriages that linked American heiresses to European titles. "The manners of European nobility fascinated Americans who, having the dollars, felt they should buy continental culture and station. Though only a few Americans could afford the grand marital alliance, the Grand Tour of the grand house, . . . more could attempt to satisfy their desires through the medium of romantic fiction."[26]

In *American Wives*, a comedy of manners, Atherton turns the fad into an opportunity to lightly satirize types from both sides of the Atlantic: the priggish, impersonal Oxford man, the pushy Chicago-born female social climber, the blasé California debutante. Her sympathetic San Francisco-bred heroine Lee Tarleton combines a Southern aristocratic lineage with Californian individuality; she diverges from type in not being the daughter of a millionaire. When we first meet Lee, in her shabby-genteel phase, she lives in a Market Street boarding house much like the one Gertrude had lived in with her mother and stepfather after their financial fortunes had begun to slide.

At the boarding house Lee meets and promises to marry some day Cecil Maundrell, whose father, the Earl of Barnstable, typifies broken-down British nobility married to crass, commanding American money. Cecil makes it clear from the start that in England, where Lee will live when she becomes his wife, the English women cater to the men. In America it is quite the reverse: "My mother always told her husband and brothers to do everything she wanted, and they always did," Lee says.[27]

American Wives takes up and develops a theme Gertrude had touched on in the newspapers: the differences between the sexes in England compared to those in the United States. Not long after moving to England she had sent a letter to the *London Daily News* comparing English men with their American counterparts. Picked up by American newspapers, the letter claimed that American women "practically own London" because they possess a vitality shared by

English men but unknown to English women. "American women," she boasted, "are alive to their finger-tips; they have cast off the yoke of conventionality, cut-and-dried religion and all the old forms and traditions." Mentally, spiritually, and sexually they were the natural companions of English men, whom she crowned "the most dominant, perfectly balanced . . . and highly developed race of men the world has ever known." By comparison, American men seem primitive, composed merely of "money-greed and sensuality."[28]

Gertrude knew very well that her remarks would create a stir. She gleefully revealed to Bierce,

I've been raising Cain in the newspapers again. You know that always amused me. I'm never happy if people are entirely pleased with me. . . . I will confide to you that I was neither married to an Englishman, engaged to or in love with one. But they have interested me immensely as a study and I do like them. I'd like to see a few people in America but I don't care if I never see the place again. . . . It's never treated me decently and the cads on the newspapers drive me wild. (October 3, 1896)

None of her feathers had been ruffled by the replies to her letter that Hearst published in the *San Francisco Examiner*—by such figures as the dancer Loie Fuller and novelist Edgar Fawcett—but Bierce's response gave her a turn. He dredged up his old cavil that she was creating an uproar merely to promote her notoriety. Gertrude's hackles rose high enough to send waves across the ocean. "I did not think you would make the mistake of confounding the public and private personalities of anyone," she snapped. "You have written several tomes of abuse of women, and you might have known that what I said about delighting in the wrath of my countrymen was in joke." She had *not* written the letters on American women and English men in a bid for notoriety; rather, "they were dragged out of me. I must have been asked six or seven times before I consented to put my ideas on the subject in print." She writes what she believes to be true, she said in her defense, "and of course I knew what the result would be—knowing the vanity of man." Hearst had finally cabled her for a more developed essay on the subject, and by that time, she said, "I was so angry that I said far more than I would have done in the beginning. It is a remarkable fact, mon ami (ex- I suppose) that these letters hit no harder than many—otherwise directed—

that I wrote while on the Examiner—all of which incurred your approval." This time the breach with Bierce did not really heal, and letters between them became increasingly rare. But Gertrude had by no means exhausted what she had to say about American men and women compared to British.

In a piece for a British women's magazine, she credits the American girl—who in many minds, during the 1890s, would conjure an image of the famous Gibson Girl—with creating a climate of freedom which had benefitted British New Women: "Volumes have been written about the revolt of the British maiden, her demand for the latch-key, the vote, and for the husband of her critical choice; her statement in bald English that she can bicycle alone with a man, she can go with him unchaperoned to a party. . . . The invasion of the American maiden, both in fact and fiction, may have something to do with it." Unlike her British counterpart, she continues, repeating a point she had made in her article on American divorce, the American girl has been encouraged from childhood "to form and express her own opinions." Europeans who see hordes of noisy, gum-chewing American girls in hotel lobbies should not be fooled. The best type of American girl has an atmosphere of "splendid independence" that allows her to pounce with audacity "upon the greatest ideas under heaven."[29]

By the time she came to write *American Wives* Gertrude had lived outside the States for several years, and her ideas about British and American men had crystallized. The novel depicts American men, as the various pieces of journalism do, as mentally undeveloped, concerned mainly with making money. But the American male, unlike the British, tends to indulge his wife or sister. Lee Tarleton has an American suitor who competes with Cecil for her favor. She tells Cecil, "If I married Randolph, he would spend his life buttoning up my boots. If I married you, I should spend my life pulling off yours."[30]

When Lee grows up, she not only marries the loving, brilliant but self-absorbed Cecil, she briefly sacrifices her individuality to him, totally submerging herself in his career in Parliament and his emotional needs. But inevitably she rebels, telling Cecil that she feels "I adapted myself, and you took me for granted," and that she desires to return to California for a year to reclaim her separate self. In the end she gives up the plan, realizing that she has changed and could never be content with her old life; and that, since she does love Cecil, his need for her overrides all other considerations. But he has been made aware that she has needs, too, and that he cannot continue to ignore, as he has in the past, her well-developed individuality.

In fiction that accommodates the fantasies of readers, Gertrude Atherton could create a truce in the war between the sexes, allowing Lee and Cecil to stay lovingly married while acknowledging their separate personalities and needs.[31] In real life—as when she observed the submergence of Elodie Hogan in domestic duties and the ego of Hilaire Belloc—she realized such resolutions within marriage were hard to come by.

American Wives received extravagant praise from British reviewers, who responded not only to its verve and compression (a rare virtue in an Atherton novel) but its depiction of a palatable New Woman. "Mrs. Atherton," wrote the reviewer for *The Athenaeum*, "has achieved effortlessly what Sarah Grand [author of two extremely controversial New Woman novels] labored to express: the equality of women to men.... She brings her heroine from America, where the women are, as a rule, far better educated than in England, and where they have far more independence of thought and initiative."[32] In the New Woman era, the American woman of independence seemed Newest.

The boom Gertrude had been promised seemed about to materialize. Dr. Robertson Nicoll wrote to say she must now take herself seriously as the leading woman novelist. Richard Le Gallienne said that "with the two obvious exceptions of Mr. Meredith and Mr. Thomas Hardy, he doubts if there is another English [language] novelist living who is so unmistakably a novelist from Nature's hand. She has, he said, spontaneous story-telling and character-drawing instincts in combination with a serious and witty philosophy and a brilliant literary gift."[33]

One reviewer who had not found *American Wives* beyond reproach was Henry James. He could not obscure with circumlocution his opinion that it lacked depth and artistry. He felt the novelist not only failed to see the situation she wished to evoke, "but leaves us wondering what she had supposed herself to see instead." James could not have liked the fact that Mrs. Atherton in this book was treading on his turf, the theme of American interaction with European culture. Unfortunately, he thought, "the conflict of character, or tradition . . . is reduced to proportions so insignificant that we never catch it in the act."[34] Gertrude read this review, but pretended not to understand its negative intent. Henry James had reviewed a book of hers once, she wrote (overlooking another negative review he had done of *His Fortunate Grace*), "and I do not know to this day whether he liked it or not."[35] She was an excellent selective listener.

The publication of *American Wives* marked another milestone in her career, and it was time to take stock and regroup. In a scant four years of living abroad she had accomplished a great deal. She had published an amazing amount: six novels, including, to be sure, one rewrite of an earlier work and a number of "absurd and tasteless fancies" (Percival Pollard's words) like *The Valiant Runaways* and *His Fortunate Grace*, but also including work of substantial originality, energy, and timely social comment, like *The Californians* and *American Wives*. She found herself interviewed, paragraphed, photographed. "I was now made," she told herself (*Adventures*, p. 292).

She had certainly been noticed and, in Britain, widely praised. But her need for approval, attention, and constant renewal through publication worked against any strategy of artistic integrity. She refused to stop, to take time to discard inferior work or revise it until it achieved its best possible form. When sympathetic critics advised her to take things a bit slower, she paid no heed, preferring to glory in the flattering things they said. As she had once admitted to Bierce, she did not know her good work from her bad.

No words of praise pleased her more than those she received in a letter from her countryman and fellow novelist, Harold Frederic, who was London correspondent for the *New York Times*. Speaking of *American Wives*, he said, "It has a kind of vitality of its own which forces recognition even if it eludes analysis. When I had finished it I said . . . 'she has a clearer vocation to write novels than any woman I know of.'" He commented on the growth in her writing that was manifest in the gap between *Patience* and *American Wives*, but at the same time issued a warning: "I should harangue you about the peril, not perhaps of writing too much, but of writing too easily. You have in extreme degree the talent of lucidity—but melody is an acquired gift with all but the laurel-wreathed few. Do take the pace a little more slowly, and listen with a more solicitous reflective ear" (*Adventures*, p. 313).

Do take the pace a little more slowly. Listen with a more reflective ear. It was good advice, but she would not hear it.

Despite her sense that she had "arrived," Gertrude remained alert to any social slight, real or imagined. Pearl Craigie, an American-born writer whose father had made a fortune manufacturing patent medicines, had lived in England many years before Gertrude's arrival. She was a close friend of Lady Randolph Churchill, and she wrote novels under the pseudonym "John Oliver Hobbes." For Gertrude she became the object of a small personal vendetta for having "turned her back on me pointedly one night when she was receiving with the hostess at a literary party." Gertrude overreacted. She became convinced that Mrs. Craigie was arranging that her books be constantly slammed in *The Academy*, a weekly owned by Mrs. Craigie's father, and that her malice was motivated by a spirit of petty competition between two American women novelists: "She had been born in the U.S. . . . and until I appeared had been the only American pebble on the literary beach" (*Adventures*, p. 390).

According to the Irish-American writer Vincent O'Sullivan, a firsthand observer of the London literary scene of the 1890s, Mrs. Craigie lacked the power to monitor critical comment in *The Academy*. "The editor was Lewis Hind, and he was perfectly capable of arranging what slams he wanted done himself. Mrs. Craigie . . . had no reason to be jealous of Mrs. Atherton, who at the time she speaks of was generally unknown, [not true, if the snub took place after 1897] whereas Mrs. Craigie was very well known indeed. Neither was Mrs. Craigie 'the only American pebble on the literary beach' till the arrival of Mrs. Atherton. There were Elizabeth Robins, Anne Douglas Sedgwick."[36]

We can conjecture that the extremely anglicized and somewhat pretentious Mrs. Craigie took a view toward Mrs. Atherton that resembled that of Henry James. Gertrude's aggressiveness, her willingness to publish drivel along with good books, and her hunger for publicity might well have appeared "vulgar" to Mrs. Craigie.

Gertrude had her own version. She had been snubbed by a social insider, a person who consorted with the very people to whom Gertrude herself wanted entrée. A very raw spot had been pressed, and she would not forget it. When John Lane, who published Mrs. Craigie's books as well as Mrs. Atherton's, offered to serve as fence-mender, Gertrude would have none of it: "Mrs. Craigie was extremely rude to me when she had every reason to be otherwise, for I . . . had been introduced to her by a lady who held a high social position while she was still known as the daughter of a pill-vendor."[37] After Mrs. Craigie's death she would take her revenge by basing a character in her 1906 novel *Ancestors* on the rival novelist, turning the woman into a deceitful vixen who expresses herself in epigrams and snubs fellow Americans.[38]

Rejection from another quarter—American critics—had become such a sore point that after reading the American reviews of *Patience Sparhawk*, Gertrude suspended her subscription to a New York clipping service and kept herself in blissful ignorance of American opinions about her. She spared herself reading in *The Critic* that *American Wives* gave the world an utterly inaccurate picture of American society, but she also missed learning of some sentiments that would undoubtedly have pleased and surprised her: that *The Californians*, for example, was "distinctly superior in vitality and attractiveness to most of the fiction of the day," or that Mrs. Atherton was incapable of writing anything commonplace or dull.[39]

When Gertrude decided to return to the United States early in 1899, it was not because of the recent change in her family's configuration. Muriel had married Albert B. Russell, who was then a clerk in a sugar refinery, in a quiet ceremony at the San Francisco home of her aunt, Florence Atherton Eyre, on January 4, 1899,[40] and was already expecting a baby. Certainly Mrs. Atherton, the outspoken American novelist, was not returning to the States to spend time with her daughter or grandchild or to meet her new son-in-law. The name Albert Russell does not appear a single time in *Adventures of a Novelist*.

Nor did she decide to return out of any conviction that she and her books would be greeted by friendly critical winds. Since her next book was to be about an exemplary American senator, however, there can be no doubt that she wanted to correct the impression, articulated by the likes of Ambrose Bierce in private and the *New York Times* in public, that she had nothing good to say about American men. And she wanted to test her hunch that Americans would begin to honor her after the British had begun to do so.

She said she wanted also to explain America to her British readers, whose questions about American politics she did not know enough to answer. (One British reader, Oscar Wilde, would read her *Senator North* on his deathbed in Paris and would tell Reggie Turner it was a fine study of the American politician and ask what else the lady had written.)[41] In order to write her American political novel, she would have to acquaint herself with Washington D.C. Within weeks of her crossing, she had established herself as a daily visitor to the gallery of the U.S. Senate.

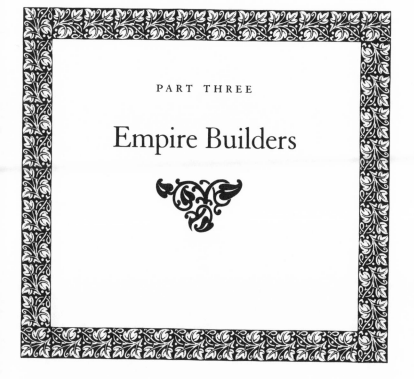

PART THREE

Empire Builders

CHAPTER NINE

Superheroes

"We go to Europe to become Americanized," said Emerson. As the nineteenth century drew to its close, Gertrude Atherton began to think of herself as a novelist with a purpose: she would entertainingly teach the British and fellow Americans about her country's social and political life. Placing herself now in a national and international rather than regional context—as a Europeanized American instead of a Californian—she selected Washington D.C. as her new arena. Here she would watch senators and presidents, observe their wives, daughters, and mistresses, attend receptions, read the *Congressional Record*, and absorb as much "background" as she could. "I met everybody, from cave-dwellers [old Washingtonians] and diplomats down to minor 'representatives.' I went to crowded 'days' of senators' and congressmen's wives, where you merely walked in one door and out the other; dined where talk was as political as in London; attended receptions at embassies and the houses of Cabinet officials, elbowing queer looking persons, tourists from the backwoods who marched in uninvited" (*Adventures*, p. 307).

Gertrude had become a frightful snob. Her mutinous spirit subsided as she identified with those who have power rather than those —like divorcees, sequestered daughters, or rebellious wives—who are shut out. Somehow her long residency in Britain, her New England ancestry, her growing celebrity, her early association with the Athertons, and her inherent tendency to hold herself aloof from others combined in a way that allowed her to think of herself as displaced British aristocracy, horrified at the presumption of the plebs. She wrote for Lady Randolph Churchill's sumptuous *Anglo-Saxon Review* (whose contributors, it was said, had to use blue-blood ink) and argued a pro-British, anti-Boer line with Washington acquaintances. In her 1901 novel *Aristocrats* she took the point of view of an English noblewoman—sister of a duke—who is vacationing in the Adirondacks and recording her observations on American foibles in a series of letters home. As Lady Helen Pole she is superior to everyone else and at the same time free to expose the hypocrisy and pretentiousness of the American ruling class.

In her Washington novel *Senator North*, servants who adopt an over-familiar tone with their employers take a drubbing, as do "The Great Commoner" William Jennings Bryan and his supporters. The novel is set against a background of national debate over the Spanish-American War, which is viewed as a caprice of the ignorant mob; "the people" want it, but "the people" are shallow, excitable, trigger-happy, and easily manipulated. The book's heroine, Betty Madison, observes: "As for 'government by the people,' the phrase should be translated today into 'tyranny of the people.' England under a constitutional monarchy is far freer than we are."[1] Senator North himself believes with Alexander Hamilton—who appears before him in a vision—that the United States should be ruled by a powerful, educated elite, forming an aristocratic government with a strong centralized core. Hamilton tells North, "in you . . . I seem to have lived on" (*Senator North*, p. 346). The two superheroes apparently share not just a philosophy but a soul.

Gertrude expropriated the methods of a journalist when she researched *Senator North*. Like a reporter in search of an "exclusive," she combed the Senate for a figure around whom she could weave her fable, the newspapers for political background, and Washington salons for her novel's social milieu. With the help of letters of introduction from her brother-in-law Lawrence Rathbone she obtained from Vice President Garret Hobart (who would die before the year's end) a card admitting her to his private "pew" in the Senate Gallery which overlooked a sumptuous space full of light, furnished with 90 desks and easy chairs and warmed by a large fire. Young senators and congressmen were not much in evidence; from the gallery Gertrude found herself looking down on a sea of bald heads.

On the whole the senators impressed her as "men of worthy purpose," with more education and more distinguished backgrounds than she had imagined, even if they did chew gum and use spittoons. But the prevailing disorder appalled her. During the debate over the peace treaty for the Spanish-American War, no one seemed to pay the slightest attention to the senator who held the floor. The other senators would talk in groups or couples, write letters, or even read the newspaper. She told Charles Culver Johnson, whose interview-article "Woman in the Senate" was syndicated in newspapers across the country, "You are not quite sure . . . whether the senators are in sessions until you see Mr. Hobart bring his gavel down in an orderly way to command silence. If you have been in the House and heard Speaker [Thomas B.] Reed hammer his desk and bellow for order you are amazed at the contrast until you see the effect is about the same—little comes of it."[2]

Not only did she find her way into the Senate Gallery, she got herself invited to a reception for the triumphantly returning hero of Manila Bay, Admiral Dewey, and to more than one glittering White House event. She was introduced to President McKinley, whose manners she admired but whose character she found ambiguous. "No two people agree . . . whether he is weak or strong, McKinley or [Republican party boss] Hanna," she wrote.[3] McKinley struck her as a little bit too congenial, "a politician of the approved 'glad hand' tradition, who made every one feel that he, or she, was the one person he had waited all his life to meet." Since Mrs. McKinley was an epileptic, she did not stand in the receiving line with the Cabinet wives, but instead sat silently behind the President, who showed a touching devotion to her. If she had a seizure, he deftly threw a handkerchief over her face. "Such was high life in Washington" (*Adventures*, pp. 307–8).

Although social life and the personalities of women she met engaged her interest, although she continued her ongoing assault on conventional marriage, it was the men in this man's town who captured her most assiduous attention. The Washington novel she had in mind was going to signal a new direction for her. In a marked departure from her previous novels, she would focus on male characters and endow them with heroic qualities—dominance, power, strength —that she had worshipped since the days of William Ralston. Again she had her finger on the public pulse, for the jingoistic and national-istic spirit, after the Spanish-American War, was at its zenith. Teddy Roosevelt, who had won the public's zealous approval in his fabled Rough Rider charge up San Juan Hill, personified the virile, West-ernized, action-loving masculine ideal of the moment. But he was by no means the only heroic icon before the public. Imperialist ex-pansion sanctioned the prevailing British and American notion that mighty nations, dominated by manly white military and political chiefs and capitalist barons, rule by divine right. The United States itself, not just its president-to-be Teddy Roosevelt, was seen as an invincible North American strong man. The "yellow" press con-tributed its share to the hero-worshipping climate. With its banner headlines and staged events, its brawny comic-strip good guys and dastardly villains, it purveyed and thrived on an atmosphere of con-stant excitement and heightened reality.[4]

Long before she returned to the United States in 1899, Gertrude —who held weak men in utter contempt and grew increasingly blithe about referring to her late husband as "unlamented"—in-dulged in Superman fantasies. The more passive, unsuccessful, or irresponsible men she encountered in daily life, the more she made a fetish of exaggerated masculinity and mastery. In her room in Bushey, in England, she had posted a clipping of Cecil Rhodes, with his picture. She dreamed of meeting him and in that hope cultivated the acquaintance of his tweedy, "amazonian" sister Edith in London. They never did meet, and after the Boer War broke out she lost her illusions about him, but in the mid-1890s, when he had amassed a fortune in diamonds and seemed to personify Empire as prime min-ister of South Africa's Cape Colony, she thought of him as a rugged idol, a kind of ultimate Forty-Niner who had "opened up a new and savage country by the sheer insolent force of one great man's person-ality."[5] She told her friend Horace Vachell that she ranked power in men above any other quality.

Gertrude announced her return to the United States, and affirmed her contempt for men less heroic than Cecil Rhodes, with a satiric newspaper piece—surely read by her recently married daughter in San Francisco—about husbands. "There are two ways of managing a husband," she wrote in the *San Francisco Call*. "One is muscular and the other by mental force."[6] To her, relations between the sexes, as between nations, easily became reduced to a power struggle between the weak and the strong, the Darwinian tough survivor and the pitiful, expendable milksop.

An actual senator, Eugene Hale of Maine, served as the model for Senator North. After attending the Senate regularly for some weeks, Gertrude was struck one day by the appearance of a man who seemed both virile and typically American. He stood squarely on his feet, and his speech was curt and concise. As usual, she was drawn in by this aura of virility: "He was a rather short, square man, but authoritative in bearing. He had a beard, . . . close-clipped, trim and iron gray like his well-cut hair; the face it framed was rugged and powerful, with piercing black eyes" (*Senator North*, p. 306). In her eyes, his age—he appeared to be about 60—merely added to his impressiveness.

When she met Senator Hale, she found him to be "a man of the world, an interesting talker," with fine manners and enormous personal magnetism. He seemed flattered to have been chosen as a model and pleased to offer himself as consultant, becoming quite involved with the actual creation of the novel. Gertrude wrote to her publisher, John Lane, "Senator Hale has been trying to think up a big scene for Senator North behind closed doors. . . . He is as much interested in the book as if he had written it himself."[7] When the novel came out, he reported with amusement that everyone in Washington was calling him Senator North. He praised it for its "forceful and logical attack on democracy" and for its success in "concentrating all the tragedy of the white-negro race in one of the characters."

The embodiment of this tragedy is the character Harriet Walker, half sister to Betty Madison and the illegitimate child of Betty's now dead father and a beautiful octoroon. After Harriet's mother and guardian both die, Betty agrees to take her in and help educate her. She hopes to conceal the family connection and Harriet's "taint of blood."

Although she fights against it, Betty Madison succumbs to a primitive, "inherited" horror of "black" blood, which her creator unfortunately shared. Harriet appears to be white but her "taint" tells; she becomes the receptacle for every conceivable racial stereotype. She is dishonest, indolent, "barbaric," and incapable of improving herself except in externals. When Harriet breaks into a gloriously sung Methodist hymn, Betty is terrified that the servants will discover the unspeakable truth about her ancestry and warns: "You have a magnificent voice, and you must have it cultivated. But never sing another hymn" (*Senator North*, p. 116). Betty also advises her never to smile, for her wide grin "was the fatuous grin of the negro." When Harriet thanks her for the "kindness" of her advice, the present-day reader shivers at the display of bigotry and cruelty.[8]

Atherton presents Betty's racial prejudice as something inborn, inevitable and unalterable. "The repulsion was physical, inherited from generations of proud and intolerant women, and she could not control it" (*Senator North*, p. 80). In Betty's universe, a drop of concealed black blood carries a curse more dreadful than the one on the house of Atreus. The Southern gentleman who marries Harriet, unaware of her "taint," commits suicide when he learns the truth, and Harriet drowns herself in remorse.

When this grim melodrama has been played out, the novel proceeds matter-of-factly to narrate the saga of the unconsummated love affair between the married Senator North and the ambitious Betty, who has turned her mother's stately Washington home into a political salon. The Senator's invalid wife obligingly dies at the end, making way for a hastily arranged marriage between the previously repressed lovers, who have been allowed to hold hands and kiss, but nothing more. Betty, we're asked to believe, "hated the thought of sin as she hated vulgarity." For her to commit adultery would be "to violate the greatest of social laws," a prospect "abhorrent to every inherited instinct" (*Senator North*, p. 156).

What is a modern reader to make of the moral quagmire that is *Senator North*? Certainly racism was more widespread, more openly expressed, and more socially acceptable in 1900 than now, and greater novelists than Gertrude Atherton—among them Frank Norris and Jack London—exhibited it. But even in 1900, some American reviewers expressed dismay at the treatment of Harriet. "The author abhors the taint of blood as thoroughly as she condones the taint of sin," wrote the critic for the *New York Times*, tossing in a charge of sensationalism.[9]

The relationship between Senator North and Betty provoked additional critical outcry. *Lippincott's*, previously a bastion of support for Mrs. Atherton, fulminated at the disregard shown to the invalid Mrs. North, charging the Senator with violation of the seventh commandment in thought and word if not in deed, and Betty with cruelty, immorality, and immodesty. "*Senator North* should be included in the Index Expurgatorius of every healthy mind. . . . Wealth and luxury are sapping the morals of the American people rapidly enough. Shall we encourage novels which tend to accelerate the corruption of private life and the destruction of the family relation?"[10]

Confronted with these charges, Gertrude protested, as she had done in the past, that her only crime was telling the truth. *Senator North* was "current history . . . written at first hand, after personal study and accurate observation of the leading characters in the political life of today."[11] Responding in a published letter to the attack in the *New York Times*, she defended her own courage and objectivity: "Perhaps I am the only woman who has ever dared to write of the world exactly as she has seen it. (I do this because I live for my work and nothing else, having practically no personal life.)"[12]

What a bundle of defenses and contradictions! For years she had been attacking Howells and his brand of tame realism as "Littleism" that glorified the commonplace. Novelists, she had argued, should depict what is extraordinary and exceptional. Now, as a new, broader, and more naturalistic kind of realism was emerging in books like *McTeague* (which she called "powerful but loathsome"), she was again proclaiming herself the champion realist, as she had in defending *Hermia Suydam* against its attackers.

She had also gone on record against writers who court mass popularity. Responding in the *San Francisco Examiner* to Edwin Markham's hugely popular poem "The Man with The Hoe,"—a paean to the working man—she asked, "Why waste a beautiful gift in groveling for popularity with the mob? Striving to please the common mind has a fatal commonizing effect on the writing faculty."[13] But popularity, in the form of large sales, was exactly what she had sought with every previous novel and especially with *Senator North*, whose publication had been timed precisely to coincide with the climax of the 1900 presidential election.

A few months after its release she was so despondent over what she considered poor sales that she told John Lane she was contemplating abandoning her career as a writer:

I have been thinking seriously of throwing over the whole business. "Senator North" is a failure. It is the most American novel that has been published in this country and it has sold less than any dialect story, machine made historical novel, of the year. . . . In fact of all the books which have been published in the U.S. this year and sold at all, "Senator North" has sold the least. 13,000 in a country and a period [when] all sorts of books are selling by the ton . . . is a failure. I must say I don't see the use of hammering away any longer. . . . I can make all the money I want at newspaper work. Or, I can marry.[14]

The threat to give up novels for journalism, or to marry for an income, should not be taken at all seriously. But she *was* angry and disappointed that *Senator North* was selling so slowly, and she was keenly aware that other political and historical novels—like those of Paul Leicester Ford—were raking up huge receipts.

By June she was singing a different tune. Lane's assistant Temple Scott was promoting the book with significant success; by the end of the year, according to *Publishers Weekly*, it had sold 25,000 copies. It had also received that most coveted of prizes, a favorable notice from Ambrose Bierce in the *New York Journal*. Gertrude assured him that his high opinion coincided with the views many British critics had expressed and that the book was at last doing well, "selling as fast as they can print it and that is all I really care about. It is a true and artistic piece of work and all the reviewers in the country couldn't convince me to the contrary."

As she had planned before coming to Washington, Gertrude returned to Europe to write *Senator North*. She thought of England as her base and expected to return to it between wanderings but had arranged to do her actual writing in Bruges, Belgium. She stopped in London en route, during the summer of 1899, and found it darkened by mourning for sons, brothers, and fathers killed in the Boer War. Since the London atmosphere depressed her, she returned directly to Washington from Bruges and began casting about for yet another locale that could provide a novel setting for the next book.

She then took an unexpected tangent. Cuba, no longer under the yoke of Spain, was now a U.S. military protectorate. Frederic Howland, part-owner of the *Providence Journal* and its Washington correspondent, persuaded Gertrude that she must go there "to write *the* book of that country. He says that every book and every story, including those by [Stephen] Crane and R. H. Davis, have been failures because they cannot get the atmosphere. I should go with a knowledge of the Spanish character and an experienced handling of the 'atmosphere.' . . . I'll take letters to the governor and all. Mr. Howland says no one who has not been there can imagine the romance and beauty, and when you take into consideration the recent tragedies and the political side, you can see what a big book can be made."[15]

For a woman to travel alone to Cuba from the United States was virtually unheard of at the turn of the century. Gertrude had tried to persuade her sister Aleece to accompany her—she offered to pay for the $70.00 round trip from New York—but when Aleece declined, she went ahead alone, sailing in February 1900. She wrote to John Lane, "You cannot imagine the discomfort and tediousness of travel to Cuba. . . . As I am apparently the first woman who has ever travelled alone here, and as they have the Spanish idea about such things, it is often very disagreeable. Still, it has to be done or there will be no book."[16]

Obstacles abounded. On board ship they were driven back six hours by a severe storm. Once docked in Havana she learned of the yellow fever epidemic. Although a massive clean-up effort was under way, sanitation was more primitive and health-threatening than in any city she had so far visited. "There is a stream that runs through the middle of Havana from the slaughter house to the bay and today I saw it *red*. I won't get over it for a month."[17]

She carried with her a letter of introduction to "the grande dame of Havana," a woman who had lost $1,600,000 during the Spanish-American War and "did not have bread to cut in her palace while the Spanish were here," and who took Gertrude to board "in a marble palace, the handsomest private house in Havana, with a court full of banana trees in the middle and a large garden full of every sort of tropical plant, including palms sixty feet high.... There are curious double corridors with lofty ceilings.... The home looks something like the Treasury Building in Washington."[18] Her newly impoverished hostess promised to introduce her guest to "everybody of note" and "show her the life." She arranged for Gertrude to visit a sugar plantation and a battlefield where one of the significant insurgent battles had been fought.

Gertrude favored independence for Cuba. She told Lane, "What I want to accomplish is to prevent annexation [to the U.S.]. It would be a crime after people have struggled for fifty years for their liberty." Cuba escaped annexation, as she had hoped, but her Caribbean adventure proved a total failure. The trip spawned no literary progeny. The planned novel had to be scrapped when Gertrude's habitual fortitude gave way and she began to feel ill. She hated the heat, her teeth were bothering her, "and last night there was a rat in my room. A rat fills me with horror, and he went off with my best cake of soap."[19] Although she had been introduced to some important people, she lost interest in a man she had initially liked and developed an active antipathy to the American army personnel she encountered everywhere.

She was ready to leave by April, having stuck it out almost three months, but leaving presented its own set of obstacles. There were quarantine restrictions, and all her clothes had to be fumigated. She tried to send a trunk ahead and preserve its contents: "I must avoid fumigation for my velvet dresses. They burn and spoil things generally."[20] Her irritability peaked when she learned she would have to defer her anticipated return to London and sail instead for New York, where Lane wanted her on hand to help publicize *Senator North*. She berated him roundly for this restraint on her liberty and also for his failure to make good on her request to forward some money from her royalties to Aleece in San Francisco.

At last out of Cuba and resettled in New York in June, she apologized to Bierce for having been so long incommunicado, explaining, "if you had ever been in Cuba you wouldn't write to anyone either—you would probably forget how." The Cuban escapade, an unqualified disaster, was soon no more than a bad memory, one she did not even rekindle briefly in her autobiography.

The tropics and the Caribbean were to beckon again, however. While working on *Senator North* in Bruges, Gertrude had come upon a passage in James Bryce's *The American Commonwealth* that gave her pause. It concerned her grandfather's hero, Alexander Hamilton. Hamilton, Bryce had written, was "to Europe the most interesting figure in the early history of the Republic," yet his countrymen denied him due recognition. George Washington stood alone and unapproachable, like a snowy peak, but Hamilton, "of a virtue not so flawless, touches us more nearly, not only by the romance of his early life and his tragic death, but by a certain ardor and impulsiveness, and even tenderness of soul, joined to a courage equal to that of Washington himself."

Reading this, Gertrude experienced another of her creative thunderclaps. Bryce's words seemed to be "written in letters of fire." She recalled her grandfather's discourses on Hamilton, "but it needed this summary, this splendid tribute from a great authority to excite my imagination as it never had been excited before, rescue him from the undeniable obscurity into which he had fallen, give him back his fame. It seemed to me that all my training as a novelist had been but toward this end" (*Adventures*, p. 310). Early in 1901 she began to formulate a plan: "I don't know what my next novel will be about, but I do know that I never can be content to write about ordinary, everyday men again. That is the reason I want to study the life of Hamilton, to write it."[21]

She determined on an innovative course, one that would allow her to combine the techniques and imaginative prerogatives of fiction with a biographer's research methods. In throwing the graceful mantle of fiction over the "sharp hard facts" of history, she hoped to attract a wide audience and accomplish her lofty goal: nothing less than the "raising from the dead of Alexander Hamilton."

She went first to Washington for a close look at the portrait of Hamilton in the Treasury Building, "and was agreeably surprised to find that he had been as handsome as he was gifted." She would keep a copy of this portrait—as she had done previously with pictures of Bierce and Cecil Rhodes—on her dressing table, mantelpiece, or wall. Her icons are always a clue to her current ideals and imaginings.

In New York, where she had furnished an apartment at the Iroquois on West Forty-Fourth Street, she began reading everything she could find by or about Hamilton and his contemporaries. She made contact with Hamilton's grandson, Dr. Allan McLane Hamilton, who showed her some private papers and "such relics as he possessed," but discouraged any mention of the rumored illegitimacy of his famous forebear. To find out the facts of Hamilton's birth and early life she would have to do what no prior biographer of Hamilton had yet troubled to do: visit his birthplace, the island of Nevis in the West Indies, and the other scenes of his childhood, St. Kitts and St. Croix.[22]

From her friend Senator Hale she obtained letters to the various American consuls in the West Indies, explaining her purpose and requesting their cooperation. Since she did not want to repeat her Cuban mistake of traveling alone, she persuaded a friend and fellow resident of the Iroquois to come along. This was Grace Lounsbery, a relative of Edith Haggin (of an old San Francisco family) and a poet whose work Gertrude was pressuring John Lane to publish. "There is no question of her ability," she told him, "and no question that she has made up her mind to have the literary career, so the thing to do is to get her started. . . . She lives in this apartment house and I find her so solidly clever and so natural and unassuming that I feel a personal interest in seeing her started."[23] Lane published a volume of Lounsbery's verse, *An Iseult Idyll*, the following year.

On February 19, 1901, the two women set out. "The boat was a mere cockle-shell and little used to passengers; it was one of a 'fruit line.' The food was bad; there were rats. And we nearly turned upside down in a storm off Cape Hatteras" (*Adventures*, p. 318). After touching at St. Thomas and St. Croix, they landed at St. Kitts and established themselves in the one boarding house on the island, a place infested with three-inch cockroaches, where the bath was a hole in the ground in a pitch-dark room on the other side of the court.

On St. Kitts, where they had a scare concerning a resident ghost, and later on Nevis, Gertrude and Grace Lounsbery had to share a bed, a fact Gertrude tosses into her autobiography with casual good humor and no hint of sexual innuendo. (Elsewhere, commenting on a too-demonstrative woman friend, she says, "I never held a woman's hand in my life.") However, Grace Lounsbery apparently was a lesbian who had known Gertrude Stein during student days and would know her again in Paris. Alice Toklas liked her better than Gertrude Stein did and wrote of her: "She was small and not unimpressive in her funny little way. She considered herself a Greek scholar and wrote Greek plays. When she was young she came to Paris . . . [and lived in a flat] painted in the fashionable manner of the day in black. Later, she moved, with beautiful Esther Swainson, down to the rue d'Assas."[24]

Gertrude considered the athletic Miss Lounsbery "an ideal travelling companion, always ready for anything." She was "a valiant gallant little thing whose intellect had been trained at Bryn Mawr [and who] detested feminine weaknesses, and dressed herself in severe tailor-made frocks in the fond belief that they made her look like a boy" (*Adventures*, p. 326). Clearly, she was aware of her friend's mannish appearance and—initially at least—completely accepting of it. (In the autobiography she tactfully omits direct reference to the proclivities of any of her several homosexual or bisexual friends, though she many times recoils at effeteness and preciosity. If she herself had ever felt, as Bierce once suggested, attracted to other women, she probably would have fancied the "Romance Queen" type, like Lady Colin Campbell.) We will never know if Lounsbery's sexual preference drove a wedge into their friendship or if the two women simply lost touch. Gertrude, as we have seen, allowed many once intense connections to dwindle into extinction. She manages to misspell Miss Lounsbery's name in *Adventures*, never refers to her after the West Indian part of the narrative, and almost surely failed to look her up when she visited Paris in the 1920s. But during the trip they seem to have remained on the best of terms.

If the accommodations on St. Kitts were primitive, the setting proved exotically beautiful: "a long green island fringed with palms and rising to a volcanic mountain in whose crater lava moved sluggishly" (*Adventures*, p. 318). Monkeys leapt around banana and coconut trees, and terraces overflowed with "the intense red and orange of the hibiscus and the croton bush, the golden browns and softer yellows of less ambitious plants, the sensuous tints of the orchid. . . . The slopes to the coast were covered with cane-fields, their bright young greens sharp against the dark blues of the sea."[25]

When she began making inquiries about records concerning Hamilton's birth, Gertrude learned that her task would not be an easy one: the church in Nevis, the neighboring island where he was born, had been burned by the French in 1782. If any records had survived, Gertrude was going to have to dig them up for herself. Charged with excitement, she and Grace Lounsbery set out for Nevis in a large sailboat. As they approached the island, they could see the ruins of great houses that had been built by wealthy planters and the remains of the once thriving Charles Town. The American vice-consul greeted them at the landing and promised to take Gertrude to the Court House the following morning.

There she combed the unindexed "ponderous volumes" of Common Records, turning over the tomes page by page in search of three names: Fawcett, the maiden name of Hamilton's mother Rachael; Levine (or Lavien), her married name; and James Hamilton, his presumed father. Toward the end of the long search she came upon her first clue: a deed of separation between Hamilton's maternal grandparents, the John Fawcetts.

Returning to St. Kitts, she haunted its Court House, where the clerks had begun to call her "Mrs. Hamilton." After days of scrutinizing volumes that unaccountably bore the scent of opium, she found a deed from Mary Fawcett bequeathing three slaves to "My beloved daughter Rachael Levine." The document was dated eight months before the verified date of Hamilton's birth, indicating that at the probable time of the infant's conception Rachael had not married James Hamilton.

As Gertrude learned about Hamilton's mother Rachael, she began to identify with her more and more closely. Rachael had been brilliant, isolated, and vilified for immorality. She was the victim of a miserable early marriage to an oaf from whom she separated but could not (Gertrude believed) divorce. Rachael had no memory of her father, and she possessed intellectual powers that "in a later day might have taken the form of mental creation." Rachael's eyes, the very carriage of her body, "expressed a stern aloofness from the small and common exteriorities of life."[26] She was assuming the shape of an eighteenth-century Gertrude Atherton.

On the Danish island of St. Croix Gertrude found in the Burial Register a record of Rachael's death at age 32, and searched in vain for her grave at the Grange estate where there was a family cemetery. Before leaving St. Croix (and also before her trip to Denmark, where she learned that Rachael had served a jail sentence for adultery and *had* been divorced by Levine) she had a monument erected to Rachael Fawcett Levine, identified as the mother of Alexander Hamilton. It stands in the plot in the old Lytton Grange house, "under the ancient mahogany trees in a glade below the St. Croix hilltop."[27]

If she regarded Rachael as a version of herself, Gertrude viewed young Hamilton as a precocious, idolized son. Maternal feelings that she had denied her children—and herself—came pouring out of her in a flood of romantic idolatry. Her attachment became "so strong, so maternal, that I could not bear to part from him. In fact, I rewrote the last chapter three or four times before I could bring myself to sever the relation between us."[28] *The Conqueror* makes no attempt to be restrained or objective. It gushes adoration, showing Hamilton to be more brilliant, passionate, industrious, and far-seeking than any other leader of his generation. Despite his illegitimacy, his blood is the bluest, his hands and feet the smallest, his energy and spirit the highest that imagination can conceive. Physically small, he is in every other way a giant, a colossus, a lion. His faults—infidelity to his wife, rigidity, a hot temper—only confirm his genius, for "brain and character cannot grow side by side to superhuman proportions." Geniuses should not be expected to observe such bourgeois conventions as marital fidelity. "To expect a man of Hamilton's order of genius to keep faith with one woman for a lifetime would be as reasonable as to look for such genius without the transcendant passions which are its furnace." He embodies "all that is greatest in the American evolution," including an iron will to succeed. "To him failure was incomprehensible . . . for self-confidence and indomitability were part of his equipment."[29]

Compared to him, Jefferson and Monroe "had the spirit of the mongrel." Only Washington emerges as a hero of equal stature, and Hamilton is shown to be his most trusted aide, his substitute son, and the author of his Farewell Address. Gertrude was so competitive herself and so prone to thinking in polarities that she was not content to crown her hero the greatest; she had to diminish other contenders.

So deep was her love for Alexander Hamilton that she assuaged the pangs of separation she felt on finishing the book by promising herself she would some day write a conventional biography of him. She never did, but she went on to Denmark to continue her research on his early life, incorporating her findings in an edition of documents and letters called *A Few of Hamilton's Letters* (1903). She returned to Nevis several times in fiction, using it as the scene for *The Gorgeous Isle* and a part of *Julia France*. And she appointed herself custodian of Hamilton's image, exploding in a rage when a photograph of "that hideous old" George Arliss in a 1920s film version of Hamilton's life was placed without her consent on the cover of a Stokes reprint of *The Conqueror*. For the frontispiece of *A Few of Hamilton's Letters* she picked a bust of Hamilton that shows "his most striking likeness to the Caesars."

She completed the actual writing of *The Conqueror* in New York and in the Adirondacks in the summer and winter of 1901. It was brought out not by John Lane, but by a publisher with which she began a new affiliation, Macmillan. Signs of strain in her relationship with Lane had surfaced when she was in Cuba. It deteriorated beyond repair when he fired his New York assistant, Temple Scott —his most aggressive sales promoter—and when he bungled the release of *The Aristocrats*, a book Gertrude had completed just before setting out for the West Indies.

About the firing of Mr. Scott she fulminated in a letter to Lane: "He is the only person connected with your firm . . . who has shown sufficient energy and business ability to sell a respectable number of *my* books, at least. He raised your firm over here from a dilettante concern into a business house of some pretensions. . . . He advertised you like any other first class house, . . . paid accounts when they were due, sold our books as no one connected with your house has ever sold them before." She lamented having sunk some of her best books "with a publisher who considers himself first, last and always," and who had the nerve to send proofs collect. Now, with Scott gone, the old business of delayed payments and inadequate promotion would resume, and she wanted out.[30]

And what a mess Lane had made of her carefully orchestrated ruse involving the anonymous publication of her satiric epistolary novel, *The Aristocrats*. He had brought it out in early April of 1901, more than a month late, and she exploded at him: "I arrived from the West Indies this morning to be greeted by the information that *The Aristocrats* has only been out a week. The contract said March 1. Do you really imagine that you can have your own way in everything? I insist that you pay me $250 advance royalties, as indemnity for the loss of spring trade."[31] To make matters worse, Lane had been so fearful that the book might offend people, he had considered making some alterations in the text, which aroused the predictable furies: "Don't you presume to make the slightest alteration or there will be trouble. The contract gives you no such liberty. . . . This is the last book which will ever subject me to any annoyance from you."[32]

Meanwhile she had her little joke at the expense of the American literary elite. Reviewers praised the book's wit, spirit, and cleverness, even though they themselves were being exposed in it as emasculated prigs, snobs, hypocrites, and bloodless cowards, afraid of real passion and incapable of making independent judgments. American critics could swallow such sentiments as "a woman has passion exactly like a man," or "to be great in American literature you've got to be a eunuch," so long as they were expressed by an unnamed, possibly British author. They would have been unforgivable coming from the acknowledged pen of Gertrude Atherton.

Eastern literary journals joined in a spirited guessing game about the writer's identity. "We think it is the work of an American woman who knows a great deal about England rather than an English woman who knows a great deal about America," wrote Harry Thurston Peck of the New York *Bookman*. M. H. Vorse surmised in *The Critic* "that the author must have suffered at the hands of the aristocrats." Several reviewers commented that the author came down harder on the foibles of women than of men.[33]

With her accustomed theatricality, Gertrude plotted the timing and placement of the revelation of her authorship. "Please do not use my name till I say the word," she advised Lane. "If an anonymous book is selling it is often fatal to satisfy curiosity."[34] Later she revealed, "I have given *The Bookman* exclusive permission to announce it in the September number. . . . They are very much delighted with what they call 'the bomb,' will open the magazine with the announcement."[35] It read:

There has been so much surmise and controversy about the authorship of *The Aristocrats*, and so many absurd guesses have been hazarded that we are very glad to be at liberty to put the matter at rest. *The Aristocrats* was written by Gertrude Atherton. Ever since she began to publish, her work has been greeted in this country with a certain amount of abuse, and in consequence it has been with a very keen relish that she has found that those newspapers which have been most consistent in denouncing her have been loudest in their praise of *The Aristocrats*.[36]

As usual she basked in the publicity she had generated and verbally boxed John Lane's ears for missing a unique advertising opportunity: "It is now a month since the authorship was announced in *The Bookman*, and it has received a large amount of additional free advertising by the press. . . . And yet with an extraordinary lack of business enterprise you have not taken advantage of this."[37]

Her decision to switch to Macmillan—she was now in a strong enough position as a writer to direct her own course—undoubtedly owed something to publisher George Platt Brett's reputation as an excellent merchandiser who brought business acumen and meticulous attention to detail to the prestigious Macmillan imprint. Brett was the publisher of James Bryce as well as that best-selling American author of historical romance, Winston Churchill. He had recently signed on a promising new author from California named Jack London.[38]

Brett thought the title *Alexander Hamilton* too flat and proposed a list of alternate titles, of which *The Conqueror* was one. He praised the completed manuscript when Gertrude sent it down from Tarrytown, but he asked her to cut 150 pages of it before sending it on to the printer. Defiant, and too vain and impatient to think she might make her book better by considering his editorial advice, she sent it on without even opening the package, a characteristic but unfortunate move. The book would have benefitted hugely from a rigorous pruning, particularly of the tedious latter half. The comment in the British *Saturday Review*, "she has given us a long book instead of a great one," must be heartily seconded, with the qualification that the opening section on Hamilton's background and upbringing in the West Indies still makes exciting and atmospheric reading.

The Conqueror received mixed, sometimes patronizing reviews. Praised for her scholarship and vigor, Mrs. Atherton was chided for "feminine" emotional exaggeration and hero-worship, "violent partisanship" and "lack of judicial poise." Perhaps Hamilton's illegitimacy might be forgiven, but not his moral lapses as an adult. The book contained too many "antiquated Byronic disquisitions upon the inalienable right of genius to be as immoral as it pleases."[39]

She was accused of unfairness to Thomas Jefferson, who is portrayed as physically repulsive, deceitful, and vindictive and blamed for an antiaristocratic bias that launched the United States on its deplorable egalitarian course. In a responding letter to the *New York Times* she admitted that she was "a good hater" who was "subject to intense enthusiasms." But she claimed she had started the book "with no prejudice against the Father of Democracy, little as I like his child." She acknowledged Jefferson's great mental and creative powers, but accused him of having "plebeianized this country with such thoroughness that it is more uncomfortable to live in than any Kingdom in Europe." What she seems to be saying in defense of her attack on Jeffersonian democracy is that Europe outclasses America, since in Europe servants know their place.

As for Hamilton, "It is possible that I idolize him, but I have not idealized him. As I brought him up from babyhood, I should like to ask who should know him better?" She freely confessed that she saw Hamilton as a romantic hero and thanked Burr for having provided him an appropriately dramatic death; if Burr had not shot him in a duel he would have "breathed his last prosaically in bed a year or two later."[40]

With *The Conqueror*, a book that owed its very existence to a disdain for the common herd, Gertrude Atherton at last achieved significant and sustained public success in America. Mr. Brett of Macmillan had been unsure of the sales potential of a fictionalized biography of Alexander Hamilton and had offered an advance of only $500. Within a week after publication the book had passed the

25,000 mark and earned its author another $3,000. Within a year it had sold 70,000 copies. Never allowed to go out of print, it passed the half-million mark by 1938, and by 1940 Gertrude was boasting that she, unlike Ellen Glasgow and Willa Cather, had written a book that sold over a million copies.[41]

Gertrude had a well-oiled mechanism for handling rejection or failure. She could point to the hostility of American critics, East Coast resentment of her Californian insurgent spirit, or her independence from the editorial mainstream. In private, during the early 1890s, she could occasionally look inward, blaming failures on her own inadequacies. When she was struggling to find a voice and an identity that would at the same time allow her to make a living and a name, she could sometimes admit her self-doubt to herself, and sometimes to Bierce. But now that she had one big seller, her English renown, and a long list of published titles under her belt, she puffed up with pride. Self-congratulation became the order of the day, and worldly success the shrine she worshipped at. Now that she considered herself a winner, her Social Darwinist beliefs were set in concrete: life was a competition in which victory rewarded talent. People got what they deserved. Finally the world had come round to placing Gertrude Atherton among the conquerors.

Gertrude Atherton, frontispiece for *The Bell in the Fog*, 1904 (California Historical Society)

(*Left*) Reginald Birch cartoon showing Gertrude Atherton driving a chariot made from a book and drawn by a four-in-hand of four continents, Munich, 1903; inscribed by Poultney Bigelow (Florence A. Dickey)

Gertrude Atherton with George Sterling, about 1902 (Bancroft Library)

(*Far left*) Ina Coolbrith (Bancroft Library)

(*Left*) Cora Older (Bancroft Library)

HARPER'S WEEKLY

EDITED BY GEORGE HARVEY

SAN FRANCISCO'S TRAGIC DAWN

By GERTRUDE ATHERTON

LOOKING DOWN CALIFORNIA STREET FROM NOB HILL

HARPER & BROTHERS, NEW YORK
MAY·12 1906   PRICE 10 CENTS

Harpers Weekly cover, May 12, 1906: "San Francisco's Tragic Dawn" (California Historical Society)

Maude Fay in Munich Opera
(Bancroft Library)

Gertrude Atherton as "California Welcoming the World," Albert Herter mural for Hotel St. Francis, 1913 (California Historical Society)

Vol. I   AUGUST, 1918   No. 7

THE
AMERICAN
WOMAN'S
MAGAZINE

PUBLISHED BY THE
VACATION ASSOCIATION, Inc.   58 West 49th Street, New York

YEARLY SUBSCRIPTION $1.00   SINGLE COPY 10 CENTS

Pupils of Isadora Duncan
dance for War Relief Fund,
1918 (Leider)

"American Woman in War-
time," cover by Stacy H. Wood
for *The American Woman's
Magazine*, edited by Gertrude
Atherton, 1918 (New York Public
Library)

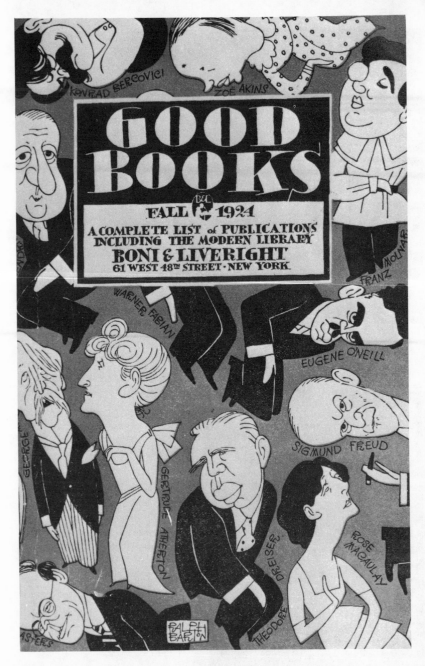

Ralph Barton cartoon cover for Boni & Liveright's fall 1924 catalog,
showing Atherton and other Liveright authors, including Freud, Dreiser,
George Moore, and Edgar Lee Masters (Reproduced with the permission of
Liveright Publishing Corporation)

Dr. Eugen Steinach injecting a cow with female sex hormone; from his book *Sex and Life: 40 Years of Biological and Medical Experiments* (Viking, 1940; New York Public Library)

Gertrude Atherton, signed and dated 1916 (Bancroft Library)

Dr. Harry Benjamin, by Bruno (Harry Benjamin)

Corinne Griffith, center, as Countess Zattiany in the 1924 First National/ Frank Lloyd Productions film *Black Oxen* (Museum of Modern Art, New York)

(*Below, left*) Muriel Atherton Russell with her daughter Florence, 1920s (Bancroft Library)

(*Below, right*) Gertrude Atherton with Helen Wills (Bancroft Library)

Approaching Villa Montalvo (Bancroft Library)

November 1926 luncheon at Montalvo for Pueblo Indian leaders; Gertrude Atherton is at right, opposite Senator Phelan, and Helen Wills is at extreme left (Bancroft Library)

Gertrude Stein de-
planing, 1935 (Bancroft
Library)

Gertrude Atherton
posing for a portrait
(Bancroft Library)

Gertrude Atherton at 89, standing before her books and a portrait of her earlier self; *Life*, November 11, 1946 (Photo: N. R. Farbman. Life Magazine, © 1946, Time, Inc.)

CHAPTER TEN

San Francisco, 1902-1907

After her success with *The Conqueror* Gertrude showed a new willingness to weave San Francisco back into the fabric of her life. Having stayed away from her native city for nearly ten years—and missed her mother's death, her daughter's wedding, and the arrival in 1899 of her first grandchild—she began in her mid-forties to make annual migrations of several months' duration.

Her new acclaim partly explains the altered pattern. Previously she had felt herself "a mere notoriety" in California; now she was being hailed—at least by some—as a scholar, patriot, and best-selling celebrity author. Coming home on her own terms, she could boast to George Brett at Macmillan, "They are making a good deal of fuss over me, and the editor of the *Bulletin* [Fremont Older] and others are getting up a banquet for me, to be given at the Bohemian Club. The other day at the Women's Press Club they overwhelmed me, as they looked upon me with horror a few years ago. I have had as many flowers as a prima donna."[1]

"As a prima donna." Perfect! She reveled in her new glory, for it forced her previous detractors to eat a bit of crow. During the years when she was struggling to make her mark, the Athertons for the most part judged her harshly; she had failed George as a wife and Muriel as a mother. Now she swelled with satisfaction when informed by her late husband's brother Faxon Jr. that everyone "keeps asking him if he's a relation of mine."

Where once she had been shunned by elite clubs like the Century, now she sat in the chair of honor. The Sequoia Club feted her at a reception attended by the poet Ina Coolbrith, the painter Maynard Dixon, and an obscure young woman of gypsy-like appearance, Alice B. Toklas, who perceived Gertrude as the embodiment of everything she was not: beautiful, daring, free.[2]

Gertrude found San Francisco improved—much built up, prosperous, full of tourists, and teeming with restaurants and theaters—but still small-townish compared to London, New York, or Munich, where she was living most of the time now. She exclaimed in a letter to Brett, "*Dios de mi alma!* it is provincial! Two girls interviewed me today for two of the leading papers and they wouldn't keep a job two days in New York. Such ignorance, such out-of-touchedness. Even their grammar was shaky." She went on about a new addition to the family: not her son-in-law or grandchild, but Aleece's second husband: "my sister's new husband Ashton Stevens is considered the brightest young man in San Francisco journalism."[3]

Ashton was one of the few male relatives Gertrude genuinely liked, despite the fact that as a drinker he rivaled her father and S. S. Chamberlain. The waggish, banjo-playing Ashton (who supposedly gave banjo lessons to his boss, William Randolph Hearst) worked as drama critic for the *San Francisco Examiner*, and Gertrude, even in this haughty phase, always relished the lively company of newspaper types. Fifteen years younger than Gertrude, he was convivial enough as critic and carouser to win the friendship of many a playwright and leading lady. When Sarah Bernhardt came to San Francisco after the earthquake, it was Ashton Stevens, together with photographer Arnold Genthe, who shepherded her through the ruins.

He even charmed Gertrude out of her adamantine belief that a married man should be his wife's financial provider. Gertrude continued making generous contributions to the Stevenses support long after their marriage. She instructed Brett, while she was in Munich, to "send my sister Mrs. Ashton Stevens a thousand dollars of my coming royalties. . . . I want Ashton to knock off work for several months before he collapses altogether and have offered my sister the money on condition that he goes to the country and takes an absolute rest, doing no newspaper work whatever."[4] Gertrude was also sending money regularly to her other sister Daisy. By 1903 Daisy was alone with a daughter after two failed marriages and a bout with morphine addiction—developed from being overmedicated for rheumatism (*Adventures*, p. 412)—and was living the restricted life of a cardiac invalid. The money being sent to Aleece was also meant to cover some of Daisy's medical emergencies. "I have a younger sister who is at death's door with a complication of horrors and a worthless husband (California style.) I have been supporting her for some time but Aleece might need a larger amount suddenly. I have a daughter who is rich—she inherited what I would have had half of if my husband had outlived his mother—but she is inclined to be closefisted and her husband more so. She and Aleece had a grand row some time ago but have now made up on my sister's death-bed."[5]

Never once in any of her letters from San Francisco or Munich in these early years of the new century does Gertrude allude to her grandmotherhood. She so resisted this role that, although she often stayed with Muriel's family when she visited the Bay Area, her grandchildren were taught not to address her as "Grandmother" or "Grandma." Florence, born in 1903, and her older brother George were instructed to call her "Mrs. Atherton," which they simplified to "Middy Addie" after the youngest grandchild, Dominga, was born. "When we were little," Florence recalled, "if she'd come over and stay with us, she was usually writing, and we were told to be very scarce, stay out of the way and be quiet and not disturb her. As a consequence we didn't really feel that she was a grandmother. So my brother first used to call her 'my mother's mother' as a name. . . . So then this nick-name was changed to just plain 'Mrs. Atherton' and eventually to 'Middy Addie.' "[6]

Muriel herself—who lived with her husband and children part of the year in San Francisco and part in the Marin County community of Belvedere—had emerged in young adulthood as a maternal, domestic, unambitious woman of the sort her mother often disparaged in print. A devout Catholic (although her husband was not), she was forbidden by the church to read many Atherton novels, as were her children as they grew up. According to granddaughter Florence, *A Daughter of the Vine*, whose alcoholic heroine bears an illegitimate child, was singled out as particularly wicked. Hospitable, nurturing, conventionally feminine, and submissive, Muriel was no match for her formidable mother. Few people were.

When Gertrude was away in Munich or elsewhere, she rarely heard from Muriel, who was not much of a letter writer and whose portion of Spanish blood, Gertrude felt, carried with it a certain lassitude: "I hear seldom from California," Gertrude wrote to Ina Coolbrith from Munich. "Mrs. Russell [Muriel] has inherited the manana characteristic of the race and writes about four times a year."[7] If Muriel harbored resentment for having been abandoned by her mother—and it is hard to imagine she did not—perhaps this reticence was the only acceptable way she found of expressing it. However, when her mother visited, Muriel offered unstinting and attentive solicitude, often providing a temporary home for the woman who had never stopped long enough in one place to make a home for her.

As the end-of-year holidays for the year 1905 approached, Gertrude settled in for a long season in California. She was at work on not one but two California novels, after having sought other locales for her books since 1899. The reason for this renewed interest in Californian themes, and a compelling additional motive for her resumption of lengthy visits to San Francisco, may have been her deepening friendship with James Duval Phelan. About him she would write "although I have had many friends among men, never have I had one so devoted, consistent, loyal—and valued. He was a man of strong character, high ideals tempered with worldly cynicism, a broad and charitable outlook, and while one side of his mind was intellectual, with a great love of literature and particularly poetry, the other was shrewd, far-seeing, financial; and he was Nature's own politician" (*Adventures*, p. 415). Phelan was Ralston, her grandfather, Senator North, and Alexander Hamilton—with a bit of Ballard Smith blarney thrown in—all rolled into one.

James Duval Phelan, son of an Irish immigrant who made a fortune in San Francisco banking and real estate, had served three terms as reform mayor of San Francisco before the Union Labor Party, after a series of crippling strikes, put him out of office in 1902. A lover of beauty, of European culture and cities, a patron of the arts who himself wrote verse and essays, the Jesuit-educated Phelan ardently promoted California and especially San Francisco, doing everything he could to reward citizens who enhanced the fame or contributed to the glory of either.

When he and Gertrude—always "Mrs. Atherton" to him—first met in 1902, they did not immediately warm to one another. As she put it, "I don't think . . . he was (initially) attracted to me personally. Although but little over forty at that time [she was four years older], he was the old-fashioned type of male whose preference was for a less independent type of woman, one more exclusively feminine, leaving to man the honors and kudos of life. But I had added to the prestige of his beloved California, and therefore [was] worthy of homage. . . . I told him once that the reason he had never married was [that] . . . his one true love was California. He was not one to give away any secrets and merely smiled" (*Adventures*, p. 415).

When he heard she was at work on a romance concerning Count Nikolai Rezanov, the Russian trader and diplomat who fell in love, in the early 1800s, with Concepcion Argüello, young daughter of the commander of the San Francisco Presidio, Phelan dispatched librarian-poet Ina Coolbrith to uncover what she could on the subject; the result was typed and sent to Mrs. Atherton. She thanked him with characteristic formality, masking genuine emotion: "I am indeed a thousand times obliged for the papers. . . . It was most good of you to take all the trouble and I shall not forget it. I am very anxious to write a psychological rather than a narrative novel about Concepcion Arguello, but of course the more facts and color the better."[8] Phelan's solicitude reinforced her sense of connection with him; she also felt gratitude toward Ina Coolbrith. Their help enabled her to throw herself at once into the new novel, the popular *Rezanov*, her second historical romance.

Ancestors, the other California novel she was working on, had a contemporary 1904–6 setting, although its characters have links with "old" American, English, Spanish-Californian, and San Franciscan families and with previous Atherton novels about San Francisco. The heroine, Isabel Otis, is a descendant of Sam Adams and Don Jose Argüello, and a cousin of Helena Belmont; she currently manages a Petaluma chicken farm that she has inherited. Unlike previous Atherton heroines, she engages in the practical, workaday activities that provide her absolute economic independence and allow her to make a show of her superb competence and practicality.

Gertrude selected Petaluma, a poultry center in Sonoma County, as a good setting for a modern California novel when she went on a driving tour with Muriel—who owned and drove an early model automobile. Once settled there for the winter, Gertrude wrote to Phelan—who also owned a car and adored "motoring"—inviting him to drive up for a visit: "If you come up here, I would take you up in the cupola of this hotel and show you how charmingly the unjustly slandered Petaluma is situated. I would also give you a very good dinner, for the hotel is kept by a Swiss who has a French chef. It is cold here in the mornings but as soon as the sun comes out it is as warm as summer, and there are palms and oranges, magnolias and pepper trees in the gardens."[9] Clearly, they had become close friends by this time. That pleased her, as did the fact that she was getting a lot done, if quantity counts. The printed version of *Ancestors* runs beyond 700 pages. When the overweight manuscript was nearly complete, Gertrude left Petaluma, stored the bulky tome with Ashton and Aleece in San Francisco, and went over to the East Bay's Berkeley Inn to continue work on *Rezanov*.

The celebrated Mrs. Atherton enjoyed having her likeness preserved by artists. Early in 1905 she sat for sculptor Robert Aitken, who had molded the bronze Victory high above San Francisco's Union Square, commemorating Admiral Dewey's victory at Manila Bay, and who now carved Gertrude's portrait in marble. Aitken had an instinct for heroic subjects, monumentally interpreted. The portrait bust of Mrs. Atherton, said a reporter in the *Bulletin* who had seen it exhibited in the Bohemian Club, showed the influence of Rodin; "it is a strong portrait study; the expression of light and power over the firm, regular features is excellently caught."[10] The bust was bought by *Bulletin* editor Fremont Older and his writer wife, Cora, who lived in the hotel William C. Ralston had built but never lived to see completed, the luxurious Palace, in downtown San Francisco.

Newspaper advertisements of the day boasted that one of the Palace's luxury features was its sturdy resistance to earthquakes, but on the morning of the Great Earthquake—April 18, 1906—the

Palace Hotel, with its celebrated glass-roofed Palm Court, hydraulic elevators, and bay-windowed bedrooms, was an instant disaster area. The Olders escaped to safety, but the marble bust of Gertrude Atherton toppled from its pedestal and shattered on the floor.

Across the Bay, the actual Gertrude was awakened "by a noise like that of a regiment of cavalry charging across the world. . . . I sprang out of bed and opened the door. . . . There was a sound of crashing china and glass all over the house, a few screams. The shock was comparatively brief, and I was about to return to bed when the fun began. The earth danced, and leaped, and plunged, and roared. 'This is the end of California,' I thought. 'We are going to the bottom of the Pacific.'" Gertrude prided herself on her fearlessness, the mark of a California thoroughbred. Surrounded by falling chimneys and grinding rafters, she stood calmly in a doorway, which is considered the safest place to stand during an earthquake. When the quake seemed to wrench to a conclusion with a sudden violent twist, she turned "and saw a New York woman leaning against the wall, pallid and gasping. 'Quite a shake, wasn't it,' I said nonchalantly" (*Adventures*, pp. 404–6).

Although loathe to admit it, she did worry about her sisters in San Francisco and Muriel's family in Belvedere. Determined to get across the Bay to San Francisco, she found her way to the Oakland ferry and pushed her way on board. Surrounded by passengers who muttered about God's judgment against San Francisco's sinful ways and the approaching end of the world, she reassured herself that Belvedere remained intact. "So, apparently, was the city, sitting serenely on its hills." She had her first misgivings when she saw a column of smoke rising in the windless air. San Francisco was on fire (*Adventures*, p. 407).

Greeted at the San Francisco Ferry Building by a curtain of smoke and flame that obliterated the city, she asked a policeman how she could get to the Occidental Hotel on Montgomery Street, where Aleece and Ashton had rooms and where Gertrude had stored her trunk containing the almost-complete manuscript of *Ancestors* (which she would soon expand to incorporate an account of the earthquake and fire) and assorted memorabilia, including Bierce's letters to her (only *Ancestors* was saved). The policeman said the hotel had been evacuated and pronounced the city doomed. He advised her to return to Berkeley, which she did after encountering by chance a woman who had just come from Belvedere who assured her that Muriel was all right.

Late in the morning, safe in Berkeley, she lost the option of returning to the city when General Frederick Funston issued an order prohibiting anyone from entering San Francisco. She spent the night watching the hills of her native city burn, and listening to the incessant booms of the dynamite being used in an attempt to arrest the progress of the fire.

Next day, determined to reach Belvedere, she persuaded a man with a motor boat to ferry her to Marin in exchange for her $50 check on a New York bank. Since no one trusted a San Francisco bank, and she carried only a few dollars in cash, the New York account had saved her. "For years after I carried a hundred dollars in a money bag strapped to my waist, and of course had no use for it" (*Adventures*, p. 411).

From the private ferry she saw the place of her birth, Rincon Hill, as a mass of toppled chimneys, South Park a shambles. It was all "like some horrid picture by Doré, the smoky darkening atmosphere, . . . the square masses of flame, each seeming to embrace a block if not more, . . . the broken dislocated houses, the great haughty defiant buildings, with the superb conflagration behind them."[11] What remained of the Palace Hotel succumbed to flames when its private water supply ran dry. Old San Francisco, the San Francisco of her past, was gone.

In *Ancestors*, the bohemian painter Lyster Stone proposes a champagne toast to the lost San Francisco: "He held the glass high, pointing it first towards the middle of what had been Market Street, and was now a river of fire, then slowly shifting it along towards Kearny and Montgomery, as he named the restaurants that had given San Francisco no mean part of her fame. 'Here's to Zinkand's, Tait's, The Palace Grill! The Poodle Dog! . . . Coppa's! . . . And here's to the Cocktail Route, the Tenderloin, and the Bohemian Club! And here's . . .' By this time his voice was dissolving, and the glass was describing eccentric circles. 'Here's to the old city, whose like will never be seen this side of hell again'" (*Ancestors*, p. 698).

The earthquake crystallized Gertrude's thinking about San Francisco. Back in the days when she was writing "Letters from New

York" for the *Argonaut*, she had argued that the Pacific slope's temperate climate spawned talent, but failed to nourish it; a gifted person —like Sibyl Sanderson—had to leave in order to flourish and gain recognition. Now she saw the same argument in even more emphatic outline. Living on the brink—not just of a geographic continent, but of disaster—discouraged planning ahead or discipline while it encouraged fads, dilettantes, and dissipation. Again Lyster Stone—a tippling, not very focused or hard-working artist—explains how so many San Francisco writers, musicians, painters, and editors prefer sitting in restaurants, talking and drinking, to working: "A few are born with a drop of iron in their souls. They resist the climate, and the enchantment of the easy luxurious semi-idle life you can command out here on next to nothing, and clear out, and work hard, and make little old California famous. . . . Never was such a high percentage of brains in any one city. But they must get out. And if they don't go young, they don't go at all. San Francisco is a disease. You can't shake it off. And you don't want to. To Hades with ambition anyhow" (*Ancestors*, p. 369).

The earthquake also clarified her feelings about James Phelan, who found new opportunities to demonstrate his civic-mindedness, generosity, and rectitude. As one of the relatively few in town who owned an automobile, he took it upon himself to carry loads of dynamite wherever they were needed as part of the attempt to stop the fire. "It was during the first day that he had a singular experience. He was resting for a few moments on the lawn of his house out near the Mission, listening to the detonations, when he saw a piece of paper sailing before the wind. It fell at his feet and idly he picked it up. It was one of his canceled checks, and he knew that the Phelan Building, one of the finest office structures in the city, had been blown up. . . . He shrugged, and went forth to pack his car with another load of dynamite."[12] Gertrude cast her Mr. Phelan as the White Knight, rescuer not of damsels but of cities in distress. Never before much interested in local politics, she now found that her closeness to Phelan thrust her—when she was in town—into the very center of the hive that post-earthquake San Francisco became.

In the four years since Phelan's last term as mayor, San Franciscans had watched their city government set a new standard for venality and corruption. Boss Abraham Ruef, a highly intelligent lawyer who had written an undergraduate thesis on "Purity in Politics," ruled covertly as master of the shakedown. His puppet in the mayor's chair was "Handsome Gene" Schmitz, a violinist and theater orchestra leader who headed the musician's union at the time he secured the nomination as candidate of the Union Labor Party. During the Schmitz administration, as Phelan put it, "the red flag of anarchy turned out to be the red flag of the auctioneer—everything was for sale."[13] The Ruef machine collected payoffs from French restaurants, prostitutes, gambling halls, saloons, corporations, businessmen, Pacific Gas and Electric, and the United Railroads. Ruef in time admitted that the Board of Supervisors that had been swept into office in the 1905 election consisted of men so hungry for boodle they would "eat the paint off a house."[14]

Crusading *Bulletin* editor Fremont Older spearheaded the effort to throw the rascals out. He found moral and financial support from two reform-minded millionaires, Rudolph Spreckels, of the prominent sugar-business family, and James D. Phelan. Aided by President Theodore Roosevelt—who sent out a special prosecutor named Francis Heney and a famous detective named William J. Burns—the Graft Prosecution was launched.

But the earthquake intervened. Mayor Schmitz took the helm, moving swiftly to try to stop the fire, evacuate refugees, shelter the homeless, and suppress looting. He formed a committee of citizens to manage the relief effort, the Citizens Committee of Fifty. Phelan, who was trying to unseat him, became head of the Finance Committee, empowered to disburse the more than nine million dollars that would be donated for relief.

If Gertrude Atherton had been in charge, she would have given Phelan absolute authority. "I wish you could be elected a sort of dictator," she wrote from Belvedere, "for the next ten years. This is where the advantages of monarchy come in."[15] And from Munich she rhapsodized, "If I were out there I should prepare a Vigilance Committee with you as its head. No one else could manage it. If I outlive you I shall certainly be the first to propose that you have a monument—of reinforced concrete!"[16]

Gertrude's admiration and deep affection for Phelan shine through every word she ever wrote to or about him. Her letters to him are the frankest and most open of any since the days of her liveliest correspondence with Bierce; they have less wit and pointedness, less explosive energy than the Bierce letters, but more warmth. With Phelan she stood on much surer ground. She knew she held a secure place in his affections. Many who knew both have speculated on whether they became lovers as well as intimate friends. The question will never be resolved with certainty, because Atherton and Phelan shared a gift for covering their tracks. Both were emotionally reticent, willing to hide behind the masks of formal dress and address, and to use the conventions of etiquette as a language for feelings. From his deathbed he would dispatch a letter to her—dictated to his secretary—beginning "Dear Mrs. Atherton."

At the time she got to know Phelan, Gertrude was nearing the age of 50—an age she never, of course, mentioned or acknowledged to anyone. By then she does not seem to have prized a sexually active life, if she ever did. With George, the initial strong attraction had eventually given way to resentment at her enslavement to a man she did not respect, then separation. In the days of her early widowhood she did fall under the spell of men she considered powerfully "magnetic," like S. S. Chamberlain, Fred Somers, Ballard Smith, and Bierce himself. She never gave herself an easy time for having such feelings and sensations; they reminded her she did not have absolute control, and that alarmed her. If she slept with any of them, the evidence of novels like *Hermia Suydam* and *Ancestors* and of the letters to Bierce suggests she suffered pangs of remorse, for "free love" offended her Puritan moral inheritance.

Moreover, living in her head and in books, as she had from the time of her adolescence, pleased her more than sustained attachment to any person or place. And the body itself seems often to have offended her with its relentless indifference to the proprieties. In *Ancestors*, the sight of her former lover's corpse (he has died of Bright's disease, and Isabel unexpectedly sees his coffin in a Munich cemetery) provokes an outburst of revulsion: "I never dreamed that a brilliant mind could leave so miserable a shell behind, that the body was such a mean poverty-stricken thing. . . . I shrank and curdled with horror that I had loved that hideous clay" (*Ancestors*, pp. 268–

69). Isabel has kissed and embraced this one-time swain, but she tells Gwynne, the new man in her life, "that side of love seemed to me much over-rated. I was happiest when sitting alone in a sort of trance and thinking about him" (*Ancestors*, p. 340).

The courtly and magnanimous Mr. Phelan gave his ally Mrs. Atherton many lavish gifts and entertained her constantly at Montalvo, his country estate, where she had her own room after it was completed in 1914. He remembered her and members of her family in his will. Though an appreciator of beautiful women who was rumored to have had several mistresses at different times in his life (his will left one dollar to any self-proclaimed illegitimate heir), Phelan was also a dutiful, if less than devout, Catholic who was wary of marriage and well-established in his bachelor habits. He did not live a celibate life, but Mrs. Atherton was probably not a woman he chose to sin with; not because he found her unattractive, but because, by the time he met her, she had become so repressed and untouchable.

"Divine, austere . . . / Pride set upon her brow a barrier." These words of his from a poem called "Lines to a Bust of the Fifth Century B.C.," which Gertrude used as the epigraph to *The Immortal Marriage*, could refer to her as easily as to the sculpted head he ostensibly addressed. Mr. Phelan and Mrs. Atherton were probably not lovers, but they loved.

In San Francisco, in the summer and fall of 1906 and on into the next year, private love was not the only kind in evidence. In the wake of their city's destruction, San Franciscans banded together, commonly aware of human insignificance against nature's destructive power and of the size of the task of rebuilding that lay ahead. People were buoyant, hopeful. The *San Francisco Call* quoted Mrs. Atherton's opinion that the big quake "brought out the best in everybody who was going along in a rut, and created a new set of capable pioneers."[17] What they called "earthquake love" burst into bloom like a flowering plum. William James, who was teaching at Stanford at the time, wrote to his relatives in the East that he could feel "a kind of uplift in the sense of the common lot" that took away from the sense of loneliness.[18] In an era when class divisions and violent confrontations between capital and labor were at a peak, suddenly everyone seemed the same, equally bereft, equally responsible for facing the task of rebuilding from the ground up. As Lincoln Steffens, who wrote a series of muck-raking articles on the Graft Prosecution, put it: "With property destroyed and money worthless, there was no incentive to selfishness, so all men became good."[19]

Needless to say, the bloom faded. Money refused to remain worthless, and selfishness came back into style. People with insurance windfalls went on spending sprees, displaying their wealth as ostentatiously as possible. *Town Talk*, a San Francisco weekly, reported that at a Spinners Club reception for Mrs. Atherton, the guest of honor "stood out in sane and sober relief to the overdressed throng of women," some of whom made a show of diamond necklaces and ropes of pearl.[20]

To Gertrude and others who had known San Francisco from its infancy the atmosphere recalled the old gambling spirit of the 1850s. Citizens "bought out the shops, invaded the restaurants in gorgeous attire, packed the theaters and flew up and down the hills in automobiles."[21] They heatedly debated how the city should be rebuilt, how wide the streets should be, and whether trolleys should have overhead or underground wires. Energy and optimism seemed boundless.

The rest of the country hungered for firsthand accounts of the disaster that had reduced a Pacific coast metropolis to rubble and ash. Gertrude Atherton, along with such others as Jack London and Will Irwin, supplied some of the magazine articles that fed this appetite. Writing for *Harpers Weekly* in a piece dramatically titled "San Francisco's Tragic Dawn," Mrs. Atherton voiced her hope that the new San Francisco would be built along the lofty and aesthetic lines suggested by "City Beautiful" architect Daniel Burnham at the behest of Phelan's Association for the Improvement and Adornment of San Francisco. A few days before the earthquake, she reported, Mr. Phelan had sent her a book of the Burnham plans—plans which, if carried out, would make San Francisco, then a picturesque but haphazard, shabby, and unaesthetic city incomparably situated, into a metropolis as beautiful as Athens at the height of her glory. Phelan had told her how difficult he thought it would be to translate the design into a reality. "'How could you wake all these people up? How would you ever get all those signs off Market Street, all those hideous rows of houses out of the way? You couldn't even persuade their owners to put new facades on them. It will take fifty years!' And then," she continued, "Nature stepped in. She employed an unpleasant method, but she disposed of the signs and about three quarters of the buildings."[22] The Burnham plan, if implemented, would render the city "as classic and imposing as Nature had dreamed of when she piled up that rugged amphitheater out of chaos" (*Ancestors*, p. 179).

Time and again, when Atherton and other writers described the ruined city, they did so by summoning images of the beautiful ruins of classical antiquity. In *Ancestors* she likens San Francisco's post-earthquake eastern slopes, "with their arches and columns, towers and broken walls," to the Roman Forum and the Palatine Hill. She had so often looked to Europe for monuments eloquent of history, etched in time. Now, by becoming a ruin, the young city of San Francisco took on an ancient aura. Suddenly it suggested a rich and limitless past, remembered but forever lost. If the Burnham plan took hold, the city would cease to be a ruin, but it could retain an antique grandeur linking it with Periclean Athens and the Rome of the Caesars.

The phoenix-like rebirth of San Francisco after the disaster seemed all the more striking to Gertrude because she left for Munich (via Sitka, Alaska, and New York) three months after the quake and remained in Europe for nearly a year. She reported in *Harpers Weekly*: "When I left San Francisco . . . all of the business and a great section of the residence district was a waste of smoldering ruins. From the island of Belvedere . . . where I had been living, the hills of the city looked as if scattered with brown teeth, old rotting tusks." While in Europe she continued to picture it "still a forlorn waste of bricks and twisted wire. . . . I even fancied people still living in tents."

When she returned in the summer of 1907, she was instantly

"struck with the fact that the lower part of the city—I spent the night at the St. Francis Hotel—was no longer a wilderness, and that the streets were clean; but I was too much absorbed with my companions [she does not name them] to pay much attention to my surroundings. What was my amazement upon reaching Belvedere to look across the water and see the hills of San Francisco covered with houses."[23]

Although the Burnham plan was being ignored, she had only good things to say about the rebuilt city, which she now found "fresh, handsome and bustling." "The streets no longer looked dusty and old fashioned. . . . There are smart restaurants and there are great plate-glass windows." The brusque, get-on-with-it pace matched her own temperament, and she forgave businessmen who were too eager to get back in the swing to bother about conforming to an architectural overview. The remarkable speed of the rebuilding confirmed her Social Darwinist conviction that "progress is automatic. . . . The enterprising unit goes doggedly to work to retrieve his fortune on the spot."[24]

Municipal planning took a back seat to the exhilaration of reconstruction and the daily drama of the Graft Prosecution, which had resumed while Gertrude was in Europe. In the interim, Mayor Schmitz had been arrested on 27 counts of graft and bribery, and a new mayor had been appointed. Before the trials ended, Heney, the prosecutor, was shot, and Fremont Older kidnapped. "Boss" Ruef was the only one sentenced, Schmitz's conviction having been overturned on appeal. And the social fabric of San Francisco came apart.

When the prosecution began sniffing out bribes and pay-offs made by rich, socially prominent men, the business community turned against it. "Members of the prosecution were not bidden to entertainments where people of fashion gathered," wrote Cora Older. "Old friends fell away. Men in the clubs . . . fraternized with the corruptors of the city's government. Rich people withdrew their accounts from [Rudolph Spreckels's] bank. The *Bulletin* was boycotted by advertisers."[25] When Patrick Calhoun, president of the United Railroads, was indicted, "old friends ceased to speak to each other, people entertaining were given to understand that one party or the other must be invited at a time, and one went so far as to demand the sympathies of her guests as they entered her drawing-room; if they declared for the prosecution they were requested to withdraw." San Francisco had become a house divided.[26]

In the midst of all this strife and melodrama, Gertrude and Phelan were able to accomplish one worthy goal: the rescue of a lady in distress. Ina Coolbrith, the unofficial poet laureate of California (until 1915, when Senator Phelan officially crowned her with laurel at the Panama-Pacific Exposition) had lost her home and possessions in the fire. More than the author of commemorative stanzas and wistful lyrics, more than a well-known librarian who had guided the early reading of Isadora Duncan and Jack London and aided Mrs. Atherton's research on Rezanov, she was the state's literary matriarch. Everyone knew of her special place in early California literature, how she had been an editor of the *Overland Monthly* and, with Charles Warren Stoddard and Bret Harte, one of the "Golden Gate Trinity." Tall and grey-eyed, she had a dignified beauty matched by a generous heart. "The Sappho of the Western Sea," Edmund Clarence Stedman called her. "The sweetest note in California history," said Bret Harte. "A daughter of the gods," sighed Joaquin Miller, "divinely tall, / and most divinely fair."

Born Josephine Donna Smith of Mormon parents in Illinois, she had emigrated to California by wagon with her family in 1851 when she was ten. In her early twenties, after a catastrophic marriage and the death of her only child in Southern California, she came to San Francisco, adopted her mother's maiden name of Coolbrith, and began publishing poetry. As an *Overland* editor she developed friendships with Mark Twain, Bierce, and Miller, along with Stoddard and Harte. Her Russian Hill flat became a favorite literary gathering place, with the twilight-and-fresh-violets atmosphere of a small salon.

Calamity had a way of finding Ina Coolbrith. Though her reputation as a poet grew, she struggled to earn a living, not just for herself but for the new dependents she kept acquiring. She assumed responsibility for her mother, for the two children of her dead sister, and agreed to provide a home for the daughter of Joaquin Miller and a

Native American woman. Ina Coolbrith formed a wreath of Marin laurel for Byron's grave, but it was Miller who went to England and placed it there. As the writers she had befriended left, one by one, for wider arenas, she remained in the Bay Area, toiling for meager pay as a librarian, first in Oakland and then in San Francisco. Arthritis plagued her increasingly as she grew older; she lived with constant, at times incapacitating, pain. Her name became synonymous with the lost glories of early San Francisco, a poignant reminder of past associations, steadfast commitment to the literary life, and sorrows endured.

At the time of the earthquake she was in her mid-sixties and a near-invalid, able to work only part time as librarian for the Bohemian Club. She devoted much of her energy to a book of literary reminiscences she was writing, a firsthand history of California literature. In the flat she shared with her companion Josephine Zeller she stored manuscripts and a valuable file of letters from many writers, including Mark Twain and George Meredith.[27] Of these, only her scrapbook of clippings and a small box of letters were retrieved from the earthquake rubble. So were Zeller and Coolbrith herself, found "shivering in an open space" at Fort Mason by editor Harr Wagner.

Gertrude felt a personal debt to Ina Coolbrith, a fact that surprised the poet, who had heard stories about how prickly Mrs. Atherton could be, "especially [with] members of her own sex, with whom she did not largely affiliate. So I stood rather in fear of her, and more in awe." When they first met, at a Sequoia Club reception, Gertrude quashed any shyness on Ina Coolbrith's part by greeting her warmly, with both hands extended. Coolbrith continued to find her gracious in subsequent encounters, and "wholly unaffacted, with an easy dignity . . . ; witty, certainly, and a little caustic at times, but no more so than her knowledge of human life and nature, and her not always honey-rose-and-nightingale experience might warrant and develop; with the absolute courage of her convictions; a frankness not always an attribute of her sex . . . ; a more than usual feminine sense of justice and honor; generous and unselfish to a degree, and [with] a faith in, ambition for and love of women such as I wish were more largely shared by her sisters."[28]

Gertrude's display of warmth and generosity toward Ina Coolbrith does stand out as something quite different from her usual competitive and combative posture toward other women writers. The reasons are several, but the primary one is that Gertrude did not see the older, invalid Coolbrith as a threat. The fact that Coolbrith wrote poetry, not fiction, helped too; so did her association with a part of San Francisco's history that Gertrude genuinely valued. Mrs. Atherton could be bountiful and welcoming to other women writers—as we will see in her hospitality to Gertrude Stein—when she occupied a secure position of power and could take the role of the bestower of favors. When she felt she and another woman writer were contenders in the same ring and for the same trophy, her caustic, less than generous side—the "bad" profile she never liked to display in photographs—showed itself.

Two months after the earthquake and fire, Gertrude, through a third party, sent an anonymous check to Miss Coolbrith, declaring her own losses minimal and adding: "I think all California writers should feel a responsibility regarding Ina Coolbrith, for she was the first California woman to distinguish herself, her genius has never been questioned, and [her losses] are one of the chief tragedies."[29] She wrote to Coolbrith, urging her to try to continue writing, despite the lost manuscripts. "Of course the poetry is gone; inspiration does not come twice, but perhaps the history—and possibly the memories. . . . I do wish it were possible, as much for our sakes as for your own. . . . I wish I could do something."[30]

Gertrude could and did hatch the idea for holding a benefit Authors' Reading whose proceeds would go wholly and directly to Ina Coolbrith. A previous effort to help Miss Coolbrith had ended in disaster when a group called the Spinners launched a fund-raising effort in her name. They solicited contributions from the public and from the literary community received donated short stories that would be published in an anthology called *The Spinners Book of Fiction*. The writers came through handsomely, handing over their stories—many of which would have commanded high sums on the marketplace—in the belief that any money raised by the publishing venture would benefit Ina Coolbrith directly. George Sterling wrote a dedicatory poem comparing Coolbrith's verse to the music of the nightingale, wafting over "fallen marble pale." Stories by Jack London, Mary Austin, Charles Warren Stoddard, and Gertrude Atherton were printed in elegant type designed by John Henry Nash and published by bookseller Paul Elder. California artists donated color plate illustrations.

The Spinners' plan backfired when they used the funds they raised to purchase a bond. Interest it earned would be paid to Ina Coolbrith as "first beneficiary." She would receive, in addition, two cents for every book sold at a retail price of two dollars. It worked out that the profit to the "first beneficiary" came to less than fifty dollars a year, a token sum. Authors who had donated their work to the book were outraged, and the proud Ina Coolbrith, still without a permanent home after having been paraded before the public as an indigent invalid, felt wounded and demeaned. Eventually she returned in full the trivial amount the Spinners had bestowed.

Gertrude was incensed and made a prompt display of her celebrated frankness. She wrote to Ina Coolbrith that the Spinners were nothing more than a group of "good, fussy women who got a real sensation out of their scheme, bustled about, felt important," and then "made the worst bargain possible with the book—giving it to an amateur publisher, and at ten percent!" She vowed to press them to give the poet "the entire profits. If they don't do as I wish there will be war."[31]

Not one to sit on her hands, Gertrude set about the task of arranging an alternative benefit plan: an Authors' Reading. "I think it would be a good idea," she wrote Coolbrith from Belvedere, "as soon as the business tide turns again and the people are feeling happy, to have an 'Authors' Reading.' Joaquin Miller, [George] Sterling, Mary Austin, myself and several others should draw a full house of the curious."[32] She wanted to make it a fashionable affair, with press notice. Enclosing a check drawn from the advance she had received from Harpers for *Ancestors*, she reported to Coolbrith that "Porter Garnett [an artist] and James Phelan both think highly of the Authors' Reading scheme and the latter will take hold of it should the Spinners fail to raise money. I said that I would not go into it unless it was understood that the money raised would go directly to you."[33] Although she sought enough newspaper publicity to draw a good crowd (the event was being billed as San Francisco's first Authors' Reading), she tried to be discreet and to avoid that kind of invasive, patronizing comments on Coolbrith's situation that the Spinners had circulated.

A date, Thanksgiving eve, and location, the reopened Fairmont Hotel, were agreed upon. Cora Older was asked to join the roster of readers. "She would make a stunning figure on the stage," Gertrude wrote to Phelan, and "I should hate to see her left out." The *Bulletin* could be relied on to provide publicity, and the *Call* and *Chronicle* might publish some notices too. But Hearst's *Examiner* could "go to ————, where it belongs. Did you ever know anything so disgusting as its neutral attitude during the greatest crisis in the history of the city?"[34]

Naturalist John Muir was invited to read, but had not responded. Neither had Mary Austin, whose early work Ina Coolbrith had published in the *Overland Monthly* and who had subsequently made her name with her desert-evoking *The Land of Little Rain*. A member of Carmel's bohemian literary community who liked to wear her long hair loose and her garments flowing, she may have been put off by the formality of the Fairmont affair. Besides, Mrs. Atherton was doing the inviting, and they were not friends, particularly. "Of course *I* am the greatest woman writer living," she once (according to Gertrude) announced, to which Gertrude replied, "The hell you are, Mary."[35]

Jack London was off on his *Snark* expedition, sailing across the Pacific, but it is doubtful he would have appeared anyhow, despite his expressed gratitude to Ina Coolbrith. His fame would have outshone all the others'—Gertrude would *not* have liked that—and his socialism jarred with the patrician ambience (though he did belong to the less-and-less bohemian Bohemian Club). But an impressive array of writers had agreed to appear, and "unless the country goes entirely broke"—there was a brief economic depression throughout the United States in the fall of 1907—"we expect a brilliant affair." In fact, even excluding the "unknowns" who, according to Gertrude, clamored to get themselves included, the program was already too long, with too many readers scheduled.

On November 27, 1907, the night of the Reading described by the *Bulletin* as "the most notable gathering of Western literati ever known in San Francisco," a throng of formally attired guests jammed the newly restored gold-and-white Louis XV style ballroom of the Fairmont, whose classic Ionic pillars and Florentine mirrors bespoke imperial grandeur, Renaissance magnificence. Programs, expensively printed on fine paper, announced the carefully prearranged sequence of recitations and musical interludes. An array of prominent family names (Mrs. M. H. de Young, Mrs. Sigmund Stern) and prestigious clubs lent their cachet as patrons. In all, the event looked more like an opera opening than a literary soirée.

The guest of honor, however, failed to appear. Although Mr. Phelan sent a carriage for her and reserved a room at the Fairmont for her use, she remained cloistered with Miss Zeller at their temporary quarters. Miserable with rheumatism, she was also caring for her companion, who had been injured that day in a streetcar accident. Perhaps too she cringed at appearing in public as the recipient of charity. Or maybe, with all those promised eulogies, it seemed too much like attending her own funeral.

If Ina Coolbrith's presence was missed, at least her poetry was heard; her "Hymn of the Nativity," set to music and performed by a soloist with chorus, immediately followed an opening tribute by the dignified, whistle-clean new mayor, Dr. Edward Robeson Taylor. After the Coolbrithian glimpse of heaven, more somber thoughts intruded. George Sterling, up from Carmel, made a melancholy appearance. People often compared his darkly handsome, bony face to Dante's, but as Van Wyck Brooks suggested, it was Dante in hell. A Bohemian Club regular, drinker (Gertrude's pre-Reading letters to him kept reassuring him that cocktails would be served at the Fairmont), womanizer, and socialist, Sterling was then at the height of his (never great) fame as a poet. His friend and mentor Ambrose Bierce, whose literary judgments sometimes took a hyperbolic turn, had recently used his column in Hearst's *Cosmopolitan* to pronounce Sterling's *A Wine of Wizardry* on a par with Milton's *Comus* and Spenser's *Faerie Queen*. He anointed Sterling "a very great poet— incomparably the greatest that we have on this side of the Atlantic."

A reporter for *Sunset* magazine who knew of Bierce's accolade wrote that on the night of the Reading the slender and boyish poet did not appear spoiled by recent glory. The notes Sterling sounded from the platform were flute-like, plaintive, full of sadness and yearning. He mourned both the destruction of old San Francisco and a more recent tragedy, the death by suicide two weeks before of Nora May French, friend, lover, and fellow poet, whose love poem to death, "The Outer Gate," he recited. He also read his own sonnet "Romance," in which a crusading king returns home to confront his past. The king's brow is lit by sunsets, his glance is backward, and his heart fed "with music of the dead." Sterling expressed for many the feeling that, despite the terror, grief, and havoc it brought, there was something noble in the earthquake, something majestic and sadly beautiful.

Not noted for the brevity of her works, Mrs. Atherton read a story she called the shortest she ever wrote.

Luther Burbank had been persuaded to briefly abandon his Santa Rosa greenhouse—mercifully spared by the earthquake—and read a paper. He arrived well after the readings had begun and promptly fell asleep in the back of the room. Some of the press accounts reported him a no-show, but he was there, in fact, and was roused from slumber in time to read his piece and be acknowledged by resounding applause.[36]

The last reader on the program brought the crowd to its feet. He was Ina Coolbrith's old friend Joaquin Miller, the posturing poet and professional Westerner (born Cincinnatus Hiner Miller, in Indiana) acclaimed in England as "the Byron of Oregon." Decked out in trousers tucked into his boots, a lace tie, and flowing coat, his long white hair and matching beard shook as he intoned his poem "Columbus": "What shall we do when hope is gone? / Sail on! Sail on! and on!" There had been enough melancholy and lament. Now was the time to break into buoyant affirmation of hope for the future. San Francisco, like Columbus, would persist in a dauntless quest. "Sail on!" The crowd cheered.

Next morning, Gertrude wrote to Ina Coolbrith: "You don't know what you missed by being absent last night!" She told of the "great and brilliant crowd assembled to do you honor. The big ball room was packed to the doors and I am sure a fine sum of money was taken in. You certainly had a great personal triumph." She added a rare flourish of modesty: "To my mind Mr. Phelan deserves the larger share of the credit for last night's accomplishment."[37] One thousand dollars was handed over to Ina Coolbrith. Together with other dona-tions, it made the down payment on a Broadway lot on which she built herself a home. As for who deserved "the larger share of the credit," Ina Coolbrith had no doubt that it was Gertrude Atherton. "It was *her* idea, *her* plan, which Mr. Phelan and others . . . kindly assisted in carrying out. The ground upon which my home stands . . . is thus largely *Atherton* ground." [38]

Gertrude never entirely let go of her self-image as a firebrand, but in San Francisco she had worked her way to a long-coveted position close to the centers of power, wealth, and respectability, as a venerable public personality. Secure now in a way she had never been before, she showed herself capable not only of receiving homage but, when the moment and circumstances were right, of bestowing it.

CHAPTER ELEVEN

Munich: Magnificent Repose

In the years between *The Conqueror* and her feminist novel *Julia France and Her Times* Gertrude commuted every six months or so between the San Francisco area and her flat in Munich—the closest thing to a real home she had allowed herself since those barely remembered days of setting up house with George and the babies in the San Mateo woods near Valparaiso Park.

Why did she choose Munich? Partly because it was new to her and would afford her an opportunity to get to know the Continent as well as she knew England. She had the American's addiction to fresh starts, and a fresh start in a beautifully situated, culturally rich, and elegant European capital seemed an enticing prospect. Though her ties to San Francisco were now well secured, the United States still alienated her enough so that she did not want to make it her primary home; she did not feel she entirely belonged.

Although much more identified with America than she had been before her investment in the lives of Senator North and Alexander Hamilton and the forging of her close bond with James Phelan, Gertrude still nurtured an expatriate mentality. She preferred not to think of herself as part of the American literary scene, even though, of course, she in some ways epitomized it. American writers, she complained in a much publicized article called "Why Is American Literature Bourgeois?" in the *North American Review*, feel "no necessity to see the world." Shrinking from the "larger life" of the cosmopolitan arena, "they spend their years comfortably describing the little life about them. . . . Their utmost range is after dialect and local color."

"Timidity," she continued, "is a leech at the throat of originality. American literature today . . . is the most timid, the most anaemic, the most lacking in individualities, the most bourgeois, that any country has ever known." Renewing her old quarrels with Howells, the New England tradition, middle-class realism, and the blandness of American magazine fiction, she complained that American writers shared none of the audacity common to its politicians and millionaires. There was no comparison between American writers and "such men as [Theodore] Roosevelt, Pierpont Morgan, . . . Cleveland, or even Crocker—between our imminent financial supremacy, our devouring commercial inroads, our gigantic trusts violating many laws, our utter contempt for the survival of the monarchical superstition of the Old World—and our literature."[1]

One of the curiosities of this irritable outburst is that it might have been written in the 1880s or early 1890s, instead of 1904; it doesn't acknowledge the impact on the early-twentieth-century American fiction scene of a new breed of popular, ambitious, acclaimed, Western, and by no common definition "bourgeois" American realist—like Jack London and Frank Norris. Nor does it do more than give the nod to that most eminent Europeanized American novelist, Henry James, or even mention the names of the several well known American authors who, like Gertrude Atherton, had spent considerable time living and writing abroad.

As usual, Gertrude's various arguments and accusations failed to add up to a consistent or well-thought-out point of view. She wanted American writers to display the daring of the Robber Barons, but at the same time she objected to the commercialism besetting the New York publishing scene. She went to Munich, she said, to get away from other Americans and from from the "money-making atmosphere, the everlasting and demoralizing talk of 'best-sellers' and new geniuses."[2] If she had been more self-aware, she might have acknowledged a point made by Upton Sinclair, who published an angry rejoinder to "Why Is American Literature Bourgeois?" in *Col-*

liers. Gertrude Atherton herself, he asserted, "is one of the most bourgeois of our writers. We have no writer more readily impressed with bigness than Gertrude Atherton, more ready to accept it as greatness."[3]

She might also have realized that the competitive spirit that she prized so highly in herself and other Americans was in her own life taking a bit of a holiday. The frenzy of production that had dominated her existence since the death of Georgie, some twenty years earlier, and the accompanying zeal to prove herself a Somebody abated during the Munich years, in part because she felt satisfied—though by no means sated—with the success she had already achieved. For the first time, she organized her days around pleasure, as much as work. Merely being in Munich, she thought, enlarged her perspective and expanded her horizons, while delighting her senses.

She held fast to an essentially naive notion that her range as a writer would increase in proportion to the breadth of her European travels; and that writing about aristocrats, millionaires, potentates, and castles provided a resonance, excitement, and color that could serve as a corrective to the thinness she so lamented in American fiction. It did not occur to her that the narrow range of her human and class sympathies muzzled her own fiction, limiting it far more than geographic confinement might have. Poor people, obscure people, people who work and cook dinner, figure not at all in her argument about class. It is as if they did not exist.

She considered Munich the most beautiful city in Europe. It offered urban amenities—opera, restaurants, art galleries—without a hint of grime, menace, or blight: "It has none of the appearance of a business city, no poverty, scarcely a factory; it has a university, . . . [and] an atmosphere of independence and beauty, beauty everywhere." The old city had been rebuilt by King Ludwig in the grand style of the Italian Renaissance. And the natural surroundings matched or surpassed the architectural grandeur: the azure sky, the low-lying white clouds, the beryl-green Isar winding its way through the Englishergarten. "Situated on a high plateau in sight of the Alps, down from whose snow-fields came a gentle wind, [its] air was so bracing one's feet felt winged, and the sky was the richest blue I have ever seen."[4]

Pleasure-loving, artistic, and luxurious in a way that contrasted strikingly with the rigidity of Prussia to the north, Bavarian Munich enjoyed its reputation as the new Athens. Loyal enough to its resident Prince Regent, it paid small homage to the Kaiser when he visited, turning out to view him and take his measure in stony silence. There was "a prevailing belief that life was made to enjoy, not to take with the fatiguing seriousness of northern climes. The Bavarian understands Italy far better than he will ever understand Prussia."[5] The sensuous ease of the life she made for herself in Munich seduced Gertrude while she lived it; in retrospect, after the horrors of the Great War, it took on even more powerful and poignant associations. Pre-war Munich seemed like a dream: what she remembered turned out to be the Belle Epoque's last, languorous sigh.

Even though Bavarian Munich distanced itself, as far as Gertrude could tell, from the Kaiser and Prussian military arrogance, Gertrude did not view imperial, nationalistic Germany with alarm. On the contrary, her 1904 novel *Rulers of Kings*, "an historical novel of the present day," took the daring and controversial step of using Kaiser Wilhelm II as a character who, if haughty and greedy for territory and power, is nonetheless depicted as a likable chap; his eagle eyes and his flinty appearance—"as if hewn out of finely tempered steel" —are made to seem laudable. Using information furnished her by her friend Poultney Bigelow, an American writer, traveler, and adventurer who lived in Munich and who, as son of the U.S. minister to France, had made a boyhood friendship with Wilhelm II, she was able to draw a likeness of the German ruler taken—albeit at second hand—"from the life."

She pictures the young Wilhelm as the friend and admirer of an American millionaire just out of college, a youth named Fessenden Abbott who was raised in the Adirondacks in hardship, ignorant of his father's enormous wealth. As a child he was taught to constantly repeat the words: "Life is a fight. Millions fail. Only the strong win. Failure is worse than death."[6]

Devoted, like Teddy Roosevelt, to the strenuous life, Fessenden Abbott emerges as the American counterpart of Wilhelm of Germany; they are two faces of the same imperial coin, two practical, powerful, charismatic captains—one of finance and industry, the other of a nation. Abbott credits the Emperor with "making an American [modernized and industrialized] city out of Berlin" and for being "an autocrat with a Yankee head on his shoulders." The American and the German, viewed by Atherton as the two "controlling forces" in the world, agree to divide the earth's spoils. "You can have Europe," says Fessenden to the Kaiser, "but you can't have South America."[7]

By the time she came to write her virulently anti-German postwar novel *The White Morning*, Gertrude reversed herself and took a stingingly antagonistic view of the Kaiser and the patriarchal militarism he came to symbolize. For now, he was just another of her virile superheroes, an attractive embodiment of male energy, industry, and combativeness.

Introducing a living European ruler into *Rulers of Kings* cost Gertrude Atherton the disapproval of Baron Tauchnitz, whose inexpensive paperback editions of Atherton novels enjoyed wide popularity among English-reading travelers in Europe, and an even more costly opposition: George Brett, the Macmillan editor who had scored such a financial triumph with *The Conquerer* refused to publish *Rulers*. It offended his belief that the modern novel should not exploit current leaders and events, a view that left Gertrude baffled, hurt, and exasperated.

"I am astonished," she wrote Brett, "at your reason for declining the book . . . for I both told you and wrote you beforehand the subject matter. . . . And if Macmillan & Co. in England do not object why on earth should you over there [in the United States]? Roosevelt has been mentioned and quoted in more than one story. . . . So it is impossible for me to believe that you have given your real reasons. I can only think that you falter before a new thing. Why on earth shouldn't the same liberty be taken with a living as with dead monarchs, particularly if there is nothing offensive. The Emperor of Germany can only be flattered. Are not these monarchs in the newspaper every day? Why are they fair game for the novelists less than for the reporters?"[8]

A few days before informing him that Harpers had accepted *Rulers of Kings*, she wrote Brett that she had been canvassing her titled English friends in London and they all shared her belief that living monarchs had a place in fiction, "especially those who are always prancing on the public stage. These people give themselves to the public, to history."[9] Gertrude showed a very American disregard for the privacy of public figures and an ability to turn "news" into "entertainment" prophetic of the era of instant books and television docudramas.

She made it clear to Brett that the scruples were all on his part; she would have been supremely content to stay on with Macmillan. "I had not the slightest desire to leave you; in fact I had the pleasant feeling of being settled for life."[10] Even as she wrote she was living on the profits from *The Conqueror*—$10,000 in royalties had been invested in October of 1903—and was able to send sizable sums to both her sisters in San Francisco, while living in great comfort herself.[11]

In 1903, the same year Isadora Duncan performed and lectured in Berlin on "The Dance of the Future" and Gertrude and Leo Stein established themselves on the Left Bank in Paris, Gertrude Atherton rented a large flat in the Kaulbachstrasse. Its location was choice, and it came equipped with electricity and plumbing and suffused with wonderful light, all for a thousand marks (roughly $250) a year. "As my landlord was a cabinet maker I bought from him some charming Gothic furniture he had copied from pieces in the museum. It was a bedroom set, and to reach my stately couch I had to climb a little flight of steps. I had brought with me an old-rose rug. I had the walls papered to match, and found an old-rose silken cover for the bed" (*Adventures*, p. 360).

The flat was four flights up, with no elevator, "but from my window I could see the Englischergarten," described in *Ancestors* as "that wonderful imitation of a great stretch of open country, with fields where they made hay, and bits of wild woods, and crooked pathways, and bridges over a branch of the Isar. . . . And then the little beer-gardens, where people are always sitting and listening to the band—and beyond the tree-tops, the spires and domes of the beautiful city" (*Ancestors*, p. 260).

During her first two weeks' residence, she was hounded by the Munich police, who took a suspicious view of her motives for establishing a home there. Investigating her as a possible spy or radical, they visited her daily, "singly and in pairs, with papers, which as a resident I was forced to sign. They wanted the status of my ancestors, and were extraordinarily inquisitive regarding my reasons for living in Munich. Students they understood, but why a woman alone, and yet not a student, should sign an eighteen months' contract for a flat and furnish it, passed their comprehension." She agreed to sign every document they presented, and at last they seemed satisfied. Gertrude was later "convinced that only my light hair saved me from being put under surveillance as a possible anarchist." [12]

If one person could be credited with casting a rosy glow on all of Gertrude's Munich associations, that person would be her servant, Elise Palmert, a multilingual Swiss woman who answered an ad for a housekeeper during her own first days in Munich. Not since childhood, when Rose Stoddard took her under her ample wing, had Gertrude felt so cared for and protected. Elise "took all household affairs off my hands and I never entered a provision shop during the years I lived in Munich; she was a good cook, and the apartment fairly shone. As time went on, I had guests frequently for luncheon and dinner, but when I asked her to get some one in to help her she would reply seriously, 'No, madame, I fear we should come to blows. I do not wish to kill any one'" (*Adventures*, p. 360). Gertrude understood perfectly.

Like her employer in her younger days, Elise was both solitary and fierce. It was rumored she carried a knife. Her one diversion was the bicycle. With "a tiny, round hat perched on the top of her funny untidy coiffure, a loden cape streaming behind her, a savage frown on her face, careering down the stately Ludwigstrasse," she made one of the sights of Munich (*Adventures*, p. 361).

An educated woman, well-read in German, French, and Italian classics, Elise had seen every opera in the standard repertory many times. Although more cultured, according to Gertrude, "than any servant ever was in the United States . . . , or than many of one's friends, for that matter," she made no presumptuous intrusions. Gertrude valued her all the more highly because, unlike American servants, she "kept her place." In a seven-year period, "she never once addressed me directly, took a liberty of any sort, nor failed in any duty."

Elise insulated her from workaday Munich so effectively that one could argue Gertrude did not really live there. For one thing, she made regular trips to San Francisco and Britain, sometimes staying away for months at a time. For another, she never learned German, and the circle of friends she eventually acquired in Germany consisted wholly of English-speakers like the Scots-born novelist Marie Hay (married to diplomat Herbert von Hindenburg) and the Southern American Leila von Meister, also married to a wealthy German, who played the guitar and sang "plantation songs" (perhaps spirituals) to the Kaiser.

Since she had a spacious apartment, ample means, and a housekeeper, Gertrude generously invited family members to come and visit. Muriel stayed only briefly, loathe to leave her family for too long. But a niece, Daisy's daughter Boradil Craig, came for an extended stay after her mother died. Gertrude sent her to art school (and expressed disappointment when Boradil decided she wanted to become a nurse, sending her back to the United States to train) and took her on several expeditions to castles, accompanied by Boradil's charming and exuberant young friend Philip Sassoon. Gertrude seems to have enjoyed having Boradil around. She reported in a letter to Ina Coolbrith that Boradil showed decided artistic talent. "It is very interesting to make something of somebody, and she does not talk too much and is pretty. I never could stand an ugly or chattering girl." [13]

What contact she did have with ordinary Germans aroused a sort of bemused condescension. "The streets and less fashionable restaurants were always full of students with their duel-scarred faces. I used to hear them under my windows at night trying to be riotous; but they were too well seasoned to be able to get really drunk, and the effort was rather comic. They were picturesque objects in their colored caps, and so were the peasants who came in from the villages on Sundays and sauntered stolidly through the streets" (*Adventures*, pp. 363–64). During intermissions at the opera it was not uncommon to see a stout, middle-class Bavarian woman turning back her overskirt to extract from the capacious pockets of her petticoat an apple, sandwiches, and chocolate.

For Gertrude, as for so many other residents of pre-war Munich, opera was the great draw. Almost every night throughout the year audiences thronged to the six o'clock curtain at the Hof-und-

National theater, which boasted a classic dome, blue-and-white interior decorations, blue lights whenever royalty attended a performance, and a fresco above its portico depicting a blue-and-gold vision of Apollo among the Muses. "There one heard not only the Wagnerian operas—with the exception of *Parsifal* to which Bayreuth clung greedily—but practically every opera ever written. . . . The incomparable Fassbender was the dramatic soprano, Morena the lyric, . . . Bender basso. The conductor was Felix Mottl" (*Adventures*, p. 362).

Gertrude could make the journey from her flat to the Hof on foot. It was a mile along the broad Ludwigstrasse and entirely safe. "I not only was never spoken to, I never met any one. . . . There was no crime that I ever heard of." If she had no plans for a late dinner, she would arrive home by ten.

She became an opera insider when she befriended the California soprano Maude Fay, a friend of James Phelan, who made her Munich debut in 1906, replacing Morena as Elizabeth, Elsa, and Sieglinde at the Hof. After hearing her as Elizabeth, Gertrude reported to Phelan that "her voice is simply magnificent. It peals out like a great chime of silver bells. And her appearance is such a relief! All the rest of the women [singers] have the *mistress* look . . . , but Maude Fay is *la jeune fille* personified. This is not an unimportant consideration when you consider what a hash Sibyl made of her life and it is an immense thing for California to have produced a really great voice that will never deteriorate through any fault of the owner." [14]

Comparison with Sibyl Sanderson was inevitable, and Gertrude elaborated at some length: "Sibyl sang like a lark . . . , Maude had what the Germans called the lyric dramatic. It was a 'white voice,' but full, large, round." [15] Maude Fay, she had written to Phelan earlier, was Sibyl "with the badness left out."

Sibyl had died, not yet 40 years old, in Paris, attended by soprano Mary Garden, in 1903. Massenet had helped bear her casket through the Paris streets, and the French government ordered a portrait of her as Manon painted on the ceiling of the Opéra Comique. She had not sung in public during the year immediately preceding her death, and her American tour in 1901 had failed to please either audiences or critics. She had married once—a wealthy Cuban named Antonio Terry who promptly died and left her a widow—wrangled over her husband's will, suffered a stroke, returned to the stage briefly, and shortly before her death become engaged to Count Paul Tolstoi, a cousin of the novelist.[16] Instead of grieving for the friend of her youth, Gertrude seemed to feel Sibyl's early death provided a kind of retribution for sinful living.

But, at the same time, she faulted Maude Fay for her lack of fire or allure. Perhaps hoping to douse any romantic interest Phelan might have shown in Maude Fay, perhaps merely making a show of her sexual competitiveness, she told Phelan Fay's voice was "as sexless and coldly sweet as a choir boy's soprano. It is almost remote."[17]

Gertrude wanted her divas to be, like the heroines of her novels (and like Gertrude herself), seductive and passionate by nature, but untouchable. The diva—who has captured the imaginations of many novelists, including George Sand in *Consuelo* and Willa Cather in *The Song of the Lark*, as an arresting heroine—held a special fantasy appeal to women writers and readers, because on stage, she dominates. "She is a queen of the performance and a ruler of the audience," as Cather suggested when she referred to the Wagnerian soprano Nordica as a "splendid Amazon warrior," and when she praises her diva-heroine Thea Kronborg for being "uncommon, in a common, common world."[18]

Margarethe Styr, Atherton's Wagnerian soprano, who dominates the Munich novel *Tower of Ivory*, fairly sets the stage on fire when she sings. Her Isolde suggests "a yearning that is not all bliss and a torment that is not all pain . . . , surge upon surge of aching passion" (*Tower*, p. 157).

Styr empitomizes the Atherton heroine who is powerful, melodramatic, gifted, solitary, independent, and alluring, but whose sexuality is all suggestion, no consummation. She has a sordid New York past, a buried life of squalor and prostitution, which we hear about but do not see. At the time we meet her, she has held herself aloof from men for years. "The natural passions of an uncommonly lusty woman were turned back upon themselves" (*Tower*, p. 462). Now comes Ordham, the great love of her life, a young British aristocrat married to a shallow young American beauty he despises. Although Styr and Ordham embrace and kiss in one scene, they never become lovers. At the end of the book Styr as Brunhilde rides into real flames and immolates herself. *Tower of Ivory*, Gertrude's own favorite among her novels, reaffirms a conviction that art is sublimation and sexual satisfaction best realized in fantasy.

As she often did when she wrote fiction, Gertrude based the leading characters of *Tower of Ivory* on actual people. She never met Zdenka Fassbender (who spoke no English) but could see and admire her in performance as "the risen Isolde and Brunhilde." According to one report, Fassbender knew of the book and had an English-speaking friend read her translations of selected excerpts, chosen with an eye to sparing Gertrude a libel suit.[19]

John Lambton, a young British aristocrat of impeccable manners, indolent habits, extravagant tastes ill-suited to his modest income, well-developed intellect, and considerable charm, served as model for the character Ordham. The real-life Lambton, in Munich to learn German in preparation for a career in diplomatic service, eventually became Earl of Durham. For the status-hungry Gertrude, a large part of his appeal and fascination resided in his patrician lineage. "What is the secret," muses the American Mrs. Cutting in *Tower*, "of the fascination of England for the well-born of the United States? Perhaps it is mere picturesque contrast to our republican institutions. . . . Perhaps some harking back of the blood. Perhaps it is an unconscious attempt to live the literature of our childhood, where all the fascinating characters were kings and queens, lords and ladies. Perhaps the sleepless American instinct to go straight to the top. . . . No doubt, however, the reasons . . . are given complete and final expression in that one hideous little word, 'snob'" (*Tower*, p. 363).

In her autobiography Gertrude describes Lambton as intellectually alert and sophisticated, but physically lazy, accustomed to being waited on and reluctant even to walk; he preferred cabs. "If he had chosen to study he could have mastered German in six months"— the same could have been said of Gertrude—"but he preferred to read what interested him instead." This "sybarite on a small income" might have enjoyed a larger income "if his uncle Durham had approved of him. But he hated killing things and refused to shoot when staying at any of the ancestral estates—a gesture of contempt

in the face of a sacred tradition. A British nobleman is a sports-
man or nothing. His entire family regarded him as a deflection from
the normal because he preferred books and art to potting birds and
racing around the country in pursuit of a desperate fox" (*Adventures*,
p. 428).

In the 1890s Gertrude had praised the virility and worldliness of
British gentlemen and expressed her contempt for "effete" and "over-
civilized" Decadents. Now she seems less judgmental, more willing
to accept deviance from the masculine norm—at least where well-
mannered and discreet aristocrats like Lambton were concerned.

The Ordham in *Tower of Ivory* succumbs to a powerful passion
for an older woman. The real-life Lambton preferred the company
of strong women twenty or more years his senior who would take
him in tow, but present no sexual threat. He relished Gertrude's
lively company and made no protest when she told him she was
studying him for future use in a book. She took him to Bayreuth to
hear *Parsifal*. "Took is the correct word, for I had to buy the tickets,
rescue the luggage, find the porters, settle him in his room when we
got there." Other friends, the American singer Marcia Van Dresser
and her companion Gertrude Norman, had arrived earlier, securing
the tickets and engaging the rooms. "All three of us . . . had to wait
on him, see that he got his bath, that his room was properly aired,
rout him out of bed in the morning; in fact we did everything but
dress him and put him to bed. But he was so grateful, . . . his manners were so beautiful, and he made himself so charming, that we
felt quite rewarded" (*Adventures*, p. 431). Lambton clearly awakened
in Gertrude the maternal qualities that she so often disclaimed.

Gertrude's solicitude and affection for Lambton, though genuine,
did not inhibit her from using him in a way he found insulting. Her
portrait of him in *Tower of Ivory* did not flatter; Ordham emerges a
man polished on the outside, but brutal at his core, capable of abandoning his wife when she is close to death in childbirth in order to
go off to an assignation with the prima donna Styr. Gertrude told
herself—and probably Lambton too—that although based on observations "from the life" her fictional portraits were always composites,
never exact likenesses. She made an exception in the case of Phelan
and a few family members, but in general she cared not a whit for
the feelings of those who became grist for her fiction mill. If friends

and acquaintances took offense—as Ambrose Bierce had—that was their problem, not hers. Fiction writing was like reporting: everyone was fair game, but not everyone was interesting enough to be singled out, studied, and brought to life on the page. Those who were should be flattered.

A review of *Tower of Ivory* that appeared in the *Atlantic Monthly* cited Ordham's cold-bloodedness and his creator's apparent endorsement of it as evidence of a Europeanized American's cynicism and cosmopolitanism gone to seed. It was fatal, implied the reviewer, for American writers to cater to the fad for depravity. American writers should leave passion to the Europeans. Mrs. Atherton's "second-rate novel"—her most commercially successful since *The Conqueror*—revealed her as "morally and artistically underbred."[20]

The accusation of human callousness carried more weight than the charge that Mrs. Atherton had been won over by slack European standards or aesthetics. She brought her ethics with her to Europe, and they were American to the core. As for morals, though she was indeed more relaxed than she used to be about the life of pleasure, she could hardly be called a voluptuary. And she was anything but favorably impressed by the modernist aesthetic innovations so hospitably received by Munich during the years she lived there.

In 1908 and 1909, when she was writing *Tower of Ivory*, Wagner was no longer the revolutionary figure in European music, Richard Strauss was. Although set in the 1880s, *Tower* finds Ordham musing on Munich's turn-of-the-century position as a center of the avant-garde, the first to welcome, as he puts it, "all that was distempered in the arts." He refers in particular to "the gifted but dislocated brains of Richard Strauss, Wedekind and the ultra Secessionists" (*Tower*, p. 139). The book registers discomfort at the unshockability of Muncheners, "good, homely, soft-waisted people . . . [who] relished the indecencies of the stage, their expression much the same as when they sat with their elbows on a table in a restaurant and devoured a dinner lasting two hours without raising their eyes." Returning from an evening of Wedekind or Strauss, they "supped on sausage, black bread and beer, and snored in stuffy ugly rooms without a dream" (*Tower*, pp. 139–40).

The very Gertrude Atherton who once courted scandal by creating heroines who were frankly provocative and willing to challenge social conventions about "decency" was now clucking away like another righteous Mrs. Grundy over the scandalous Strauss *Salome*. She reported in a letter to Phelan her delight that Maude Fay had refused to sing "that stinking Salome," and added, "all the musical Germans here are delighted that New York [the Metropolitan Opera, bowing to public outcry] has turned it down and openly admit that they are ashamed they did not have the courage to do it themselves."[21] She seems to have seen (and heard) in Strauss no more than the clamor and sensationalism of a misguided Wagner disciple.

Nor could she sympathize with the "hideous New Art" emerging in Munich. If Kandinsky, a resident since 1896, was feeling his way toward abstraction in painting; if, as *Jugendstil* artist Herman Obrist put it, "the first act of the drama of the art of the future is being played out here," Gertrude elected to shun the performance. As she identified increasingly with the entrenched European past and its traditional, representational forms, she recoiled from innovation and artistic insurgency. Modernism, abstraction, nonlinear structures confused and repulsed her. In her 1907 novel *Ancestors* she describes a piece of decorative art made in "the latest" Munich manner: a lamp in which the light is filtered through "an opalescent globe upheld by a twisted bronze female of the modern Munich school, that looked like nothing so much as Alice elongating in Wonderland" (*Ancestors*, p. 99). It is part of the decor of a promiscuous woman's boudoir, and it betokens decadence.

Gertrude also flinched at the open displays of homosexuality and transvestism common in Munich cafes and restaurants. A young Hungarian count she met at the home of her friends the von Hindenburgs frequented the Munich bars at night with painted lips and mascaraed lashes, waiting to be picked up "by gentlemen of similar proclivities" (*Adventures*, p. 435). Despite its rising militarism and its outward devotion to the cult of masculinity, Germany, Gertrude heard, was considering legalizing homosexual marriages. She did not herself frequent places like the Maximilia after midnight, but

Lambton told her about the painted young men from noble families who came, rubbing elbows with army officers and their "almost respectable partners." Like San Francisco, Munich was a city "too artistic to have a moral life" (*Tower*, p. 65).

Gertrude's distrust of what was truly unconventional or experimental qualifies as another of her jarring inconsistencies. In "Why Is American Literature Bourgeois?" she had protested against writers whose fiction presented an American image "as correct as Sunday clothes and as innocuous as sterilized milk." In Europe, she pointed out, Americans are associated with "all that is unique, startling, unexpected," and with "dangerous and unfathomed power." When given the opportunity, in future years, to respond to innovative American artists like Gertrude Stein, she balked, again failing to draw a connection between revolutionary aesthetics and the buccaneering qualities she championed. Writing about one's friends and about living rulers: yes; writing in a style that was elusive, new, and hard to understand: no.

Her own reputation was undergoing changes she only partially perceived. In Edwardian England, which she visited from time to time, she now held a secure social position. Elise would help her pack her many gowns and would accompany her on weekend visits at the country homes of Sir Ian and Lady Hamilton near Stonehenge or the lordly Dillons of Dytchley, Oxfordshire. At Althop, Northampton, she met Mrs. Humphrey Ward, the Dutch novelist Maarten Maartens, and Violet Hunt, a novelist and suffragist who was the companion of Ford Madox Ford. In London, Lady Randolph Churchill, now Mrs. George Cornwallis West, extended a friendly hand, including Gertrude in several entertainments at her home and introducing her to her son Winston, who so impressed Gertrude that she used him as the model for Gwynne in *Ancestors*. Mrs. Patrick Campbell, "the most popular actress in London," invited her for luncheon; they had met previously, through Ashton Stevens, in California (*Adventures*, p. 397).

She accepted many invitations from the hospitable Lady Jeune, afterwards Lady St. Helier, who specialized in "mixed" parties that brought together celebrities from different spheres of life. One night her guest list included Prime Minister Arthur Balfour, "possessed of a leisurely, almost indolent manner"; Pierpont Morgan, whose "immense red distorted nose" overwhelmed any other impression of him (*Adventures*, p. 378); and Elinor Glyn, the sensational novelist who had written *The Visits of Elizabeth* (1900) and would become infamous with *Three Weeks* (1907).

Gertrude had only kind things to say about the red-haired Mrs. Glyn, whose siren's looks, aristocratic connections, literary popularity, and scandalous air struck a chord. The sister novelists exchanged compliments as Gertrude attempted to fathom the secret of her new acquaintance's flawless alabaster complexion. They would meet again in Hollywood a little more than a decade hence.

Gertrude's literary social life in London included encounters with "boyish" Edmund Gosse, salons at her old friends' the Corkrans, and a luncheon at the home of Shakespeare critic Sidney Lee, where she had one of her several meetings with Henry James—perhaps the one that emboldened her to write to ask him if she might dedicate to him her 1905 short story collection *The Bell in the Fog*, whose title story obliquely warns James that he was losing touch with his public.[22] James, she told a reporter for the *New York Times* in 1905, "is the biggest literary figure in London. Anthony Hope [whose *Prisoner of Zenda* had started the fad for costume romances, back in the 1890s] is still going to parties and sitting on staircases talking to pretty girls." Hope, she averred, was all façade. There was "nothing behind the man of charming manner."[23] James was the exact opposite, a penetrating psychologist who "fills every crevice—so *thick*; I use this word because the prevailing characteristic of American literature is thinness."[24]

American readers could learn about Gertrude's London successes by reading *The Critic*, which reported: "Mrs. Atherton is in London for the present. She is having a gay time now; everybody seems to be receiving her and giving her dinners, etc. The Women Writers' Club in London gave her a luncheon—the first thing of the sort they have ever done. No American woman's work has been so popular in London. Of course it is *Senator North*, *The Aristocrats* and *The Conqueror* that have done it."[25]

Socially at least, London did not seem to distinguish between the kind of literary celebrity whose books sell well and the kind who competes in the High Art sweepstakes. A famous writer was a famous writer, and hostesses scurried to fill their guest lists with "notable" names.

But by 1910, when she gave up her Munich home for more or less permanent residence in the United States, Mrs. Atherton no longer ranked, beyond San Francisco, as a preeminent literary novelist. Some might argue she never had. But in England especially, from the 1890s through the first few years of the new century, she had been taken quite seriously, and she had taken herself so, selecting the Brontës as her models. And though Gertrude always assigned a high importance to making a living, to sales figures and commercial success, she continued to set her sights on enduring renown for—at the least—her historical fiction.

Her persistent willingness to publish potboilers as well as more finished and accomplished books did not strengthen her critical standing. Neither did her penchant for exaggeration, garish publicity, hasty composition, prolixity, and melodrama. As early as 1899, young Willa Cather was writing reviews that sneered at Mrs. Atherton's "fervid pen" and addiction to "hectic" subjects; Mrs. Atherton, to Cather, had relinquished her claims as a serious artist. She was a "scribbler," an American Marie Corelli.[26] Corelli, along with Ouida, Rhoda Broughton, Mary Elizabeth Braddon, and Elinor Glyn, belonged to the still flourishing tradition of romantic or sensational "lowbrow" women's fiction. For many "highbrow" readers, women as well as men, Gertrude Atherton also belonged in this spirited but hardly lofty company.

However, there were those on both sides of the Atlantic who insisted on placing her on a plane with Edith Wharton, who with *The House of Mirth* had made an indelible mark in American fiction. Wharton had also—most unforgivably, from Gertrude's point of view—created with that novel a best-seller. For all her whining about the commercialism of the American literary marketplace, Gertrude hungered for one of those. She wrote to a friend in San Francisco, "I have yet to find the person above . . . being a best seller . . . if he could. And why not? As many good novels have been best sellers as trash. *Tower of Ivory* is second on the March list (given in *Bookman*) and first in New York and the Northern states."[27]

Between New York's Edith Wharton and California's Gertrude Atherton—who never met, although they sometimes found themselves in London, Paris, or New York at the same moment—there were resemblances. Both wrote novels of manners that focused on the upper class and especially on woman's confinement in narrow social roles; both had published in the *Anglo-Saxon Review* and with the British house of Macmillan; both befriended Lady Jeune; both traveled freely between Europe and the States, quarreled with mainstream American culture, and lived restless, cosmopolitan, international lives. They shared the experience of failed marriage and had been stung as young women by the disdain of the conforming social elite for intellectual, independent, or ambitious women.[28] A typical comment linking the two (during the decades when they were both publishing) came from critic John Underwood, who wrote: "Few can or will dispute with Mrs. Atherton the title of our leading lady novelist, for Mrs. Wharton is in many ways in a class by herself."[29]

A closer look reveals profound differences. Edith Wharton shuddered at raucous publicity, though she liked her books to sell. She chided her publisher for advertising on the book jacket that in *The House of Mirth* for the first time "the veil has been lifted from New York society," saying, "I thought that, in the house of Scribner, the House of Mirth was safe from all such Harperesque methods of *réclame*."[30] Mrs. Atherton published four books with Harpers between 1904 and 1907 and relished its boisterous publicity, though she complained it didn't do as good a job of marketing her books as did Macmillan. An advertisement for *Ancestors* read: "Mrs. Atherton has done for old San Francisco what Hugo did for Paris, what Dickens and Thackeray did for London."

Edith Wharton found an acceptance by the Eastern American and European literary and social establishments of a kind unknown to Gertrude Atherton. Socially, she ranked much higher, since her family descended from blue-blooded Old New York stock. (When Gertrude met Wharton's sister-in-law Mary Cadwalader Jones at a summer resort in the early 1890s, she told Ambrose Bierce she had met a "howling swell.") Wharton possessed from birth what

Gertrude Atherton struggled to acquire: roots that had stayed rooted in the most hallowed ground and access to the innermost elite circles. Edith Wharton dined at the White House with Teddy Roosevelt. Her artistry had earned her the respect and friendship of "The Master" himself, Henry James—who privately considered the admiring Mrs. Atherton tawdry. Edith Wharton loved houses—owned, built, decorated, and received guests at several in her lifetime. In contrast to the nomadic Gertrude, she loved gardens and gardening. What better testimony to her essential rootedness?

In her writing Edith Wharton served a scrupulous muse, an uncompromising aesthetic. She made a fetish of "taste." No one would ever accuse her, as Frederic T. Cooper had Mrs. Atherton, of faulty technique and arbitrary methods, "riotous freedom of style and construction." Or as a reviewer for *The Dial* did, of flinging at her readers "the garish coloring of Ouida." In reviewing *Senator North* for *The Dial*, Morton Payne damned Atherton by praising Edith Wharton's superior "delicacy of texture and distinction of style." Mrs. Atherton, by contrast, "in the place of delicacy has a sort of rude energy; in the place of distinction she has a form of expression which is rough in sound and crude in coloring."[31] In what Virginia Woolf would call "The Battle of the Brows," Edith Wharton came up the undisputed winner.

Very much threatened by Mrs. Wharton's eminence, Gertrude Atherton tried to convince herself, and others, that her rival's superior reputation derived from the critics' favoritism and the public's compliance. To George Brett, before *The House of Mirth* came out, she wrote, "Mrs. Wharton has got ahead of me on reviews although I don't believe she has made so great an impression on the reading public. People are like sheep. I don't like to hear said to me, 'According to the critics, Mrs. Wharton is the best woman writer.'"[32] She urged her publisher to tout *her* in advertisements as the leading American woman novelist.

Edith Wharton could not be ignored, and Gertrude spoke of her in print with guarded respect, calling her, after the publication of *The House of Mirth*, "by far the most uncompromising critic of New York Society," and "a remarkably clever woman who is a close and accurate observer."[33] Placing Wharton—as many readers did—among the imitators of Henry James, she found her wanting: Mrs. Wharton lacked The Master's objectivity and "background" (whatever that means). "Her stories are hung up in the air, and her people mentalities whose names one immediately forgets."[34] To *New York Times* interviewer Clifford Smyth she complained, "Mrs. Wharton has made the same mistake that Mrs. Craigie made: dull. They are good draughtsmen but they can't paint."[35]

For anyone familiar with Gertrude's loathing for Pearl Craigie, the comparison is a giveaway. In private, Gertrude bridled at the mere mention of Edith Wharton's name. According to Carl Van Vechten, she even disparaged Wharton's best work. When defenders would protest, "What about *Ethan Frome?*" she gathered herself up, "gazing directly at her interlocutor with her beady green eyes," to ask, "Do you really believe that Mrs. Wharton actually *wrote Ethan Frome?*"[36]

By surrounding herself with acquaintances who had famous names or aristocratic connections, Gertrude propped up her self-regard. If she sometimes wondered whether her books had any lasting worth, if she felt eclipsed by Edith Wharton, at least she, Gertrude Atherton, as a personality, an opinion maker, and a formidable presence in the "best" Munich, London, or San Francisco circles, had earned her place of honor.

Gertrude might have lingered indefinitely in the comfort and luxury of Munich had not Elise, on whom her domestic arrangements wholly depended, been called away to nurse her elderly father in Leipzig. "Elise had done more than run my household smoothly; she had saved me all unnecessary contacts, and even from taxation" by haranguing a magistrate and telling him "*meine dame* will leave rather than pay taxes to keep up your army" (*Adventures*, p. 445).

While there, she was having too good a time to notice, but in retrospect Gertrude suspected that Munich had softened her up to a harmful degree. She produced "only" six books in six years there, and one, the short story collection, contained little new work. She had successfully withdrawn to her own "Tower of Ivory," where she encountered the outside world infrequently and then only on her own terms. "One forgets the world in that dream city. I rarely looked

at a newspaper; I wanted to go every night to the opera . . . , roam
about the city and the wonderful country, talk art, music and literature with an ever-widening circle of acquaintance. . . . Why work
when it is so delightful to play?"[37]

Toward the end of 1909 she returned to a United States gripped
by momentous changes. In the White House, Roosevelt had been
succeeded by Taft. D. W. Griffith had made his first films, and
movie-going had become a favorite American pastime. A locomo-
tive on the Pennsylvania Railroad established a new world's record
—a fraction more than 99 miles an hour—for steam locomotives,
and Wilbur Wright had set a new record for flight, staying aloft in
an airplane for more than an hour. Dr. Freud had visited America,
lecturing on psychoanalysis at Clark University in Massachusetts.

The world of writers had on a new face. The muckraking journalism of Ida Tarbell and Lincoln Steffens had triggered significant reform. Willa Cather, already the author of a first collection
of short stories and a book of poetry, took over as managing editor
of *McClure's*. Dreiser's *Sister Carrie* had been written and printed,
but withheld. Upton Sinclair had exposed the Chicago meat-packing
industry in *The Jungle*. Frank Norris had died, but Jack London
continued to publish fiction that marked him not just as the leading
California author, but a dominant voice in all of American fiction.
Mark Twain, an imposing figure on the literary landscape from the
time of Gertrude's girlhood, was close to breathing his last.

By spring of 1910 Gertrude was writing to Phelan from New
York's Algonquin Hotel that she was doing her best to promote
Tower of Ivory, that she had been to see dance performances by Ruth
St. Denis and Isadora Duncan, and that she was attending the re-
hearsals of actress Minnie Maddern Fiske in Ibsen's *Pillars of Society*.
She was hoping to learn something, she said. "I have an idea for a
play."[38]

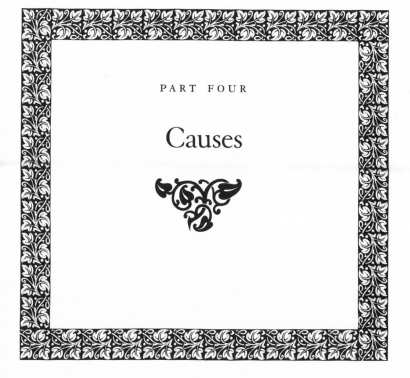

PART FOUR

Causes

CHAPTER TWELVE

Mrs. Fiske, 'Julia France,' and the "Clamoring Bell of Woman's Equality"

The celebrated stage actress Minnie Maddern Fiske, famous for her crisp, spirited, and life-like portrayals of Becky Sharpe and Ibsen heroines, wanted Gertrude Atherton to write a play for her on the most timely of themes: modern woman. In England, the actress/writer Elizabeth Robins had rallied the public with her 1909 play, *Votes for Women*. Mrs. Fiske hoped to find a similar vehicle, but she lacked a script; for that she enlisted Mrs. Atherton, who had said in print that woman's insistent demand for a voice was at last being heeded. From the moment in the remote past when the first queen ascended a throne, she had written, "the first low, tiny silver bell of woman's equality and enfranchisement began its tinkle, and that tinkle has never paused, until today, after many recastings, the primitive toy is a mighty brazen bell whose determined clamor fills the world."[1]

Gertrude had never tried her hand at a play and—as it turned out, with good reason—doubted her capacity to write successfully for the stage. But she loved the challenge of anything new. In addition, she both admired and identified with Mrs. Fiske, a friend of Ashton Stevens and Aleece who seemed to Gertrude to epitomize the best of modern womanhood.

Everyone who knew both the actress and the writer commented on the two women's physical and temperamental resemblances:

Arnold Genthe, who had photographed them both, called them "two Royal Bengal tigers."[2] A *New York Times* reporter who interviewed them together spoke of "the tawny hair and the violet eyes of the one, the light-gold hair and gray eyes of the other; the strong, modern, intellectual personality of both."[3] They shared a certain briskness and detachment. Mrs. Fiske, it is interesting to note, did not like playing love scenes, and the characteristic of her acting style was "intense repressed force."[4]

Looking for a starting point in this new venture, Gertrude focused first on material she had already used: a scene set in Nevis and dominated by a character based on Alexander Hamilton's mother, whose youthful intelligence and promise were sacrificed on the altar of matrimony; her ambitious mother marries her off at a tender age to a man of wealth and rank who proves to be a moral monster. This unfortunate young woman, transplanted to London, became the Atherton suffragist heroine—first in the play and then the novel— named Julia France.

How to learn to write drama? Gertrude's method was to immerse herself in the study of one good Ibsen play, to read it constantly and use its form as a model: "I have selected *Rosmersholm*," she told Mrs. Fiske, "as it is a fine piece of construction." Her modest ambition was to show "the development of woman up to this time, as Ibsen did in the *Doll's House*." "Since Ibsen's time," she told one reporter, "there has been a steady advance in the development of women. It will be of these new conditions and advancements that I shall write."[5]

"The Woman Question," it might be argued, had preoccupied Gertrude Atherton from the moment she first set pen to paper. She had invested her career in the glorification of female independence of spirit and the denigration of maternity, subservience, and monotonous domestic routine. But she had managed to stay clear, so far, of organized feminism. Competitive, self-serving, and individualistic, she had little use for joiners or their groups, hated meetings, and found polemics a bore. "Women make too much fuss," she had Patience Sparhawk say. "If they don't like their life, why don't they alter it quietly, without taking it to the lecture platform or the polemical novel?" (*Patience Sparhawk*, p. 295). When Charlotte Perkins Stetson (later Gilman) had tried to enlist her support in San Francisco in 1891, Gertrude rebuffed her: "As I had so far been able to take care of myself and owed nothing to any organization, I was not interested in her plans for the general emancipation of women" (*Adventures*, p. 211).[6] In London she had been similarly dismissive of Mona Caird, although willing enough to take credit when May Sinclair hailed her as a pioneer of New Woman fiction.

The world had changed, and so had Gertrude's attitude. Now focused on the struggle to win the vote, and dissociated from earlier alliances with temperance, feminism had become, by 1910, the subject of the hour. British Militants made headlines with their radical tactics: violent confrontations with the police, disruption of public meetings, hunger strikes in prison. In the United States women organized around voting rights, and the Western states led the way. Although Gertrude considered suffrage but one step in the inevitable "sweep of women from the backwaters into the broad central stream of life," she joined the campaign for suffrage in California, lending her name to organizations and penning newspaper articles in which she called the anti-suffrage campaign "the final appeal of the unintelligent female to the unenlightened male."[7]

Her stature as a public figure allowed her to think that what she did and said might make a difference. "I was fired with a holy enthusiasm to do something for my downtrodden sex! I had always resented the calm assumption of men that they were the superior sex, and their very real dominance. . . . I had succeeded in spite of them, and it was up to me to use what influence I might have to help liberate those unequipped to conquer life for themselves" (*Adventures*, p. 453).

Work on the play began slowly, partly because of her lack of experience and partly because, now back in San Francisco, Gertrude found herself uncharacteristically preoccupied with family cares. Muriel and her brood were still living in Belvedere. Muriel's youngest, the baby Dominga, was a great favorite with her grandmother, who used to rock her in a rocking chair, something she'd never done with the other grandchildren.[8] And the oldest, George, came down with pneumonia. In the midst of it all, Muriel broke her arm while cranking up her car.

For once, Gertrude briefly allowed family obligation to displace the claims of work. "I have been constantly interrupted," she complained to Mrs. Fiske. Her concern over young George's health—he was still sick after spending six weeks in bed—prompted her to consult an astrologer, Mrs. Bell, who predicted that by a particular date he would be convalescent. She proved correct, and Gertrude—who harbored under her no-nonsense exterior an attraction to the occult —was so impressed that she found a role for an astrologer in her work-in-progress. She turned Julia France into a child of Uranus, destined, according to an old woman's prediction, for prominence and power.

When George had recovered enough strength to be taken to southern California for the winter, Gertrude set out for a few month's writing in South Carolina. She half hoped Mrs. Fiske and her producer-husband would reject the draft of the play she had sent. Gertrude felt in her bones that it was no good and wished they would free her of the undertaking. But no, for the present they expressed satisfaction and supported Gertrude's plan to go to England to study at close range the British Militants whose sister-in-struggle the character Julia France was slated to become.

Like the American suffrage leader Alice Paul, Gertrude felt American women had much to learn from the radical and confrontational tactics of their British models. British women had more to be fierce about than their American counterparts because they suffered lower status and fewer rights. American husbands, according to Gertrude, both indulged and neglected their wives, while British men expected service and subservience. Moreover, divorce was all but unattainable in Britain. "English women may need the vote to redress their wrongs, but American women need it to give them stability of character and responsible minds."[9] Even if she had not found British feminism more dynamic than the American version, Gertrude still would have chosen a British setting for her Militant novel. "I was glad of any excuse to go to England" (*Adventures*, p. 453).

In London, her Militant friends Sophy Hall and Mrs. Cavendish Bentick launched her into the midst of things, supplying her with pamphlets and newspapers from the Women's Social and Political Union and bringing her along to meetings at the Albert Hall to hear Mrs. Emmeline Pankhurst, her daughters Christabel and Sylvia, Mrs. Emmeline Pethick-Lawrence, and Annie Kenney. She reported to the San Francisco drama critic Edward O'Day, "I am studying the women. They mean business, I can tell you. I have heard them speak (wonderfully), and this week am to meet Mrs. Pankhurst and others privately." [10]

From Queen Anne's Mansions, St. James' Park, she wrote to Mrs. Fiske: "I am meeting all the leaders of the suffrage movement . . . and have received much enlightenment. For instance they particularly do not want to go into Parliament or to hold office, merely to get the vote that they may send men up to Parliament who will reform certain laws and abuses. I am going tonight to the great meeting at Albert Hall and shall imagine Julia on the platform." [11] The leadership so impressed her that she became convinced if she returned to Britain 50 years hence she would find it being governed by women.

Sympathy for the working class had never been a component of her character, but the suffrage cause in Britain bound itself to Fabian Socialist principles in a way she found compelling. For the moment she was moved to wave the banner for complete social equality, not just the vote, and to endorse the Militants' commitment "to improve the condition of the millions of working women and children, who are miserably underpaid and have no pleasure in their lives whatever, nothing but work. Their ultimate hope is the elimination of poverty." [12] Fabian concerns found their way into her work. When *Julia France* was in rehearsal, she urged Edward O'Day to write in his column about it that the primary objective of the Militant women whose cause she championed was "to raise the status of the working woman. Her wage is almost two-thirds less than that of the man and she often has as many to keep." [13] In the novel, Julia joins the

Woman's War on Poverty; she haunts the London slums and visits women factory workers in Manchester, where she is appalled by the conditions she sees.

Gertrude attended a debate between feminist journalist and playwright Cicely Hamilton, who "ranted about the necessity of women rising superior to feminine charm," and G. K. Chesterton, who "with much urbanity confessed that woman might rise above it but that man could not." Chesterton, she told Edward O'Day, "is a great thick man with a fat head covered with curls, and he speaks with a squeaky voice. Cicely is a slab-sided sunken-in creature who screeches. For all the world they looked like a eunuch and a sterile nymphomaniac."[14]

Reducing a debate about ideas to a comic-opera beauty contest was a typical Gertrudism. She simply could not put aside the matter of a person's physical attractiveness, and she considered the British Militants—with a few exceptions—to be devoid of feminine appeal, impersonal, sexless. "They had grim mouths, clairvoyant eyes, were worn to the proportions of a shingle, and filled with a cold enthusiasm that had drained their egos of all human feeling. . . . They were fanatics on ice. Even the gray-faced girls, speaking at street corners, looked like the embodiment of cold intellect and had about as much charm as an embryo in a bottle" (*Adventures*, pp. 468–69).

When she wrote about feminists during the 1890s Gertrude had ridiculed their dour looks. Now she could find pragmatic value in such plainness and the single-mindedness it bespoke. Every word the Militant leaders uttered "was the product of thought, not of passion. They were detestable as women, but as scientific martyrs they were a commanding success." And such martyrs had spearheaded all the significant reforms throughout history. "I would remind myself and others that such great women as Susan B. Anthony were thought quite as pestiferous in their day, and yet it was such women . . . who forged the priceless tools of liberty which have freed women from the shackles of the centuries. They were held up to ridicule, reviled, persecuted, but so have been the martyrs of every revolution since the world began."[15]

Gertrude made her own suffrage heroine a stunning beauty. Julia France wears her flame-colored hair coiled on top of her head. She has transparent white skin, immense gray eyes, thick black lashes. As she rises to prominence as a Militant leader, making speeches, storming Parliament, and getting herself thrown in jail, the other Militants come to view her magnetism and good looks as a political plus. One of them says to her, "You've got the born style. . . . You've got just the air and the beauty to attract the crowd at the street corners. . . . But ugly little things like me can do the heckling." [16]

Unlike the "sexless" suffragists wholly dedicated to the Cause, Julia tries to balance her rage at property and divorce laws that turn a woman into no more than her husband's subject, her need for autonomy and meaningful work, and her submerged but undeniable craving for love, children, and human connection. The dramatic version of *Julia France* has not survived, but Mrs. Fiske's biographer tells us that the play concluded with a renunciation of love by the heroine; she defers to a younger woman in love with her fiancé and vows to devote herself to suffrage work.[17] But in the novel, Julia is allowed in the final chapters to "have it all." After the death in England of her insane brute of a husband, to whom she has been bound by unjust and decrepit divorce laws, she marries the young San Franciscan Daniel Tay. With him she will move to America, where she will help his political career while continuing her own work as an advocate for women.

Having completed her three-month-long study of English Militants, Gertrude returned in June 1911 to the United States. Mrs. Fiske wanted her to be on hand for rehearsals. Despite the tug of reluctance she always felt when she left Europe, Gertrude found, once back, that she enjoyed traveling through North America in a private train with a caravan of itinerant players. And she got on famously with Mrs. Fiske, whom she found eminently sane, generous, and alert, even though the actress's biographer claims they disagreed on some ramifications of the woman question. "The novelist believed that women should be able to stand alone and that an Amazonian society was in the offing; she found her work a thoroughly satisfactory substitute for a family . . . and confessed to having no maternal instincts. Minnie, on the other hand, looked on [her husband] Harry

as the stabilizing influence in her artistic life; she regretted her early
decision not to have children."[18]

The play proved a fiasco.

Plans were to bring it to Broadway, where several other Californian women writers, among them Geraldine Bonner and Cora
Older, had recently opened plays. When Mary Austin's *The Arrow
Maker* closed in rehearsal, Gertrude wrote to Ina Coolbrith: "I hope I
shan't have the bad luck which seems to be pursuing other California
playwrights."[19]

After rehearsals in Cincinnati and Chicago, *Julia France* opened
in Toronto before an audience of moderate size. Gertrude looked
on from a stage box as the audience sat politely, the men applauding only "at the sarcasm of men in the play anent suffrage."[20] After
"one perfunctory curtain call, the audience drifted out into the snowy
street without calling for the author."[21] The Toronto press performed burial rites, the *News* declaring that Mrs. Fiske had seriously
damaged her reputation by producing the dreary work of an ambitious amateur. There would be no second performance.

The well-defended Mrs. Atherton declared she hadn't stood a
chance, that "if Pinero brought the best play of his life to Canada
it would be damned by the critics."[22] But she professed no love for
the play. Although she considered one performance insufficient, she
disclaimed any interest in resurrecting it or in writing again for the
stage. She told the press that nothing it could say about *Julia* could
be worse than her own opinion of it,[23] and wrote to Macmillan's
Mr. Brett, who had contracted to publish the novelized version of the
play: "Mr. Fiske says that I am a born playwright with a true theater
sense, and wants me to abandon the novel. But you need not worry,
for I hate everything about playwriting except traveling around with
the company."[24]

She trained her attention on the novel, which she hoped, because
of its timeliness, would attract attention and sell briskly. Macmillan
released it in the spring of 1912, despite Brett's misgivings about the
commercial appeal of suffrage fiction. Gertrude protested, "I don't
see how you can assume that a suffrage novel is bound to fail when

that is the subject women are most interested in today. No adequate suffrage novel has heretofore appeared, that is all." [25]

Once the book came out, Mr. Brett suggested it be sent to American suffrage leaders who might promote it. True to her upper-class bias, Gertrude sought out Mrs. Alva Belmont, once married to William K. Vanderbilt and the mother of the unfortunate Consuelo, whose much-publicized international marriage proved disastrous. After the death of her second husband, Mrs. Belmont had traded in the tiara she had worn as a queen of New York society for the banner of Women's Rights. She received *Julia France* favorably, agreeing to lunch with Gertrude after reading it and telling her she was certain it would do much to further the cause.

Sales were disappointing (Gertrude complained vociferously that only 11,000 copies had been sold in the first month, and asked Macmillan for more aggressive advertising), and reviews mixed. While the *New York Times* called *Julia France* the best suffrage book to date, Frederic Taber Cooper in the New York *Bookman* faulted its loose-jointed construction, excess of melodramatic incident, and confusion about ideas.[26] At least the first two of Cooper's judgments hold water. As for the confusion, a better word would be ambivalence. Julia France as suffrage heroine had to be at once a victim—of her mother's social ambition and a brutal, imprisoning marriage— and a devastating siren, ready to restructure her existence, move to America, and exchange tailored suits for tea gowns when the right man comes along.

In the end Gertrude wrote the book off as a failure, pleasing to no group. "The English feminists [objected] because the heroine 'went through the Movement and out of it,' marrying an American instead of going to prison and being fed through the nose; the American crusaders resented the fact that the scene was England and none of their own leaders exploited; the general public on both sides of the water didn't care to read about Votes for Women in a novel; they had enough of that subject in newspapers. Nevertheless, it was admitted that *Julia France* gave a comprehensive picture of the Movement in England. . . . I have no love for it myself" (*Adventures*, pp. 470–71).

No one would quarrel with her assessment. It is an inferior book. But Gertrude was by no means finished with the Woman's Cause, or her role as public advocate and opinion maker.

CHAPTER THIRTEEN

Platforms and Mineshafts

One reason *Julia France* fails as a feminist polemic is that in the end it undercuts group action and glorifies the commanding and beautiful Queen Bee who sets herself apart from the other suffragists and the mass of womankind. In the presidential election year of 1912, Gertrude Atherton the public figure remained true to the Queen Bee role. Ever the attention-seeking, highly visible individualist, she behaved in a manner that countermanded the efforts of organized feminists.

In California, James Phelan was preparing to run for the U.S. Senate in an upcoming campaign. Despite his record as an anti-graft, pro-reform "progressive" San Francisco mayor, he intended to run for national office on the Democratic rather than the Progressive Party ticket, and he needed to cultivate allies in the state and national Democratic camps. Above all, he wanted to see Woodrow Wilson, the Democrats' candidate for president in 1912, elected. As a shrewd, pragmatic politician, he knew that California women, who would be voting in a national election for the first time since passage in California of the amendment for Woman Suffrage, would play a pivotal role. If Woodrow Wilson was going to take California, the newly enfranchised woman voter was going to have to be won over. Perhaps Mrs. Atherton could be persuaded to lend her name and influence to the Wilson cause.

Privately, Gertrude was partial to Theodore Roosevelt, who had bolted from the Taft-led Republicans to run for president on the Progressive ticket, with California governor Hiram Johnson as his running mate. Roosevelt's combination of intellect and physicality, his identification with adventure, the outdoors, and military heroics, made him supremely attractive to Californians in general and to Gertrude in particular. She had little feeling for Wilson, and she cared not a whit for party loyalty. She had always voted for the man, not the party. But James Phelan, her best friend and most devoted supporter, was asking a favor of her. "It was difficult to stand up against Mr. Phelan. He was no dynamo; on the contrary he was always calm, suave, diplomatic, but he could talk the hind legs off a donkey, and when he applied himself to win a point he won it" (*Adventures*, p. 474). She agreed to make her debut as a "platform woman" and to go on the stump for Woodrow Wilson.

Anticipating her first public appearance, she suffered pangs of premature stage fright and even consulted a Christian Scientist for help in overcoming her fears. The consultation armed her with a bit of useful advice: she must tell herself, "I am nothing, the Cause is everything. . . . I won't, *won't* be frightened" (*Adventures*, p. 475). The eve of her first talk found her still tremulous. To the poet Witter Bynner she agonized in a letter, "Tomorrow, alas! I will give a speech! My first! Political!!! I can't get out of it and would rather die."[1]

In a few days the *New York Times* ran a story headlined "Mrs. Atherton a Spellbinder" summarizing her talk before an audience, composed mainly of women, gathered in the Rose Room of San Francisco's Palace Hotel. Showing no sign of terror or inexperience, she had galvanized every person in the room.

A problem she faced as she courted women voters was Wilson's opposition to the Woman Suffrage amendment. Wilson had repeatedly stated his belief that suffrage was an issue to be decided at the state, not the national, level. Roosevelt, on the other hand, had spoken out in favor of woman suffrage and, more important, had agreed to a plank of woman-supported platform measures for social and industrial reform. Many American feminists who had held fast to the belief that they should stay clear of partisan politics had been won over by the Progressive reform platform. At the Progressive convention, Jane Addams of Hull House, probably the most admired woman of the day and never before an endorser of any political candidate, had seconded Roosevelt's nomination.

In her speech at the Palace, the *Times* reported, Mrs. Atherton questioned the sincerity of Roosevelt's conversion to the women's cause. She also questioned his support *from* women. Women's positive response to Roosevelt, she intimated, was hormonal rather than intellectual. "Seventy years ago Charlotte Brontë invented Roosevelt in the character of Rochester. Since that time women have loved Rochester, the man who was 100% male. I confess I have a sneaking affection for the type. Rochester was a colossal bluffer—the self-sufficient man. Roosevelt is of that sort. Woodrow Wilson is a man who always exercises self control. He will never be found acting like a bull moose. . . . Recently Roosevelt has burst out for suffrage for women. Wilson is opposed to woman suffrage, and is too honest to say that he is for it. He has a few old-fashioned prejudices. But the best way to correct this is to vote for Wilson and convince him by that means that suffrage for women is a good thing."[2]

Expounding her position from a soapbox provided by the Letters section of the *New York Times*, she called Roosevelt a johnny-come-lately to the field of social reform who did not deserve Jane Addams's support. "Throughout the former seven years of his incumbency," she argued, "he did nothing for labor, child or otherwise"—the Progressive platform called for prohibition of child labor for those under sixteen—"although children then as now were working sixteen hours a day in the southern cotton mills, women were the victims of 'speeding up' wherever there were factories and wages shamefully low for shop girls." (Roosevelt's platform also promised regulation of hours and conditions for working women.)[3]

Writing from Progressive Party headquarters, a woman counter-charged in the *Times* that "Mrs. Atherton's criticism of Miss Addams but emphasizes her own inability to make a fair criticism of any woman. We are quite content that Mrs. Atherton should stay on the side opposed to us, and we are equally content to have Miss Addams remain on ours."[4]

Certainly anyone trying to make sense of Mrs. Atherton's public stances could only be baffled by her inconsistencies. How could she campaign for suffrage one year, making a point of returning from a trip to New York in time to cast her vote for the first time in California, only to turn around and take a stand against the only presidential candidate committed to both suffrage and social reform? Her real devotion was to Phelan (which the public had no way of guessing), to the spirit of adventure that forever urged trying things she had never tried before, and to getting her name in the papers.

Twice during the campaign—once at the South Shore Country Club in Chicago and again in Los Angeles—she caused a stir by smoking in public, in violation of a taboo against women who smoked that was by then being frequently tested. "Mrs. Atherton Puffs Derision at Critics: Novelist Says Only Provincials and Backwood Natives Get Excited at Women Smoking," one headline read. When a Los Angeles Democratic women's group convinced her that her smoking was hurting the Wilson cause, she relented: "Novelist and Campaigner Will Associate with Lady Nicotine Only in Private." In the news story accompanying this last headline she is quoted as saying that in giving up smoking while campaigning "for the first time in my life I feel I am doing something useful." As for her nicotine habit, she confessed she never inhaled, nor did she imbibe much alcohol. Among women, she said, she thought drinking a more serious problem than smoking.[5]

When election day came, Gertrude claimed partial credit for Wilson's strong showing in the popular vote. She seems not to have realized that despite the closeness of the race, the Roosevelt-Johnson ticket and the Progressives won in California. She treasured a note from Wilson thanking her for her efforts on his behalf, but decided the "amusing and instructive experience" of political campaigning had served its purpose. It was time for her to return to the business of novel writing.

For her newest venture, the novel that would be called *Perch of the Devil*, she chose the setting of Butte, Montana. Montana seemed "the realest thing left in the world," recalling the excitement of Gold Rush California. It had a wide-open quality, a rawness, a sense of rugged adventure that the settled California of the second decade of the twentieth century could no longer claim. And, unlike New York or California, which had been "done to death," it had rarely been written about. American fiction, Gertrude told a *New York Times* interviewer, needed "undiscovered interest" and outdoor settings: "There is no story now in social success; the story is in the beginning."[6] Since she thought of novelists as literary prospectors, always on the lookout for new quarry to explore and exploit, she hoped to strike in the prosperous mining town of Butte a rich vein that had not yet been plundered.

Butte, "a long scraggy ridge of granite and red and grey dirt rising abruptly out of a stony uneven plain high in the Rocky Mountains,"[7] was a noisy, bustling, stay-up-late town, where trucks, laden with ore, shook the houses as they clattered by on the cobbled streets. Since it was ruled by what went on beneath its surfaces and since she intended to situate much of the action of her novel at a mining camp, Gertrude insisted on finding out for herself what a miner sees during a day's work. She descended into a copper mine, 1,800 feet underground, where "the atmosphere was so exhausted, the heat so oppressive, that I wondered how the miners could endure it. . . . Everywhere were signs: SAVE YOURSELF, which added nothing to one's mental comfort. The props were always threatening to snap under tremendous pressure, and sometimes did. Inspection was unremitting, but accidents happened all the same. The vast mine, ramifying in all directions and farther than the eye could follow, was lighted by electricity and one heard the constant pulsing of the dynamo. Miners were at work everywhere, and trolley cars laden with ore sped up and down in passages so narrow we were obliged to flatten ourselves against the wall." Even the intrepid Mrs. Atherton found her pulse quickening, her spine tightening, until her safe return to the surface. "Never before nor since have I been so glad to see the light of day" (*Adventures*, p. 490).

Gertrude devoted considerable energy to the study of the technologies of mining engineering and metallurgy, so that she could talk authoritatively to her reader about chalcopyrite deposits, float, faulted veins, and copper glance. She befriended a geological engineer who contributed to her education and read the manuscript for accuracy. Old-fashioned in many respects, the Montana novel breaks new ground in its ability to find beauty and mystery in science and technology, music in the roar of machinery and the crash of rock dumped from buckets. "The mystery down there is more romantic than your medieval dungeons," says the hero.[8]

Perch of the Devil, written not in Butte but in the sparkling mountain town of Helena, uses the underground setting for several key confrontations: between the lovers Gregory Compton and Ora Stratton, both married to others; and between aristocratic Ora and ambitious, humbly born Ida Hook, rivals for the love of the taciturn, strong-jawed, mining tycoon Gregory, Ida's husband. For an astute inward-looking psychological novelist, the mine would have provided a natural metaphor of the characters' unprobed depths. The narrator does speak of "unsuspected bulbs" in Ora's inner garden, but she is suggesting Ora's submerged physical beauty and sexuality. Like Hermia Suydam in the past and Mary Zattiany in the future *Black Oxen*, Ora undergoes a transformation only of externals, surfaces. A beautician (modeled on a young woman Gertrude met on the train to Butte) will work her over and turn her into a stunning temptress.

Ida Hook undergoes another kind of outward transformation. She too is a Galatea of sorts, one whose metamorphosis is to a higher social class. The daughter of a miner and a laundress, Ida starts out as a vulgar, brassy beauty with a mouth full of slang ("I need new duds the worst way") and chewing gum. Tutored in speech and manners by the "American princess" Ora, exposed to the culture and sophistication of Europe, pursued by an English lord and maintained in opulence by her increasingly neglectful and work-obsessed husband, she emerges as a finished, socially "advanced" matron, a woman who has fought to keep her husband, earn his respect, and prove her worthiness of him.

Neither one of the rival heroines can qualify as feminist ideals, since both organize their existence around men. Ora, who is named after a mine, actually owns a mine and expresses an interest in running it herself. But when she moves into her own mining camp, her motive is not to learn to work it but rather to put herself in close proximity to her best friend's husband, and entice him into divorcing Ida to marry her. Echoing sentiments that Gertrude had expressed in her 1912 *Harpers Bazaar* article "Woman Will Cease to Love," Ida claims at the end of the novel that the day will come when women no longer live for love and they "will really be able to take men as incidentally as men take women," but she demonstrates that for her and the other women she knows that day has not yet dawned. "I'm the sort that hangs on to her man like grim death."[9]

Gertrude considered *Perch of the Devil* her first novel "of the great American Middle Class." It does break from earlier novels in its celebration of Ida's ascendance from "crude" poverty into "polished" affluence and of her triumph over Ora, who despite advantages of birth and breeding, shows herself to be both parasitic and predatory. For once, Gertrude betrays no sympathy for a woman's designs on another woman's husband and shows divorce in an unfavorable light, as an easy out. For the first time too, a heroine's inherited privileges count for little in the end; endowment matters less than accomplishment.

The real hero of this novel is the competitive Western capitalist ethic, embodied in Gregory Compton, that says: commit yourself to a goal, work hard, stand alone, take on all comers—even giant trusts—and prevail; measure your success in wealth and power. Gregory, the apotheosis of the self-made man, starts out an obscure rancher and becomes a nationally recognized colossus of property and prosperity. He is the 1913 incarnation of the Atherton superhero. As the narrator effusively puts it, "the boldest imaginations and the most romantic hearts are sequestered in the American 'big business' men of today."[10]

In the *Californians*, written in the late 1890s, Gertrude had taken a far less sympathetic view of the greed of wealth-obsessed venture capitalists, writing: "Men came to kiss California and stayed to tear away her flesh with their teeth." There is no hint in *Perch of the Devil* that mining tycoons are despoilers of the earth. They are its conquerors.

By the time she left Montana, Gertrude had permanently retired any sympathies for the poor, the working class, or Fabian socialism and had temporarily retired her sympathy for the radical tactics of British Militant feminists. *Perch of the Devil* gives the nod to self-supporting young women of the West, but barely acknowledges the miners, dismissing them either as well-paid, thriving American laborers who had no cause for complaint or Southern European "Bohunks" who live like pigs and deserve nothing but contempt. Her drift to the right may have been assisted by what she saw of IWW agitation among Butte miners. During her stay there the Union Hall was blown up, and anarchist Emma Goldman made an appearance. Gertrude reportedly went to hear and see her, saying "I want to get a look at the creature before she's run out of town." [11]

Her friend Cora Older, back in San Francisco, had allowed herself to be converted to the cause of the Industrial Workers of the World. Encouraged by her, and anticipating Mabel Dodge's efforts to include "dangerous people" at her Fifth Avenue salon evenings, Gertrude had in 1912 invited IWW leader "Big Bill" Haywood to have dinner with her in New York. She had reported to Mrs. Older, "Your friend Mr. Haywood asked me to send you his love. I had him to dinner last night as I wanted to get from headquarters a statement of his policy of destruction and construction. He talked from about 8 till 11 and was most interesting and likable," adding that she thought he would ultimately be defeated by "his own optimism, jealousy of other leaders, drink and the Catholic Church." She predicted, "the working class will never get everything and there is no earthly reason why it should. However, such things make life more interesting—if the world had not been full of trouble from its dawn where would be our histories?" [12]

Between the time she dined with Bill Haywood in New York and her encounter with Emma Goldman in Montana, she had become decidedly less tolerant. There were limits. She believed in trade unions, but syndicalists went too far. In the same way, she thought the British Militants' most recent extremist methods showed that they had "gone mad." How dare they slash a great painting? "20,000 militants are not worth one Valasquez," she told the *New York Times*.[13] Revolutionaries, anarchists, violence-prone organizers, and advocates of mob rule were a menace, and women like Cora Older were dupes who had been seduced by a radical fad. Referring, in a letter to Phelan, to a threatened railroad strike, she said, "I suppose Mrs. Older is rejoicing in it. Like all people who allow fanaticism to warp her mind she is now convinced that the working class is the one and only class in the world." [14]

She now acknowledged her own unalterable loyalty to the ruling class, which she considered her class. She told Upton Sinclair, who had dedicated *The Jungle* to "the workingmen of America," that though she wanted to see poverty eliminated and favored a more equable distribution of wealth, "still I am frank to say that if it came to a showdown, that is to say civil war, I'd stand by my own class." [15]

But another kind of war—not between men and women, opposing candidates, or the haves and the have-nots, but the most destructive war among nations known to history—was to intervene. The publication of *Perch of the Devil* in the summer of 1914 coincided with the outbreak of World War I.

CHAPTER FOURTEEN

The Great War

 Gertrude was more than a casual observer of the cataclysm that was World War I. In 1916 she joined a small band of American women covering the war.[1] As a reporter for *The Delineator* and the *New York Times*, she stood on the battlefield of the Marne and saw fields of grain broken by faded flags marking the graves of the fallen. In Paris during the first week of the battle of the Somme, she could hear the guns firing day and night. In a railroad station near Verdun a drunken soldier flung a loaded gun on the floor in front of her. And at a Versailles sanatorium on a private estate she heard the cries of an inconsolable child who stared ahead as if in a trance, "like one of the broken stone nymphs in the woods."[2]

Even before she traveled as a journalist to France to view the heroism and carnage at close range, the war had affected her in the most visceral of ways: she became physically ill. Her bleeding ulcer—the direct result, her doctor thought, of the "poisons" generated by her passionate hatred for Germany—hospitalized her in the spring of 1915 and then confined her to bed in her apartment in the Morningside Heights district of New York City. "How terrible is this *Lusitania* sinking—the loathsome brutes," she wrote from her sickbed to James Phelan—who had recently been elected the first Democratic senator from California since 1897. "The warships are sailing up the Hudson today. I can see them from my window."[3]

Her fury over the Germans had been slow to ignite. At the outbreak of the war, Gertrude, like most Americans, took her time registering the full reality of the catastrophe awaiting Europe and the culture she equated with civilization.

The eve of the Great War had found her at a professional and personal crossroad. She had agreements with three different publishers dangling on strings of varying lengths. Stokes had brought out *Perch of the Devil*, promising to promote it aggressively and, she reported, to advertise "as if it were a new brand of soap." Macmillan had issued *Julia France*, but since its botched handling of new plates for *The Conqueror* had incurred her wrath, she allowed Stokes to buy the plates for that perennial big seller and washed her hands of Mr. Brett. And she had promised her old friend Elizabeth Jordan, now an editor for Harpers, a book on California history that would exploit the interest in the subject sure to arise from the Panama-Pacific International Exposition to be held in San Francisco in 1915. In fact, she had rented the apartment in Morningside Heights to be near Columbia University's libraries for her research on California.

Because of the Byzantine complexity of her relations with publishers, she wanted to keep her work on the California book for Harpers under wraps. "Please don't tell a soul that I am writing this book," she begged Phelan, who was sending information to assist her research, "as I want to be safely on the Atlantic before my present publisher, Mr. Stokes, or my recent publisher, Mr. Brett, knows that I have given a book to Harpers."[4]

She planned to depart for Europe as soon as she finished the California book; Muriel and the children were spending the year there. Muriel's marriage to Albert Russell was foundering under economic pressures combined with mother-in-law trouble. Russell was not earning enough to support his family, and Gertrude had taken them on as dependents. By her lights, Russell forfeited all claims as husband and father when he ceased paying the family's way. "I have had to support his family since last May," she wrote to Phelan in March 1915, "and while I do not resent this, . . . still I think that a man should support his family. And Muriel would prefer this herself. I do not believe that Al will ever do anything on his own. He utterly lacks the money making talent.... He is a born clerk."[5] Two months later she pronounced him a "complete failure" and wondered to Phelan who would provide for the children if anything happened to her. Russell, she had decided, would henceforth be considered Muriel's ex-husband. Muriel's own voice, through all this, remains inaudible; she seems to have mutely deferred to her mother.

In August 1914, when the German army began its march through Brussels, Muriel and the children were vacationing in Ostende, Belgium. Gertrude's first concern of the war was for their safety. With the help of Secretary of State William Jennings Bryan, she learned that they had escaped unharmed to London and would soon embark for New York, where they would join her on Morningside Heights. But the magnitude of the conflict had not yet become evident. Gertrude worried about practical things, relatively minor things, like having to alter her own plans to go to Europe and whether the war would keep people away from the Panama-Pacific Exposition.

Since she had spent so many years in Germany and still had friends there, Gertrude bent over backwards at first to see the German point of view. She published a letter in the *New York Times* maintaining that although democracy naturally abhorred autocratic power, she would not allow her sympathy with Great Britain to break her friendships with individual Germans. She quoted a letter to her from an unnamed German friend, claiming that Germany had not wanted war and was being misrepresented in the British and American press. She didn't agree, but she was willing to state the case.

Neutrality was President Woodrow Wilson's policy, and at first she agreed with it. She joined such luminaries as Elihu Root and Ida Tarbell on a newly organized Committee of Mercy, a "strictly neutral organization for the collection of funds for the destitute women and children of Europe."[6] But after the Germans torpedoed the unarmed *Lusitania*, killing more than a thousand civilians, all pretense of neutrality gave way. Now she beat the drum for preparedness, and spoke out against pacifist opposition to American military involvement in

the European conflict, parting company with social feminists with
whom she had already differed during the Wilson campaign. She
told the *New York Times* she could not oblige a request Jane Addams
had made in a telegram "asking me to strengthen the appeal to President Wilson urging a conference of neutral nations to find a just
solution to the war." Though she professed "the highest admiration
for Jane Addams as a humanitarian," she now believed neutrality
meant allowing Prussia to brutalize Europe.[7]

When she learned the Germans were guilty of such atrocities as
germ and chemical warfare, her fury exploded. Germany became
a venomous snake, strangling its enemy by gas-bombing unforti-
fied towns, "the most arrogant, ruthless and brutal power since the
Huns," and the pacifist doctrine of nonresistance became "the one
thing more abominable than war."[8]

A letter to the *New York Times* accused her of inconsistency; why
was German terrorism any worse than the methods of the British
Militants she had championed? Gertrude answered that she had
never defended extremists who slashed paintings or destroyed ancient ruins. "What I did uphold was fighting brawny policemen in
order to gain entrance to the House of Commons, heckling at public
meetings, smashing windows or even burning empty houses. Even
at their most violent the suffrage efforts were 'pygmy' compared to
outrages like the German devastation of Belgian cities, slaughter of
civilians, wasting of northern France, torpedoing of the *Lusitania* or
Zeppelin raids over London."[9]

It galled her that singer Maude Fay, a fellow Californian, had
chosen to remain in Munich through all of this. Making use of her
ready access to the columns of the *Times*, she published Fay's personal letter to her—a breach of confidence Fay never forgave—in
which Fay claimed "you would be pro-German if you were here. . . .
This terrible war has shown me the real Germany, and for this I am
happy to have remained."[10]

Although Gertrude pretended to forgive Miss Fay on the grounds
that German propaganda had clearly brainwashed her, the harm had
been done. Maude Fay's pro-German sympathies and the fact that
she had stayed in Germany, continuing to perform *Parsifal* to sold-
out Munich houses, had been broadcast to the increasingly incensed
American public. When Fay finally did return to the United States

in 1916, she had difficulty getting booked on the American opera or concert circuit and turned to Senator Phelan, an old family friend, for financial help. Gertrude probably did not know this. She confided to Phelan that she had never really liked Fay, who "likes no one but herself and pays not the least attention to anyone whom she cannot make some sort of use of." [11]

The repatriated Maude Fay found Western Americans more forgiving, or perhaps simply less aware of her pro-German past than were Easterners, who tended to identify with the Allied effort in a way the West did not. Gertrude chided her fellow Westerners for yawning if they found too much war news on the first page of their newspapers: "The distance of a thousand miles or so from the Atlantic seaboard seems to make all the difference in the world between human sympathy and stupid indifference." Perhaps, she speculated, Californians resented the British blockade that had robbed California of its export trade. [12]

Anti-German passions ran high, and Gertrude herself came under fire for sending her older granddaughter Florence to the "German" Elizabeth Duncan School in Westchester County. Elizabeth, sister of Isadora Duncan, moved her school from Darmstadt, Germany, to escape the war, bringing with her several young German girls who were pupils. She also brought as music teacher and pianist, her pro-German lover Max Merz, who aroused considerable suspicion.

Gertrude did not allow the rumors to bother her. It was she who selected the Duncan school for Florence, who had run away from the rigidly structured Sacred Heart convent school—the same school Muriel had attended. No doubt Gertrude sympathized with Florence's show of rebellious mettle, and she had heard of an educational alternative that seemed suited to Florence's temperament and talents. Marcia Van Dresser, who had known Elizabeth Duncan in Germany, told Gertrude that the Duncan school was re-forming in Croton and that she expected wonders of it. Florence enrolled as the first American pupil, exchanging Sacred Heart's black uniform with black stockings and shoes for Duncan's flowing, liberating blue tunic, blue cape, and bare feet. She was ready to imbibe Elizabeth

Duncan's philosophy of life as a daily work of art based on nature's rhythms and the Greek ideal of beauty, ready to be taught how to "touch the hills" with her fingertips.[13]

Visiting from France, the great Isadora would occasionally sweep down to observe Elizabeth's students, and when she performed in New York, the pupils were given box seats. Gertrude joined Florence at the Metropolitan Opera House on the memorable night when Isadora concluded her performance of the "Marseillaise" by bearing her breast and shoulder, in imitation of a figure representing Liberty on the Arc de Triomphe. Isadora won an ovation, but Gertrude sat aghast.

Florence thrived at the school, and her grandmother held this most unconventional, innovative, and frequently destitute academy in the highest esteem. Gertrude even recommended it to the daughter of a wealthy San Francisco society matron, touting it as "such an ideal place—on a hill above Tarrytown in a mansion surrounded by a park [the school relocated several times], bought for Miss Duncan by Vanderlip. The children are always in perfect health and learn all that children do at other schools as well as dancing out of doors and making their own clothes. They wear simple little Greek garments."[14]

She refrained from adding that the sole male student at the school was John Evans, the son of Mabel Dodge, whose Greenwich Village salon had made her the center of New York's bohemian and intellectual circles. Mabel had a genius for recognizing and cultivating "movers and shakers," the personalities that announce radical political movements and new artistic directions. In Europe she had befriended Gertrude Stein, and in 1913, newly resettled in New York, she had helped to organize and promote the landmark Armory Show of Postimpressionist art. John Reed, Lincoln Steffens, Bill Haywood, and Emma Goldman had animated her living room. Now, with the world at war, Dodge felt herself turning away from the foment and dissension of political radicalism and looking to nature and art for solace. A school devoted to the celebration, rather than the destruction of life, earned her unstinting financial and emotional support.[15] Of course she would want her only child to attend it. More than that: because her next husband, Maurice Sterne, had become the school's

resident drawing teacher, she sometimes spent nights at the school.
Her room adjoined Florence's.

Mabel Dodge and Gertrude Atherton may well have met during
this period. Surely the Dodge salon served as a model—along with
the salons of Madame de Staël and Madame Récamier—for the Sunday receptions Gertrude held on the third Sunday of every month,
which were attended by what she called "people of interest" in the
literary, journalistic, theatrical, and academic communities. Among
the guests were Carl Van Vechten, who would become a good friend,
playwright Avery Hopwood, Charlotte and Robert Hallowell of the
newly formed *New Republic*, actresses Ina Claire and Emily Stevens,
and writers Charles Hanson Towne, Sinclair Lewis, Fannie Hurst,
Frances Hodgson Burnett, Amy Lowell, Mary Austin, and Ellen
Glasgow. Senator Phelan came up from Washington when he could.
Unlike Mabel Dodge's intellectually charged evenings, designed to
stimulate lively exchanges on controversial issues like birth control
or anarchism, the Atherton salon served a primarily social function.
What was discussed mattered less than the convivial atmosphere and
the stellar guest list.

There were several reasons for this flurry of sociability. One was
that Muriel was around to see to the arrangements, food, and housekeeping—tasks she enjoyed as much as her mother found them oner-
ous. Another may have been that the war itself made people want to
gather together in the comfort of conviviality. And a third was that
this kind of entertaining suited Gertrude's present very public position as commentator, campaigner, Manhattanite, and—most recently
—advocate for writers. A charter member of the Author's League,
she now sat on its council (some of the regulars at the Sunday receptions—Gelett Burgess, Rex Beach, Kate Douglas Wiggin, and
Hildegarde Hawthorne—were fellow council members) and chaired
a fund to provide financial help to writers down on their luck.

If the social impulse pulled in one direction, the war and the
hatred it unleashed pulled in another. The 1916 topical novel *Mrs.
Belfame* deflects through satire some explosive anger. Germany is

one obvious target. When the heroine, a respected suburban New York clubwoman, goes on trial for the murder of her drunken lout of a husband, the German servant, "surly, large-footed" Frieda, exhibits the alleged oafishness of her nation by trying to blackmail her employer.

For Mrs. Belfame, the German flouting of all commonly held standards of decency provides an excuse for her own lawless impulses. When the novel opens, she is attending a lecture at the Friday Club on the topic "The European War vs. Woman." The idea of murdering her husband takes shape in her mind as the speaker touches on the recent war atrocities. Mrs. Belfame abhors her husband and has been longing, as she puts it, to "remove him." She has ruled out divorce as simply not respectable. But if she could get away with quietly, bloodlessly murdering him? As the lecture progresses, her inhibitions about taking someone's life are overcome, and she reasons, "Why not? Over there men were being torn and shot to pieces by whole-sale, joking across the trenches in their intervals of rest, to kill again when the signal was given with as little compunction as she herself had often aimed at a target, or wrung the neck of a chicken that had fed from her hand. And these were men, the makers of law, the self-elected rulers of the world." [16]

By the time Mrs. Belfame has heard the whole lecture she has persuaded herself that doing in one expendable husband counts for little when measured against the "stupendous slaughter in Europe." In her mind she has turned German swinishness and the failure of nations to effectively quell it into an indictment of the entire male sex. The war offered proof "that not civilization but man was a failure." [17]

Some of the stimulus for *Mrs. Belfame* came from a much publicized trial of the day, which Gertrude covered for the *New York World*. An upper-middle-class woman, Mrs. Florence Carman, had been accused of murdering a woman patient of Mrs. Carman's physician husband. In common with Mrs. Carman, the character Mrs. Belfame appears refined, respectable, well-spoken, and composed. The accounts of the Carman trial in the New York newspapers refer often to her tailored suits, white-gloved hands, and straw hats, and also to the courtroom crowded with the well-dressed women of her prosperous community. Gertrude borrowed the suburban, affluent ambience and adopted the premise of a respectable clubwoman on trial for murder. But in a significant switch, she changed the sex of the victim from female to male.

The wife with murderous designs on her husband crops up at regular intervals in Gertrude's imagination, offering an antidote to her overdeveloped hero-worshipping proclivities. We have met her in Patience Sparhawk, in Julia France, even in those early, Biercian columns for the *Examiner* that caused such a furor. Undoubtedly she owed her existence partly to George Atherton (or more precisely, to Gertrude's wish to be rid of him while she still chafed at the marital bit) and partly to Gertrude's cipher of a father and his disastrous replacement, Mr. Uhlhorn. Most recently, Muriel's husband had renewed her fury at the male of the species. Husbands were a tribe she found it easy to despise.

The murderous wife, then, is an old story. But never before had Gertrude draped a married woman's homicidal impulses in ideological cloth. Now it was not just particular husbands, but tyrannical or ineffectual Man who stimulated the homicidal itch. Germany, the Germany of Prussian Junker militarism and the Kaiser, became for her the embodiment of male aggression and paternalistic tyranny. Forgetting the place of honor that she had so recently reserved for the Kaiser and her own weakness for what she called the "100% male," Gertrude let her strain of Medea-like fury run riot. She did not actually injure anyone except herself, but in speech and in print allowed "this cormorant in the mind" free course. Referring to *Mrs. Belfame* (which takes its epigraph from *Medea*) in a letter, Gertrude wrote: "My new novel deals with murder. This sudden development of murderous inclinations on my part, relieved only in fiction, I ascribe to the War."[18]

Her second war novel, *The White Morning*, written after her visit to the French War Zone and just as the United States prepared to enter the war, takes place in the starved, shattered Germany of 1918. It envisions a revolution led by German women that dethrones the Kaiser, establishes a German republic, and brings the war to an end. The heroine of this most radical of Atherton novels, Gisela von Niebuhr, the daughter of a dictatorial Prussian, has foresworn mar-

riage and distinguished herself as a feminist playwright before the
war. During four youthful years spent as a governess in the United
States, Gisela carried on an affair with Franz von Nettelbeck, an
erect blond German diplomat of haughty military bearing. With
him she has formed the deepest of bonds; he is the love of her life,
her "other part." Transformed by the war into a feminist terrorist,
Gisela decides she must murder Franz in order to accomplish the
goals of a Woman's Revolution that will topple Prussian militarism. Women will blow up munitions factories, seize the telephone
and telegraph stations, and destroy miles of railroad tracks. Before
committing murder, Gisela cooly reasons that she cannot afford distraction or weakness borne of sexual desire. The war has made her
freer and more passionate than ever, but her responsibilities as a
leader take precedence.[19] Revolution is everything, her private needs
and emotions nothing; therefore Franz must die. On the eve of the
first act of terrorism in the Woman's Revolution, after a night of
ecstatic lovemaking, she drives a knife into his heart as he sleeps,
"the hilt of the dagger thrusting forward the rows of medals on his
breast."[20] In the most erotically charged chapter in an Atherton novel
since *Hermia Suydam*, the woman warrior has aped her male lover,
thrusting a weapon that destroys not only Franz, but male potency.

Gisela descends from "the old race of goddesses of her own Nie-
belungenlied." In the Arnold Genthe photograph of her prototype
on the book's cover she wears a helmet like Brunhilde's, and Atherton likens her explicitly to Brunhilde on her rock, awakening after
long sleep "not at the kiss of man, but at the summons of Germany
in her darkest hour."[21] She is Atherton's wrathful goddess, a Wagnerian heroine turned against Siegfried's passion and Wotan's might.
She and her female army, somber in grey uniforms, unfurl a flag
whose emblem shows "a hen in successive stages of evolution. The
final phase was an eagle. The body was modeled after the Prussian
emblem of might, but the face, grim, leering, vengeful, pitiless, was
unmistakably that of a woman."[22] The nurturing mother hen has
evolved into a menacing bird of prey.

Gertrude insisted that her fantasy of a German Woman's Revolution had solid grounding in reality. German women, she proclaimed,
had been in secret rebellion against their male oppressors for years
before the war. Editing her own experience in Germany, she now

emphasized the grumbles of discontent she had heard from the mouths of German women resentful of male domination. She wrote that while she lived in Germany, several young girls had confided to her their secret determination never to marry. "Having grown up under one House Tyrant . . . why in heaven's name should they deliberately annex another?"[23]

Soon after publication of *The White Morning*, the press reported strikes in the German munitions factories. Gertrude rejoiced at this first evidence of the uprising she had predicted: "It means," she wrote to the *Times*, "that the women of Germany are in revolt at last . . . for practically all the workers are women. . . . Let us pray for their success, for it would be the crowning humiliation of the wicked men who have destroyed the flower of Europe if their downfall were hastened by the sex they have never made any bones about despising."[24]

Gertrude's new willingness to countenance revolution earned her the unexpected applause of her once and future antagonist Upton Sinclair, who was publishing a monthly newsletter during the war. "It appears," he wrote in his column, "that her views have radically changed. She seems willing to contemplate revolution as a not wholly undesirable thing." Sinclair welcomed her to the fold and said he looked forward to seeing her apply her talents "to the tasks of social reconstruction."[25]

Gertrude rushed to clarify her somewhat unclarifiable views. She explained that the redistribution of wealth she envisioned in Germany shared nothing with the goals of either the IWW or the Bolsheviks, whose revolution had recently toppled the Russian Czar, and whose tyranny, she felt certain, would be several times worse than that of the Romanovs. (She hoped the Germans and the Russians, equally malevolent powers, would destroy one another.) Instead of adopting revolutionary tactics, American workers, she thought, should better their lot through legislation that would improve working conditions and education that would refine their skills.[26]

Eventually Gertrude "flew into a towering rage" with Sinclair over his pro-Bolshevik sympathies, but at the time he praised *The*

White Morning they were on friendly terms, which his support only enhanced. He considered it remarkable that Atherton, "our premiere exponent of the aristocratic tradition" had turned against at least the male half of the aristocracy. "She tells about a heroine who organizes a successful revolution of German women. The heroine is of course *hochwohlgeboren*—it is not yet possible for Mrs. Atherton to imagine a heroic person who is poor. The heroine is a rich German lady, and she kills rich German men." Sinclair held that in the end class loyalty would surpass sex loyalty: "I will venture to say to Mrs. Atherton: When the revolt in Germany comes . . . you will not see rich German women killing rich German men; you will see rich German women killing poor German women—and calling on rich German men to help." [27]

Her reply reveals her essential condescension toward the working class. She said that in Germany, only a rebel leader from the top stratum would be able to hold sway. In the United States, workers could hope for a fairer shake only after they overcame their ignorance and laziness. The IWWs were secret shirkers who only wanted to work two days a week. As for herself, she held no brief for the idle of any class. "Work has always been my play and I fancy I do a good deal more of it than most of these talking boxes." [28] And yes, in a showdown she would stand with her own class, the upper class.

Upton Sinclair was not the only critic to challenge her class sympathies. Commenting on *The Living Present*, Atherton's collection of essays on the activities of French women she met and observed during her visit to France in 1916, an anonymous reviewer for the *New Republic* protests the book's overemphasis on the war's implications for aristocratic women. "Her book is a curious although intriguing jumble of prejudice, keen swift insight, merciless observation, and a good deal of perhaps unconscious snobbery. Only Mrs. Atherton could have written it without misgivings." [29]

The essays in *The Living Present*, most of which had been written from France for *The Delineator*, do lavish attention and praise on aristocratic types like Countess d'Hassonville, president of one section of the Red Cross; the Duchesse d'Uzès, the once frivolous beauty who had founded seventeen hospitals; and the Marquise d'Andigné, the American-born founder of Le Bien-Être Du Blessé, a relief organization Gertrude adopted as her personal crusade. But what impressed her about these titled ladies—in addition to their titles—was their ability to throw off the mantle of privilege to take up tireless, selfless work on behalf of France. Salons full of gilt and filigree were being furnished with cots and turned into hospitals, workrooms, and refuges for homeless children. A former lady of the manor now harvested her own hay and cut her own wood.

Nor did Gertrude ignore the efforts of French women of the bourgeois, peasant, and industrial classes in this country so class-conscious that its Red Cross divided into groups based on the social status of its leaders. She describes peasant women delivering produce to Les Halles in carts they drove themselves, their bright coifs and cotton blouses black with dirt, their faces impassive. She speaks of munitions workers whose physically taxing jobs were transforming them into Amazons capable of tossing 40-pound shells; and young girls "of good family" being taught the skills of inn-keeping at the school in Passy, run by feminist journalist Valentine Thompson, where Gertrude lived for several months.

In common with other women who saw the war as the climactic episode in the ongoing battle of the sexes,[30] Gertrude recognized the sense of release and exhilaration at large among women enlisted in the war effort. The women she observed felt energized and liberated by the essential work they performed, independent of men and sometimes in the place of men. "Never," she wrote, "prior to the Great War, was such an enormous body of women awake after the lethargic submission of centuries, and clamoring for their rights. Never before have millions of women been supporting themselves; never before have they even contemplated organization and direct political action."[31]

Speculating on the war's long-term consequences for women, she foresaw a reversion to prehistoric Mother-Age, in which inheritance of property passed through the mother. In preparation for such a time women should henceforth be trained to be economically self-sufficient. Perhaps, at least for the generation still young at the end of the war, European women would choose to live their lives independent of male interference. "Thinking women . . . may emerge from this hideous reversion of Europe to barbarism with utter contempt for man. They might despise the men of affairs for muddling Europe into the most terrible war in history, in the very midst of the greatest civilization of which there is any record. They might experience a secret but profound revulsion from the men wallowing in blood and filth for months on end, living only to kill." Women might grasp the folly of bringing into the world more children "to be blown to pieces on the field of battle or a burden to their women throughout interminable years." The maternal instinct might subside "under a heavy landslide of disgust."[32] What she saw in France made plausible the prospect of an Amazonian Herland in which men count for little and children hold no sway.

The physical revulsion "from men wallowing in blood and filth" that she projected onto the entire female sex originated in her own responses to the maimed and mutilated men she saw in war zone hospitals and on the streets of Paris. At a military hospital devoted to the care of men whose faces had been disfigured, the sight of the unbandaged face wounds upset her so much she could neither eat nor sleep. She firmly believed that her body was protected by some "mysterious force" from enemy guns, but she lacked protection from her own violent responses to the injuries other had sustained.

The intensity of her gut reactions may have unconsciously influenced her decision to make Le Bien-Être Du Blessé her chosen cause. Her friend the Marquise d'Andigné enlisted her to head an American committee to raise funds to improve and supplement the diet of wounded Belgian and French soldiers who were hospitalized. Founded at the request of the French Ministry of War, Le Bien-Être Du Blessé, Societé France-Américaine pour Nos Combattants (The Well-Being of the Wounded, French-American Society for Our Soldiers) provided items like concentrated beef juices, cocoa, oranges, ingredients for gruels, preserves, and condensed milk to hospitalized soldiers.

Gertrude readily sympathized with the wounded who were being cared for in hospitals lacking dieticians, special kitchens, or provisions suited to individual needs. She wrote to Phelan thanking him for his donation; it would help fill an overwhelming gap: "In the military hospitals there are only milk and eggs in the dietary kitchens. . . . Many men, weakened already by loss of blood and unable to swallow a diet that disgusts them, have died of inanition, when a diet of bouillon, rice, cocoa and gruel would have saved them."[33] With her help, the relief organization eventually supplied not only provisions, but a squad of American dieticians and a fleet of Ford delivery trucks.

Charity work had once been as alien to her as political causes used to be, but she threw herself into fundraising for Le Bien-Être without stint. Moved by genuine fervor, she responded to the additional spur of competition with Edith Wharton, whose efforts on behalf of orphans, destitute women, and tubercular soldiers had already won her the cross of the Legion of Honor. Aided by the Letters column of the *Times*, which printed her appeals, and by a Bien-Être Du Blessé letterhead that included names like Mrs. William K. Vanderbilt, Miss Elsa Maxwell, Kate Douglas Wiggin, Mrs. Schuyler Van Rensselaer, and Mrs. Charles Dana Gibson, she continued to meet her goal, raising $5,000 a month despite the stiff competition among relief organizations.

For the first time since her novel-writing career began, as America entered the war, Gertrude Atherton willingly stopped producing fiction, telling Ina Coolbrith, "Affairs are so tremendous now that Art must take a back seat, and as for the individual, the less he thinks of his little ego the better."[34] The caption under her photograph in the June 1917 *Literary Digest* read: "Withstands the lure and lucre of novel-writing to raise funds to benefit the French wounded." When she did return to fiction, she predicted, she and other novelists were going to have to begin anew, rather than pick up where they had left off. "Types that were appealing before the outbreak of the war are insignificant now. . . . Everything that has contributed to literary certainties becomes uncertain now [amidst a] disastrous confusion of human nature."[35] The novel she produced right after this two-year hiatus—*The White Morning*—does stand apart for its polemical intent and scalding intensity.

If Le Bien-Être consumed the bulk of Gertrude's energy, it was not her only pro-Allies outlet. She briefly edited a propaganda organ called *American Woman's Magazine*. Its motto was "Service-Loyalty-

Responsibility" and its cover—the same for each of the eight published issues—showed a heroic American woman astride an eagle,
its wings spread against the horizon, soaring above the New York
skyline.

One of her editorials praises the Vigilantes, a group of writers and
artists (including her old acquaintance James Montgomery Flagg,
popular historian Mark Sullivan, and her editor-writer friend Charles
Hanson Towne) who sought to drive "the peace-at-any-price men
to cover, and to carry on propaganda that will thrill the country in
what they call their hour of peril." [36] In her Vigilante guise, Gertrude
blasted "the cowards and slackers who called themselves Pacifists
or IWWs" and backed all efforts by the government, the press, and
the motion picture industry to mobilize public opinion as "a solid
body (joined) for one purpose only, the winning of the war." [37]

The war had turned her into a new kind of flag-waving American
patriot, a creature far removed from the Gertrude who had so often
expressed her contempt for American provincialism and its tepid literary expression. Now she bristled when Ellen Glasgow complained
in public about American readers who demand in fiction "an eva-
sive idealism" and "sham optimism." This was the time to champion
American literature, not fault it. The old citadel of convention and
timidity, Gertrude claimed, lay in ruins. American magazines now
received new writers eagerly. We must "read and encourage our own,
for they are doing magnificent work, fearless, vital, informing." [38]

In wartime she considered it the duty of American artists to stay
in America; their country needed them. What she said about Henry
James's decision to become a British citizen we can only guess, but we
do have her response to Isadora Duncan's declaration, made during a
U.S. tour, that America was too narrow-minded to appreciate art and
she intended to return to Europe. Gertrude felt Isadora was right
concerning the intractability of American puritanism, but at least
Americans could be taught aesthetics. "As Miss Duncan is American
born, and has acquired a very high degree and unique quality of art
in Europe . . . , it is her duty to remain in her own country for a
few years and create in the minds of her compatriots those ideals of
beauty which nearly all men and women crave and few know where
to find. . . . So, let us pray she will abide among us." [39]

Isadora went back to France to live, but Gertrude would never again return to Europe as anything but a visitor. In fact, despite her efforts on France's behalf, she managed to insult the French government when she returned a citation she had received, explaining that it was her pleasure to serve France without reward. She did accept the Médaille de la République Française, but enraged the French ambassador to Washington, J. J. Jusserand, by writing to tell him she wished no further recognition, for "the only way left in this world to be distinguished . . . is NOT to be decorated by France" (*Adventures*, p. 531). In 1925, when Jusserand was no longer ambassador, she finally was offered—and condescended to accept—the cross of the Legion of Honor.

In 1919, with the war finally finished, the *New York Times* sent Gertrude to Paris to cover the peace conference. The French capital, which she had called "Our Lady of Sorrows" in 1916, was now "Once More the Gayest City." Despite rain-darkened skies, she reported, the French had gone on a dancing spree, and there were diamond tiaras in the window of every Parisian jeweler.[40] But her journalistic mission was destined to be cut short. At the start of the Peace Conference she suffered another inflammation of her ulcer. She sailed back to New York and the Morningside Heights apartment, where she remained only briefly. Within a few months, facing surgery, she decided to return to California.

Muriel, it turned out, also had a great deal to do with the decision to leave Morningside Heights. Her marriage over, she found she needed to work. The fragility of her mother's health made it clear she must develop her own financial resources. The war had prompted her to take a course in massage, which lead to a job in a military hospital in Louisville, Kentucky; after the war she planned to return to California. Her absence from the big New York apartment meant that Gertrude's life there had lost its domestic center. The Sunday salons were no longer practical without Muriel to run them. Florence would be facing major changes too; the Duncan school would be relocating, without her, in Europe. A momentous chapter was coming to an end.

PART FIVE

The Twenties

CHAPTER FIFTEEN

Lady Lazarus

 For Gertrude as for so
many others, the war served as a Great Divide, separating experience from callowness, mature women of judgment from vapid
jazz-babies. The new worship of flaming youth, "the everlasting succession of empty-faced girls" paraded on magazine covers, she considered absurd. Though she praised the new generation of American
women for its lack of moral hypocrisy—"Modern Youth Championed by Gertrude Atherton. 'Doing in Open What Older Generations Did in Secret' "[1]—she chided its rudeness and superficiality.
Flighty, egocentric Sally Montgomery, in *The Horn of Life* (a post–
World War I novel written during World War II), can't compare
with her older sister Lynn, who nursed French soldiers for three
bloodstained years and has emerged sad, sober, competent, and responsible. The war-seasoned woman, with her keener awareness of
suffering and of history and her immunity from the fad for fast
parties and bootleg liquor, towers above her younger flapper sister,
who blithely dismisses the past—"Anything back of 1918 is older
generation to us"—and proclaims youth's dominion: "The world is
ours. We'll say and do and be everything we damn well want to."[2]

When she returned to California from New York in 1919, Gertrude was approaching her sixty-second birthday. Although she disliked the feeling of remoteness from the world's nerve centers that living in California always awakened in her, she had reason to feel optimistic about her new life. Her health problems, a constant trial during the war years, seemed to have been put behind her. Surgery freed her of painful attacks and allowed her to eat anything she pleased, "including mince pie, fried eggs, . . . and my favorite vegetable, cabbage. It is exactly like being born again," she told a friend.[3]

While recuperating at Montalvo, she got a call from Samuel Goldwyn inviting her to come to Hollywood to try her hand at writing for the screen as one of his "Eminent Authors." She saw the offer as a chance to "cut a new groove" in her mind and to greet the new decade and the mood of eager expectation with a new challenge. In the past year, her novel *The Avalanche* had been turned into a film in which Elsie Ferguson starred, but she had had nothing to do with its adaptation for the screen. She jumped at the opportunity to become a full participant, a screenwriter and a member of the burgeoning Los Angeles film community.

From the Hollywood Hotel, where the "haughty" Somerset Maugham and the "sensational" Elinor Glyn were also ensconced, she wrote to Phelan that although she regretted her recent relocation had made it impossible for her to vote for his reelection (which he would lose in the Harding landslide), Screenland seemed full of promise. "It grows more interesting here. Goldwyn has the most brilliant editorial men on his staff to be found anywhere . . . and they have all adopted me. I have an idea they tried me out at first, fancying I might be conceited or egotistical or snobbish or unable to assimilate. However all is well."[4]

Goldwyn had her partnered with another writer, Lewis Sherwin; together they were expected to come up with a story that would in turn become a scenario for a silent film. Even though Sherwin seemed preoccupied with "chasing gas [which was scarce] and the elusive bootlegger," Gertrude had no doubt they would "strike fire and produce something."[5]

All of Goldwyn's Eminent Authors—writers like Mary Roberts Rinehart, Rupert Hughes, Alice Duer Miller, Rex Beach, and Gouverneur Morris—were, like Gertrude Atherton, successful working professionals with backgrounds in theater, popular fiction, or magazine writing and a healthy respect for the anticipated advances of $10,000 per film. None minded being called Eminent, and none objected to the full-page ads Goldwyn's publicist placed in magazines like the *Saturday Evening Post*, proclaiming them the greatest American writers of the day.

Goldwyn, a Polish-born former glove merchant, combined a shrewd business sense with total intellectual naiveté. To him, any successful writer was a good writer, and all famous writers occupied the same plateau. He tried to entice George Bernard Shaw, and later Sigmund Freud, to come to Hollywood to write for him. He even suggested that Washington Irving should write a screenplay for *The Legend of Sleepy Hollow* and had to be gently advised that Mr. Irving no longer dwelt among the living.[6]

Most of the Eminent Authors and the writers for other studios soon found themselves at loggerheads with their bosses and non-writing colleagues. They saw their stories rewritten and often altered beyond recognition by producers, actors, and scenario departments who complained about uncinematic writers who failed to think in visual or dramatic terms. The writers balked at losing control, and the studios felt they had imported a bunch of literary prima donnas who adapted poorly to the demands of a new medium. Film historian Kevin Brownlow says that continuity writers, who were despised as hacks, "were called in to rescue many an Eminent Author from many an elementary muddle."[7]

Failure to think cinematically signaled one problem for writers. Failure to think in dollar signs was another source of friction with the studios. Gertrude protested when her chosen title *Noblesse Oblige* was changed to *Don't Neglect Your Wife*, probably to echo a successful 1920 comedy called *Why Change Your Wife?* She complained, "My picture was given [this] awful title. They got into a panic because it was a period picture . . . and they feared the public was wedded to the present and gave it a title that is modern to excess."[8] Nor was she pleased later when the film version of her Munich novel *Tower of Ivory*, about an expatriate American opera diva and an English duke, was transformed into a movie about convicts that was banned in Philadelphia because it was thought to contain too many tips on jail-breaking.

Several other Atherton novels—*Perch of the Devil, Black Oxen,* and *The Crystal Cup*, in addition to *The Avalanche*—became films, but only *Don't Neglect Your Wife* resulted directly from her script work in the Goldwyn studio. Although it featured Gertrude's granddaughter Florence Russell, renamed Jane Atherton, in a small acting role, Gertrude found *Don't Neglect Your Wife* a disappointment unredeemed by box-office or critical success. The film critic for the *New York Times* astutely detected evidence that Mrs. Atherton, creator of the story, had "some experience in the cinema world not entirely to her taste." He thought the film less successful in plot and action than in character and setting and found little to praise: what started out as "history touched with romance" degenerated into "uninspired movie melodrama, incredible, homiletic, conventional."[9]

Within a year after the release of *Don't Neglect Your Wife* Gertrude had parted company with the Eminent Authors and succumbed to cynicism and disenchantment about the Hollywood she abandoned for Northern California. When she first arrived in Hollywood, she had defended it against charges that it had become a mecca of sin and depravity. An opponent of Prohibition who considered attempts to legislate morality a waste of time, she could not sympathize with bluenoses who regarded flapper bobs and dance crazes as signs of devil worship, or motion pictures as teachers of vice. She claimed in print that for all the brouhaha about Hollywood decadence, the city of Los Angeles took its tone from its ultrarespectable Methodist and Midwestern inhabitants, who were swarming into Southern California.[10]

Now she had second thoughts: maybe Hollywood was the new Gomorrah after all. Gertrude had seen for herself that skirt chasing, promiscuity, drug and alcohol abuse, back-alley dealings, and a willingness to measure every kind of value in dollars were more than gossip; they did exist. One of the most sensational of the several movie-star scandals that rocked the country in the early 1920s had come uncomfortably close to her. Two suspects in the headline-grabbing murder of director William Desmond Taylor were Mary Miles Minter, a young actress being ballyhooed as the new Mary Pickford, and her ambitious and possessive mother. All murders are unsavory, but the Taylor case—which remains officially unsolved—involved especially lurid allegations about drug connections, blackmail, jealousy, and sexual hanky-panky among the film community's rich, beautiful, and famous. During the commotion immediately following the murder, Mary Miles Minter hid out at the Pasadena home of Gertrude's granddaughter Florence.

Florence had married a screenwriter named Philip Hurn, had a baby, temporarily shelved her acting career, and settled in for a cycle of domesticity. After the murder, Minter needed to be shielded from the ever-inquisitive reporters who knew that she had seen Taylor on the night of his death and had kissed the corpse after the funeral. Although never named as a suspect by the district attorney, Minter's love letters to Taylor and her monogrammed silk nightgown had been discovered in Taylor's bungalow.[11] The press pursued her relentlessly, and she desperately sought a safe haven. Lewis Sherwin, who had worked with Gertrude at Goldwyn Studios, was a friend of Minter's. He suggested she stay with Florence and her husband; no one would think of looking for her there. Innocently, they had agreed.

Florence hoped to get some free baby-sitting out of the arrangement, but Minter proved incompetent and irresponsible. She couldn't be trusted to take proper care of herself, much less a baby. She simply closeted herself in Florence's home, not going out at all for weeks at a time. The task of fending off reporters, who had somehow gotten wind of Minter's presence, fell to Florence, who became less and less patient with the intrusions and with Miss Minter herself. After several months, the Hurns finally escaped to New York, leaving Minter behind in Pasadena.[12]

Gertrude had told a reporter, just as her stint in Hollywood was beginning, that she hoped to discover "the soul of Los Angeles."[13] By 1922 she had given up the search: it had no soul. She compared its atmosphere to the wine caves of Italy, where those who descended became intoxicated by the fumes.

Gertrude's disenchantment with Hollywood coincided with more general feelings of stagnation and despondency. Her books continued to sell well, especially in Europe where American travelers preferred paperback Tauchnitz editions of Atherton titles to those of any other American author, including Sinclair Lewis and Edith Wharton.[14]

In the United States she remained a commercial success—in 1921 *Sisters-in-Law* made it to ninth place on the bestseller list—but she was more and more widely regarded as a formula writer and a hack. Only older readers who remembered her firebrand reputation at the turn of the century or those aware of her feminist revolutionary fervor during World War I thought of her as a renegade, and no one in the literary community ranked her an artist comparable to Cather or Wharton.

Nor did readers think of her, any longer, as a social critic. Baiting the complacent middle class had become the perogative of H. L. Mencken, who found much to mock in romantic, escapist fiction of the day. He placed Mrs. Atherton among "the heaven-kissing heroes of the $1.08 counter," who saw writing novels as a chance "not to interpret life, but to varnish, veil and perfume it."[15]

Gertrude found herself alienated from both mainstream culture and its most vocal critics. She attacked Mencken for his "pounding, yelling, screeching style" and his sympathy for such purveyors of the commonplace as Dreiser and Sinclair Lewis. She held Lewis responsible for anatomizing the small town and giving it more attention than it deserved: "I am only protesting the deification of the common and vulgar."[16] She sat gingerly—aware she did not truly belong—at the Algonquin Round Table where, during stays in New York, she sometimes lunched with the celebrated wits. Their smugness irritated her. The Young Intellectuals—dubbed by her "The Sophisticates"—created at their stylish gatherings "an excellent forcing house for ideas and vocabulary," but they tended to take their own pronouncements too seriously. "They consider themselves the most important group in New York—in America—at present: the life-giving group of suns round which far-off planets humbly revolve."[17]

No writer, no movement, no popular trend, seemed worthy of her respect. Such blanket negativity was nothing new for Gertrude; finding fault, hitting out, casting aspersions were almost reflex acts. But far less usual was the self-reproach, the dissatisfaction with her own recent work she privately voiced. She fretted about the way her "fiction tract" had been functioning; no novel she had produced since the pre-war *Perch of the Devil* pleased her. In fact, she felt certain that something was seriously amiss.

She begged a friend's forgiveness for the imperfections of *Sleeping Fires*, a cliché-ridden potboiler that serves up the tired theme of alcoholism in post–Civil War San Francisco society, and the more successful *Sisters-in-Law*, which follows a San Francisco family from the earthquake through the Great War. "I wrote *Sisters-in-Law* too soon after an illness and operation," she explained, "and felt it was lacking in vitality. *Sleeping Fires* was written (in Hollywood) with the thermometer ranging from 85 to 90 degrees and in utter discomfort." [18]

Sisters-in-Law is actually a far more vivacious novel than she realized. ("It belongs," critic Henry Seidel Canby wrote, "not with the fine art of American fiction that Mrs. Wharton and Miss Cather have been attaining; and certainly not with the mediocre, the facile, the merely sensational. It belongs with the imperfect, which yet has the girth, the vitality and some of the truth of the best in literature.") [19] But Gertrude harshly judged it "the most shallow and uneven novel I had written since my earliest period" (*Adventures*, p. 542). Depressed and uncharacteristically self-abasing, she found nothing positive to say on any subject.

Gertrude's sense of well-being required constant novelty and the stimulation of new settings and projects. Fallow periods were rare. When they did come, she panicked. Had the springs of her creativity run dry? No ideas for new books came to mind, and she was finding it hard to concentrate. Casting about, she fled Northern California for New York and took a room in a hotel overlooking Madison Square, close enough to where the circus played so that she could hear its lions roar.

Years before, in Rouen, her temporary inability to come up with an idea for a book had caused her to fall on her knees in prayer at a church frequented by pilgrims; she had been rewarded with the conception of *American Wives and English Husbands*. Once again a supplicant, she found her prayers answered this time, not by the Almighty, but by His replacement, Science. A newspaper story had inspired her very first book, and again would offer deliverance. As she scanned the New York papers, her eye caught an account of a seemingly miraculous rejuvenation. A Viennese surgeon, in whom the privations of war had induced premature senescence, had been restored to his former level of youthful vigor by a surgical procedure performed by Dr. Eugen Steinach, Professor of Physiology at the University of Vienna. The revivified surgeon told the Associated Press that Steinach had found a "modern scientific fountain of youth." Although close to 70, he now boasted the energy and endurance of a strong man of 40 and could work fourteen hours a day.

Dr. Steinach's New York based disciple, Dr. Harry Benjamin, was quoted in a statement that struck Gertrude with the impact of a thunderclap. "Women were running to the Steinach clinic from all over Europe, among them Russian princesses who sold their jewels to pay for treatments—women were not operated upon—that might restore their exhausted energies and enable them to make a living after the jewels had given out" (*Adventures*, p. 556). "After the jewels had given out" was a phrase she would not forget. Gertrude decided at once to contact this Dr. Benjamin and place her own treasures—both her weary body and her creativity—under his care.

The patient, sixty-four years old, for several years had complained of an increasing lack of mental activity; power of concentration was waning, also imaginative ability. Mental sterility would perhaps best sum up her chief complaint. Outside of occasional sleeplessness, requiring a veronal, there was no physical disability.

Treatment was begun in February, 1922. Three more treatments were given at intervals of one week. The patient felt very dull and tired for a few days after each treatment. About six weeks after the first treatment this very intelligent patient, not at all hysterical, stated that she slept better than in many years; that she felt her brain clearer; that she had begun to do considerably more work and that she felt more 'sustained' in it. New ideas had come to her 'like a flash,' as rarely before. During the following months the patient was unusually active, working intensely from ten to twelve hours each day—a strain which she had not been able to endure in many years.[20]

Although Dr. Benjamin attempted to disguise Gertrude's identity by referring to her as "an educator" and omitting any mention of her name, there can be no doubt that Gertrude Atherton is the patient he is describing.

The Steinach Treatment, as administered in 1922 by Dr. Benjamin, consisted of mild X-ray stimulation of the ovaries. (In 1925, when the harmful effects of radiation were acknowledged, the treatment was altered, and diathermy substituted for X-rays). The theory was that while women who underwent the treatment would be rendered sterile (a negligible loss in the case of post-menopausal patients), the ovaries would resume their hormone-producing capacities. Women in their sixties would regain the youthful glow, the sexual allure, the smooth skin and bright eyes, of those half their age. Their energy, their capacity for work, would also rise, Lazarus-like, from the post-menopausal crypt.

Gertrude experienced a sudden, near-mystical rebirth, similar to a religious conversion, but centered on changes within the physical body. At first her brain was torpid. She slept sixteen hours a day. "I saw no one, for I was too stupid to sustain a conversation, and could barely read a mystery story." After her eighth treatment, "I had the abrupt sensation of a black cloud lifting from my brain. . . . Torpor vanished. My brain seemed sparkling with light. I was standing in the middle of the room when this miracle happened and I almost flung myself at my desk. I wrote steadily for four hours. . . . It all gushed out like a geyser that had been 'capped' down in the cellars of my mind, battling for release" (*Adventures*, pp. 558–59). She had begun the treatments in February. In May she wrote to Charlotte Hallowell that she had started a new novel, "and have written 30,300 words. I haven't felt so thoroughly well-equipped for writing for years."[21] *Black Oxen*, one of her most powerful and accomplished efforts and her biggest commercial success, was under way.

As far as Gertrude was concerned, a scientific miracle had occurred. She was absolutely convinced—although some members of the scientific community considered the Steinach Treatment bogus and its benefits the result of nothing more than auto-suggestion—that Dr. Benjamin had resurrected her youthful vitality and creative energy. She looked and felt better than she had in years, and she knew with a certainty that the new book would be a success. Her self-confidence surged. She immediately abandoned Frederick Stokes, her publisher for the past seven years, in favor of Horace Liveright, the most innovative and up-to-date publisher in New York. She felt in absolute command as a writer—a feeling she had feared she might never again have. And in the midst of a youth-worshipping decade, she had accomplished an age-old fantasy. At age 64, without losing any of the experience and knowledge of the world those years had given her, she was young again.

In a 1980 interview, Dr. Benjamin—nearly blind and almost a century old—said in a steady, matter-of-fact voice tinged with the faintest traces of a German accent, that his patient Mrs. Atherton cared far more about her regained ability to work than any renewed sexual vitality. He had doubts about her interest in sex and used the word "frigid," although he knew about her closeness to Senator Phelan. The creative process, he thought, became Gertrude's substitute for procreation. She would joke about strange food cravings she experienced while hatching a book—just like those in the folklore of pregnancy. The inscription she wrote in Dr. Benjamin's copy of *Black Oxen* merely expresses general gratitude. But in private she told him: "I am the mother and you the father of this book." [22]

CHAPTER SIXTEEN

'Black Oxen'

 "I do not merely *look* young again, I *am* young. . . . I am the age of the rejuvenated glands of my body" (*Black Oxen*, p. 176). These astonishing words are spoken by Countess Zattiany, the mysteriously youthful ash-blonde, 58-year-old heroine of *Black Oxen*, a novel of contemporary New York that Gertrude conceived several weeks after she began treatment with Dr. Benjamin.

Black Oxen topped the best-seller lists for 1923, sharing the roster with Emily Post's *Etiquette* and outstripping *Babbitt*. Movie and mass-market rights were quickly sold, and Gertrude again, to her delight, found herself financially flush—she banked more than $31,000 in royalties in one year—and in the news as a celebrity author viewed by some as a threat to public morality. *Black Oxen* was denounced from the pulpit and banned from the Rochester, New York, public library for being "unfit for young minds." For the first time since the days of *Patience Sparhawk*, the *New York Times* found Gertrude Atherton newsworthy enough to prompt editorials. It claimed to be more disturbed by the book's science than its morality and argued that the Rochester library's censorship had inadvertently given *Black Oxen* an excellent free advertisement for which its publisher "will be duly grateful."[1]

Publicity was Horace Liveright's strong suit. The book's huge success owed something to Boni & Liveright's state-of-the-art marketing techniques and the talents of its publicist, Edward Bernays. Bernays, who invented the term "press agent," initiated the practice of distributing circulars to major bookstores each week, offered newspaper book editors free books, and handed out ready-made articles, which he called press releases, on current books and authors. The goal was to turn books into news events and authors into stars.[2]

The appeal of such an approach to a literary diva like Gertrude Atherton is easy to comprehend. But Liveright, whose list included titles by Theodore Dreiser, George Moore, Ezra Pound, Dorothy L. Sayers, and Sigmund Freud, had to feel *he* had something to gain. Eager for controversy, he rushed in where other publishers feared to tread, with books on provocative subjects: socialism, psychoanalysis, sex. With a gambler's daring he would invest in books he thought both worthy and potentially profitable. *Black Oxen*'s contemporary New York setting, its glimpses into elegant opera boxes, sophisticated literary soirees, and boozy flapper carouses, were sure to attract a public eager for insider information. Its focus on the youth-worshipping Twenties and on the explosive and timely topics of sex, warring generations, and aging women made it a potential block-buster.

Black Oxen is, among other things, a propaganda novel with a message directed at women no longer young: ladies, go out and find yourselves a doctor who will restore your youth via the Steinach Treatment. Countess Zattiany, the regally elegant young "European but subtly American" siren whose uncanny resemblance to a former Old New York belle named Mary Ogden has perplexed and agitated all of New York society, turns out to be, not the ghost or illegitimate daughter of Mary Ogden, but Mary Ogden herself, rejuvenated. A widow who has returned to New York after many years in Europe, Mary Ogden Zattiany reveals to a group of gaping, gasping, post-menopausal Gramercy Park matrons ("We're still human if we are old and ugly") that after the war she had suffered a profound sense of exhaustion and demoralization: "Life had seemed to me to consist mainly of repetitions. I had run the gamut" (*Black Oxen*, pp. 135–37).

During the war, she performed a vital function, running a hospital. Sick and displaced children in Vienna still needed her help, but in the war's aftermath she felt too depleted of energy, too world-weary, to have much to offer them.

A Viennese physician (Gertrude calls him Dr. Leinbach) advised her that her despondency had a simple physiological explanation: her ductless (endocrine) glands "had undergone a natural process of exhaustion." The cure was equally simple: X-ray stimulation of the ovarian cells, which caused "the other glands to function once more at full strength and a certain rejuvenation [to] ensue as a matter of course."

All of the women find the account of the resurrection of "that section which refined women cease to discuss after they had got rid of it" fascinating, but a few express outrage; such tampering with the natural processes strikes them as indecent or immoral "interfering with the will of the Almighty" (*Black Oxen*, pp. 139–43). Countess Zattiany's very appearance contradicts and mocks their scruples. She argues that one day rejuvenation will be taken as a matter of course, like vaccination. Only the rigid, the fear-ridden, the hopelessly hidebound will fail to seize the miraculous restorative gift bestowed by science.

The autobiographical underpinnings of Countess Zattiany's experience of rejuvenation are obvious to anyone who has read Gertrude's account of her own transformation. The same sensation of a "lifting" is common to both Gertrude's and Mary's accounts, and for both the "lift" follows a period of torpor. But while Gertrude's primary concern was the effect of "mental sterility" on her creative output, for Mary Zattiany the change in her appearance becomes the primary benefit of the Steinach Treatment. True, Countess Zattiany has a political calling and finally forsakes the transient gratifications of a romantic marriage for a clear-eyed alliance with a European suitor who appeals to her need to serve a useful function. But on the stage where we see her playing her part, her restored beauty is what empowers her and sets her apart.

Before her rejuvenation, Mary Zattiany tells Lee Clavering, the 34-year-old New York drama critic who wants to marry her, she watched the sad deterioration of her once celebrated allure. "I seemed slowly to dry up—wither. . . . It seemed to me that I had ten thousand lines." Someone who had known her as a belle in New York spotted her at the Paris Opera after the war and pronounced her a faded beauty, a dethroned idol. Now her sexual magnetism has returned with such force that she becomes the sensation of New York. At the opera, the entire audiences fixes on her, rather than the stage. A hushed gasp follows her entrance to a social gathering. Young men throw themselves at her feet. Newspaper columnists write about her. Desirable young women turn on her in jealous fury. A romance queen of unrivaled sexual power, she gleams and dazzles, outshining every other star in the firmament.

To a veteran reader of Atherton novels, Mary Zattiany's transformation reprises a familiar theme. The metamorphosis of ugly duckling into beautiful swan had occurred in her books from the time of Hermia Suydam, who invests a million-dollar inheritance in a course of health and beauty treatments that render her irresistible. Ora Stratton in *Perch of the Devil*, after a beautician's makeover, evolves from a drab matron into a temptress. In a short story called "A Monarch of Small Survey," published in 1905, a 70-year-old maiden invests her windfall in a quest for the allure she never enjoyed when young. She installs a trained nurse who steams and massages her face and body "with spirits of wine and unguents" until she feels revitalized. If she cannot reclaim her youth, at least she will have "all that belongs to youth."

The preoccupation with remaining young-looking took root in Gertrude's psyche long before she ever heard of Dr. Steinach. As a child she watched her mother become habituated to cosmetic rituals designed to preserve her complexion and figure. "As far back as I can remember," wrote Gertrude, "she made a fetish of her beauty and preserved it in every way she knew how.... She resented bitterly the passing of youth" (*Adventures*, pp. 33–34). So did Gertrude herself. By the time of her stay in Hollywood, she had become so sensitive about her age that she concealed from everyone her true relationship with her granddaughter Florence. She did not want the people she met to think of her as old enough to have a grown granddaughter, and so introduced the young actress Florence (who had taken the name Jane Atherton) as her niece. She used massage to keep her skin supple and walked around Los Angeles carrying a black parasol, which she opened to keep off the sun's harmful rays. She did her best to suppress any photograph that showed her in what she considered to be an unflattering pose.

Unfortunately for Gertrude the woman and Gertrude Atherton the novelist, she convinced herself that changing the way you look supersedes any other kind of change: intellectual, social, psychological, or spiritual. She indulged in a kind of magical thinking that seeks one-step solutions to complex problems. A fighter, she viewed the Steinach Treatment as her superior version of her mother's Cameline powder, her scientific defense against time's relentless assault. She seemed, as H. L. Mencken put it in his review of a later Atherton novel (whose heroine miraculously sheds frigidity and mannishness under an endocrinologist's care) to "find the primary springs of human character in the ductless glands."[3]

In *Black Oxen*, the women in their fifties and sixties who are Mary Zattiany's contemporaries but have not benefited from the miracle of rejuvenation make a dismal showing. The Gramercy Park matron Mrs. Oglethorpe retains not a trace of her former handsomeness. With a heart still young, she craves the love of young men, but they want none of her. She's an "old husk," with the face of an aged warhorse. "Her hands were skinny, large-veined, discolored by moth-patches and her large aquiline nose rose from her sunken cheeks like the beak of an old eagle" (*Black Oxen*, p. 186). She and other feminine representatives of Old New York—the patrician enclave so often visited in the fiction of Edith Wharton—make no concessions to current fashion. "They all have that built-up look, with hats too small and high for their bony old faces, which they do not even soften with powder" (*Black Oxen*, p. 27). Mary Zattiany laments the fact that in America, unlike Europe, women who are no longer young rarely attract romantic interest. She and Lee Clavering invite us to consider the possibilities of "autumnal love." But in *Black Oxen*, no older woman, other than Mary Zattiany herself, arouses anything but physical revulsion.

The withered matrons at least retain dignity, a quality their flapper granddaughters wholly lack. Dizzy Janet Oglethorpe, who was played by Clara Bow in the 1924 silent movie of *Black Oxen*, is a mean-spirited "near-strumpet," eighteen years old. Rude, jealous, conniving, and an embarrassment to her distinguished family, Janet drinks to excess, throws herself at men, and paints her face with heavy makeup that attempts to disguise the fact she looks like a child, "a greedy child playing with life." With her bobbed hair, slangy speech, rolled stockings, and gutter morality, she embodies the worst qualities of emancipated, post-war young womanhood set loose in an anarchic, pleasure-worshipping society. In this world, the "democratic flu" is epidemic; time-honored standards and traditions have no place, and old notions about aristocracy have fallen away. In a previously select enclave, anything goes.

Janet and her contemporaries hold one card Mary Zattiany will never again play: they can have children. Although Mary insists she is as young as the rejuvenated glands in her body, she acknowledges to her would-be husband Lee Clavering that she is sterile. Clavering finds Mary's beauty and fascination more than enough compensation for her inability to conceive. He shows an enlightened willingness to separate a woman's romantic and sexual appeal from her biological function. But without directly saying so, the book denigrates the child-bearing capacity. There are no children, no young families, in this novel about the war between generations. Mrs. Oglethorpe's many children represent her life of duty and service. Every young woman we encounter pales by comparison with Mary Zattiany, whose beauty, restored by the most modern scientific advances, harkens back to a turn-of-the-century feminine ideal.

When Clavering catches his first glimpse of Mary in the audience at an opening night, he associates her sloping shoulders and the "haughty poise of head" with family portraits in the gallery of his Southern home. He suspects she has a profile, though profiles are out of date nowadays. "Probably she was the only woman in the house who wore gloves. Life was freer since the war" (*Black Oxen*, p. 6). For him she is a revivified icon from the past. Madame Zattiany's patrician elegance makes a last stand for a vanishing feminine aesthetic and a system of rigid class distinctions that in the 1920s were fast becoming obsolete.

If Mary Zattiany's beauty—a heightened and idealized version of Gertrude Atherton's—returns us to the age of aristocratic Edwardian formality, its static, "posed" quality suggests another kind of stasis. Like Gertrude, Mary has traveled widely and lived at many different addresses, but she projects an image of statue-like immobility. A stranger to the flowing, curved lines that marked the sensuality of an Art Nouveau image or an Isadora Duncan dance, she seems to be made of marble. The arrogant pose of head says keep your distance, do not touch. She holds her chin high, the universal attitude of the snob. Her austere carriage conveys her inherent superiority and comments negatively on the flapper's dervish-like gyrations.

Clavering sees her as a Nordic princess sweeping northward over the steppes of Russia as ice caps retreat. We are meant to think of her as one of nature's chosen, a manifestation of the hegemony of Nordic ancestry. A Snow Queen, she appears once wearing a diamond necklace "that seemed to frost her gown. She was smiling and gracious and infinitely remote. The effect was as cold and steadying [to Clavering] as his morning's icy shower" (*Black Oxen*, p. 84).

Mary's sexual magnetism becomes all the more extraordinary when we consider that—in addition to being almost 60, frosty, queen-like, and aloof—she expresses a sexual disinterest that approaches revulsion. For decades she has "looked upon love with abhorrence. . . . Sex was not only dead but a detestable memory." Weary in body, mind, and spirit before her rejuvenation, she finds, now that she looks and feels young again, that "the bare idea of that old game of prowling sex fills me with ennui and disgust. The body may be young again, but my mind, re-energized though it is, is packed with memories, a very Book of Life" (*Black Oxen*, p. 172).

Gertrude bestowed on the young Mary none of her own sexual inhibitions or scruples—the "fastidiousness" she referred to in her revealing letters to Bierce. Instead, she dealt the beautiful, unhappily married countess a generous portion of lovers, with whom she amused herself while her husband sought his pleasures with mistresses. She tells Clavering, "for a woman of my type—what may be called the intellectual siren—the lover phase is inevitable" (*Black Oxen*, p. 171). But her lovers eventually bored and disgusted her (here she does begin to resemble Gertrude) as much as her husband did. Prey to a profound cynicism, she comes to regard young love as "a blaze that ends in babies or ashes." A hysterical outburst by a repressed 42-year-old virgin leaves her nauseous and overcome with loathing "for all women and all men."

Mary plays a few passionate love scenes with Clavering. In one, his kiss makes her forget both past and future; the present moment's happiness and communion obliterate everything else. But she senses immediately that "life was being drained out of her." The embrace makes her feel "that her entire body was encircled by flexible hot bars of iron and her face, her mouth, were being flagellated" (*Black Oxen*, p. 162). Sex offers fleeting excitement, pleasure, transcendence, and release, but beyond the moment it becomes a prison, a threat to freedom and autonomy that saps the elixir of life.

When she throws herself into the role, opposite Clavering, of romantic heroine, Mary only proves herself a victim of delusion and common human folly. She abruptly terminates her engagement to Clavering when persuaded by a former lover—Prince Hohenhauer of Austria—that she has been fooling herself if she thinks romantic love can endure in a marriage to a young American. Hohenhauer's successful countersuit does not proffer love or passion. Rather, it puts romantic love in its place as "merely one more youthful delusion of the senses," soon shattered by daily intimacy.

Prince Hohenhauer does not ask her to stop acting, only to switch roles. Instead of using her restored beauty, intelligence, and wealth to manipulate men in the "commonplace unworthy" game of love, he asks her to place these same gifts at the service of sterner tasks. If she returns to Europe as his wife, she can look forward to a position as the most famous and powerful woman in Europe. The prince plans to rule Vienna, making it the capital of a great Austrian republic. Together they will save Europe, and—since Europe represents all that is precious in human history—civilization.

Hohenhauer prevails because he truly knows Mary, understands her as a creature to whom power is the breath of life. He knows that her restored beauty matters so much because it allows her once again to successfully control and manipulate people. His perceptions validate those of a character named Gora Dwight, a successful novelist (carried over from *Sisters-in-Law*) who has told Clavering that Mary would be a fatal choice as wife for him because he could never dominate her, and she would sap his creative energy and ambition to write plays. Gora sees marriage as a power struggle in which Clavering would lose to the indomitable Mary, who conceals ruthless force behind her charming manners. The proper mate for Mary would be a statesman, not an artist. Ambitious and successful herself, Gora believes that "power, after sex has ceased from troubling, is the dominant passion in human nature." As a novelist, she knows a thing or two about the sweet taste of power. "After all," she says, "a novelist has things all her own way" (*Black Oxen*, pp. 336–37).

Gora Dwight and Mary Zattiany voice the disillusionment with romantic love and rapid social change that Gertrude experienced in the early 1920s. *Black Oxen* has enormous vitality, but its vision is a dark one. Gertrude's old sparring partner, Upton Sinclair, took the book as proof of the moral bankruptcy and vapidity of the New York upper crust. "A more devastating picture of waste, futility, and above all, boredom, could not be drawn by a muckraker's pen," he wrote.[4] Gertrude saw an unraveling of standards everywhere, not just in the upper crust. She saw a society rushing to destroy the conventions, morality, and class structure of the past, without offering anything of substance in their place. And she saw love between man and woman as a mirage, offering neither durability nor an alternative to isolation. In *Black Oxen*, what conquers is not love, but solitary strength; a strong woman can triumph even over time. The Steinach Treatment's glory is that in the Darwinian struggle to survive and dominate, it provides a competitive edge. Mary Zattiany, as the narrator says, "marched off with the flag" (*Black Oxen*, p. 232).

Gertrude found the title "Black Oxen" in a Yeats play, *The Countess Cathleen*:

> The years like great black oxen tread the world
> And God the herdsman goads them on behind
> And I am broken by their passing feet.

She told Phelan that in the epigraph of her new book's title page she would omit the last of these three lines, the one about being broken by the years, because it would misrepresent the book. "The characters are pretty well banged about, but not broken. I don't take any interest in weak characters." She regarded growing old as another of life's battles. If you let the years defeat you, you could blame yourself.

When *Black Oxen* first began making a stir, Gertrude made an effort to distance herself from its heroine. Mary Zattiany may have undergone the Steinach Treatment; that did not prove her creator had. In a letter to Phelan, she seems startled by his response to an advance copy she had sent; he assumed that she had written from personal experience. Ingenuously she asked, "What on earth put the idea into your head that I had taken the treatment? It was my heroine. But mind you don't breathe it until the book comes out." After Phelan told her he found Mary a most unsympathetic character, she protested, "Mary Zattiany created herself. I had nothing to do with her. No novelist worth his salt 'makes' his characters. To me she is perfectly logical. The trouble was that she had too much intellect and had had too much experience."[5] The same disclaimer appeared in the press. "Gertrude Atherton Denies Being Own Heroine" ran the headline for a story in the *San Francisco Chronicle* that quotes the author saying even if she *had* had the treatment, she would deny it, because she would be ridiculed. The reporter who interviewed her in her California Street apartment noted "an autographed photo of Steinach is prominent on the mantel."[6]

When a literary agent asked her, in 1925, to write an article based on her personal knowledge of "reactivization" (the word she and Dr. Benjamin both preferred to "rejuvenation"), she flatly refused, explaining that she always made a point of "telling the public as little as possible about myself, not only because I am jealous of my privacy, but because the less the public knows about a writer the more [it] is interested. I am always rousing their curiosity—however unintentionally—but never gratifying it."[7] Her lack of candor here—and of self-knowledge—reaches epic proportion.

The intrepid Upton Sinclair approached her after a literary dinner in San Francisco and frankly asked "some personal questions about the cause of her youthful appearance, and she replied that it was none of my damn business."[8] But the public persisted in connecting Mary Zattiany and her creator. Gertrude was besieged with letters—mostly from career women eager to prolong their capacity to work—imploring her to share her secret with them. A few chided her for giving women false hopes. She usually answered with a recommendation that they consult Dr. Harry Benjamin, who became successful enough to move his New York practice from Central Park West to Park Avenue and eventually opened a summer office in San Francisco.

The "real" identities of Countess Zattiany and her doctor became more and more of an open secret. The novelist and critic Carl Van Vechten, champion of anything avant-garde or bizarre, wrote a review of *Black Oxen* for the *Nation* claiming that "the resemblance between the Californian and her own heroine will be apparent to many readers." Both were well endowed, he said, with glamour and vitality, qualities he prized, and found entirely absent in Mrs. Atherton's artistically scrupulous rival, Edith Wharton. For him, the spontaneity and fire of *Black Oxen* could not be separated from Gertrude Atherton's unique and vibrant personality.[9]

By the 1930s Gertrude lost all inhibition about confessing she had undergone the Steinach Treatment. She promoted "reactivization" vigorously and pressed for the nomination of Dr. Steinach for the Nobel Prize. In articles with titles like "Science After Fifty" and "Defeating Old Age," she attempted to annihilate all scientific opposition to the controversial method of forestalling old age, and in her autobiography she carped at the "narrow-minded, ignorant, moronic, bigoted, Puritanical" Americans "who soothe their inferiority complex by barking their hatred of anything new" (*Adventures*, p. 561). Appearing for a 1935 *New York Times* interview in a black satin gown with a feather-trimmed pink satin jacket, "her nails carmined to match her lips" and "her straight golden hair in a pompadour," she claimed that "reactivization" kept her productive and young looking, and made it possible for her to adopt the point of view of an eighteen-year-old in her latest book.[10]

In fact, by the 1930s she had availed herself of several other experimental regimens that promised to turn back the clock. Dr. Benjamin kept in close touch with Dr. Steinach. When Steinach recommended to Dr. Benjamin that he try Gertrude on a course of treatments featuring high-frequency stimulation of the pituitary gland, she eagerly submitted. She also sought out a Dr. H. Lyons Hunt for surgical implantation of ovarian tissue from sheep—an adaptation of the notorious "monkey gland" experiments of Dr. Serge Voronoff. Dr. Hunt incensed her by failing to match the miraculous results Dr. Benjamin had produced. His surgery—helped along by injections of female anterior lobe hormone—produced no new best-seller or resurgence of creative energy. Dr. Hunt begged her not to blame "a couple of innocent inoffensive sheep glands . . . simply because there is no bet-

ter or more interesting subject in the world to write about than what
you have already written of." He added, "I was afraid to transplant on
you because you are very impatient and if you did not get the effects
within a month . . . you would vote thumbs down on glands." [11]

For the rest of her life, Gertrude would turn to the medical profession for cosmetic and psychological—as well as physiological—
remedies. She elevated Dr. Benjamin to divine status, making him
the high priest of a new religion. Having endowed him with the
power to raise the dead, she remained dependent on his care and
counsel in her day-to-day bouts with insomnia and occasionally flag-
ging energy. He rewarded her devotion by serving as a constant and
attentive friend to her and eventually her entire family. One of her
last letters, written when she was 90 and addressed to him, reports,
"I take your hormones regularly as directed." [12]

Almost everyone who wrote about Gertrude Atherton in her later
years commented on her extraordinary youthfulness, attractiveness,
and vigor. A *Newsweek* article, "Seventy-Eight Year Old Novelist
Feels Thirty Years Less," throws cold water on the Steinach Treatment, but concludes, "Whatever the cause . . . Gertrude Atherton
has enormous capacity for work. She moves, acts and speaks with
decision. . . . She talks rapidly, and her swift conversation reflects a
brilliant, supple brain." [13] An earlier press account stresses her Mary
Zattiany–like glamour: "She was regally beautiful in black silk with
a cloud of aquamarine tulle about her milk-white shoulders," and six
young men curled about her chair. [14]

A minority opinion—not widely publicized—came from Edward
Weston, who photographed her in 1928 on the day Herbert Hoover
defeated Al Smith in the presidential election. Weston had been
looking forward to meeting "some forceful Amazon." Instead he met
"a watery, washed up, squat scrubwoman, bursting out of her bespangled evening gown." Amazed when he learned that his subject
was 71, Weston wrote, "I would have guessed under sixty. Of course
she has had her face lifted, tried gland rejuvenation, and I'm sure
wants to simulate fifty. This lying about one's age nauseates. . . . Such
people only fool themselves." [15]

Dr. Benjamin himself took an ironic, affectionate, somewhat
amused position on his former patient's vanity, though he prized
her intelligence and vitality. At age 96, meditative and weary, he re-

sembled Tennyson's Tithonus, who had been granted his wish for eternal life but had forgotten to ask for eternal youth. Pressed for his perspective on rejuvenation, nearly 60 years after he introduced the Steinach Treatment, he demurred. He said simply that he thought the single most important contributor to sustained, productive, and healthy life was heredity.

CHAPTER SEVENTEEN

Select Society: Montalvo, PEN, and 'The Immortal Marriage'

Gertrude often said she spent the most delightful days of her life at Montalvo, James Phelan's country estate, where she took frequent refuge during the 1920s and where, in the nineteen-room villa, at the top of a sweeping staircase, she had her own pink-painted suite, her own little balcony, which in spring became fragrant with violet and white wisteria. If she had two contrary impulses, one to gravitate towards a throbbing center of activity like New York and another to withdraw to a fantasy landscape, then Montalvo served the second, escapist inclination.

In planning the landscape, architecture, furnishing, and functioning of his country estate, Phelan turned to models from the past. He saw himself as part Renaissance prince—a patron of the arts who creates a "new Athens" by bringing together the most talented and prominent people of the day in the most beautiful setting imaginable—and part Spanish-Californian don, whose ideal of hospitality he hoped to revivify. He borrowed the name "Montalvo" from Ordoñez de Montalvo, the sixteenth-century Spanish writer whose *Las Sergas de Esplandian* was set in a fictitious terrestrial paradise called "California" populated by Amazons who rode around on griffins which they fed to captive men. Phelan incorporated the griffin motif into Montalvo's architecture and decoration: a griffin, surrounded by Amazons on either side, spouted water from a bronze fountain; griffins carved in stone greeted visitors at the entrance gates.

"The house," according to Gertrude, "stood on a steep rise, and from the broad terrace that ran around the front one had the most superb view. Below stretched the long sloping lawns, with a Greek temple separating them from the heavy undergrowth beyond, and then came the great Santa Clara Valley, . . . set with orchards always green save in the spring when it was a mass of white blossoms, varied here and there by the pink of the almond tree and the vivid yellow of the acacia. Far away were the high mountains of the Coast Range, delicately colored in pastel shades of blue and pink. . . . Unless the valley were swimming in a blue haze quivering with heat, the town of San Jose, eleven miles away, was also clearly defined against the foothills" (*Adventures*, pp. 546–47).

At Montalvo Gertrude found herself within a few miles of the Ranch, where as an attention-greedy child she had been left with her grandparents while her mother amused herself in the city, but emotionally she dwelt light-years away. Under Phelan's Mediterranean-style roof her needs were lavishly attended: she was cherished, catered to, and protected from every intrusion of prosaic or unpleasant reality. Her fame and distinction were taken for granted, her preference for privacy respected. In the richly carpeted library, in a bookcase of Circassian walnut, Phelan kept his collection of inscribed Atherton novels. Whenever she added a new title, or in honor of her birthday, he would pin a little flag on the shelf, in celebration.[1]

Even today, when the villa houses a gallery and public arts center, even without Phelan's personal furnishings or his jovial presence, one senses the enormous care he took with aesthetic details and for the ease of guests. A generous, welcoming spirit prevails, and the volunteers who run what is now the Montalvo Center for the Arts speak of Senator Phelan in reverential tones.

Although his official political career ended in 1920, Phelan continued to function as a public figure devoted to civic virtue. He used Montalvo as the reception center for distinguished guests to

California, like Franklin Roosevelt, who visited while he was Assistant Secretary of the Navy, Congressman Nicholas Longworth, and author-adventurer Richard Halliburton. Always partial to performing artists, Phelan extended his red carpet for Ethel Barrymore, Will Rogers, tenor Tito Schipa, and baritone Lawrence Tibbett, who rewarded his hospitality with a recital.[2]

An inveterate booster of California, Phelan kept his carved Granada doors wide open to those whose achievements reflected glory on the state. Gertrude herself ranked high among these. So did poet George Sterling, who after his wife's suicide in 1918 became increasingly despondent and alcoholic. Phelan took a paternal interest in him, inviting him to Montalvo for ceremonial poetical events, like the crowning with laurel of prize-winning poets in the redwood circle presided over by bronze busts of Joaquin Miller and Edwin Markham. Phelan prized Sterling's poem about Montalvo that begins:

> The hills go down to the east and the hills go down to the west,
> And here between bay and ocean is a place where men may rest;
> But the clouds and the winds they pass and the waters change and flow,
> And Beauty, even when captive, seems ever about to go.[3]

The poet had paid tribute to his creation, and he in turn delivered a eulogy to Sterling at the funeral following his suicide in 1926.

Phelan himself wrote lyric poetry, most of it stilted and arcane by modern standards ("Fair Goddess come, Minerva-like, a Greek"). His light verse has aged more gracefully; this comic epigram, for example, about the diffident young tennis champion named Helan Wills—one of Phelan's particular favorites—who had been presented a bronze plaque at a Jubilee banquet in Paris: "To honor Helen—how amazin' / The fools presented something brazen."[4]

Wills was a dark-haired young beauty who began collecting tennis trophies for national competitions while a high school student in Berkeley and went on to win eight Wimbledon singles championships and two Olympic gold medals. She visited Montalvo often, sometimes to play tennis and refresh herself in the wonderful air and lush gardens; sometimes to dine in splendor at a celebrity lunch or dinner. She always found the atmosphere restorative and romantic. She and Phelan shared a special rapport. To her he represented warmth, support, culture, hospitality; and to him she was paragon of a new, Californian ideal of American young womanhood that combined classic beauty with athletic prowess and grace. He introduced her to influential people, sent her books, commissioned her portrait, underwrote some of her expenses, and went to see her play Suzanne Lenglen in Paris. Wills's biographer Larry Engelmann calls their relationship a passionate though platonic one.[5]

Wills rarely acknowledged her emotions—the press called her "Little Miss Poker Face"—but they ran deep. The letters she wrote Gertrude after Phelan's death suggest that she had really loved him and that things might have gone differently had they not been separated by so wide a gap in age. What endures, she now realized, "is not so much that which is expressed as that which is felt."[6]

Wills and Atherton were not intimates—an impossibility for two such circumspect women—but they shared a sense of kinship and mutual respect. Wills did not smoke, drink, or use make-up. In Gertrude's eyes she represented the younger generation's highest type, the antithesis of the garish, out-of-control flapper she reviled in *Black Oxen*. And Wills admired Gertrude's independence of spirit and her ability to surmount obstacles. When she injured her back, Gertrude visited her at Stanford Hospital, and Wills was "struck with the thought of all she had accomplished. . . . Without 'training' for writers, that is in the sense of a formal education, she had by the brilliance of her mind made her name known through her work, in every country of the world."[7] She clearly felt Gertrude's trailblazing had eased her own path.

Wills had verbal and visual gifts—she painted and wrote—which Gertrude encouraged. In her memoir she deftly sketches Gertrude with a few strokes, seating her at the table during a Montalvo luncheon: "with her corn-colored hair and blue eyes with their frequent look of meditation, her black hat with its black feather, her cigarette in a long ivory holder from which the smoke curled."[8]

There were many luncheons, many dinners. Phelan loved celebrations and ritual observances of all kinds. He was forever entertaining groups at Montalvo: Boy Scouts, cadets from Annapolis, Pueblo Indian chiefs, members of the Edwin Markham Poetry Society and the writers' organization PEN, or prize-winning poets from nearby San Jose Normal School.

On less formal occasions, the inner circle of overnight guests

might include Phelan's nephew Noel Sullivan, a music lover and
the intimate of many musicians, who had an otherworldly manner described by some as saintly and by others as effete; Charles
Fay (brother of Maude Fay), who had managed Phelan's campaign
for the senate and who functioned, as Gertrude put it, as Phelan's
fides Achates; Mrs. Downey Harvey, whose husband apparently spent
most of his time at the Bohemian Club and did not seem to mind
that his wife had established residence at Montalvo; writers Kathleen
Norris and Ruth Comfort Mitchell Young; the Fremont Olders;
sometimes Muriel, who since her separation from her husband went
by the name "Mrs. Atherton Russell"; and Mrs. Harvey's daughters,
Anita Cooper and Genevieve Barron.

Although Mrs. Atherton and Mrs. Harvey might have seemed
obvious rivals for Mr. Phelan's favor, there is every evidence of good
will between them. Gertrude certainly had no interest in running
anyone's household. She praised Mrs. Harvey's domestic gifts in *Adventures*, saying "Mrs. Harvey had two passions, music and housekeeping, and she had taken pity on her bachelor friend, whom she
had known from childhood, and gradually assumed the responsibility for Montalvo in all its domestic phases. As no more expert
housekeeper ever lived, it was the most perfectly run house that I,
at least, have ever visited. And she was a gay and animated hostess
—when she liked the company! Once, when we had one hundred
and ten Democrats down for the day, during the Democratic Convention, she basely locked herself in her own room, leaving Mrs. Fay
and me to bear the brunt" (p. 551).

Gertrude's granddaughter Florence, a frequent Montalvo guest,
had the impression the two women were "very good friends, *very*
good friends. In fact, people used to say that Mrs. Atherton and
Mrs. Harvey were his two girl friends."[9] Phelan's balancing act seems
to have worked. At formal Montalvo dinners, Gertrude always sat at
his right, Mrs. Harvey at the foot of the table. Even after Phelan's
death, people close to him tended to divide his deepest affections into
two equal portions. Cora Older wrote to Gertrude in commiseration,
"You and Mrs. Harvey were closer to him than any one else."[10]

Attentive but unobtrusive, Phelan made a practice of leaving overnight guests to their own devices for much of the day: "You might die
and be buried and resurrected between meals, and he none the wiser.

He did nothing, mercifully, to 'entertain' us" (*Adventures*, p. 549). Dinner was announced for half past eight, but he rarely made an appearance before nine.

Phelan's festive, relaxed style survives in his scrapbooks and photo albums, left by his nephew Noel Sullivan to the Bancroft Library. There are several pictures of him—a short, elfin figure with a pointed beard—at the side of the swimming pool, in a tube suit, grinning broadly. One shows him dressed up in sombrero and serape. His love of fancy cars and fast driving is enshrined in the cartoon Gertrude presented him as the Phelan Coat of Arms: a roadster on a field of belly-up (run-over) bodies, over the emblem "Arriver À Tout Prix" (Arrive at Any Price).

Very much a loyalist—to California, San Francisco, the schools he attended, his family, and friends of long standing—Phelan could not be relied on to make discerning judgments. In literature, for example, he tended to lump all poets together, placing Olympian William Butler Yeats on the same peak with Edwin Markham. At Montalvo he extended the laurel branch to quite a few pompous second-raters.

Gertrude had much to do with the prevailing confusion between good writing and polite society, at Montalvo and elsewhere in the Bay Area literary community. She founded and presided over the San Francisco branch of PEN, the international organization of poets, playwrights, essayists, editors, novelists, and other literary professionals which began in England under John Galsworthy's leadership. Under her domination it became little more than a social club that might have been called Friends of Atherton and Phelan.

A West Coast branch of PEN was not established without a struggle. Galsworthy himself wrote to ask for Mrs. Atherton's assistance in forming regional American PEN branches in literary communities outside New York. She told him she would do her best in California. Her ally, San Francisco short-story writer and novelist Charles Caldwell Dobie, volunteered to help with administrative duties, which were not Gertrude's forte. But Maxwell Aley, an editor who controlled New York PEN and believed he should control the entire

American operation, balked, refusing to recognize a San Francisco chapter as an affiliate. He may have disliked Mrs. Atherton or resisted the notion that writers might live in California—or both.

Incensed, Gertrude and Dobie decided to form their own organization for writers, which they would call the Writers' Dinner Club. She wrote to Galsworthy in England: "I found it impossible to start a San Francisco branch of the PEN club . . . particularly as Charles Caldwell Dobie . . . could get no promise of recognition from Maxwell Aley. . . . I took it up with him [Dobie] and we determined to start a club exactly on the same lines, call it the Writers' Dinner Club temporarily, and hope that Mr. Aley would see the light! A number of established writers live out here, or are here part of the time: Stewart Edward White, Harry Leon Wilson, Peter B. Kyne, . . . Ruth Comfort Mitchell, etc. We also have many young aspirants who have begun to publish, and seem to be doing things worthwhile." They held their first dinner at the Bohemian Club, and "since then we have been besieged by applicants, but are determined that none but those who are doing professional and really good work shall belong."

About the recalcitrance of the New York PEN, she continued: "It is rather a small attitude on his [Aley's] part, and if I wrote to Booth Tarkington [titular head of the American PEN], of course he would agree at once. But as Aley really runs the PEN, I thought it only right to pay him that courtesy. Whether in the circumstances you feel you could make us a branch officially, I do not know, but as you asked me to form one here, I can do no less than tell you I have . . . done so."[11] Within two months, her pleas and machinations overruled the will of Maxwell Aley. The San Francisco Writers' Dinner Club became an affiliate of the PEN American Center.

But the socially elite, insular nature of the group did not change. Gertrude viewed the organization as her own private duchy, and she showed less interest in recruiting the best writers around than in forming a congenial social circle. For starters, she made Senator Phelan a member. He *had* published a travel book, after all, and with him on board meetings could be held at Montalvo or the Bohemian Club. To make absolutely certain that bohemians of that other, raggle-taggle sort would stay away, she stipulated that women attending PEN dinners must wear formal evening gowns.

In addition to the writers Gertrude mentioned in her letter to
Galsworthy, the San Francisco PEN membership included people
like Cora Older, George Sterling, Charmian London (who wrote
about her life with her late husband Jack), Charles and Kathleen
Norris, Lionel Stevenson, Berkeley English professor Benjamin
Lehman (a close friend of Noel Sullivan), writer-historian Oscar
Lewis, Stanford professor Albert Guerard, poet and Phelan pro-
tegé Dorothé Bendon (who later became known as critic Dorothy
Van Ghent), and Hildegarde Hawthorne, Nathaniel's granddaughter, who became Gertrude's avid friend. More important writers like
Robinson Jeffers, or later, Dashiell Hammett, never joined. Neither
Hammett's politics nor his books appealed to Gertrude. Jeffers chose
to keep to himself, though he, at least, was invited. A letter from
Dobie explains, "No, Jeffers is not a member. He never replied to an
invitation to join and I do not know him personally. He is said to be
more difficult than most poets."[12]

Although he belonged, Oscar Lewis said privately that he did not
think much of the group, calling it "a social supplement not important to anybody except maybe Charlie Dobie and Gertrude Atherton."[13] A writer for the *American Mercury* concurred. San Francisco
PEN dinners, he harshly concluded, "quickly degenerated into as-
semblies of obscure ladies, each clinging to some forgotten one-book
success. Mrs. Atherton herself has done her generous share in contributing to the degeneration of California letters. With genuine gifts
as a story-teller, and with a vitality and gusto that carried her free
of the genteel taboos, she has become our contemporary American
equivalent of the Victorian Englishwomen who delighted servant
girls with their titillating fictions."[14] Gertrude's response to this, and
to other assaults from Mencken's launching pad, was to conclude
that the *Mercury* crowd were simply out to get her and would never
publish any favorable comment on her. "Their pet is Willa Cather
and they resent my existence—as does the Wharton claque."[15]

As doyenne of the San Francisco literary world she looked her
best not when she showed her petty, competitive side (toward Peter
Kyne for poaching on what she considered her literary turf or toward
Lionel Stevenson for trying to start a PEN chapter in Los Angeles)
but when she could offer lavish, Phelan-style California hospitality
to other writers. When Ellen Glasgow traveled west, Gertrude (then

in New York) furnished her with a letter to Phelan that assured her warm reception. And when Gertrude and Phelan happened once to be in New York at the same time, they invited Rebecca West—also visiting—to join them and agent Lawrence Giffen at a prize fight in Madison Square Garden. West had written to tell Gertrude that Atherton novels had been the favorite reading of her mother, a pianist who said after reading one, "If that woman played—how she could play Beethoven!"[16] Gertrude could hardly help feeling favorably disposed.

She joined writers of the stature of Willa Cather and Mary Austin on the Executive Committee of the PEN American Center and on a hastily formed literary support group for Al Smith in the 1928 presidential campaign, which included Mary E. Wilkins Freeman, Susan Glaspell, Dorothy Parker, Walter Lippmann, Edgar Lee Masters, and Mencken. With Richard Halliburton she formed a committee of artists and writers against Prohibition. But by and large the Montalvo years saw her more and more removed from the prevailing American literary culture. She tended increasingly to mingle only where she could preside as queen.

She and Phelan both liked to feel the past beckoning, pulling them back to an earlier, golden age, a more accomplished and beauty-loving time. They saw themselves reviving the glory days of Periclean Athens or Augustan Rome. Phelan had once hoped, with the Burnham plan, to turn San Francisco into a city-state modeled on the great centers of classical antiquity, and the life he envisioned at Montalvo refocused his fantasy of a California Renaissance of splendor, beauty, order, and good works.

After she had published *The Immortal Marriage* and *The Jealous Gods*—both set in fifth-century Athens—Gertrude often remarked on the connection she felt existed between modern California and ancient Athens. San Francisco had the same sky as Athens, "the same girdle of sea and hills. The same open-door and out-of-door life," even a huge open air Greek theater and a flourishing community of artists and writers. She told a reporter for the *San Francisco News*, "California seems to be approaching something of the ideal of

Greece's glorious age of Pericles. History never repeats, and that age cannot be duplicated, but externally at least, how like that scene is the setting of our California. Our climate and our scenery are like those of the Attic plains and hills. We have the courage to reinstate the human body. The state is dotted with stadiums, swimming pools, golf links and tennis courts. Our athletes, from Helen Wills down, are earning laurels from the world, and soon we will stage the first Olympic games in the new world. The Platonic ideal of poise, spiritual, mental and physical fitness is being approached." [17]

In the last years of the 1920s she published three novels set in classical Greece or Carthage. At the same time, while imaginatively immersed in the past, in 1928 she managed to participate in the present enough to serve as delegate-at-large pledged to vote for Al Smith at the national Democratic Convention, and to dash off some pro-Smith journalism. These gestures did not fully engage her; the past exerted a mighty pull. She told Carl Van Vechten that Ancient Greece embraced her "like the tentacles of an octopus," and that she had lost all desire to write about the modern world. [18] Repeating the sentiment to Upton Sinclair, she confessed, "I am so bored with my own time that I neither want to write about it nor read about it—although I do the last, because my mind is too curious to miss anything." [19]

But something more than escape was operating here. In addition to losing herself in the past, she was finding herself in it. Although she stopped short of directly saying so, she came to believe she had lived a previous life as the brilliant beauty Aspasia who consorted with Pericles. The notion that she had once been Aspasia came to her first from a former actress (Gertrude saw her perform in New York in the 1880s) named Cora (Mrs. James Brown) Potter. They met in Monte Carlo in 1925, during the same extended European sojourn that included the visit to Gertrude Stein in Paris and the presentation of the medal of the Legion of Honor for her work on behalf of France during World War I. In Monte Carlo, on the way to a tea, Cora Potter drew Gertrude aside to impart some startling information that explained why she had been staring at Gertrude so intently that Gertrude had begun to wonder "if I had applied my lipstick in the wrong spot or if the rough drive had displaced my hat" (*Adventures*, p. 563).

It seems Mrs. Potter had studied the occult sciences in Paris and India for several years and had given herself over to mysticism. A strong believer in reincarnation, she was persuaded that she herself possessed the soul of Mary, Queen of Scots. Now she told Gertrude, "The minute you entered the room I knew you were some great woman out of the past . . . but I couldn't place you. After you left I could think of nothing else. When I went to bed I couldn't sleep. 'Who was she? Who was she?' I kept saying to myself. I'll never sleep until I know. And then suddenly it came to me. I sat up in bed and exclaimed aloud: *She was Aspasia*" (*Adventures*, p. 564).

Gertrude's account in her autobiography is corroborated and embellished by letters and by the diary Phelan kept jointly with Col. Harry S. Howland when the two men traveled to Monte Carlo the following year. Equipped with a letter of introduction from Mrs. Atherton, they got themselves introduced to Mrs. Potter, who took it upon herself to warn Phelan "not to go on living in Materialism and to remember his soul—as it was all that lasted."[20] She repeated to Phelan and Howland that she knew, after 24 hours of deep concentration, that Mrs. Atherton had been Aspasia in a previous life. Though Gertrude had apparently initially recoiled at the suggestion she had ever possessed "the questionable character of the rare jewel of the Athenian hetaerae," Mrs. Potter was not to be dissuaded and made a great point of Aspasia's intellectual brilliance. "She said Mrs. A. had all the physical characteristics of Aspasia; her classical head and well-knit hard body. She told Mrs. A. she had not yet attained the full perfection of her work of which she was capable and that this was an opportunity to reveal herself and give the world a great picture of an extraordinary woman. She told her that Lord Northcliffe had embodied the spirit of Pericles, which seemed to please Mrs. A because . . . Northcliffe was a particular friend of hers and they understood each other. Mrs. A went away promising to dig into her inner consciousness and find her soul as it existed five hundred years before Christ."[21]

Apparently Gertrude was at least convinced she was destined to write about Aspasia. After leaving Monte Carlo, she scrapped her plans for a novel about the League of Nations set in Geneva. Instead she would go to Greece, and she would prepare for the trip by reading everything she could about Periclean Athens. Separating from her traveling companions—Muriel, youngest granddaughter Dominga, and cousin Inez Macondray—she stopped in Lausanne and plunged into her Greek studies. Books, however, could only take her so far. She must visit Athens, and she must attempt a kind of psychic remembering. Mrs. Potter sent her a letter that she took to heart: "Place your subconscious mind under the orders of your conscious mind. Your mind will instinctively find its way back to the truth. Remember *O great Aspasia* that everything your soul has lived through psychically is in the subconscious ready to be called up. So my advice is, 'of all the books that lie on your shelf, read and study the book of self.' "[22]

Gertrude made her way to Greece, but stayed for two weeks only. Although she responded rhapsodically to a sunset seen from the Acropolis, silvery olive groves, and the sapphire color of the Gulf of Corinth, ruins depressed her as emblems of decay, and her attempt to "see" ancient Athens clashed with the modern city before her, with its screeching automobiles and Standard Oil signs.

Before leaving Athens, however, she consulted a Professor Oeconemon of the Numismatical Museum, who profoundly influenced her thinking about Aspasia. The professor questioned the widely held assumption that Aspasia had been a hetaera, or courtesan. No, he insisted, she was what later came to be called a morganatic wife, a wife of inferior social status, married to a royal or noble husband, whose children would not inherit the father's high rank. Comic writers like Aristophanes had perpetuated the image of Aspasia as little more than a prostitute, but Professor Oeconemon referred her to the work of German scholar Adolf Schmidt, whose book on Pericles and Aspasia lists 27 reasons why Aspasia could not have been a hetaera.

For Gertrude, a great deal hung upon this point, because she so identified with Aspasia that she felt she was establishing her own virtue; she was making an honest woman of Gertrude Atherton. Since she too had been the victim of scurrilous attacks, back in the days of *Hermia Suydam*, she found it an easy matter to put herself in Aspasia's place. In her note at the end of *The Immortal Marriage* she compares the slanders of the comic Attic poets to those of the modern yellow press, who would despise any woman said to possess the "manly" virtues of intellect and power. Gertrude enshrines Aspasia as history's first emancipated woman.[23]

She now attempted total immersion in Aspasia's world. She read voraciously in New York for several months, interrupting her studies to visit the Greek antiquities of the Metropolitan Museum of Art. She haunted the New York Public Library, but preferred libraries like the Mechanics, which allowed her to take books back to her hotel room. Just as she disliked ruins, funerals, and old age itself, she found oppressive the "emanation of death and decay" that came from musty volumes on library shelves. Her whole effort was to breathe life into the past, to believe in it as something alive and present.

When she returned to San Francisco to continue her reading, she hung the walls of her workroom with enlarged photographs of the temples, statues, and vases of ancient Greece. The here-and-now receded as the past took hold. "I lived in those ancient streets and dwellings, dawdled in the *aulas* with the secluded women, listened to the sonorous voices of the men in the Agora . . . , heard the owls hoot at night, tasted the resin in the wine, wandered through the temples with their colored statues of gods, goddesses and eminent citizens" (*Adventures*, p. 575). In *Adventures* she asks us to believe "I never deluded myself that I was Aspasia," but she admits to a feeling that she was uncovering layers of experience that were already there. She told a reporter for the *San Francisco Examiner*, "the more I delved into the past of Athens . . . the stronger the feeling grew in me that somehow I had known all this before. It was as if, in a previous incarnation, I was a woman of Athens." "As if" indeed. To her family, her identification with Aspasia was a near certainty: she seemed to believe what Mrs. Potter had told her. She *was* Aspasia.[24]

Belief in reincarnation offered one more path to denying death, a denial made more urgent by the recent passing of her sister Aleece. Just as the Steinach Treatment perpetuated youth, so now she could submerge herself in a continuum of time that substituted cycles for finales. In a sense she was reborn as Aspasia, a woman combining intelligence and beauty who could cross mental swords with Socrates, who had descended from Athene and carried that goddess's immortal soul and crystalline intellect. Aspasia differs from other Atherton projections in one important way: she lives for Pericles. Her union with her husband is total. We can only guess who Gertrude in her thoughts placed in Pericles' role as leader, husband, and soul mate. It was surely not Lord Northcliffe.

The scholarly command she demonstrated in *The Immortal Marriage* earned her the kind of applause she most valued. Dr. Benjamin thought it her best book to date. Senator Phelan greatly admired it. His spirit suffuses it, and it is no accident that his poem on a Greek head thought to be Aspasia found its way to the front of the book. Classicist Paul Shorey, in a review for *Classical Philology*, found it "much saner and better informed than the chapters on Greece of H. G. Wells or Spengler."[25] High school and college teachers assigned it to their students. Gertrude finally felt she had legitimized her claims as a learned woman of letters who had surmounted the handicap of a limited formal education.

Horace Liveright would have preferred another *Black Oxen*. Not that he didn't praise *The Immortal Marriage* lavishly; he just voiced doubts about its money-making potential. The book in fact made quite a respectable showing, going into six editions, getting printed in braille and translated into Swedish. It sold 30,000 copies in its first years, but that was less than a third of *Black Oxen*'s record.

Gertrude thought she was onto something. Fast on the heels of *The Immortal Marriage* she produced *The Jealous Gods* (1928), about Alcibiades, and *Dido, Queen of Hearts* (1929), written at the request of the Classical League of America to commemorate Virgil at his bimillenium. This last, released only weeks after Wall Street's collapse, proved a financial disaster, selling fewer than 12,000 copies. Liveright blamed the books, not the stock market crash of 1929. He thought three historical novels on the ancient world from the pen of Gertrude Atherton, in quick succession, made poor business sense.[26]

Liveright pressured her to write a new book with a modern setting, and Gertrude went to New York in search of one—and also for a course of pituitary diathermy with Dr. Benjamin—in the spring of 1930. Very soon after establishing herself at the Madison Square Hotel she had disturbing news from Montalvo: Senator Phelan had been taken ill with bronchitis and gastritis. He wrote to her, urging her "to benefit from my experience and not over-work or over-play," which he apparently felt he had done.[27] She responded from her cool tenth-story room with an admonition to him to take better care of himself, sounding a note of alarm that would prove justified.

In June he wrote that he had had a stroke and was a dangerously sick man, attended by six doctors and three nurses. His last letter to her, typed by his secretary Belle Driscoll and signed with the faint signature of a weak patient, begs her to underplay the highly charged emotion of the situation. "When you reply, please do not express sympathy or solicitude, as it only excites me. . . . What I am interested to hear is news of you and your activities in New York."[28]

Her reply—her last to him—skims lightly over family news, the progress of her book, and European politics. She hopes to heaven Mussolini (with whom Phelan had had an audience in Italy a few years before) won't start another European war. She urges him not to feel obliged to answer her. Signing herself "Affectionately, Gertrude Atherton"—what a symphony of repression!—she closes with a postscript, her final words to him: "Splendid Helen [Wills] is still unbeatable."[29]

But to his secretary, Mrs. Driscoll, she addressed a letter that conveys a truer picture of her emotional state. Since Phelan now lay in a stupor, partly paralyzed, she wrote: "I don't know that I want him to live now. . . . Selfishly, I would, for I cannot stand the thought of losing him altogether. Even if he had to spend the rest of his life in a chair, it would be something to be able to talk with him occasionally. But he would hate it."[30]

Helen Wills called at Montalvo, but did not see her dying friend. In the orchards, from which the apricots, plums, and cherries had already been gathered, "the leaves were green, but drooping in the heat. The gardens on the hillside I had never seen so beautiful. . . . The leaves were large and luxuriant, the flowers so bright and crowded in their borders. Verbena and orange blossoms scented the air and ripe oranges weighed down the branches. The wide sweeping valley below drowsed in a light haze of heat, while the drone of bees in the flowers was continuous in the air. Senator Phelan was too ill to see anyone. It was impossible to realize that in this garden where nature had seemingly enthralled the place with a dream of beauty, there could be anything as contrary as death. I talked with Mrs. Downey Harvey in the cool library, and then drove back to San Francisco."[31]

When she received the news that Phelan was dead, Gertrude said it was "almost a relief, for I had no hope after [Mrs. Driscoll's] last letter. It is dreadful to see his pictures in the newspaper, knowing what it means."[32]

Mrs. Harvey wrote of the grand funeral: "Such tribute as was paid to him in every possible way. Even the laborers on our way to Holy Cross [Cemetery] stood without hats and caps as he passed. It was touching to a degree. Montalvo—no soul—all gone with his last breath. Never have I had such a friend." She thought Gertrude should write his biography: "Who better fitted, and what love you could put into it and how pleased he would be could he know."[33] But Gertrude was too distraught to even think of undertaking such a project. The brief tribute she paid him in the *Overland Monthly* is strangely tongue-tied.[34]

Cora Older's letter of condolence cut to the heart. She had been one of those present at Montalvo on the day before Phelan had his stroke. She wrote that on that day, after speeches, Phelan "arose and read a little verse of Markham's that ends: 'Give other friends your lighted face, / The laughter of the years: / I come to crave a greater grace, / Bring me your tears.'" No one had ever seen him weep before, "but he wept, and within thirty-six hours he was mortally stricken." All of his guests felt "that we have lost not only a dear friend but that we have lost a home. Without him California will never be quite the same."[35]

Phelan's will left to Gertrude Atherton, as "California's great authoress," a bequest of $20,000 and an additional $5,000 to Muriel and each of the three grandchildren. He left Villa Montalvo "to be maintained as a public park open to the public, . . . the buildings and grounds immediately surrounding the same to be used as far as possible for the development of art, literature, music and architecture by promising students."[36]

Gertrude vowed she would never visit Montalvo again, "and if it were not for my family I'd not return to California either." [37] She felt orphaned, outcast. Like Aspasia bereft of Pericles she stood "alone in the path, her arms hanging listlessly."

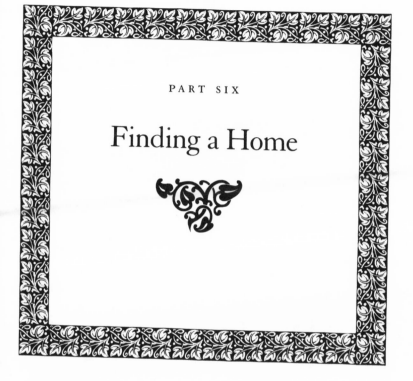

PART SIX

Finding a Home

CHAPTER EIGHTEEN

Herland

"I don't know what to do with myself, unless I write, now that Mr. Phelan has gone," Gertrude wrote in the last, bereft days of 1930.[1] Again she found her own resources her most enduring and reliable friends.

Her next major book, her autobiography, not only draws upon her independence and pluck; it mythologizes them. The Gertrude Atherton who narrates *Adventures of a Novelist* hides behind an armor of crisp irony, self-confidence, and invulnerability. She becomes one of her own spirited Californian heroines: icily beautiful, adventurous, courageous, combative, and nobody's fool. Her American West shares little with the mysterious and spiritual landscape that awakened the souls of Willa Cather, Mary Austin, and Mabel Dodge Luhan. Urbane, social, and pleasure-loving, it is a place for looking outward, not within; a place to either kindle or thwart ambition and worldly success. Here the individual will—Gertrude Atherton's will —becomes a force in nature, overwhelming every other force.

Neither introspective nor confessional, the book's omissions have their own eloquence. Although Gertrude's ability to remember amazed her, there were certain doors she did not open. She has very little to say about men she may have been romantically involved with, and makes no mention at all of her grandchildren (although a photograph of each appears in one edition) or of family secrets like her sister Aleece's drinking problem. Feelings such as self-doubt, hurt, loneliness, guilt, and confusion—which we know she could suffer —find no expression at all. Neither do failures, like the aborted trip to Cuba at the turn of the century. Interestingly, at the time she was writing *Adventures*, Gertrude was reading Emma Goldman's *Living My Life* and was as repelled by its sexual candor as she was attracted to Goldman's originality, brilliance, and ruthlessness.[2] Her own brilliance and ruthlessness she was more than willing to display; but no one was going to say of Gertrude Atherton that she did not know the meaning of reticence.

Published reviews praised her wit, clarity, and outspokenness. The *Times Literary Supplement* found "more truth and certainly less flattery in these pages than in any book of memoirs published in recent years."[3] The *New York Times* discovered in the narrator "the personality of a brilliant, very unusual woman, a woman with a clear and capable brain, swift perceptions, social charm and a will of steel."[4]

Friends applauded her for having finally captured the uniqueness of her personality on the page. Carl Van Vechten, who had persuaded her to undertake the autobiography, told her after he read it how proud he was of his role in generating a book "trembling . . . with that special lively quality of yours."[5] The influential Yale professor William Lyon Phelps confessed he had always been conscious of a discrepancy between the quality of her books and the dimension of her native endowment: "I have always thought that you—your mind, character, intelligence, personality—were so very superior to any book you have ever written. You hold an enviable position as a writer, . . . and yet I do not think any of your books has ever fairly represented the actual wealth of your mind and art. That is why your novels never seem to me first-rate, although *you* always do. That is why I like your autobiography so much better than any of your stories."[6]

Negative comment focused on the woman Gertrude Atherton rather than her book. "She is disdainful, ungenerous, undisciplined," wrote Dorothy Van Doren in the *Nation*. "She has no heart."[7] Mary Ellen Chase complained of "egoism and cocksureness, repelling through its bad taste, barren because of its total lack of anything even remotely spiritual."[8] The *Saturday Review* reviled her "rather hit or miss combativeness" and quarreled with her peripatetic lifestyle: "If we grow so mobile as to have no home, unrooted in any soil, we shall all grow superficial and hopelessly bored."[9]

The truth is that by the time she sat down to write her auto-biography, in her mid-seventies, Gertrude had finally settled into a reasonably fixed pattern of living in San Francisco. The Depression, and diminished income from book sales, put a damper on her mo-bility. "My income has not been reduced to the extent where my usual method of living is affected," she wrote a friend, "but it leaves no margin for travel."[10] She would visit New York again, but her days as a dervish were behind her.

Until she was well into her eighties, when she moved into the top floor of Muriel's house, Gertrude maintained independent quarters in an apartment on California Street (very near the Victorian man-sion Dominga Atherton built in the 1880s), which she regarded as more of a work space than a domicile and which she had occupied intermittently since the 1920s. She turned the dining room into a study, furnishing it with desk, filing cabinet, pivot chair, and two stands for dictionary and atlas. "There is a fine kitchen, but tea (or hot chocolate) is about all that will be made in it, for I intend to take my meals out."[11]

As in the past, she relied on others to free her of domestic cares, and in particular on Muriel to serve as nurturer and family mainstay. The world she inhabited now was a matriarchy similar to the one she described in her novel *The House of Lee*, in which three genera-tions of women from the same prominent San Francisco family— a powerful and elegant grandmother, jokingly called the "General," her widowed, fortyish daughter, and her emancipated, Berkeley-educated granddaughter—share a household and together face the social changes and economic hardships of the 1930s. Muriel provided in her Green Street home (which Gertrude helped her to buy) a place where family dinners were shared and guests entertained. She would invite to family dinners Gertrude's half brother William P. Horn, forging a link with the scarcely acknowledged paternal side of her mother's family. She gave PEN receptions for her mother's associates and saw to it that she was looked after when she was sick. With each passing year she functioned more like Gertrude's parent, like the mother Gertrude had never been to her.

Most evenings, grandson George, who lived with Muriel, would be dispatched to pick Gertrude up in his car and take her to dinner. Never independent until after his mother's death in 1962, George worked in real estate and accepted his household role as fetcher and carrier. The only male in a family of women, he seems to have followed his mother's lead in recognizing his grandmother as She Who Must Be Obeyed.

Granddaughter Florence, after the failure of her Hollywood marriage, had returned to San Francisco with her young daughter and resumed her stage career. She remarried and settled into an offstage role as Mrs. William Duvall Dickey the same year Phelan died.

The youngest grandchild, Dominga, held a special place in her grandmother's affections. Always sensitive and otherworldly, she went through an emotional collapse in her early twenties after a romance ended unhappily. Muriel wrote from Europe, where they had been traveling in 1930, "Dominga has been ill. It is a sort of a nervous breakdown. Being in love has been too much for her."[12]

Within a year of her breakdown Dominga made the decision to become a teaching nun of the Dominican order. An article in the *San Francisco Chronicle* announced to the world: "Plans Life in Convent. Postulant Made Debut December 15, 1928."[13] Gertrude accepted Dominga's renunciation with sympathy tinged with sadness. Nuns had often appealed to her romantic imagination, but she told Dominga she was too innocent and free of sin to embark on a life of prayer and asceticism. Dominga answered: "You said you thought past sins essential for the religious life. I had them, but even without having them . . . I am sure I would choose this life. It is peaceful and happy. In the religious life one is aided to achieve the very best one is capable of and I always had a hard time managing myself."[14]

Dominga implored her grandmother to write books the church would allow her to read. The autobiography, she knew, would be forbidden, as had been both the book and screen versions of *The Crystal Cup*, in which a mannish young woman acquires femininity after undergoing endocrine treatments. The kind of Atherton novels she treasured were those—naturally—featuring nuns as heroines.

When she lived as Sister Mary Dominga at St. Dominic's convent in Benicia, she delighted in the link with Concepcion Argüello, the first woman in California to take the veil, whose story Gertrude had told in *Rezanov* and who had lived and taught at the Benicia convent.

She prayed for her worldly grandmother's immortal soul. Only the saintly Dominga would think of addressing Gertrude Atherton with the words: "Today should be your feast day. St. Gertrude lived from 1253 to 1334, in Saxony. She was a writer and for forty years Abbess of, I think, a Benedictine convent. . . . Today I have placed you under her special care."[15]

Dead from a brain tumor before she reached the age of thirty, Dominga is buried near Concepcion Argüello in the Benicia convent plot. Gertrude never referred—at least not in any surviving letter—to this devastating loss. While Dominga was confined to a Stockton hospital bed, Gertrude continued to write to her and send her gifts, though visits were infrequent. She preferred to think of Dominga as the teaching nun she had often gone to see at the Dominican convent school in San Rafael, once in the company of another admirer of nuns—Gertrude Stein.

The two Gertrudes made unlikely friends, but friends they were, within strict limits. They had met for the first time in Paris in 1925, at the instigation of playwright Avery Hopwood, who wanted "the two Gertrudes whom I so much love to know each other."[16] He brought Mrs. Atherton with him to call one day at the famous household at 27, rue de Fleurus, fulfilling a childhood fantasy of Miss Stein's companion Alice Toklas, who had grown up in San Francisco idolizing the renowned and fearless Mrs. Atherton.

Stein and Toklas viewed the novels of Mrs. Atherton with a certain condescension, as specimens of an inferior kind of writing designed to "tell of the new generation in the words of the last generation." Linear plots and orthodox punctuation worked against the kind of linguistic experiment and innovation in form Stein championed. Nonetheless, Alice found when she reread some Atherton novels that "though markedly dated they held one's attention to the end."[17]

For her part, Gertrude Atherton greeted the prose of Gertrude Stein, as she greeted all modernism, with an exasperation she never expressed to Miss Stein. She sided with those who saw in nonrepresentational, experimental art a threat to social norms that provide individual and community coherence. She could find no excuse for what she considered to be Stein's "childish, uneducated, utterly rotten English" and confided to Joseph Henry Jackson, book editor of the *San Francisco Chronicle*, that it was all the more unpardonable from the pen of a woman who "had the best of education and associated all her life with accomplished people." Gertrude Stein was "little better than an assassin" to "so debauch the language, seek to deprive it of all the beauty and subtlety it has accumulated throughout the centuries." Her prose was a "clever hoax," perpetrated by one who "realized early in life that she had no gift to make her famous so decided to be a freak. One must respect her for putting it over." [18]

Literary differences aside—and they could put them aside—the two Gertrudes liked one another immensely. "I don't think any one could help liking her," Atherton wrote to Jackson of Stein. "A less affected, nicer woman you couldn't ask to meet." They shared sharp intelligence, high spirits, a sense of fun, delight in witty company, childish egotism, and an appetite for fame—their own and other people's. Each felt that being Californian brought a special destiny, one that fostered do-what-you-please independence and love of freedom—including the freedom to pick up and leave the place that gave you your unique identity.[19] They had what Gertrude Stein called "a strong love of starting," a passion for the new. For Atherton that meant endless new locales for new novels. For Stein, who became a hearth-loving homebody in her life with Alice in France, it meant pioneering the new aesthetic of modernism. Being alive through the birth of the new century was the counterpart in time of what coming from California meant in space.

Both Gertrudes had nomadic childhoods, multiple homes. Stein had lived in Pennsylvania and Austria before she came to Oakland at age five. Her parents died when she was in her teens, and she went to live with relatives in Baltimore, then to Radcliffe. Both identified strongly with male models, rejecting sanctioned feminine patterns of passivity and domesticity. But although Stein tagged after her older brother Leo as Atherton let herself be taught by grandfather Stephen Franklin, both future writers felt self-made. They had been left on their own so much as children that they believed they had raised themselves. Neither took to religion. You might say that each attempted to be her own mother, father, and God.

They shared the biases of social and economic privilege, although there were enough fluctuations in each family's fortunes to instill a sense of precariousness. Where Atherton always looked to writing as a means to financial independence, Stein insisted she served Art, not Mammon, and for most of her creative life had to struggle to get published, let alone paid. Her first earned commercial success came in 1933 (a year after *Adventures of a Novelist* appeared) when she was 58, with the publication of *The Autobiography of Alice B. Toklas*. Amusing, easily understood, and crammed with the famous names the public liked to hear, the book earned her copious royalties and the celebrity she craved. *La gloire* finally came, and American friends urged her to capitalize on it by returning to lecture in the country she had left more than 30 years before. At the end of 1935 she arrived in New York, excited but somewhat disturbed to be greeted by a moving electric sign at Times Square that said, "Gertrude Stein Has Come."

Miss Stein had promptly quarreled with the agent who was to arrange her tour, so she was doing without an agent, relying on the secretarial good offices of Alice, her friend Carl Van Vechten, and a network of contacts spread across the United States. In Northern California she turned to Mrs. Atherton, who complained—not to Miss Stein—that she was going to have to take time out from promoting her new book (a collection of short stories called *The Foghorn*, for her new publisher, Houghton Mifflin) to make arrangements for the visit:

I am very subtly having Gertrude Stein landed on my back. She won't have an agent, so wouldn't I speak to clubs, colleges, etc.? She is not on the make but wants enough to pay her expenses out here. The University of California won't have her at any price, and Stanford is little more interested, but I have called up the presidents of the two principal women's clubs here and across the Bay and asked them to interest enough other clubs to make a good sized purse. I'll see that PEN gives the April dinner in her honor, and of course I'll have to give her a tea or something. I like her personally, and although her stuff is tripe I am glad to do anything for her I can, but she comes at an inconvenient time.[20]

She beautifully concealed her misgivings. As far as Alice Toklas and Gertrude Stein were concerned, her performance as hostess made her the very model of graciousness and generosity. "Gertrude Atherton was to do everything for us and she did," Stein wrote.[21] Toklas remembered her as "old and very wonderful. She was then well over seventy and very beautiful in an outrageously pale blue dress."[22]

Mrs. Atherton did go to a lot of trouble. Letters flew back and forth between her and Stein, and she spent hours on the phone, lining up lecture dates and inviting guests to the various receptions. As usual she relied on Muriel to oversee the food preparation—she was not planning, herself, to cut crusts off cucumber sandwiches—but she cared enough about their gustatory pleasure to make good on her promise to take them to a fish restaurant on the Wharf, the one place in town that still remembered how to properly fry an oyster.

Aware of Stein's affection for nuns, she took her guests to the Dominican convent where Dominga was teaching and where Stein could informally address the students and meet several of the Sisters, who had been touted by Atherton as "among the most brilliant women I have ever met." It was raining in San Rafael that day, but Gertrude Stein said otherwise the visit was charming: "I said to the mother superior . . . when she said that she could not understand what did it matter if the little ones could and she said but little ones always look as if they understood and I said yes but if they look it it is pleasant."[23]

Mrs. Atherton displayed tact in her deft handling of the delicate matter of Mabel Dodge, who had by this time acquired her fourth husband's name of Luhan. Mabel had once been admitted to Gertrude Stein's inner circle, and they had written "Portraits" of one another. But the flower of their friendship had faded. Wilted, more precisely. Alice disliked Mabel, felt jealous and excluded, never forgave her for the "strong look" that had passed between her and Stein years ago at Mabel's Villa Curonia in Florence. She wanted nothing to do with the woman famous for her flamboyant sexuality, numerous couplings, and ability to draw notable people into her sphere and then write about them in her voluminous memoirs.

The lives of Mabel Dodge and Gertrude Atherton had intersected in New York during World War I, when both had held salons and become peripherally involved with the Elizabeth Duncan School. Mabel admired Atherton, but Atherton didn't return the compliment. After reading a volume of Mabel's memoirs, she called it "an extraordinary exposition of child psychology."[24]

During Gertrude Stein's much publicized visit to the Bay Area, Mabel was visiting Robinson and Una Jeffers in Carmel. Mabel saw the accident of geographic proximity as a chance to patch things up with Gertrude Stein, but Toklas intervened. She answered the phone when Mabel called with an invitation, and to Mabel's question, "When am I going to see Gertrude?" replied, "I don't think you are going to."[25] Not easily discouraged, Mabel wrote to Mrs. Atherton to see if she could get herself invited to the party being planned in honor of her old friend. "I certainly would like to see how Gertrude Stein acts nowadays after all her success & everything." If she couldn't be included on the guest list, wouldn't the two Gertrudes like to motor down the coast to Carmel together to see her? "What fun! Do!"[26]

Mrs. Atherton cautiously requested Miss Stein's own preference in the matter. Did she care to have a reunion with the High Priestess of Taos? "If you did, I'd ask her to the Cocktail party. I like Mrs. Luhan, but this is your party and I want no jarring note." The jarring note was not to be sounded; Mabel received no invitation to what promised to be *the* party of the season. Mrs. Atherton told Gertrude Stein, "I have asked the most interesting and distinguished persons in San Francisco. Not one regret have we received! They fairly sputter over the telephone when asked. Already we are up to seventy-five, and hope to stop there, for if there are too many few will get a chance to talk to you."[27]

At the PEN dinner, given at the Bohemian Club, Mrs. Atherton sat at Gertrude Stein's right. What a study in contrasts they must have made: Miss Stein with her massive girth, cropped hair, vest, tweed skirt, and sensible shoes; Mrs. Atherton dressed, quite likely, in black satin with a feather-trimmed pink satin jacket, her nails carmined to match her lips, her straight golden hair worn in a pompadour over a brow that showed no sign it would soon see its eightieth year.

Stein gave a number of lectures in the Bay Area—most of them arranged by Mrs. Atherton—and the press lavished attention on the "eccentric poet-biographer-librettist" who had lived in Oakland as a school girl and now made a point of flouting the laws governing commas, periods, and paragraphs. She told people how strange it felt to return to Oakland, a place she had never expected to see again. Stein tended to brood about identity and memory, and although returning to the scene of her childhood thrilled her, it was also unsettling, reminding her both of the brevity of life and the continuity of time. "The only difference between human nature and cable cars," she told Carolyn Anspacher of the *San Francisco Chronicle*, "is that the cable cars frequently stop. Human nature never does."[28]

The mixture of familiar and unfamiliar threw her off balance. Things both were, and were not, as she remembered them. In Oakland's Fruitvale section she discovered that "the big house and the big garden and the eucalyptus trees and the rose hedges" weren't there, and she "did not like the feeling." In musing about the experience she came up with the famous lines, "what was the use of having come from Oakland it was not natural to have come from there yes write about it if I like . . . but not there, there is no there there."[29]

When the time came, she found it hard to leave "the lap of luxury and the pleasant adulation." She wrote Carl Van Vechten, "We have just said good-bye to Mrs. Atherton and Mrs. Russell they have been perfectly charming to us and we have really all of us gotten very fond of each other, to-day they took me to see the mayor and he gave me a large golden wooden key of San Francisco all dedicated to me and signed by himself and it was all very lovely and very grand and we have had a beautiful time" . . . "and the hills are lovely and the streets are steep and the bay and ocean all there and everybody went to school with me and everybody else went to school with Alice and it is all most xciting."[30]

Fond of each other, yes, but Gertrude Atherton reserved the right to discharge a few private parting shots. She expressed misgivings about the sincerity of Stein's modernist convictions. "I wonder how much she believes it. She seems to be the most sincere of mortals, but she is also as clever as the devil."[31] And she stood in awe of the hugeness of Stein's ego. "I thought Mary Austin was about as conceited and swollen in the head as a writer could be, but Gertrude Stein [in proclaiming herself the greatest genius of the age and the prophet of a new order] goes her one better."[32] In Gertrude Stein she had finally met someone whose capacity for self-celebration dwarfed her own.

Her guests departed, Gertrude Atherton returned to her work: a column for the Hearst papers and a new novel. She was researching and beginning to write—at the request of some classicists at the University of California who wanted a novel that could be used to celebrate the 2000th birthday of Horace—*Golden Peacock*, a book about Horace's imaginary niece Pomponia. Sixteen-year-old Pomponia wears the stola and palla of Augustan Rome, but she talks and behaves like a twentieth-century feminist of the Atherton stamp, vowing she will never promise to obey her future husband and averring that "if Cleopatra killed herself it was because she had lost Egypt not Anthony."[33] Like many a previous Atherton heroine, she expresses her defiance with physical aggression. She not only carries a knife tied to her thigh, she jumps down from a tree where she has been hiding and uses it.

In the last decade of her literary career, as in the first, male critics objected to the amount of strength Atherton allotted her Amazonian heroines, finding threat in the supporting-cast roles she assigned to men. The *New York Times* reviewer of *Golden Peacock* considered "the extra-ordinarily beautiful, extra-ordinarily intelligent, extra-ordinarily strong-willed Pomponia . . . too domineering, too much the superwoman."[34] And a *Time* magazine reviewer commented, after reading the matriarchal family novel *The House of Lee*, "If the War Between Men and Women foreseen by the mad fancy of James Thurber comes to pass, Gertrude Atherton will be the Stonewall Jackson of the rebel females."[35]

She saw no need to apologize for choosing superwomen as heroines, since she continued to avow her contempt for everything "commonplace." Nor did she countenance antifeminist responses from professional critics who shared the prevailing masculine bias. When newspaper book columnist Burton Rascoe disparaged Hemingway, Gertrude applauded, telling him, "I must congratulate you on your dressing-down of Hemingway, whose vogue, I have an idea, is owing largely to the critics who admire the 100% male, and still have infantile left-overs in their own composition."[36]

Her own feminine bias showed even in her nonfiction books, like *Golden Gate Country*, which devotes many pages to the part played by women in Bay Area history. For the last time Gertrude Atherton parades before us the romanticized images of women she has written of so often in the past: Concepcion Argüello, beloved of Count Rezanov; Natalie Ivanov, mournful heroine of Fort Ross; San Francisco society queens of the 1850s and 1860s; Nellie Gordon, drink-sodden daughter of the builder of South Park.

Gertrude believed that the war between the sexes had already been won by women by the 1930s and that complete sex equality in the United States was in the offing. She thought Eleanor Roosevelt would make a fine president and that it was high time a woman occupied that office. She told the *New York Times* (repeating an idea she developed in the first of her essays collected under the title *Can Women Be Gentlemen?*) that a silent revolution was going on "which makes the struggle over communism, fascism and other 'isms' look like child's play." In the fifth century B.C. in Egypt, Libya, and Sparta, she claimed, women had gone out into the working world while men performed the tasks of housework and childcare. Such a division of labor might again occur. Women might again become the dominant sex. "I only hope women will be content with equality."[37]

Gertrude had become so politically conservative that she could not see her way to endorsing a complete revolution in the sex roles. But in her private realm, where her grandson fetched her each night for dinner and her editor in Boston jumped three feet when she expressed displeasure, a woman ruled supreme.

CHAPTER NINETEEN

Becoming an Institution

If her years as a wanderer had finally ended, Gertrude showed no interest in putting a period to her career. She published seven books after her autobiography: three novels, a collection of stories, one of essays, a personal history of San Francisco, and *Golden Gate Country*, which was part of the American Folkways Series edited by Erskine Caldwell. Work continued to be the engine that propelled her.

Her name on the spine of a book was still considered a good enough draw to make several publishers scramble to sign her after the death of Horace Liveright and the bankruptcy of his firm in 1933. Her Liveright editor, T. R. Smith—to whom *Adventures of a Novelist* is dedicated—tried to retain her when Liveright was sold for a relative pittance and reorganized under Arthur Pell's leadership. Smith expressed shock and hurt when told Gertrude chose to affiliate elsewhere—hadn't he served her well? Of course he had, but that was beside the point. She felt affectionate toward Smith, her loyal and true editor for the past decade, but she never let emotions dictate to her in business matters, and judged the reconstituted Liveright firm too risky a proposition. She wasted little time in choosing as her new editor Dale Warren of the venerable Houghton Mifflin firm (which had in 1884 haughtily spurned her earliest novel).[1]

In 1938 she was sent by Houghton Mifflin to New York for a series of newspaper and radio interviews publicizing her essay collection *Can Women Be Gentlemen?* This would be her last visit to New York, and in some ways it presaged a final leave-taking. So many of her contemporaries were gone. It is the fate of octogenarians to be left standing as the bodies of other members of their generation fall, and she wrote Dr. Benjamin, "New York is a graveyard as far as my woman friends are concerned: Katherine Blake, Mrs. Schuyler Van Rensselaer, and now Emma (Kaufman) Brunner," all dead.[2] But the trip redeemed itself despite remembered losses. Novelist Fannie Hurst hosted a party for her. Old friend and editor Elizabeth Jordan sat beside her at a tea given in her honor at the Algonquin. Ida Tarbell, the renowned muckraking journalist and editor, invited her out for "not a party, just a talk."[3] And an interview she gave the Associated Press was picked up and nationally syndicated. It made her age a matter of public record: she was 81.

After years of keeping her age a jealously guarded secret, she now allowed her birthdays to become public events. She had become a phenomenon: The Ageless Wonder, the zestful, endlessly prolific octogenarian novelist. "You carry the years like a flashing diadem," wrote Hildegarde Hawthorne.[4] Her eighty-fourth birthday celebration, organized by the California Writers Club and shared by 300 guests at a gala banquet at Oakland's Claremont Hotel, captured the notice of even the far away *New York Post*, which reported she had turned out 1,000 words on her new novel that day and had no plans to retire. "You retire when you're worn out," she said. "I've buried ten generations of critics, have written forty-five or fifty books and still have something to say."[5]

She pointed out to anyone who cared to listen that other creative types before her had continued to produce well into their eighties, and there was no reason not to follow their example. One must simply carry on. When a 70-year-old novelist wrote to say that he thought it time to fold up, "I reminded him that Sophocles was eighty-eight when he wrote *Oedipus at Colonus* and Verdi in his eighties also when he composed *Othello*." She told Upton Sinclair he should continue to write "with the same fluency, vigor and imaginative power for twenty-five years to come."[6] Edgar Lee Masters sent a fan letter, commending her unflagging productivity, "It is truly wonderful. I like to read about Goethe, who kept going at Faust with undiminished interest. 'Nor knowest thou what argument thy life to thy neighbor's creed has lent.'"[7]

Even though the family, and Muriel in particular, had become essential to her daily functioning, she persisted in presenting herself as a loner, tirelessly and single-mindedly devoted to her career, a woman so stubbornly innocent of nurturing instincts that she would let boxes of flowers people had sent pile up outside her room. ("I can't spend my time cutting stems and giving them fresh water," she explained to Carl Van Vechten.)[8] She enjoyed her adult grandchildren, but when Florence's daughter Jane made her a great-great-grandmother in 1944, she made a point of her indifference to the new generation, writing to Dr. Benjamin: "Jane's baby has black hair and is said to be a fine specimen. I haven't seen it, as I've been too busy. I don't take much interest in babies anyhow and much prefer puppies."[9] Offered the chance to sit for a five-generation family portrait, she turned it down.

She did take an interest in San Francisco, the city she once scorned, and it responded by turning her into a kind of living monument. Journalists liked to describe her as a literary "dowager duchess" or "the reigning belle of California belles lettres." She accepted seats on San Francisco's Art Commission and Library Commission and allowed herself to be photographed for *Life* magazine in front of a sprawling San Francisco Victorian that was probably some years younger than she was. At 90, after her last book, *My San Francisco*, was published, she was presented with a gold medal from the city and a kiss from Mayor Roger Lapham.

All four of the books she published in her last years cast retrospective glances at her native city. But not everybody thought her accurate, either as a local historian or an interpreter of the present. Erskine Caldwell came to regret his decision to have her write *Golden Gate Country*, because he found her retellings of familiar stories about romantic heroines of California tired and her view of society both narrow and dated. He kept urging her to "bring the book up to the present,"[10] something she would not and could not do. She concerned herself wholly with the upper class, making no mention of the WPA or labor leader Harry Bridges or the Maritime and General Strike that threw the city into turmoil in 1934. Organized labor, with its "incessant strikes and demands," was at best a disruption, at worst a menace to national security; the less said about it the better. In a book of 250 pages, she devoted only 25 to the four post-earthquake decades. She had already done her homework on the years before the earthquake, and she found that they conformed more readily to her notions about what made for picturesque and colorful narrative.

In *My San Francisco* she strains to acknowledge current urban realities by including a perfunctory chapter on slums and another on the California Labor School, but her discomfort and displeasure seep through. "Her" San Francisco remains the spirited, sociable outpost of past years, a city of quaint neighborhoods, venerable bookstores, private clubs, festive restaurants, historic banks, strong-minded women, and old families who know one another.

As a young woman she had lamented San Francisco's isolation and provincialism, calling it a "jumping-off place to nowhere," but now she greeted the new Golden Gate Bridge, gateway to the north, with dismay, calling it "an ugly reminder that beauty was going down before utilitarianism."[11] Now that San Francisco had become a burgeoning population center, spilling over with World War II soldiers and sailors and laborers to supply the needs of the expanded shipyards and new factories, she objected that everything had become too crowded, servants were impossible to find, and the new citizens were not the right sort. She wrote to Dr. Benjamin: "Better not come out here until the war is over, for no hotel would take you in for more than five days. 250,000 have been added to our population—temporarily, we hope—for a good many of them are undesirable."[12]

"Conservative" is too gentle a word for her present political posture. By the late 1930s she had turned into a reactionary, whose fears about the red menace far outstripped her concerns about the threat of fascism. She told Gertrude ("Toto") Norman, her friend from Munich days, "I wish to heaven Franco would hurry up. I don't care about him one way or another, but I don't want Communism to get a hold of Western Europe. Fascism is bad enough, heaven knows, but Communism is worse."[13]

When the League of American Writers asked American authors

to answer the question, "Are you for, or are you against, Franco and fascism?" and published the answers in a pamphlet, Gertrude Atherton was the only one, out of 414 writers who responded, to equivocate about Franco. She stopped short of an endorsement, but pronounced him the lesser of two evils. "Only hypocrites," she wrote, "or gullible Americans will deny . . . that the war in Spain is between Communists and Fascists. . . . I have no sympathy for any form of government but an honest democratic one, but if I had to cast a vote on the present Spanish question it would be for fascism, if only because fascism is frankly cynical and selfish and does not pretend to be 'democratic.'. . . So, although I have no love for Franco, I hope he will mop up the Communists, and send home, with tails between legs, all those gullible Americans who enlisted to save Spanish 'democracy.' " [14]

These remarks made her somewhat notorious. Members of the left-leaning League of American Writers protested Mrs. Atherton's "pro-fascist" stance. Always ready to join battle, she hardened her line, calling Franco "a statesman as well as a military genius," pointing out that Spanish Loyalists were getting support from Soviet Reds and charging that the League of American Writers was itself suspect, made up of second-rate talents and communist sympathizers.[15]

There is very little subtlety, depth, or intellectual content in Gertrude's red-baiting outbursts. She merely sounded off and waved the American flag, acting like a West Coast Westbrook Pegler. In a 1940 Hearst column she called Roosevelt seditious and claimed only Wilkie "could rescue the United States from the abyss on whose edge it was tottering . . . and restore Americanism to the pedestal it has occupied since the days of the founding fathers." [16] Congressional superpatriot Martin Dies won her support. She boasted to Burton Rascoe that she was responsible for putting the Dies Committee onto "that stronghold of communism, the American Writers' Guild," and had the satisfaction of seeing the organization added to the Committee's black list.[17] Communists, she declared, should be rounded up, packed into ships and wafted away "to some south sea island where they can talk one another to death." [18]

When Thomas Mann, exiled from Nazi Germany and one of its most vocal and eminent opponents, came to lecture in San Francisco at the Town Hall Forum, and Mrs. Atherton was announced as chair of the opera house event, a cry of protest went up. Wasn't Mrs. Atherton pro-fascist? Wouldn't her presence be construed as an insult to Mann? Anonymous groups threatened to picket from without and disrupt from within. Not wishing to create an incident or embarrass Thomas Mann, Gertrude bowed out, saying she had "no wish that a distinguished European should get the impression that San Francisco was a city of hooligans." [19]

After the Mann episode—and after the German seizure of Poland and Hungary—she became more outspoken against Hitler. While in New York in December 1938, she spoke at a Carnegie Hall rally organized by Mayor Fiorello La Guardia, sharing the rostrum with (among others) Msgr. Fulton J. Sheen and Secretary of Agriculture Henry Wallace. In her speech, quoted at length in the *New York Times*, she branded Hitler "the curse of the world, the direst menace to civilization since the Dark Ages." His barbarous persecution of the Jews had made modern Europe reel on its foundations. His unsatiated hate, turned on anyone who dared to criticize him, signaled an eruption of medievalism threatening to sweep the world "like another Black Death." [20]

The plight of Professor Steinach, whom Hitler attacked and deprived of his Vienna laboratory, particularly upset her. Steinach was forced to begin his work all over again in Zurich. Gertrude wrote to Dr. Benjamin, "It is rather late to begin life all over again, but who knows? He may do wonderful things yet. He must have an entire laboratory inside his head. At all events, he is where Hitler can't get his claws on him, which is something." [21] Upton Sinclair's novel *Dragon's Teeth*, about Nazi crimes against the Jews, further provoked her wrath. She wrote Sinclair, "I would revel in seeing Hitler, Goring et al boiled in oil." [22]

Inconsistent as ever, she maintained a cordial friendship with socialist Sinclair, who sent her a copy of every new book of his as it came off the press, always prompting a detailed and usually favorable response from her. His campaign for governor of California in 1934 frightened her, because she thought at one point he might actually win; he was running on the Democratic, not the Socialist ticket. When he lost she could relax, again characterizing him as an amiable and talented eccentric whose crackpot ideas would cause no serious damage. She told him, no doubt believing it, "I really don't care a damn about other people's politics, any more than I care whether other people like garlic or not, so long as they don't season their food with it when I am a guest."[23]

She certainly did care about other people's politics, particularly when the people in question were writers. Her own right-wing excesses got her into a muddle that might have turned into a major embarrassment if the press had gotten wind of it. A man named James A. Hool formed an organization called the National Academy of American Literature and announced its goals: to correct "decadent" standards in American writing and to cleanse the American language of impurities, while reaffirming respect for American law, lawmakers, and law enforcers. Letterhead stationery was printed, listing Yvor Winters, Fremont Older, Zane Grey, and Kathleen Norris among the members of the Advisory Board. Gertrude Atherton's name found its way to the top, under the heading "President." The stationery was used to solicit "subscriptions" (in the form of financial contributions) supporting the Academy's efforts to restore "normal times, normal thinking and normal methods of living."

It soon became evident that the National Academy of American Literature had duped its literary advisors and duped President Atherton. The organization was a fraud. Secretaries filed complaints that they had not been paid for their services. The printer of the impressive letterhead resubmitted his bill. Hool, who it turned out, had served time for mail fraud, simply took the subscription money and vanished. Gertrude paid the delinquent accounts out of her own pocket and did her best to pretend the fiasco had never happened.[24]

The bogus National Academy should not be confused with the august New York-based National Institute of Arts and Letters, which conferred bona fide honor on Gertrude Atherton by electing her a member in 1938.[25] Henry Seidel Canby wrote the letter informing her of her election, an irony she savored, since she considered Canby's published criticism of her books unfriendly. Ezra Pound won election the same year, though nominees John Steinbeck and Edmund Wilson failed to garner the necessary votes. The only other woman elected in 1938 was foreign correspondent Dorothy Thompson, to whom Sinclair Lewis was married. Gertrude wrote to Lewis, "I see that Mrs. Lewis and I got into the Institute of Arts and Letters on the same wave. She had luck. I had to wait until all the old fogies were dead."[26] She never stopped thinking of herself as an insurgent, persecuted by the old guard.

Although nominated in 1940 for the even more prestigious American Academy of Arts and Letters, whose membership was limited to 50 distinguished Institute members, Gertrude did not win enough support to get elected. That hurt, especially when she remembered that other living American women novelists, like Willa Cather and Ellen Glasgow, *had* been voted into the Academy. She scrawled in pencil a letter of protest, which may never have been sent, arguing her own case to the chairman of the Literature Department of the Academy. "Neither Ellen Glasgow nor Willa Cather," she claimed, "wrote a book that is now regarded as a classic. *The Conqueror* has sold over a million copies. I invented a new form."[27] Although she could be (and was) generous and helpful to a young woman novelist like Janet Lewis, who was just starting her career in the 1940s, Gertrude continued to bristle at women writers who outranked her.

She could console herself by counting off the list of honors that had come to her by then: an honorary Doctorate in Literature from Mills College, an honorary Doctor of Law degree from U.C. Berkeley, selection as guest of honor for a Gertrude Atherton Day at the 1939 Golden Gate International Exposition and as "California's most famous daughter" for the Exposition's Women's Day lunch, which also honored architect Julia Morgan, educator Aurelia Reinhardt, and fellow novelist Kathleen Norris.

An exhibit of her manuscripts and memorabilia opened at the Library of Congress in May 1943, accompanied by publicity citing her as the dean of American women novelists and the first living woman writer whose work was extensively represented at the Library of Congress.

All the accolades did not put to rest Gertrude's occasional doubts about the ultimate value of her work. Although she never seems to have brooded about what she might have been able to do with her prodigious talent if she had served a more scrupulous muse, she certainly voiced dissatisfaction about much of what she had produced. When her friend Charlotte Hallowell asked if she ever reread her own novels, she answered, "No, you may bet your life I don't read over my own books. I had to glance over several when writing *Adventures* and found it hard work. The only novels of mine that I care anything about are the historical ones, and I am glad to say those have taken a definite place."[28] Particularly proud of *The Conqueror*, she continued to view its long-term success in the marketplace as proof of true distinction.

She did admit some of her failings to Joseph Henry Jackson, who critiqued her short story "Deep Collar." "I agree with you," she wrote him. "It is dated, it is too long, it is verbose and everything else it should not be."[29] She might have broadened the comment to cover more than the particular story in question, but as far as we know, she did not. Jackson's published assessment that her greatest contribution was as an observant social historian, a panoramist, a journalistic chronicler of her own and past times who peered out of windows to "Watch the Parade: Write it All Down,"[30] no doubt pleased her.

And she continued to prize in herself her Western, aggressive, and competitive fighter's stance, her ability, even into her ninth decade, to view the world from behind raised fists. When she strained a knee ligament in 1937, she kidded that it was the kind of injury prizefighters sustain in the ring. Courage is what counts, she told an aspiring young writer, "courage to believe in yourself and your own work."[31] At her ninetieth birthday celebration she confessed she didn't expect to live more than a year longer, "But I've had a good time out of life. And I've learned that if you want something you've got to go after it."[32]

Her legendary vigor and youthfulness at last made concessions to mortality. A second knee injury at the age of 84 prompted her to give up her California Street apartment and move into an apartment on the top floor of Muriel's house at 2280 Green Street. An attack of bronchitis made her feel "like a stewed owl with mud sauce,"[33] and prevented her from attending a dinner in honor of Robert Frost, the first such public celebration in the city of his birth, at which he was to read his own poetry. (Frost made a point of stopping to call on her before he left town, and after she received him in a

flowing pink negligee, he commented on her Yankee durability.)[34]
Her sight deteriorated to the point where all she could read were
newspaper headlines. Neuritis in both hands made typing difficult.
She fell and suffered a concussion, but recovered enough of her old
spunk to resume taking Dr. Benjamin's hormone pills. She wrote
him, "Muriel thinks I am stronger, but when one has reached the
venerable age of ninety, one cannot expect too much."[35]

Aware that her days were numbered, she nevertheless continued
to think ahead. As she faced her ninety-first year she had in mind
a novel about the Almaden quicksilver mines near her grandfather's
ranch in San Jose.[36] She could hire someone to help with the typing,
if need be.

When she died of a stroke on June 14, 1948, people mourned not
just the passing of a woman, but of the embodiment of the robust,
individualistic city of San Francisco "which gave her the courage to
be herself." Oscar Lewis wrote: "More than any other San Franciscan
she symbolized those qualities that have made her city the capri-
cious, charming and paradoxical place it is." Both Gertrude Atherton
and San Francisco, he wrote, "had haphazard, unconventional beginnings, both grew to maturity amid the turmoil, violence and open-
handed generosity of the frontier. And both carried into their later
years the salient marks of their upbringing: self-reliance . . . [and] a
shrewd insight into the strengths and weaknesses of mankind." Said
the *Chronicle*'s Carolyn Anspacher, "She not only was a reflection of
San Francisco. She was San Francisco."[37]

The news of her death traveled to France, where Alice Toklas responded with incredulity, writing: "The other day when I saw in the
newspaper that Mrs. Atherton had died it was quite a shock—for
though she was very old one thought of her as going on forever."[38]

Reference Matter

Notes

The following abbreviations are used in the notes:

Bancroft   Bancroft Library, University of California, Berkeley
CHS   California Historical Society, San Francisco
HRC   Harry Ransom Humanities Research Center, Austin, Texas
LC   Library of Congress
Lilly   Lilly Library, Indiana University
Montalvo   Montalvo Center for the Arts, Saratoga, California
NYPL   New York Public Library, Astor, Lenox, and Tilden Foundations

INTRODUCTION

1. In the few years between 1915 and 1919, for example, the *New York Times Index* lists her 27 times.

2. Atherton, *Patience Sparhawk and Her Times* (New York: John Lane, 1897), p. 290. Subsequent references to this edition will be included in the text.

3. Atherton was an early enthusiast for and member of the Authors League and later served on its council.

4. Atherton, "What the Day's Work Means to Me," *Bookman* 42 (Feb. 1916): 693.

5. I owe the Weston reference to Carolyn Forrey, "Gertrude Atherton and the New Woman," *California Historical Quarterly* 55 (Fall 1976): 207.

6. *San Francisco Examiner*, Apr. 15, 1889.

7. Luhan to Atherton, Apr. 3, 1935, Bancroft; quoted by permission. Unless otherwise noted, Bancroft references are to the Gertrude Atherton Papers.

8. George Stade, "Men, Boys and Wimps," *New York Times Book Review*, Aug. 12, 1984, p. 1.

9. Atherton, *The Doomswoman* (New York: Selwin Tait & Sons, 1893), p. 21.

CHAPTER ONE

1. Atherton column, *San Francisco Examiner*, Sept. 27, 1891.

2. Atherton column, *San Francisco Examiner*, Aug. 15, 1891.

3. Lucie Burnham Miller to Atherton, undated, Bancroft.

4. Atherton, *Adventures of a Novelist* (New York: Liveright, 1932), p. 43. Subsequent references to this edition will be included in the text.

5. Atherton, *California: An Intimate History* (New York: Harper & Brothers, 1914), p. 281.

6. David Lavender, *Nothing Seemed Impossible: William C. Ralston and Early San Francisco* (Palo Alto, Calif.: American West Publishing Co., 1975), p. 204.

7. Neill C. Wilson, *400 California Street* (San Francisco: Lawton Kennedy, 1964), p. 46.

8. The Franklins were a mobile tribe. Stephen Franklin's father, Amos Avery Franklin, prospered in Oxford, New York, but he had been born in Stonington, Connecticut, and died in Patch Grove, Wisconsin. Stephen's grandfather, Thomas, was born on Block Island, Rhode Island. (There is no evidence for the myth, cherished by Stephen and perpetuated by Gertrude, that the family was related to the famous Benjamin Franklin.) Gerald Wright of the California Historical Society provided essential help on the Franklin genealogy.

9. Statement of Stephen Franklin, 1886, manuscript, Bancroft.

10. Henry J. Galpin, *Annals of Oxford, New York* (Oxford, New York, 1906), p. 205.

11. Eliza Farnham, *California Indoors and Out* (New York: Dix, Edwards & Co., 1856), p. 22.

12. *San Francisco Alta*, Feb. 4, 1851.

13. Frank Soulé, John Gihon, and James Nisbet, *The Annals of San Francisco* (New York: D. Appleton & Co., 1855), p. 362.

14. Oscar Lewis, *Sea Routes to the Gold Fields* (New York: Knopf, 1949), p. 36.

15. Farnham, *California Indoors and Out*, p. 25.

16. Albert Benard de Russailh, *Last Adventure: San Francisco in 1851*,

translated from the French by Clarkson Crane (San Francisco: Westgate Press, 1931), pp. 28–30.

17. Soulé, Gihon, and Nisbet, *Annals of San Francisco*, p. 364.

18. Quoted in Clifford Merrill Drury, *William Anderson Scott, "no ordinary man"* (Glendale, Calif.: A. H. Clark Co., 1967), p. 160.

19. Ibid., p. 177.

20. Lavender, *Nothing Seemed Impossible*, p. 123.

21. *Elite Directory for San Francisco and Oakland for 1879* (San Francisco: Argonaut Publishing Company, 1879), p. 20.

22. John S. Hittell, *A History of the City of San Francisco* (San Francisco: A. L. Bancroft & Co., 1878), p. 266.

23. Charles Lockwood, *Suddenly San Francisco: The Early Years of an Instant City* (San Francisco: A California Living Book, 1978), p. 71.

24. Agricultural Census, 1860.

25. An 1870 census taker in Ward 2, San Francisco, found Thomas Horn remarried, with a two-year-old daughter named Helen. Probably the child did not survive into adulthood; if she had, Gertrude surely would have mentioned her, along with her Horn half brothers, who do turn up as adults. If her stepmother played any role in her life, we know nothing of it.

26. These figures for the year 1863 come from Franklin Walker, *San Francisco's Literary Frontier* (Seattle: University of Washington Press, 1970), p. 19.

27. *San Francisco Bulletin*, Apr. 15, 1865.

28. Atherton, *California*, p. 267.

29. Atherton, *Can Women Be Gentlemen?* (Boston: Houghton Mifflin Co., 1938), p. 49.

30. Atherton, "Most Unforgettable Character," unpublished typescript, Bancroft.

31. Atherton, "The Shame of My Sex: Women in Saloons," King Features, November 1944, CHS.

32. *San Francisco Bulletin*, May 27 and June 22, 1870.

33. Atherton, "Most Unforgettable Character," p. 7.

34. For Byron's impact on romantic imagination, see Helene Moglen, *Charlotte Bronte: The Self Conceived* (New York: W. W. Norton & Co., 1976), pp. 28–29.

CHAPTER TWO

1. The estate eventually became incorporated in a separate town called, appropriately enough, Atherton.

2. Mabel Dodge behaved in a parallel manner when she took up with

her first husband, Karl Evans, who was already married. The comments of her biographer Lois Rudnick apply to Gertrude's situation: "Mabel felt no compunction about [his wife's] prior claim. Because she had been emotionally deprived as a child, she believed she had every right to steal love" (Lois Rudnick, *Mabel Dodge Luhan: New Woman, New Worlds* [Albuquerque: University of New Mexico Press, 1984], p. 23).

3. Mrs. Thomas Selby to Dominga Atherton, Apr. 15, 1876, CHS.

4. Doyce B. Nunis, Jr., Introduction to *The California Diary of Faxon Dean Atherton* (San Francisco: California Historical Society, 1964), p. xxx.

5. Oscar Lewis, *Silver Kings: The Lives and Times of Mackay, Fair, Flood and O'Brien, Lords of the Nevada Comstock Lode* (New York: Alfred Knopf, 1959), p. 228.

6. Atherton, "Motherhood," unpublished manuscript, Bancroft.

7. Daisy Edwards Hammond to Atherton, June 1942, Bancroft.

8. Last Will and Testament of Faxon Dean Atherton, Sept. 1, 1870. San Mateo County Clerk's Office, Redwood City, Calif.

9. Atherton estate documents, May 1879, CHS. Attorney Thomas Huster provided help in interpreting these legal papers.

10. Atherton papers, Bancroft.

11. Atherton to George Atherton, undated letters, Bancroft.

12. After the Athertons left Rancho Milpitas, a few of the dispossessed homesteaders were able to raise enough money to buy back the land they had worked. Eventually William Randolph Hearst bought the property from the Atherton estate for more than a million dollars. It is now part of the Hunter Liggett Military Reserve.

13. Atherton to George Atherton, undated, Bancroft.

14. Lois Rodecape, "Gilding the Sunflower," *California Historical Society Quarterly* 19 (June 1940): 97–112.

15. Dominga Atherton to George Atherton, July 12, 1882, CHS. My thanks to M. K. Swingle for translating letters by Dominga Atherton and Alejandra Rathbone from Spanish.

16. Dominga Atherton to George Atherton, Aug. 3, 1882, CHS.

17. *San Francisco Morning Call*, Nov. 29, 1882. I owe this reference to the late James Abajian.

18. Atherton, *A Daughter of the Vine* (London and New York: John Lane, The Bodley Head, 1899), p. 259 (a revision of *The Randolphs of Redwoods*).

19. Alejandra Rathbone to Dominga Atherton, undated, CHS.

20. Dominga Atherton to George Atherton, Dec. 10, 1885, CHS.

21. See Albert Shumate, *The California of George Gordon* (Glendale, Calif.: Arthur H. Clark Co., 1976).

22. Atherton, *The Randolphs of Redwoods*, *Argonaut*, Mar. 31, 1883.

23. Roger Burlingame, *Of Making Many Books* (New York: Charles Scribner's Sons, 1946), p. 77.

24. *Argonaut*, Apr. 14 and 21, 1883.

25. *Argonaut*, May 5, 1883.

26. *Argonaut*, Apr. 21, 1883.

27. Atherton, *The Californians* (London and New York: John Lane, 1898), p. 138.

28. *San Francisco Examiner*, Oct. 4, 1891.

29. "A Pioneer Play," *Argonaut*, Dec. 22, 1883.

30. *The Californians*, p. 321.

31. Atherton, "A Difficult Question," *Overland Monthly* n.s. 10 (Nov. 1887): 465–79.

32. Amelia Ransome Neville, *Fantastic City: A Memoir of the Social and Romantic Life of Old San Francisco* (Boston: Houghton Mifflin, 1932), p. 103.

33. Atherton, "Romance Queens I Have Known: Sibyl Sanderson," *Saturday Home Magazine*, May 3, 1947, p. 11.

34. Carlos V. Lopez, personal correspondence with author, Sept. 9, 1980.

35. *San Francisco Chronicle*, June 25, 1887.

36. *San Francisco Morning Call*, June 25, 1887.

37. Lopez, personal correspondence.

CHAPTER THREE

1. On New York in the 1880s, see: Van Wyck Brooks, *The Confident Years: 1885–1915* (New York: Dutton, 1952); Lloyd Morris, *Incredible New York: High Life and Low Life of the Last Hundred Years* (New York: Random House, 1951); Arthur M. Schlesinger, *The Rise of the City: 1878–1898* (New York: Macmillan, 1933).

2. Edith Wharton, *A Backward Glance* (New York: Scribner's, 1933), p. 69.

3. Alfred Kazin, *On Native Ground* (New York: Harcourt, Brace & World, 1942), chapter 1, p. 4.

4. Even the magnificent Yosemite fell short of Atherton's expectations. She told poet George Sterling that the place was "much over-rated," a statement that gave him gooseflesh. "She'll never get a chance to say that of Heaven," he told Mary Austin, "for that remark bars her" (Sterling to Austin, Sept. 1, 1910, Huntington Library, San Marino, Calif.).

5. *San Francisco Examiner*, Apr. 15, 1889.

6. Frederick A. Stokes, "A Publisher's Random Notes, 1880–1935," in

Bowker Lectures on Book Publishing, first series (New York: The Typophiles, 1943).

7. On Gilder, see Kazin, p. 57. Atherton's comments on editors: *Argonaut*, Nov. 25 and Dec. 10, 1888.

8. *Argonaut*, Mar. 18, 1889.

9. *Argonaut*, Jan. 28, 1889.

10. *Argonaut*, Jan. 21, 1889.

11. *Argonaut*, Dec. 17, 1888.

12. *Argonaut*, Nov. 19, 1888.

13. Until international copyright became law in 1891, American authors could be undersold by pirated British editions.

14. Ellen Glasgow, *The Woman Within* (New York: Hill & Wang, 1980), p. 141.

15. *Argonaut*, Dec. 24, 1888.

16. *Argonaut*, Dec. 31, 1888.

17. Atherton, *What Dreams May Come* (Chicago and New York: Belford, Clarke, 1888), p. 162.

18. In her professional life, Atherton never acknowledged her father's name—her own maiden name—of Horn. "Franklin" was the father she preferred.

19. *Argonaut*, Nov. 5, 1888.

20. *Publishers Weekly*, Feb. 9, 1889.

21. *Critic*, n.s. 11 (Jan. 5, 1889): 4.

22. Atherton, *Hermia Suydam* (New York: Current Literature Co., 1889), p. 26.

23. Ibid., p. 32.

24. Ibid., p. 45.

25. Ibid., p. 53.

26. On erotic novels of 1888, see Carolyn Forrey, "Gertrude Atherton and the New Woman," Ph.D. diss., Yale, 1971, pp. 98–99.

27. *Argonaut*, quoted in *Publishers Weekly*, Jan. 21, 1889.

28. *Current Literature* 2 (Apr. 1889): 267.

29. Atherton to Bierce, undated, Bierce Papers, Bancroft.

30. *New York Times*, Mar. 10, 1889.

31. *New York World*, Feb. 17, 1889.

32. Atherton to Bierce, Mar. 4, 1889, Bancroft.

33. *Town Topics*, Feb. 7 and May 9, 1889.

34. *San Francisco Examiner*, Apr. 15, 1889.

35. Atherton to Stoddart, Feb. 24, 1889, LC.

36. Atherton to Bierce, undated, Bancroft. Information about payment for her articles is from *Argonaut* financial records, CHS.

CHAPTER FOUR

1. Quoted in Julia Tutwiler, "Gertrude Atherton in New York," in *Women Authors of Our Day in Their Homes*, ed. Frances W. Halsey (New York: J. Pott & Co., 1903), p. 251. I owe this reference to Charlotte S. McClure, *Gertrude Atherton* (Boston: Twayne Publishers, U.S. Authors Series, 1979), p. 52.

2. Quoted in Carl Van Vechten, "Some Literary Ladies I Have Known," *Yale University Library Gazette* 26 (Jan. 1952): 101.

3. Quoted in Lois Rudnick, *Mabel Dodge Luhan: New Woman, New Worlds* (Albuquerque: University of New Mexico Press, 1984), p. 47.

4. Sandra M. Gilbert and Susan Gubar, *No Man's Land: The Place of the Woman Writer in the Twentieth Century*. Vol. 1, *The War of the Words* (New Haven: Yale University Press, 1988), p. 17.

5. Atherton, "A Native on the California Missions," *The Critic*, n.s. 9 (1888): 271.

6. Atherton, *American Wives and English Husbands* (New York: Dodd, Mead and Co., 1898), p. 333.

7. Atherton, *A Daughter of the Vine* (London and New York: John Lane, 1899), p. 102.

8. Carolyn Forrey, "Gertrude Atherton and the New Woman," *California Historical Quarterly* 55 (Fall 1976): 204.

9. Quoted in Joseph Hone, *The Life of George Moore* (New York: Macmillan, 1936), p. 159.

10. *Town Topics*, May 30, 1889, p. 11.

11. Atherton, *Los Cerritos: A Romance of the Modern Time* (New York: John W. Lovell Co., 1890), p. 281.

12. Ibid., p. 75.

13. Ibid., p. 303.

14. *The Academy* 36 (Aug. 17, 1889): 101.

15. Mona Caird's essays were eventually gathered in a book, *The Morality of Marriage and Other Essays on the Status of Women* (London: Redway, 1897).

16. Vincent O'Sullivan, "Gertrude Atherton," in his *Opinions* (London: Unicorn Press, 1959), p. 92.

17. James Mellow's comment on the friendships of Gertrude Stein is apropos: "She had a passion for acquaintanceship . . . but a limited capacity for untroubled friendship. Her friendships . . . were seldom priceless . . . ; they were replaceable" (*Charmed Circle: Gertrude Stein & Company* [New York: Avon Books, 1975], p. 27).

18. Atherton, "Literary London," *Bookman* (London) 16 (June 1899): 65.

CHAPTER FIVE

1. Henry James, *The Siege of London* (Boston and New York: Houghton Mifflin Co., 1882), p. 18.

2. Ibid., p. 49.

3. Ibid., pp. 109–10.

4. Leon Edel, *The Master: 1901–1916* (New York: Avon Books, 1978), p. 364.

5. Quoted by M. E. Grenander, *Ambrose Bierce* (Boston: Twayne Publishers, U.S. Authors Series, 1971), pp. 34–35.

6. Ernest Earnest, *The American Eve in Fact and Fiction* (Urbana: University of Illinois Press, 1974), p. 197.

7. Quoted in Franklin Walker, *San Francisco's Literary Frontier* (Seattle: University of Washington Press, 1970), p. 344.

8. Stanley Weintraub, *London Yankees: Portraits of American Writers and Artists in England* (New York: Harcourt Brace Jovanovich, 1979), p. 50.

9. Dominga Atherton died on September 20, 1890.

10. Carey McWilliams, *Southern California Country: An Island on the Land* (New York: Duell, Sloane & Pearce, 1946), p. 73; Kevin Starr, *Inventing the Dream: California Through the Progressive Era* (New York: Oxford University Press, 1985), p. 62.

11. Atherton to Joseph Stoddart, Sept. 27, 1891, LC.

12. *Argonaut*, Jan. 14, 1889.

13. Atherton's patronizing attitude shares nothing with that of her contemporary Mary Austin, a sympathetic and attentive observer of the desert dwellers she wrote about in books like *The Land of Little Rain* (1903) and *The Basket Woman* (1904).

14. Atherton, *The Splendid Idle Forties: Stories of Old California* (New York and London: Macmillan, 1902), p. 91.

15. Cf. Kevin Starr: "Behind nostalgia for a lost Utopia bristled the belief that something better had taken its place. In that sense, the myth of Arcadia's passing served the imperialist fantasies of the California elite in the 1890s, as they began to envision their state as the point of embarkation for American moves in the direction of Pacific empire" (*Americans and the California Dream, 1850–1915* [New York: Oxford University Press, 1970], p. 353).

16. Atherton, *Splendid Idle Forties*, p. 320.

17. Atherton to Stoddart, Sept. 27, 1891, LC.

18. William S. Walsh, "Mrs. Atherton's Novels: A Dialogue," *Lippincott's* 50 (Sept. 1892): 412–15.

CHAPTER SIX

1. Bierce's letters to Atherton, which she had carefully preserved in a trunk, were lost in the San Francisco earthquake and fire of 1906. Her letters to him survive and are now in the Bierce Papers at the Bancroft Library. Precise dating of Atherton's letters is not always possible, since she made a practice of leaving out the year, and sometimes the month, in her letter headings. Unless otherwise noted, the letters to Bierce quoted throughout this book are from the Bancroft; dates are given whenever possible. Atherton's response to Bierce's first letter is quoted in Chapter 3.

2. George Sterling, "The Shadow Maker," *American Mercury* 6, 2 (Oct. 1925): 12.

3. Bierce to Ella Sterling Cummins, May 1, 1892, CHS.

4. Sterling, "Shadow Maker," p. 15.

5. "Prattle," *San Francisco Examiner*, Mar. 23, 1890. Bierce's comments on women are conveniently collected by Lois Rather in *Bittersweet: Ambrose Bierce and Women* (Oakland, Calif.: The Rather Press, 1975).

6. Atherton, *A Christmas Witch*, *Godey's Magazine* 126, 751 (Jan. 1893): 76.

7. W. A. Swanberg, *Citizen Hearst* (New York: Scribner's, 1961), p. 53.

8. Sterling, "Shadow Maker," p. 12.

9. Adolphe De Castro [Danzinger], *Portrait of Ambrose Bierce* (New York: The Century Co., 1929), p. 162.

10. This is Atherton's earliest known reference to Aspasia, consort of Pericles, about whom she would write (believing herself to be Aspasia reincarnated) *The Immortal Marriage* (1927).

11. "Prattle," Oct. 4, 1891.

12. De Castro, *Portrait*, p. 164.

13. "Woman in Her Variety" appeared in the *San Francisco Examiner* between August and November 1891.

14. Kevin Starr, *Americans and the California Dream: 1850–1915* (New York: Oxford University Press, 1973), p. 352.

15. Atherton, *The Doomswoman* (New York: Selwin, Tait, 1893), p. 21.

16. In one of her early reviews, Willa Cather, usually critical of Atherton for her frank appeal to "summer hotel ladies" and schoolgirls, singled out *The Doomswoman* for praise: "It was spontaneous. . . . It gave one a vivid impression of the wealth and vastness and variety of old California, and a striking, if not true, picture of Spanish society" (*The World and the Parish: Willa Cather's Articles and Reviews, 1893–1902*, ed. William M. Curtin [Lincoln: University of Nebraska Press, 1970], vol. 2, pp. 694–96).

17. *Argonaut*, Mar. 25, 1877.

18. Carey McWilliams, *Ambrose Bierce: A Biography* (Hamden, Conn.: Archon Books, 1967), p. 164.

19. Atherton to Stoddart, Jan. 28, 1892, LC.

20. "Prattle," Jan. 19 and May 29, 1892.

21. Atherton, "The Literary Development of California," *Cosmopolitan*, Jan. 1891, pp. 269–78.

22. *San Francisco Examiner*, Jan. 15, 1892.

23. Bierce to Ella Sterling Cummins, Mar. 13 and Sept. 25, 1892, CHS.

24. Ella Sterling Cummins (Mighels), "California Writers and Literature," *The Story of the Files* (California World's Fair Commission, Columbian Exposition, 1893), p. 349.

25. "Prattle," Sept. 18, 1892; June 18, 1893.

26. Charles Scribner & Sons to Atherton, May 29, 1893, Beinecke.

27. Helen Bierce, "Ambrose Bierce at Home," *American Mercury* 30, 120 (Dec. 1933): 455.

CHAPTER SEVEN

1. Atherton to Stoddart, [summer 1892], LC.

2. Atherton to Stoddart, Feb. 2, 1892, LC.

3. News clipping dated Sept. 28, 1890, Neville Scrapbooks, Book 14, CHS.

4. Atherton to *Blackwood's*, June 9, [1892], National Library of Scotland.

5. Atherton to Stoddart, undated, LC.

6. Atherton, "The Theatre of Arts and Letters," *California Illustrated Magazine* 5, 5 (Apr. 5, 1894): 580–85.

7. *San Francisco Morning Call*, May 28, 1893.

8. Pollard to Bierce, July 12, 1893, Bancroft.

9. Jeanne Madeline Weimann, *The Fair Women* (Chicago: Academy Chicago Press, 1981), p. 314.

10. W. A. Swanberg, *Pulitzer* (New York: Scribner's, 1967), p. 107.

11. "The first stories of legal electrocution were written in 1892 by six New York reporters, including Arthur Brisbane for the *World*" (Frank Luther Mott, *American Journalism: 1690–1960*, 3rd ed. [New York: Macmillan, 1962], p. 488).

12. *New York Times*, Jan. 15, 1892.

13. Atherton, "Wanted: Imagination," in *What Is a Book?* (Boston: Houghton Mifflin, 1935), p. 59.

14. Atherton to Elizabeth Jordan, undated, Elizabeth Jordan Papers, NYPL.

CHAPTER EIGHT

1. Richard Ellmann, *Oscar Wilde* (New York: Knopf, 1987), p. 305.

2. Barbara W. Tuchman, *The Proud Tower: A Portrait of the World Before the War, 1890–1914* (New York: Bantam, 1976), p. 2.

3. Atherton to Elizabeth Jordan, Sept. 2 [1895], NYPL.

4. E. F. Benson, *As We Were*, (London and New York: Longmans, Green and Co., 1941), p. 315.

5. Atherton to Stoddart, Apr. 30, 1895, LC.

6. Elaine Showalter, *A Literature of Their Own* (Princeton, N.J.: Princeton University Press, 1977), p. 211.

7. Linda Dowling, "The Decadent and the New Woman in the 1890s," *Nineteenth Century Fiction* 33 (Mar. 1979): 323–53.

8. Atherton, *Julia France and Her Times* (New York: Macmillan, 1912), p. 322.

9. Atherton, *A Daughter of the Vine* (London and New York: John Lane, The Bodley Head, 1899), p. 102.

10. Atherton to Jordan, Sept. 2, [1895], NYPL.

11. Atherton, "Divorce in the United States," *Contemporary Review* 72 (Sept. 1897): 410–15.

12. James Montgomery Flagg, *Roses and Buckshot* (New York: Putnam's, 1946), p. 65.

13. *San Francisco Call*, Nov. 26, 1898.

14. A. N. Wilson, *Hilaire Belloc* (New York: Atheneum, 1984), p. 39.

15. Horace Annesley Vachell, *Fellow Travellers* (New York: Frederick A. Stokes Co., 1924), p. 82.

16. "A Talk with Gertrude Atherton," *Young Woman* 7 (July 1898): 361. Atherton projected her discomfort with anything but the simplest and smallest of workspaces onto Patience Sparhawk, who retreats from Peele Manor (read Valparaiso Park) into a studio. Likewise, Edna Pontellier in *The Awakening* retreats to a cottage so small she calls it the pigeon house.

17. Flagg, *Roses and Buckshot*, p. 64.

18. For British comment on *Patience Sparhawk*, see *Edinburgh Review* 187, Apr. 1898; *Times*, Apr. 8, 1899. For American comment, *Saturday Review*, Apr. 9, 1898, and July 17, 1897; *Critic*, Apr. 24, 1897, and Nov. 1898; *Bookman* (New York) May 1897.

19. *New York Times* review, May 15, 1897; editorial, *Saturday Supplement*, May 15, 1898.

20. *San Francisco Call*, Apr. 18 and May 23, 1897.

21. Atherton's original title of choice, borrowed from a line in Yeats,

was *The Great Black Oxen*, later recycled and shortened to *Black Oxen* for her 1923 best-seller.

22. Atherton, *The Californians* (New York and London: John Lane, 1898), p. 171.

23. London *Times*, Apr. 8, 1899.

24. Turner to Beerbohm and Beerbohm to Turner, Aug. 1897, in Max Beerbohm, *Letters to Reggie Turner*, ed. Rupert Hart-Davis (Philadelphia: Lippincott, 1965), p. 121.

25. Ellmann, *Oscar Wilde*, p. 550.

26. James Hart, *The Popular Book* (New York: Oxford University Press, 1950), p. 185. In 1895 alone, Consuelo Vanderbilt had married the Duke of Marlborough; Anna Gould, Count Boni de Castellane; Mary Leiter, Marquis Curzon of Kedleston; and Pauline Whitney, Sir Almeric Paget. Whitney's father, William C. Whitney, served as model for the father in *His Fortunate Grace*.

27. Atherton, *American Wives and English Husbands* (New York: Dodd, Mead, 1898), p. 21.

28. *San Francisco Examiner*, Oct. 4, 1896.

29. Atherton, "English and American Girls," *Women at Home* 7 (1897): 42–46.

30. *American Wives*, p. 145.

31. Carolyn Forrey, "Atherton's New Women and Traditional Feminine Roles," ch. 4 of "Gertrude Atherton and the New Woman," Ph.D. diss., Yale, 1971.

32. *Athenaeum* 3680 (May 7, 1898): 597.

33. Quoted in "A Talk with Gertrude Atherton," *Young Woman*, July 1898.

34. *The American Essays of Henry James*, ed. Leon Edel (New York: Vintage Books, 1956), p. 207.

35. Atherton, "Literary London," *The Bookman* (London) 16 (June 1899): 65–67.

36. Vincent O'Sullivan, *Opinions* (London: Unicorn Press, 1959), p. 94.

37. Atherton to Lane, Apr. 3, 1900, HRC.

38. See Vineta Colby, *The Singular Anomoly* (New York: New York University Press, 1970), pp. 184–85.

39. American reviews: *Critic*, n.s. 29 (May 14, 1898): 328–29 and n.s. 30 (Nov. 1898), 394; *Bookman* (New York) 8 (Nov. 1898): 253.

40. *San Francisco Call*, Jan. 5, 1899.

41. Ellmann, *Oscar Wilde*, p. 583.

CHAPTER NINE

1. Atherton, *Senator North* (New York and London: John Lane, 1900), p. 303. Subsequent references to this edition will be included in the text.

2. *Chicago Tribune*, Feb. 26, 1899.

3. Atherton to Mr. Stanton, Jan. 9, [1899], Clifton Waller Barret Library, University of Virginia, Charlottesville, No. 7680-b.

4. Philip Fisher, "Appearing and Disappearing in Public," in *Reconstructing American Literary History*, ed. Sacvan Bercovitch, (Cambridge, Mass: Harvard English Studies, 1986), pp. 155–88.

5. Atherton, *American Wives and English Husbands* (New York: Dodd, Mead, 1898), p. 265.

6. *San Francisco Call*, Apr. 9, 1899.

7. Atherton to Lane, undated and Jan. 16, 1900, HRC.

8. An undated Atherton poem, "Negro on the Docks at Mobile, Ala.," discovered by Charlotte S. McClure and published for the first time in *American Literary Realism*, Spring 1976, p. 167, gives a far more spiritual and human portrait of a black man.

9. *New York Times*, Sept. 29, 1900.

10. M. B. James in *Lippincott's*, Sept. 1901, pp. 168–72.

11. Atherton, undated statement, HRC.

12. *New York Times*, Oct. 6, 1900.

13. Quoted with approbation by Bierce, *San Francisco Examiner*, June 10, 1900.

14. Atherton to Lane, Nov. 5, 1900, HRC.

15. Atherton to Lane, Jan. 16, 1900, HRC.

16. Atherton to Lane, Mar. 15, 1900, HRC.

17. Atherton to H. H. Robinson, Mar. 17, 1900, Berg Collection, NYPL.

18. Atherton to Willets, Feb. 8, 1900, University of Virginia, No. 6780-b.

19. Atherton to Lane, Apr. 7, 1900, HRC.

20. Atherton to Robinson, Mar. 17, 1900, Berg Collection, NYPL.

21. Atherton to Lane, Jan. 1, 1901, HRC.

22. Harold Larson, "Alexander Hamilton: The Fact and Fiction of His Early Years," *William and Mary Quarterly*, 3rd series, 9 (1952): 140.

23. Atherton to Lane, Dec. 1900, HRC.

24. Alice B. Toklas, *What Is Remembered* (New York: Holt, Rinehart and Winston, 1963), p. 63.

25. Atherton, *The Conqueror* (New York and London: Macmillan, 1902), p. 7.

26. Ibid., p. 37.

27. Robert Hendrickson, *Hamilton I: 1757–1789* (New York: Mason/Charter, 1976), p. 18.

28. Quoted by Julia Tutwiler, "Gertrude Atherton in New York," in *Women Authors of Our Day in Their Homes*, ed. Frances W. Halsey (New York: J. Pott & Co., 1903), p. 254.

29. *Conqueror*, pp. 290, 73.

30. Atherton to Lane, Sept. 27, 1901, HRC.

31. Atherton to Lane, Apr. 17, 1901, HRC.

32. Atherton to Lane, Apr. 19, 1901, HRC.

33. Comment on *The Aristocrats: Bookman* (New York) 13 (July 1901): 443; *Critic* 39 (Sept. 1901): 262.

34. Atherton to Lane, June 27, 1901, HRC.

35. Atherton to Lane, Aug. 12, 1901, HRC.

36. *Bookman* (New York) 14 (Sept. 1901): 1.

37. Atherton to Lane, Sept. 27, 1901, HRC.

38. Charles Madison, *Book Publishing in America* (New York: Bowker, 1966), pp. 262–66.

39. *Conqueror* reviews: *Critic* 40 (June 1902): 501; *Harpers Weekly* 46 (Apr. 1902): 506; *New York Times*, Apr. 12, 1902; (London) *Times Literary Supplement*, May 30, 1902; *Saturday Review* 93 (June 14, 1902): 776.

40. *New York Times*, Apr. 19, 1902.

41. *Publishers Weekly*, Nov. 15, 1941; penciled Atherton draft of a letter to the American Academy of Arts and Letters, Bancroft.

CHAPTER TEN

1. Atherton to Brett, Apr. 3, [1902], Macmillan Papers, NYPL.

2. Interview with Alice B. Toklas by Roland E. Duncan, Regional Oral History Office, Bancroft, 1952, p. 11.

3. Atherton to Brett, [April 1902], NYPL.

4. Atherton to Brett, May 30, [1903], NYPL.

5. Atherton to Brett, July 27, 1903, NYPL.

6. Florence Atherton Dickey, "Gertrude Atherton, Family and Celebrated Friends," oral history conducted by Emily W. Leider, Regional Oral History Office, Bancroft, 1981, pp. 10–11.

7. Atherton to Coolbrith, June 1, 1908, CHS.

8. Atherton to Phelan, Dec. 16, [1905], Montalvo.

9. Atherton to Phelan, undated, Montalvo.

10. *San Francisco Bulletin*, Mar. 23, 1905.

11. Atherton, *Ancestors* (New York: Harper & Brothers, 1907), p. 656. Subsequent references to this edition will be included in the text.

12. Atherton, *Golden Gate Country* (New York: Duell, Sloan & Pearce, 1945), p. 226.

13. Quoted in Judd Kahn, *Imperial San Francisco* (Lincoln: University of Nebraska Press, 1979), p. 53.

14. Robert Cleland, *California in Our Time: 1900–1940* (New York: Knopf, 1947), p. 14.

15. Atherton to Phelan, undated, Bancroft.

16. Atherton to Phelan, Oct. 24, [1906], Montalvo.

17. *San Francisco Call*, May 2, 1906.

18. Kahn, *Imperial San Francisco*, p. 156.

19. Lincoln Steffens, "The Mote and the Beam," *American Magazine*, Dec. 1907, p. 37.

20. *Town Talk*, Nov. 9, 1907, p. 21.

21. Atherton, "San Francisco and Her Foes," *Harpers Weekly*, Nov. 2, 1907, p. 1590.

22. Atherton, "San Francisco's Tragic Dawn," *Harpers Weekly*, May 12, 1906, p. 660.

23. Atherton, "San Francisco and Her Foes," p. 1590.

24. Ibid., p. 1620.

25. Cora Older, "The Story of a Reformer's Wife," *McClure's Magazine*, July 1909, pp. 286–88.

26. Atherton, "San Francisco and Her Foes," p. 1592.

27. Josephine Rhodehamel and Raymond Wood, *Ina Coolbrith: Librarian and Laureate of California* (Provo, Utah: Brigham Young University Press, 1973), pp. 246–47.

28. Ina Coolbrith, address to the Pacific Coast Women's Press Association, Apr. 18, 1929.

29. Atherton to an unnamed correspondent, June 13, [1906], Bancroft.

30. Atherton to Coolbrith, June 6, 1906, CHS.

31. Atherton to Coolbrith, Sept. 18, 1907, Coolbrith Papers, Bancroft.

32. Atherton to Coolbrith, Sept. 20, 1907, Coolbrith Papers, Bancroft.

33. Atherton to Coolbrith, Oct. 18, 1907, CHS.

34. Atherton to Phelan, Oct. 18, 1907, Bancroft.

35. Atherton, *My San Francisco* (Indianapolis: Bobbs-Merrill, 1946), p. 92.

36. Ibid., p. 90.

37. Atherton to Coolbrith, Nov. 29, 1907, CHS.

38. Coolbrith, address to the Pacific Coast Women's Press Association.

CHAPTER ELEVEN

1. Atherton, "Why Is American Literature Bourgeois?" *North American Review* 178 (May 1904): 771–81.

2. Atherton, "The Fault I Find with America," *Delineator* 80 (Nov. 1912): 324.

3. Upton Sinclair reprinted his 1904 remarks in *Money Writes* (New York: Boni, 1927), p. 81.

4. Atherton, "The Fault I Find," p. 324.

5. Atherton, *Tower of Ivory* (New York: Macmillan, 1910), pp. 138–39. Subsequent references to this edition will be included in the text.

6. Atherton, *Rulers of Kings* (New York and London: Harper & Brothers, 1904), p. 5.

7. Ibid., pp. 92, 100.

8. Atherton to Brett, Jan. 28, 1904, NYPL.

9. Atherton to Brett, Feb. 1, 1904, NYPL.

10. Atherton to Brett, [1908?], NYPL.

11. Atherton stayed with Harpers for three of her next books: *The Bell in the Fog and Other Stories* (1905), the potboiler *Traveling Thirds* (1905), and the big California novel of 1907, *Ancestors*. She returned to Brett and Macmillan with *Tower of Ivory*, a bigger commercial success than any of the Harpers titles.

12. Atherton, "The Fault I Find," p. 324.

13. Atherton to Coolbrith, June 1, 1908, CHS.

14. Atherton to Phelan, Feb. 17, 1907, Bancroft.

15. Atherton, "Romance Queens I Have Known: Maude Fay," *San Francisco Call-Bulletin*, Sept. 11, 1947.

16. Obituary of Sibyl Sanderson, *New York Times*, May 17, 1903; "Sibyl Sanderson," in *Famous American Women*, ed. Robert McHenry (New York: Dover, 1983), p. 367.

17. Atherton to Phelan, Dec. 17, 1906, Bancroft.

18. Sharon O'Brien, *Willa Cather* (New York: Oxford University Press, 1987), p. 171. Ellen Moers suggests reasons the opera prima donna made a strong heroine: "Men adore her, but there is no other kind of heroine . . . who can so plausibly be made a chaste as well as a mature and desirable woman" (*Literary Women* [Garden City, N.Y.: Anchor Books, 1977], pp. 287–88).

19. Atherton to Juliana Haskell, undated, Columbia University Library.

20. Review by Margaret Sherwood in *Atlantic Monthly* 106 (Dec. 1910): 810–12.

21. Atherton to Phelan, Feb. 17, 1907, Bancroft. On the Metropolitan's

withdrawal of its *Salome* production, see Barbara W. Tuchman, *The Proud Tower: A Portrait of the World Before the War, 1890–1914* (New York: Bantam, 1976), p. 380.

22. See B. R. McElderry, Jr., "Gertrude Atherton and Henry James," *Colby Library Quarterly* 3 (Nov. 1954): 269–72.

23. *New York Times*, Apr. 16, 1905.

24. *Argonaut* 55 (Feb. 6, 1905): 92.

25. *Critic* 44 (May 1904): 395.

26. Willa Cather, *The World and the Parish: Willa Cather's Articles and Reviews, 1893–1902*, ed. William M. Curtin (Lincoln: University of Nebraska Press, 1970), vol. 2, p. 695.

27. Atherton to Edward O'Day, Mar. 6, 1910, Bancroft.

28. See Elizabeth Ammons, *Edith Wharton's Argument with America* (Athens: University of Georgia Press, 1980) for an excellent discussion of Wharton as social critic.

29. John Curtis Underwood, *Literature and Insurgency* (New York: Mitchell Kennerley, 1914), p. 391.

30. Quoted in R. W. B. Lewis, *Edith Wharton* (New York: Harper & Row, 1975), p. 151.

31. Fredrick T. Cooper in *Bookman* (New York) 30 (Dec. 1909): 357–63; Morton Payne in *The Dial* 99 (Sept. 1, 1900): 126.

32. Atherton to Brett, May 24 [1902], NYPL.

33. Atherton, "The New Aristocracy," *Cosmopolitan* 40 (Apr. 1906): 625.

34. *Argonaut* 55 (Feb. 6, 1905): 92.

35. *New York Times*, Dec. 29, 1907.

36. Carl Van Vechten, "Some Literary Ladies I Have Known," *Yale University Library Gazette* 26 (Jan. 1952): 100.

37. Atherton, "The Fault I Find," p. 324.

38. Atherton to Phelan, Mar. 22, 1910, Montalvo.

CHAPTER TWELVE

1. Atherton, "The Woman in Love," *Harper's Bazaar* 44 (May 1910): 305.

2. Arnold Genthe, *As I Remember* (New York: Reynal & Hitchcock, 1936), p. 110.

3. "Mrs. Atherton Writes a Play on the Modern Woman," *New York Times*, Nov. 27, 1910.

4. Garff B. Wilson, *A History of American Acting* (Bloomington: Indiana University Press, 1966), p. 230.

5. Atherton to Fiske, Apr. 13, [1910], LC; Atherton to Edward O'Day, Oct. 13, 1910, Bancroft. *San Francisco Morning Call*, July 15, 1910.

6. Atherton does not identify Charlotte Perkins Gilman in *Adventures*, but describes the woman as an "EMINENT FEMINIST" who was visiting San Francisco with her neglected child.

7. *San Francisco Call*, Oct. 8, 1911.

8. Florence Atherton Dickey, "Gertrude Atherton, Family and Celebrated Friends," oral history conducted by Emily W. Leider, Regional Oral History Office, Bancroft, 1981, p. 11.

9. Atherton, "The Fault I Find with America," *Delineator* 80 (Nov. 1912): 324.

10. Atherton to O'Day, Mar. 21, 1911, Bancroft.

11. Atherton to Fiske, Mar. 22, [1911], LC.

12. Atherton to Fiske, Dec. 14, [1911], LC.

13. Atherton to O'Day, undated, Bancroft.

14. Edward O'Day, *Varied Types* (San Francisco: Town Talk Press, 1915), p. 22.

15. Atherton, "The Present Unrest Among Women," *Delineator* 74 (Aug. 1909): 118.

16. Atherton, *Julia France and Her Times* (New York: Macmillan, 1912), p. 305.

17. Archie Binns, with Olive Kooken, *Mrs. Fiske and the American Theater* (New York: Crown, 1955), p. 255.

18. Ibid., p. 255.

19. Atherton to Coolbrith, Jan. 9, 1911, Coolbrith Papers, Bancroft.

20. Atherton to Brett, undated, NYPL.

21. Binns, *Mrs. Fiske*, p. 256.

22. Atherton to Brett, undated, NYPL.

23. Binns, *Mrs. Fiske*, p. 256.

24. Atherton to Brett, undated, NYPL.

25. Atherton to Brett, May 25, [1912], NYPL.

26. *New York Times*, Apr. 21, 1912; *Bookman* (New York) 35 (May 1912).

CHAPTER THIRTEEN

1. Atherton to Bynner, Aug. 14, [1912], Houghton Library, Harvard University.

2. *New York Times*, Aug. 17, 1912.

3. *New York Times*, Aug. 28, 1912.

4. "Alice Carpenter Retorts," *New York Times*, Aug. 30, 1912.

5. *San Francisco Examiner*, Oct. 5, 1912.

6. *New York Times*, June 14, 1914.

7. Atherton, *Perch of the Devil* (New York: Frederick A. Stokes Company, 1914), p. 56.

8. Ibid., p. 293.
9. Ibid., p. 367.
10. Ibid., p. 15.
11. Quoted in H. Hamlin, *Pony Express*, Oct. 1964, p. 8.
12. Atherton to C. Older, July 12, 1912, Bancroft.
13. *New York Times*, June 14, 1914.
14. Atherton to Phelan, undated, Bancroft.
15. Atherton to Sinclair, Aug. 20, 1918, Lilly.

CHAPTER FOURTEEN

1. Edith Wharton was writing about her war experiences for *Scribner's*; Mary Roberts Rinehart published in the *Saturday Evening Post*.
2. Atherton, *The Living Present* (New York: Frederick A. Stokes Company, 1917), p. 281.
3. Atherton to Phelan, May 8, 1915, Bancroft.
4. Atherton to Phelan, May 8, [1914], Bancroft.
5. Atherton to Phelan, Mar. 24, [1915], Bancroft.
6. Atherton to Phelan, Sept. 22, 1914, Bancroft.
7. *New York Times*, Nov. 29, 1915.
8. *New York Times*, Dec. 10, 1916.
9. *New York Times*, Jan. 16, 1916.
10. *New York Times*, Sept. 2, 1915.
11. Atherton to Phelan, Feb. 4, 1916, Bancroft.
12. *New York Times*, Dec. 10, 1916; Nov. 21, 1915.
13. Florence Atherton Dickey, "Gertrude Atherton, Family and Celebrated Friends," oral history conducted by Emily W. Leider, Regional Oral History Office, Bancroft, 1981, pp. 14–15. See also Lois Rudnick, *Mabel Dodge Luhan: New Woman, New Worlds* (Albuquerque: University of New Mexico Press, 1984), pp. 123–24.
14. Atherton to Genevieve Harvey, Oct. 6, 1918, Bancroft.
15. Rudnick, *Mabel Dodge Luhan*, pp. 121–23.
16. Atherton, *Mrs. Belfame* (New York: Frederick A. Stokes Company, 1916), p. 8.
17. Ibid., p. 14.
18. Atherton to Charlotte Hallowell, Jan. 26, 1916, Bancroft.
19. Erotic release was a common experience of women during the war. See Sandra M. Gilbert, "Soldier's Heart: Literary Men, Literary Women, and the Great War," *Signs*, Spring 1983, pp. 436–38.
20. Atherton, *The White Morning: A Novel of the Power of the German Women in Wartime* (New York: Frederick A. Stokes, 1918), p. 135.
21. Ibid., p. 133.

22. Ibid., p. 146.

23. Atherton, "Women of Germany: An Argument for My Novel, *The White Morning*," *Bookman* (New York) 46 (Feb. 1916): 632.

24. *New York Times*, Oct. 28, 1918.

25. *Upton Sinclair's*, July 1918, p. 7.

26. Atherton to Sinclair, Feb. 25, 1918, and Aug. 20, 1918, Lilly.

27. *Upton Sinclair's*, May–June 1918, p. 7.

28. Atherton to Sinclair, Aug. 20, 1918, and Sept. 25, 1918, Lilly.

29. *New Republic* 154 (Oct. 13, 1917): 310.

30. Gilbert, "Soldier's Heart," p. 424.

31. Atherton, *The Living Present*, p. 207.

32. Ibid., pp. 218–20.

33. Atherton to Phelan, Sept. 6, 1916, Bancroft.

34. Atherton to Coolbrith, Oct. 12, 1918, Bancroft.

35. "Pendennis" [pseud.], "My Types—Gertrude Atherton," *Forum* 58 (Nov. 1917): 592.

36. *Literary Digest* 54 (Apr. 14, 1917): 1061.

37. *American Woman's Magazine*, Sept. 1918.

38. *New York Sun*, Apr. 15, 1916.

39. Atherton typescript on Isadora Duncan, Witter Bynner Collection, Houghton Library, Harvard University.

40. *New York Times*, Feb. 28, 1919.

CHAPTER FIFTEEN

1. *San Francisco Call*, Mar. 8, 1926.

2. Atherton, *The Horn of Life* (New York: Appleton-Century, 1942), p. 8.

3. Atherton to Hallowell, Dec. 12, 1919, in Gertrude Atherton Letters to Charlotte Hallowell, Bancroft.

4. Atherton to Phelan, July 22, 1920, Bancroft.

5. Atherton to Phelan, July 13, 1920, Bancroft.

6. Arthur Marx, *Goldwyn* (New York: Norton, 1976), p. 98; A. Scott Berg, *Goldwyn* (New York: Knopf, 1989), p. 92.

7. Kevin Brownlow, *The Parade's Gone By* (New York: Knopf, 1969), p. 276.

8. Atherton to Hallowell, Mar. 15, 1921, Bancroft.

9. *New York Times*, section 6, July 31, 1921.

10. Atherton, "Is There a Moral Decline?" *Forum* 65 (Mar. 1921): 312–16.

11. Sidney D. Kirkpatrick, *A Cast of Killers* (New York: Penguin Books, 1986).

12. Florence Atherton Dickey, "Gertrude Atherton, Family and Celebrated Friends," oral history conducted by Emily W. Leider, Regional Oral History Office, Bancroft, 1981, p. 43.

13. *Los Angeles Examiner*, July 23, 1919.

14. Tauchnitz issued twenty Atherton titles during the 1920s, and only three by Lewis, two by Wharton. See Irene and Allen Cleaton, *Books and Battles* (Boston and New York: Houghton Mifflin, 1937), p. 215.

15. Quoted in Edgar Kemler, ed., *The Irreverent Mr. Mencken* (Boston: Little Brown, 1950), p. 45.

16. Atherton, "The Alpine School of Fiction," *Bookman* (New York) 55 (Mar. 1922): 30.

17. Atherton, *Black Oxen* (New York, Boni & Liveright, 1923), p. 150. Subsequent references to this edition will be included in the text.

18. Atherton to Hallowell, May 30, 1922, Bancroft.

19. *Literary Review*, Jan. 29, 1921, p. 3.

20. Dr. Harry Benjamin, Case One, quoted in "Women Here Made Younger, Like Heroine in 'Black Oxen,'" *New York Herald Tribune*, Mar. 16, 1924.

21. Atherton to Hallowell, May 1, 1922, Bancroft.

22. Interview with Dr. Harry Benjamin, by Emily W. Leider, Nov. 17, 1980. Dr. Benjamin, who became even more famous for his work with Jan Morris and other transsexuals than he had been for introducing the Steinach Treatment, died at the age of 101 in August 1986.

CHAPTER SIXTEEN

1. *New York Times*, Oct. 4, 1923. In April 1923, Atherton had been one of several writers drafted by Horace Liveright to testify in Albany, New York, against John Sumner's Clean Books Bill, which was defeated.

2. Walker Gilmer, *Horace Liveright: Publisher of the Twenties* (New York: David Lewis, 1970), pp. 25–27.

3. H. L. Mencken, "The Gland School," *American Mercury* 6, 22 (Oct. 1925): 249.

4. Upton Sinclair, *Money Writes* (New York: Boni, 1927), p. 83.

5. Atherton to Phelan, Oct. 25, 1922, and Apr. 10, 1923, Bancroft.

6. *San Francisco Chronicle*, Sept. 9, 1923.

7. Atherton to William Lengel, July 20, [1925], Berg Collection, NYPL.

8. Sinclair, *Money Writes*, p. 82.

9. Carl Van Vechten, review of *Black Oxen*, *The Nation*, Feb. 14, 1923, p. 196.

10. "Gertrude Atherton Claims Rejuvenation," *New York Times*, Dec. 4, 1935.

11. Hunt to Atherton, June 12, 1924, Bancroft.

12. Atherton to Benjamin, Feb. 20, 1948, Bancroft.

13. *Newsweek*, Dec. 14, 1935.

14. *San Francisco Call-Bulletin*, Nov. 20, 1931.

15. *The Daybooks of Edward Weston*, ed. Nancy Newhall (Rochester, N.Y.: George Eastman House, 1966), pp. 89–91.

CHAPTER SEVENTEEN

1. Helen Wills, *Fifteen-Thirty: The Story of a Tennis Player* (New York: Scribner's, 1937), p. 263.

2. Dorothy Kaucher, *James Duval Phelan: A Portrait* (Saratoga, Calif.: Montalvo Association, 1965), p. 34.

3. Quoted in ibid., opposite p. 43.

4. Phelan-Howland diary, Apr. 1926, Phelan Collection, Bancroft.

5. Larry Engelmann, *The Goddess and the American Girl: The Story of Suzanne Lenglen and Helen Wills* (New York: Oxford University Press, 1988), p. 295.

6. Quoted in ibid., p. 402.

7. Wills, *Fifteen-Thirty*, p. 263.

8. Ibid., p. 107.

9. Florence Atherton Dickey, "Gertrude Atherton, Family and Celebrated Friends," oral history conducted by Emily W. Leider, Regional Oral History Office, Bancroft, 1981, p. 66.

10. C. Older to Atherton, Aug. 20, 1930, Bancroft.

11. Atherton to Galsworthy, Jan. 7, 1924, HRC.

12. Dobie to Mr. [Albert] Dashiell, 1931, PEN Archives, New York.

13. Interview with Oscar Lewis, by Ruth Teiser, Regional Oral History Office, Bancroft, 1965, p. 84.

14. George P. West, "The California Literati," *American Mercury*, July 1926, p. 285.

15. Atherton to Dobie, Apr. 5, [1929], Charles C. Dobie Papers, Bancroft.

16. West to Atherton, undated [1924?], Bancroft. Quoted by permission.

17. *San Francisco News*, Oct. 16, 1929.

18. Atherton to Van Vechten, Aug. 4, 1928, NYPL.

19. Atherton to Sinclair, Nov. 17, 1927, Lilly.

20. Potter to Atherton, undated, Bancroft.

21. Phelan-Howland diary, Apr. 1926, Bancroft.

22. Potter to Atherton, [July] 1925, Bancroft.

23. Atherton, *The Immortal Marriage* (New York: Boni & Liveright, 1927), p. 466.

24. Florence Atherton Dickey, unpublished memoir of Gertrude Atherton, p. 154.

25. *Classical Philology* 22 (July 1927): 332.

26. Walker Gilmer, *Horace Liveright: Publisher of the Twenties* (New York: David Lewis, 1970), p. 218.

27. Phelan to Atherton, May 19, 1930, Bancroft.

28. Phelan to Atherton, June 9, 1930, Bancroft.

29. Atherton to Phelan, July 10, 1930, Bancroft.

30. Atherton to Driscoll, July 23, 1930, Bancroft.

31. Wills, *Fifteen-Thirty*, p. 182.

32. Atherton to Driscoll, Aug. 1930, Bancroft.

33. Harvey to Atherton, Aug. 25, 1930, Bancroft.

34. "The Soul of Montalvo," *Overland Monthly* 88 (Nov. 1930): 323.

35. C. Older to Atherton, Aug. 20, 1930, Bancroft.

36. *San Francisco Chronicle*, Aug. 16, 1930.

37. Atherton to C. Older, Sept. 17 [1930], Bancroft.

CHAPTER EIGHTEEN

1. Atherton to Mrs. Aiken, Dec. 28, 1930, Oakland Library.

2. Atherton to C. Older, Jan. 22, 1932, Bancroft.

3. *TLS*, Sept. 15, 1932.

4. *New York Times Book Review*, Apr. 10, 1932.

5. Van Vechten to Atherton, Apr. 3, 1932, NYPL. Used by permission.

6. Phelps to Atherton, Sept. 1, 1933, Bancroft.

7. Dorothy Van Doren, review of *Adventures*, *Nation*, June 1, 1932.

8. Mary Ellen Chase, review of *Adventures*, *Commonweal*, July 27, 1932.

9. *Saturday Review*, May 28, 1932.

10. Atherton to Charlotte Hallowell, Apr. 1, 1935, Bancroft. At the time of her death in 1948, Atherton's estate was valued at $34,035.

11. Atherton to Hallowell, July 30, 1923, Bancroft.

12. Muriel Russell to Atherton, May 2, 1930, Bancroft.

13. *San Francisco Chronicle*, Jan. 8, 1931.

14. Dominga Russell to Atherton, Feb. 1931, Bancroft.

15. Dominga Russell to Atherton, Nov. 15, 1931, Bancroft.

16. Gertrude Stein, *The Autobiography of Alice B. Toklas* (New York: Random House, 1933), p. 139.

17. Toklas to Rosenshine, Annette Rosenshine Papers, June 30, 1948, Bancroft. Quoted by permission.

18. Atherton to Jackson, Nov. 11, [1934?], Bancroft.

19. On Stein's identification with the West, see Elinor Richey, *Eminent*

Women of the West (Berkeley, Calif.: Howell-North Books, 1975), pp. 153–79.

20. Atherton to B. A. Bergman, Feb. 9, 1935, Bancroft.

21. Gertrude Stein, *Everybody's Autobiography* (New York: Random House, 1937), p. 289.

22. Interview with Alice B. Toklas by Roland E. Duncan, Regional Oral History Office, Bancroft, 1952, p. 11.

23. Stein, *Everybody's Autobiography*, p. 189.

24. Atherton to Charles Hanson Towne, undated, NYPL.

25. Alice B. Toklas, *What Is Remembered* (New York: Holt, Rinehart and Winston, 1963), p. 154.

26. Luhan to Atherton, Apr. 3, 1935, Bancroft. Quoted by permission.

27. Atherton to Stein, Mar. 16, 1935, Collection of American Literature, Beinecke Library, Yale University.

28. *San Francisco Chronicle*, Apr. 10, 1935.

29. Stein, *Everybody's Autobiography*, pp. 289–91.

30. Stein to Van Vechten, Apr. 12 and 17, 1935, Beinecke.

31. Atherton to B. A. Bergman, undated, Bancroft.

32. Atherton to C. H. Towne, Sept. 12, [1935], NYPL.

33. Atherton, *Golden Peacock* (Boston and New York: Houghton Mifflin Company, 1936), p. 8.

34. *New York Times*, Apr. 5, 1936.

35. *Time*, Sept. 16, 1940.

36. Atherton to Rascoe, Dec. 2, [1941?], Burton Rascoe Collection, Van Pelt Library, University of Pennsylvania.

37. *New York Times*, Nov. 7, 1938.

CHAPTER NINETEEN

1. Atherton broke with Houghton Mifflin in 1939. Her last four books issued from three different publishers: *The House of Lee* (1940) and *The Horn of Life* (1942) from Appleton-Century; *Golden Gate Country* (1945) from Duell, Sloan & Pearce; and *My San Francisco* (1946) from Bobbs-Merrill.

2. Atherton to Benjamin, Dec. 18, [1938], Bancroft.

3. Tarbell to Atherton, Nov. 9, 1938, Bancroft.

4. Hawthorne to Atherton, Oct. 11, 1937, Bancroft.

5. *New York Post*, Oct. 30, 1941.

6. Atherton to Sinclair, June 20, 1944, Lilly.

7. Masters to Atherton, July 26, 1943, Bancroft. Quoted by permission of Ellen C. Masters.

8. Carl Van Vechten, "Some Literary Ladies I Have Known," *Yale University Library Gazette* 26 (Jan. 1952): 100.

9. Atherton to Benjamin, May 15, 1944, Bancroft.

10. Caldwell to Atherton, May 22, 1944, Bancroft.

11. Atherton, *The House of Lee* (New York and London: Appleton-Century, 1940), p. 5.

12. Atherton to Benjamin, Dec. 14, 1943, Bancroft.

13. Atherton to Norman, July 9, 1938, NYPL.

14. Quoted by Malcolm Cowley in "Marginalia," *New Republic*, Mar. 27, 1944. "Writers Take Sides" was originally published by the League of American Writers in 1938. See also Cowley's "American Literature in Wartime," *New Republic*, Dec. 6, 1943.

15. *San Francisco News*, Mar. 31, 1938.

16. *San Francisco Examiner*, Oct. 25, 1940.

17. Atherton to Rascoe, undated, Van Pelt Library, University of Pennsylvania.

18. *San Francisco Chronicle*, Apr. 2, 1937.

19. *San Francisco News*, Feb. 11, 1938.

20. *New York Times*, Dec. 10, 1938.

21. Atherton to Benjamin, May 14, [1939?] Bancroft.

22. Atherton to Sinclair, May 24, 1943, Lilly.

23. Atherton to Sinclair, June 13, 1944, Lilly.

24. National Academy of American Literature file, Atherton papers, Bancroft.

25. Founded in 1898, the Institute admitted only one woman, Julia Ward Howe, before 1926, when Margaret Deland, Edith Wharton, Agnes Repplier, and Mary E. Wilkins Freeman all became members. I am grateful to Nancy Johnson of the Academy and Institute of Arts and Letters office for supplying this information.

26. Atherton to Lewis, Feb. 18, [1938], collection of American Literature, Beinecke Library, Yale University.

27. Atherton to Stephen Vincent Benet, letter fragment, [1940], Bancroft.

28. Atherton to Hallowell, Apr. 1, 1935, Bancroft.

29. Atherton to Jackson, undated, Bancroft.

30. Joseph Henry Jackson, "Watch the Parade: Write It All Down," *San Francisco Chronicle*, Nov. 1, 1942.

31. Quoted in Virginia Conroy to Atherton, Feb. 7, 1946, Bancroft.

32. *San Francisco Chronicle*, Oct. 31, 1947.

33. Atherton to Louis Mertins, Feb. 25, 1947, Bancroft.

34. Note from U.C. Berkeley publicist Garff Wilson to Araminta

Blackwelder (Atherton's great-granddaughter); courtesy of Araminta Black-welder.

35. Atherton to Benjamin, Feb. 20, 1948, Bancroft.

36. Florence Atherton Dickey, unpublished memoir of Gertrude Atherton, p. 200.

37. Oscar Lewis, "Gertrude Atherton," in *Book Club of California News-Letter*, Autumn 1948; Carolyn Anspacher, "Novelist, Non-Conformist, Intellectual Siren," *San Francisco Chronicle*, Oct. 30, 1944.

38. Toklas to Annette Rosenshine, June 30, 1948, Bancroft. Quoted by permission.

Bibliographic Note

ARCHIVES

The Bancroft Library, University of California, Berkeley, holds the largest collection of Atherton letters and manuscripts, including a few early letters to Geroge Atherton and the letters to Ambrose Bierce, James D. Phelan, and Dr. Harry Benjamin. Other major repositories are: the New York Public Library, which holds letters to Elizabeth Jordan, Carl Van Vechten, Charles Hanson Towne, and (in the Macmillan Co. Records) George Brett; the Lilly Library, Indiana University, for letters between Gertrude Atherton and Upton Sinclair; the Library of Congress, for letters to Joseph Stoddart and Minnie Maddern Fiske; the Beinecke Rare Book and Manuscript Library, Yale University, for letters to Gertrude Stein; the Harry Ransom Humanities Research Center, Austin, Texas, for letters to John Lane and Richard Le Gallienne. The California Historical Society in San Francisco has letters to Ina Coolbrith and letters and documents relating to the Faxon D. Atherton family of San Mateo County. Letters to Horace Liveright and Burton Rascoe are housed at Van Pelt Library, University of Pennsylvania.

Other repositories include: Princeton University, Harvard University, University of Virginia, Columbia University, the Huntington Library (San Marino, Calif.), Mills College (Oakland, Calif.), New York University, Temple University, the American Academy and Institute of Arts and Letters, Montalvo Center for the Arts, San Francisco Public Library, and the National Library of Scotland (Edinburgh).

BIBLIOGRAPHIES

Charlotte S. McClure is preparing a thorough bibliography of writings by and about Gertrude Atherton, to be included in *Bibliography of United States Literature: American Fiction, 1865–1918* (Columbia, S.C.: Bruccoli Clarke Layman, forthcoming). At this writing, McClure's "Preliminary Checklist of the Writings of and About Gertrude Atherton," *American Literary Realism* 9 (Spring 1976) remains the most complete account. A readily available listing of Atherton's books and major articles, as well as of secondary sources, can be found in McClure's *Gertrude Atherton* (Boston: Twayne Publishers, Inc., United States Authors Series, 1979).

NEW FINDINGS

My own research has turned up a variety of pre-1906 publications by Gertrude Atherton, including columns for *The Argonaut*, November 1888 to March 1889, and for the *San Francisco Examiner*, August to November 1891; and the following works of fiction: "A Pioneer Play," *Argonaut*, December 22, 1883; "A Difficult Question," *Overland Monthly*, November 1887; and the novella *A Christmas Witch*, *Godey's Magazine*, January 1893.

Letters not listed in McClure's 1976 checklist include those to Ambrose Bierce in the Bancroft Library, to George Brett in the New York Public Library, and to Horace Liveright at the University of Pennsylvania.

ADDITIONAL SECONDARY SOURCES

The following titles, not cited in the notes, have contributed to my understanding.

Ballou, Jenny. *Period Piece: Ella Wheeler Wilcox and Her Times*. Boston: Houghton Mifflin, 1940.

Banner, Lois W. *American Beauty*. New York: Knopf, 1983.

Bruce, John. *Gaudy Century: The Story of San Francisco's Hundred Years of Robust Journalism*. New York: Random House, 1948.

Ferlinghetti, Lawrence, and Nancy J. Peters. *Literary San Francisco: A Pictorial History from Its Beginnings to the Present Day*. San Francisco: City Lights and Harper & Row, 1980.

Fryer, Judith. *Felicitous Space: The Imaginative Structure of Edith Wharton and Willa Cather*. Chapel Hill: University of North Carolina Press, 1986.

Hart, James D. *A Companion to California*. New York: Oxford University Press, 1978.

Jordan, Elizabeth. *Three Rousing Cheers*. New York: Appleton-Century, 1938.

Kennedy, David M. *Over Here: The First World War and American Society*. New York: Oxford University Press, 1980.

Lehman, Benjamin H. "Recollections and Reminiscences of Life in the Bay Area from 1920 Onward." Interview by Suzanne B. Riess. Berkeley: Bancroft Library Regional Oral History Office, 1969.

Lasch, Christopher. *The New Radicalism in America, 1889–1963*. London: Chatto & Windus, 1966.

May, Elaine Tyler. *Great Expectations: Marriage and Divorce in Post-Victorian America*. Chicago: University of Chicago Press, 1980.

McClure, Charlotte S. "Gertrude Atherton's California Woman: From Love Story to Psychological Drama." In *Itinerary: Criticism: Essays on California Writers*, ed. Charles L. Crow. Bowling Green, Ohio: University Press of Bowling Green, 1978.

Mix, Katherine Lyon. *Max and the Americans*. Brattleboro, Vt.: Stephen Greene Press, 1974.

Mott, Frank Luther. *A History of American Magazines*. Cambridge, Mass.: Belknap Press of Harvard University, 1957.

Muscatine, Doris. *Old San Francisco: The Biography of a City*. New York: Putnam's, 1975.

Pollard, Percival. *Their Day in Court*. New York and Washington: Neale Publishing Co., 1909.

Rather, Lois. *Gertrude Stein and California*. Oakland, Calif.: Rather Press, 1974.

Rose, Phyllis. *Writing of Women*. Middletown, Conn.: Wesleyan University Press, 1985.

Sterling, George. *A Wine of Wizardry and Other Poems*. San Francisco: A. M. Robertson, 1909.

Stern, Madeleine B. *Purple Passage: The Life of Mrs. Frank Leslie*. Norman: University of Oklahoma Press, 1953.

Stevenson, Lionel. "Atherton versus Grundy: The Forty Years' War," *Bookman* (New York) 69 (1929): 464–72.

Sullivan, Mark. *Our Times*. 6 vols. New York: Scribner's, 1926–1933.

Ziff, Larzer. *The American 1890s*. New York: Viking, 1966.

Index

In this index "f" after a number indicates a separate reference on the next page, and "ff" indicates separate references on the next two pages. A continuous discussion over two or more pages is indicated by a span of page numbers, e.g., "57–59." *Passim* is used for a cluster of references in close but not continuous sequence.

Library of Congress Cataloging-in-Publication Data

Leider, Emily Wortis.
   California's daughter : Gertrude Atherton and her times / Emily
Wortis Leider.
      p.   cm.
Includes bibliographical references.
ISBN 0-8047-1820-2 (alk. paper)
   1. Atherton, Gertrude Franklin Horn, 1857–1948—Biography.
2. Novelists, American—20th century—Biography.   3. California—
Biography.   I. Title.
PS1043.L4   1991
813'.52—dc20   90-32410
[B]   CIP

⊗ This book is printed on acid-free paper.